THE CAMBRIDGE COMPANION TO
THE APOSTOLIC FATHERS

The Cambridge Companion to the Apostolic Fathers offers an informative introduction to the extant body of Christian texts that existed beside and after the New Testament known to us as the apostolic fathers. Featuring cutting-edge research by leading scholars, it explores how the early church expanded and evolved over the course of the first and second centuries as evidenced by its textual history. The volume includes thematic essays on imperial context, the relationship between Christianity and Judaism, the growth and diversification of the early church, influences and intertextuality, and female leaders in the early church. The *Companion* contains groundbreaking essays on the individual texts with specific attention given to debates of authorship, authenticity, dating, and theological texture. The *Companion* will serve as an essential resource for instructors and students of the first two centuries of Christianity.

Michael F. Bird is Academic Dean and Lecturer in Theology at Ridley College in Melbourne, Australia and Senior Research Fellow with the Australian College of Theology. He is author of several books including *The New Testament in Its World* (co-authored with N.T. Wright), *Paul and the Second Century* (co-edited with Joseph Dodson), and *The Gospel of the Lord: How the Early Church Wrote the Story of Jesus*.

Scott D. Harrower is Lecturer in Early Church History and Theology at Ridley College in Melbourne, Australia. He has published articles on Syrian Christianity, comparative hagiography, and Augustine of Hippo, as well as books on women in the early church and the Trinity. He is also co-editor of Cascade's *Studies in Early Christology*.

Other Titles in the Series

(continued after index)

THE CAMBRIDGE COMPANION TO

THE APOSTOLIC FATHERS

Edited by

Michael F. Bird
Ridley College

Scott D. Harrower
Ridley College

CAMBRIDGE
UNIVERSITY PRESS

CAMBRIDGE
UNIVERSITY PRESS

University Printing House, Cambridge CB2 8BS, United Kingdom

One Liberty Plaza, 20th Floor, New York, NY 10006, USA

477 Williamstown Road, Port Melbourne, VIC 3207, Australia

314–321, 3rd Floor, Plot 3, Splendor Forum, Jasola District Centre, New Delhi – 110025, India

79 Anson Road, #06–04/06, Singapore 079906

Cambridge University Press is part of the University of Cambridge.

It furthers the University's mission by disseminating knowledge in the pursuit of education, learning, and research at the highest international levels of excellence.

www.cambridge.org
Information on this title: www.cambridge.org/9781108429535
DOI: 10.1017/9781108554992

© Cambridge University Press 2021

First published 2021

A catalogue record for this publication is available from the British Library.

Library of Congress Cataloging-in-Publication Data
NAMES: Bird, Michael F., editor. | Harrower, Scott D., editor.
TITLE: The Cambridge companion to the Apostolic Fathers / edited by Michael F. Bird, Ridley College, Melbourne, Scott Harrower, Ridley College, Melbourne.
DESCRIPTION: Cambridge, United Kingdom ; New York, NY, USA : Cambridge University Press, 2021. | Series: Cambridge companions to religion | Includes bibliographical references and index.
IDENTIFIERS: LCCN 2020041338 (print) | LCCN 2020041339 (ebook) | ISBN 9781108429535 (hardback) | ISBN 9781108454452 (paperback) | ISBN 9781108554992 (epub)
SUBJECTS: LCSH: Apostolic Fathers.
CLASSIFICATION: LCC BR60.A65 C36 2021 (print) | LCC BR60.A65 (ebook) | DDC 270.1—DC23
LC record available at https://lccn.loc.gov/2020041338
LC ebook record available at https://lccn.loc.gov/2020041339

ISBN 978-1-108-42953-5 Hardback
ISBN 978-1-108-45445-2 Paperback

Contents

Contributors

Philip Alexander is Emeritus Professor of Post-Biblical Jewish Literature, University of Manchester, Fellow of the British Academy, formerly President of the Oxford Centre for Hebrew and Jewish Studies, and Co-Director of the Manchester University Centre for Jewish Studies. He has published widely on Judaism in late antiquity, particularly on the Dead Sea Scrolls, on Bible translation and commentary, on mysticism and magic, and on Jewish–Christian relations. Among his publications are an edition (with Geza Vermes) of the Cave 4 fragments of the Community Rule from Qumran for the *Discoveries in the Judaean Desert* series (1998), and translations, introductions, and commentaries to *Targum Song of Songs* (2003) and *Targum Lamentations* (2008) for the *Aramaic Bible* series. He is currently working with his wife, Loveday Alexander, on a major commentary on the *Epistle to the Hebrews*.

Dan Batovici is a research associate at UCLouvain and KU Leuven. He is the author of *The Shepherd of Hermas in Late Antiquity* (2021).

Michael F. Bird (PhD, University of Queensland) is Academic Dean and Lecturer in Theology at Ridley College in Melbourne, Australia and Senior Research Fellow with the Australian College of Theology. He is author of several books, including *The New Testament in Its World* (2019) (co-authored with N.T. Wright), *Evangelical Theology* (2013), and *The Gospel of the Lord: How the Early Church Wrote the Story of Jesus* (2014).

Stephen C. Carlson (PhD, Duke University) is Senior Research Fellow in the Institute for Religion and Critical Inquiry at Melbourne Campus of the Australian Catholic University. Dr Carlson is the author of two books, *The Gospel Hoax: Morton Smith's Invention of Secret Mark* (2005), and *The Text of Galatians and Its History* (2012), as well as a forthcoming edition of Papias for the Oxford Early Christian Texts series.

David J. Downs is Fellow of Keble College and Clarendon-Laing Associate Professor in New Testament Studies, University of Oxford. His most recent monographs include *Alms: Charity, Reward, and Atonement in Early Christianity* (2016) and, with Benjamin J. Lappenga, *The Faithfulness of the Risen Christ: Pistis and the Exalted Lord in the Pauline Letters* (2019).

Benjamin Edsall earned his DPhil at the University of Oxford. Since 2014, he has been in the Institute for Religion and Critical Inquiry at Australian Catholic

University (Melbourne, Australia). In 2017–18 he was at Humboldt Universität zu Berlin on an Alexander von Humboldt postdoctoral fellowship. He is the author of *Paul's Witness to Formative Early Christian Instruction* (2014), *The Reception of Paul and Early Christian Initiation: History and Hermeneutics* (2019), and of numerous articles in journals such as *New Testament Studies*, *Vigiliae Christianae*, and *Journal of Theological Studies*.

Paul Foster was awarded his DPhil by the University of Oxford in 2003 and is currently Professor of New Testament and Early Christianity at the University of Edinburgh. His recent publications include *Colossians – Black's New Testament Commentaries* (2016) and *The Gospel of Peter: Introduction, Critical Edition and Commentary* (2010).

Andrew Gregory is Chaplain at University College, Oxford. He is author of *The Gospel according to the Hebrews and the Gospel of the Ebionites* (2017) and *The Reception of Luke and Acts in the Period before Irenaeus* (2003). He is a series editor of the Oxford Early Christian Gospel Texts and Oxford Apostolic Fathers and, with Christopher Tuckett, co-editor of *The Reception of the New Testament in the Apostolic Fathers* (2005) and *Trajectories through the New Testament and the Apostolic Fathers* (2005).

Scott D. Harrower is Lecturer in Early Church History and Theology at Ridley College in Melbourne, Australia. He has published articles on Syrian Christianity, comparative hagiography, and Augustine of Hippo, as well as books on women in the early church and the Trinity. He is also co-editor of Cascade's *Studies in Early Christology*.

Paul A. Hartog is Professor of Theology at Faith Baptist Theological Seminary in the USA. He is the author of *Polycarp and the New Testament* (2002) and *Polycarp's Epistle to the Philippians and the Martyrdom of Polycarp* (2013), and is the editor of *The Contemporary Church and the Early Church: Case Studies in Ressourcement* (2010) and *Orthodoxy and Heresy in Early Christian Contexts* (2015).

Reidar Hvalvik, Dr. theol., is Professor of New Testament at MF Norwegian School of Theology, Religion and Society, Oslo. His doctoral dissertation, completed in 1994, was published as *The Struggle for Scripture and Covenant: The Purpose of the Epistle of Barnabas and Jewish–Christian Competition in the Second Century* (1996). He has edited a Norwegian translation of the Apostolic Fathers (1984) and was contributor and co-editor of *Jewish Believers in Jesus: The Early Centuries* (2007; 2nd ed. 2017).

Clayton N. Jefford graduated from The Claremont Graduate School in California (PhD 1988) and has served as Professor of Scripture since 1989 at Saint Meinrad Seminary and School of Theology in southern Indiana. Author of various books and essays on the apostolic fathers, his specialty is the Didache.

Jonathon Lookadoo completed his PhD at the University of Otago (2017) and is currently Assistant Professor at the Presbyterian University and Theological Seminary in Seoul, South Korea. He is the author of *The High Priest and the Temple: Metaphorical Depictions of Jesus in the Letters of Ignatius of Antioch*

(2018) and the English translator of Olavi Tarvainen's *Faith and Love in Ignatius of Antioch* (2016).

Kirsten H. Mackerras is currently completing a DPhil on ethics in Lactantius at St Cross College, Oxford. With a background in New Testament studies and Ancient history, she now studies the interaction between the early church and the Graeco-Roman world. Her research interests include the development of Christianity, and its ethics, apologetics, and political theology.

Janelle Peters is Visiting Assistant Professor at Loyola Marymount University. Her dissertation on Paul's construction of church polity was completed at Emory University, following degrees at University of California-San Diego and the University of Chicago. Her revised manuscript is under contract with the University of Pennsylvania Press. She has published articles on Second Temple Judaism and early Christianity in *Biblica, Journal of Early Christian History, Neotestamentica, Journal for the Study of the Pseudepigrapha, Studia Patristica*, and *Postscripts*.

Clare K. Rothschild is Professor of Scripture Studies in the Department of Theology, Lewis University, Illinois. She earned her MA from Harvard Divinity School and PhD from the University of Chicago. Her research interests include Luke-Acts, Q, Hebrews, the Apostolic Fathers, and the Muratorian Fragment. She is the author of titles including *Luke-Acts and the Rhetoric of History* (2004), *Baptist Traditions and Q* (2005), *Hebrews as Pseudepigraphon* (2009), and *Paul in Athens* (2014). She is now preparing a commentary on the Epistle of Barnabas for the Hermeneia series. She currently serves as Editor of *Early Christianity* as well as the SBL series, Writings of the Graeco-Roman World, Supplements.

Michael J. Svigel is Chair and Professor of Theological Studies at Dallas Theological Seminary. Besides publishing a number of articles and chapters on the Apostolic Fathers, his most recent books include *The Center and the Source: Second Century Incarnational Christology and Early Catholic Christianity* (2016) and *A Practical Primer on Theological Method* (2019).

David E. Wilhite is Professor of Theology at Baylor University's George W. Truett Theological Seminary. He has published several books and articles on second- and third-century Christianity, including *The Gospel According to Heresy* (2015). He has co-edited (with Todd D. Still) three volumes on the reception of Paul: *Tertullian and Paul* (2013), *The Apostolic Fathers and Paul* (2017), and *Irenaeus and Paul* (2020). He is also co-editor (with Bruce Longenecker) of the forthcoming *Cambridge History of Ancient Christianity*.

Stephen E. Young is Assistant Professor of New Testament at Fuller Theological Seminary in Houston, TX. He is the author of *Jesus Tradition in the Apostolic Fathers: Their Explicit Appeals to the Words of Jesus in Light of Orality Studies* (2011).

Abbreviations

ABD	*Anchor Bible Dictionary*
Adv. Haer.	Irenaeus, *Against Heresies*
ANRW	*Aufstieg und Niedergang der Römischen Welt*
	Ant. Antiquities of the Jews
ApCon	Apostolic Constitutions
Apol.	Justin Martyr, *Apology*
Apol.	Aristides, *Apology*
ATR	*Anglican Theological Review*
Aug	Augustinianum
Barn.	*Barnabas*
BDAG	A Greek–English Lexicon of the New Testament and Other Early Christian Literature
BZNW	Beifhefte zur Zeitschrift für die Neutestamentliche Wissenschaft
c.	*circa*
1 Clem.	1 Clement
2 Clem.	2 Clement
Hist. rom.	Cassius Dio, *Historiae Romanae*
Comm. Zech	Didymus the Blind
ed(s).	editor(s) or edition
Dial.	Justin, *Dialogue with Trypho*
Did.	*Didache*
Diogn.	*Diognetus*
Ep.	*Epistles*
ExpT	*Expository Times*
Gos. Eb.	*Gospel of the Ebionites*
Gos. Thom.	*Gospel of Thomas*
HBT	*Horizons in Biblical Theology*

Herm. Mand.	*Shepherd of Hermas, Mandate(s)*
Herm. Sim.	*Shepherd of Hermas, Similitude(s)*
Herm. Vis.	*Shepherd of Hermas, Vision(s)*
Hist. eccl.	Eusebius, *Historia Ecclesia*
HTR	*Harvard Theological Review*
Ign. *Eph.*	Ignatius, *To the Ephesians*
Ign. *Magn.*	Ignatius, *To the Magnesians*
Ign. Phld.	Ignatius, *To the Philadelphians*
Ign. *Pol*	Ignatius, *To Polycarp*
Ign. *Rom.*	Ignatius, *To the Romans*
Ign. *Smyrn.*	Ignatius, *To the Smyrnaeans*
Ign. *Trall.*	Ignatius, *To the Trallians*
inscr.	inscription
JBL	*Journal of Biblical Literature*
JECH	*Journal of Early Chrsitian History*
JECS	*Journal of Early Christian Studies*
JEH	*Journal of Ecclesiastical History*
JR	*Journal of Religion*
JTS	*Journal of Theological Studies*
LCL	Loeb Classical Library
Lib.	Pliny, *Letters*
LNTS	Library of New Testament Studies
m.	Mishnah
Med.	Marcus Aurelius, *Meditations*
Mart. Pol.	Martyrdom of Polycarp
NHC	Nag Hammadi Codices
NovT	*Novum Testamentum*
NTS	*New Testament Studies*
OAF	Oxford Apostolic Fathers
Pan.	Epiphanius, *Panarion*
Pol. *Phil.*	*To the Philippians*
P.Oxy.	Papyrus Oxyrhynchus
RB	*Revue Biblique*
repr.	reprint
SC	Sources chrétiennes
StPatr	*Studia Patristica*
Strom.	*Stromata*, by Clement of Alexandria
Suet. *Claud.*	*Claudius*, in Suetonius, *Lives of the Caesars*
Suet. *Ner.*	*Nero*, in Suetonius, *Lives of the Caesars*

Suet. *Tit.*	*Titus*, in Suetonius, *Lives of the Caesars*
Suet. *Vesp.*	*Vespasianus*, in Suetonius, *Lives of the Caesars*
Tac. *Ann.*	Tacitus, *Annals of Imperial Rome*
Tac. *Hist.*	Tacitus, *Histories*
USQR	*Union Seminary Quarterly Review*
VC	*Vigilae Christianae*
vols.	volumes
War	*War of the Jews*
WTJ	*Westminster Theological Journal*
WUNT	Wissenschaftliche Untersuchungen zum Neuen Testament
ZAC	*Zeitschrift für Antikes Christentum*
ZAW	*Zeitschrift für die Alttestamentliche Wissenschaft*
ZNW	*Zeitschrift für die Neutestamentliche Wissenschaft*

Introduction
Intriguing and Enigmatic: The Apostolic Fathers and Current Research

SCOTT D. HARROWER

The Apostolic Fathers (AF) are a para-apostolic and post-apostolic corpus of writings, a group of texts composed beside and after the New Testament. This corpus constitutes an important precursor to the Christian apologists and pre-Nicene theologians of subsequent centuries. The words *intriguing* and *enigmatic* aptly describe both the collection itself as well as the current state of scholarship on them. The AF are an intriguing body of literature because they provide an important window into the lived religion of Christians in the late first and early second century. The intrigue only deepens once we look *at* and *through* these windows. Looking at them, the AF offer colourful portraits of key protagonists – much like stained-glass windows, they provide colour but only an outline of the people depicted in the artwork. For example, we know the names and some biographical details and have depictions of Polycarp and Papias, but our knowledge of them is otherwise fragmentary and scant. Looking through the AF, we observe ancient Christian people with their practices, diversities, debates, anxieties, hopes, and worship; this leaves us with many impressions but even more questions.

The intrinsic intrigue of the AF is furthered by the seeming randomness of the collection itself. It is an artificial corpus and modern invention by church historians in the seventeenth century. The ancient church did not know of a New Testament separate from a collection of Apostolic Fathers and separate again from the Apologists. Some of these writings could conceivably be placed in the New Testament by virtue of their dating to the apostolic era, be located among the apologists because of their apologetic contents, or else identified within early Christian apocrypha because of their pseudonymity. The literary works included in this corpus have varied over time, depending on the sensibilities and tastes of the editor, with some documents like the *Shepherd of Hermas* showing a consistent history of inclusion in such a collection, whereas other writings such as the *Epistle to Diognetus* do not. Today a settled consensus includes *1 Clement* and *2 Clement*, the *Didache*, the *Epistle of Barnabas*, the seven letters of Ignatius, Polycarp's *Letter to the Philippians*, the *Martyrdom of Polycarp*, the *Shepherd of Hermas*, the *Epistle to Diognetus*, the fragments of Papias, and the fragments of the *Apology of Quadratus*.[1]

The AF is, then, a lively yet "artificial collection of somewhat disparate texts."[2] Generally, two criteria have been used to draw them into a category that can accommodate them, namely: they can be "dated roughly between the late-first and the mid-second centuries – and the view that their authors either knew one of the Twelve Apostles or were taught by somebody who had."[3] As this volume shows, beyond these two criteria most other details and referents of this literary corpus have been the subject of long-running and significant debates. Notwithstanding this, the AF were a central part of early Christian literature and they function, somewhat flexibly, as a bridge between the New Testament and the later Patristic period. However, the scholarly essays in this volume treat the AF as more than a mere sequel to the New Testament. Instead, they are representative of the growth and diversification of early Christian communities and writings that began to flower in the post-apostolic period.

These texts are largely enigmatic because we often know so little of their origins, circulation, and reception. Or else, beyond debates over content, there are questions about the connections between these texts themselves, links to the earliest Jesus traditions and apostolic writings, concerns over authenticity and integrity, and discussions over cultural influences and relationship to various Christianities.

Because of the intriguing and enigmatic nature of the AF, we should not be surprised when they generate important questions, such as about the nature and diversity of local Christian groups in the second century. This volume aims to take these questions seriously and to demonstrate the nature and shape of both the critical and constructive research on the AF collection. Thus, the volume demonstrates best-practice scholarly efforts with respect to dealing with the AF's intrigue and enigmas.

---

[1] See Paul Foster, "The Text of the New Testament in the Apostolic Fathers," Chapter 5 in this volume. On the origins of the designation "Apostolic Fathers," see David Lincicum, "The Paratextual Invention of the Term 'Apostolic Fathers,'" *JTS* 66 (2015): 139–48.

[2] Foster, Chapter 5 in this volume.

[3] Stephen E. Young, "The Jesus Tradition in the Apostolic Fathers," Chapter 4 in this volume..

Our hope is that readers will be drawn in by the AF themselves and by the best lines of scholarly research suggested by our authors.

The first section of this volume treats the generative traditions, contexts, and backgrounds to the documents comprising the AF collection. Chapter 1, "The Roman Empire in the Era of the Apostolic Fathers," introduces the complex and evolving Greco-Roman context for the communities that produced the AF. Michael J. Svigel provides an analytic survey of the Roman period from the emperors Nero to Marcus Aurelius (54–180 CE), during which most of the AF corpus was composed. Svigel sets the chronological scope for studying the AF with particular emphasis on the period of the "Five Good Emperors" (96–180 CE). With some notable exceptions, the Roman Empire during this "golden age" realized political consolidation, territorial expansion, general peace, and internal cohesion – a social context in which Christianity could steadily grow with relative ease and suffer only sporadic interference from imperial and local authorities.

In Chapter 2, "The Image of Jews and Judaism in the Apostolic Fathers," Philip Alexander tackles the portrayal of Jewish groups and Judaism in the AF. He begins by pointing out that the period from the fall of the Temple in 70 CE to the end of the Bar Kokhba war (135 CE) – the period of the AF – is not well documented. The most significant development on the Jewish side, Alexander says, was the emergence of the Rabbinic movement in Palestine – a movement, centered on the Rabbinic Houses of Study (Batei Midrash), which was eventually to dominate Judaism. But there was no sudden triumph of Rabbinism after 70 CE. The Rabbis then did not command the allegiance of the majority of Jews even in Palestine, nor did they have the resources or the standing to project their authority into the Diaspora, which continued to follow a pattern of diasporic Jewish life centered on the synagogue. Judaism was probably as diverse after 70 as it had been before. Nevertheless, there was a "common Judaism" to which most Jews subscribed based on respect for the Torah of Moses, the keeping of Sabbath and festivals, the dietary laws (kashrut), and circumcision. According to Alexander, the image of Judaism in the AF (such as it is) confirms this picture, but with two somewhat unexpected additions: it seems to point to a continuing Jewish interest in the temple sacrifices (despite the fact that the temple had been destroyed) and in fasting. This picture is probably accurate and reflects the fact that many Jews after 70 did not accept that the cessation of the cult was final but looked for its imminent restoration. The fasting was an expression of repentance aimed at moving God to return in mercy to his people. While references to Jews and Judaism appear in several writings of the AF, the *Epistle of Barnabas* is by far the most engaged with Judaism. Alexander proceeds to demonstrate that the author seems to be aware of the sentiment within the Jewish community, particularly the hope for the rebuilding of the temple. The author is burdened with the "anxiety of influence," engendered by the fact that Christianity is so heavily indebted to Judaism and has, consequently, a problem in establishing its independence and authenticity. He hammers out a radical supersessionism that was to prove influential in later Christian attitudes toward Judaism. Central to this is a massive allegorical appropriation of the Jewish law. But his aggressive anti-Judaism has to be set in its historical context: it reflects a time when Christianity was struggling to forge a separate identity in the looming shadow of a larger, more prosperous, more influential Jewish community that was bent on making life difficult for it. *Barnabas* is thus indicative of the type of internecine rivalry between Jews and Christians as the identity of these two groups were crystallizing and, eventually, drifting apart.

Chapter 3, "Second-Century Diversity," by David E. Wilhite, deals with one of the most challenging debates to do with how the AF relate to the concept of "Christianity" itself. Wilhite contends that Christian diversity can be considered along several different lines, such as a geographic diversity and a diversity of sources. The primary debate today among scholars deals with doctrinal diversity, and so this essay reviews the major "heresies" or "Christianities" known in the second century. When compared in particular to the AF corpus, some surprising results come to light. The resulting picture is one of less doctrinal diversity than has been posited by some recent studies, and yet there is also no evidence of the unanimity traditionally claimed for early Christianity.

The focus of research shifts to the Jesus tradition in Chapter 4. Stephen E. Young's "The Jesus Tradition in the Apostolic Fathers" surveys the evidence for the continuing impact of the Jesus tradition in these writings in light of recent debates about continuing orality and the textualization of the Jesus tradition. The essay pays particular attention to the *Didache*, *1 Clement*, Polycarp's *Philippians* and the *Papias Fragments* with respect to discussions about oral versus textual tradition, the flexibility and stability of the Jesus tradition, various contexts of preservation and transmission of tradition, and secondary orality. It shows that Jesus' words were very much paramount in the post-apostolic church even if no consensus has been reached regarding the media in which those words were transmitted.

Chapter 5 deals with the relationship between New Testament texts and the AF. Paul Foster's "The Text of the New Testament in the Apostolic Fathers" makes it clear that the continuous text for any New Testament writing cannot be reconstructed from the scant citations and allusions contained in the writings of the AF. Instead, this study looks to establish which New Testament writings might have been known to the authors of the various AF texts under consideration. The discussion moves through the texts that became the New Testament in their final canonical order with the goal of showing which writings from among the AF might cite or allude to the New Testament text in question. The table at the end of the discussion presents, in summary fashion, the results of this enquiry. It reveals that several of the texts that later became the New Testament cannot be detected among the writings of the AF.

In Chapter 6, "The Reception of Paul, Peter, and James in the Apostolic Fathers," Benjamin Edsall points out and explores the markedly limited presence of Paul, Peter, and James in the AF collection. These writings appeal to Peter and Paul in a variety of contexts – pertaining to their authority as teachers, their noble deaths, and their connections with Jesus and the other apostolic and non-apostolic leadership figures – though these appeals are not evenly divided among the writers. Ignatius and *1 Clement*, for instance, appeal to both figures while *Hermas* makes no mention of either. James, moreover, is almost entirely absent from the collection. All this amounts to the fact that roughly half of the authors or writings of the AF do not feel the need to appeal explicitly to any of these apostolic figures in the course of their arguments, however much they may be indebted to them on the level of broader early Christian discourse.

A number of highly controversial and long-standing issues are treated in the next three essays. Chapter 7, "Between Ekklēsia and State: The Apostolic Fathers and the Roman Empire," by Andrew Gregory, discusses the AF in the context of the Greek-speaking Roman Empire. Gregory begins by surveying a range of approximately contemporary sources that show how other authors understood or negotiated the boundaries between followers of Jesus and the wider society in which they lived. In the first part of this survey he considers non-Christian texts that reveal how some Roman authors viewed followers of Jesus, and what they expected of them if they were to take their part in the civic life of the Roman Empire alongside their pagan contemporaries. In the second, he considers a range of Christian sources, including some of the writings of the New Testament, as well as some of the earlier texts usually labeled as Early Christian or New Testament Apocrypha, and writings of the Apologists. Gregory then turns to the AF themselves, noting whether and how they refer to the relationship between their communities and the wider world in general, and the functions of the Roman State and Roman imperial or civic religion in particular. Most of the texts are focused on the internal life of the communities that they address, but tensions between their addressees' exclusive allegiance to the God whom they variously associate or identify with Jesus and the competing demands of Roman religion and civic life surface in a number of ways, not least through their fear or experience of martyrdom for refusing to participate in the imperial cult.

Chapter 8, "Church, Church Ministry, and Church Order," by David J. Downs, employs three questions to explore representations of the church in *1 Clement*, *2 Clement*, the *Letters of Ignatius*, the *Letter of Polycarp to the Philippians*, the *Martyrdom of Polycarp*, the *Didache*, the *Epistle of Barnabas*, the *Shepherd of Hermas*, and the *Epistle to Diognetus*: (1) How is the identity of the church presented? (2) What is the work of the church? (3) What, if anything, is said about the ordering and structures of the church?

Chapter 9, "The Apostolic Mothers," by Clare Rothschild, focuses on Christian women of the first four centuries either named as apostles or playing the same role as apostles, or remembered as having done so, in direct line of succession to the companions or early followers of Jesus. Sixteen women are identified, who represent the under-acknowledged group of apostolic mothers of the church. This provocative essay is likely to generate further research into the presence of women in the early church.

The next section of this volume deals with particular documents. This begins with Chapter 10 by Janelle Peters, "*1 and 2 Clement*." Peters argues that *1 Clement* develops the place of the offices of bishop and presbyter from earlier texts such as Philippians and 1 Peter. The author situates the legalistic language of codicil and the contention over the roles, not to the interpersonal strife often found among Greco-Roman associations but to the contemporary shift in Roman Greek priesthoods from temporary to lifelong appointments. Given that the Pauline Corinthian house-churches were not the only example of discord and that Clement feels free to only loosely and sporadically cite the contents of 1 Corinthians, Peters disagrees with the theory that *1 Clement* is a general letter with fictionalized churches. Though *1 Clement* does indeed use generalized language, Clement's chosen location is not merely a text-based one. Peters does not find evidence for a conflict between wealthy patrons and other members of the churches. Instead, she follows the text in arguing that the issue at hand is the stated conflict of a dispute in how leaders may be selected. For *2 Clement*, by contrast, almsgiving is a central feature of the text, with repentance and eternal salvation being the goals of this almsgiving. *2 Clement* shares many of *1 Clement*'s foundational texts but it is written by a different author, speaking more generally and probably later.

Chapter 11, "The Letters of Ignatius." by Jonathon Lookadoo, outlines three broad positions on the much-disputed and interrelated topics of when the letters were composed and whether they are authentically Ignatian. The essay considers what the letters say about the communities that Ignatius addresses as well as the opponents who may have circled in and around Ignatius' audiences. Unity provides a key way in which Ignatius exhorts his readers regarding who Jesus is, how God's people should relate to one another, and what their lifestyles should look like. Lookadoo reflects on two further matters of interest within the letters: the sources that may have influenced Ignatius, and the question of whether the letters are best read individually or as a corpus. While there is much that is uncertain or debated in studies of Ignatius' epistles, the letters continue to be an important part of the collection known as the AF.

Chapter 12, "Polycarp's *Epistle to the Philippians* and the *Martyrdom of Polycarp*," by Paul Hartog, deals with the ecclesial context, life, work, and death of one of the most influential Christians to follow the canonical apostles. The burden of the essay is on the ethical dimensions of the roles that the figure of Polycarp played in early Christianity. Following a crucial evaluation of sources to do with Polycarp, Hartog proceeds to examine important aspects of the self-understanding of early Christian groups in relation to Polycarp. These include their views on virtue and community boundaries. The *Martyrdom of Polycarp*, its relationship to New Testament literature, and contemporary critical debates receive special attention, with the conclusion that it was produced with a view to enshrine particular communal and individual virtues within what at the time were marginal religious communities.

In Chapter 13, "*Didache*," Clayton N. Jefford argues that the *Didache* likely arose in first-century Syria, featuring catechetical training and liturgical rituals from an anonymous cluster of early messianic groups. The text as known from later manuscripts also features directives on worship and community rules, concluding with apocalyptic warnings. Variously referenced by patristic authors, the tradition eventually yielded to the norms of post-Constantinian Christianity.

In Chapter 14, "*The Epistle of Barnabas,*" Reidar Hvalvik discusses the standard introductory issues, focusing especially on the much-debated questions of date and provenance, proposing that there are no decisive arguments that can settle these questions; we have to speak about a probable date (most likely 130–2) and place of origin (Syria-Palestine or Alexandria). There is also a critical evaluation of the traditional view that *Barnabas* is a treatise/tract, accentuating the epistolary features and the traits that seem to be reminiscent of a preaching or teaching situation. Hvalvik highlights the author's anti-Jewish polemic and his commitment to the right understanding and interpretation of Scripture. Special attention is also given to the question of occasion and purpose of *Barnabas*, this being a key issue in several recent contributions to the writing. The essay concludes with a short presentation of the major trends in *Barnabas* research during the last century, showing that scholars' interests and approaches have changed radically: from focusing on sources to a focus on the epistle itself. Moreover, from being a literary foil, the "Jews" in the text have been perceived as reflecting real people and social realities.

Chapter 15, "The *Shepherd of Hermas,*" by Dan Batovici, examines one of the most historically popular documents within the AF. Batovici offers an introduction to the *Shepherd of Hermas* and the range of problems it raises – textual, compositional, theological, and reception historical – surveying current approaches in the scholarship devoted to this peculiar text. Batovici presents first the issues posed by the literary outlook of the *Shepherd* that lead to various theories of redactional layers in the composition of the book and the solutions proposed for identifying its type of apocalyptic genre. This is followed by a survey of the main themes of the book: church, baptism, repentance, and its intricate Christology. In the next section Batovici discusses the title of the book in its transmission, the author as identified in later traditions and as it transpires from the narrative, its provenance and dating, and briefly the community behind the *Shepherd*. The essay concludes with an overview of the reception of the book in its Greek manuscripts, ancient translations, patristic works, and canonical lists.

In Chapter 16 Michael F. Bird and Kirsten H. Mackerras survey lesser-known documents. In their "The *Epistle to Diognetus* and the *Fragment of Quadratus,*" Bird regards *Diognetus* – notoriously disputed concerning integrity, authorship, date, and provenance – as a mid-to-late second-century apology for Christianity to a real or imagined pagan enquirer, written quite possibly in Alexandria. *Diognetus* is distinguished by its account of Christians as a "new type of people" and the "soul" of the world; it has a robust theology of God's redemptive plan and the Son's incarnation and a memorable account of the atonement; its ethical exhortations have analogies with Stoicism, while the homiletic section illustrates a growing tradition of allegorical interpretation of the Old Testament. Mackerras describes the *Fragment of Quadratus* as part of an apology written in the early second century, whose author was one of the successors to the apostles' ministry. The fragment, preserved by Eusebius, describes Jesus as a miracle worker of genuine power; *Quadratus* probably responded to the charge that Jesus did miracles by sorcery. Mackerras does not think that there is sufficient evidence to identify Quadratus' apology with *Diognetus* confidently.

The volume concludes with Chapter 17, Stephen C. Carlson's groundbreaking work on "The Fragments of Papias." Carlson argues that the "The Fragments of Papias" are the remains of a five-volume exegetical work on the "dominical oracles" by Papias of Hierapolis who flourished in the first decades of the second century and passed on traditions from the last decades of the first century. Among the most important of the surviving fragments, Papias passes on traditions about the writings of Mark and Matthew, as well as materialistic speculation about the future kingdom of Christ. Unfortunately, his work has perished, leaving only scattered quotations of varying reliability. Despite significant obstacles and challenges to research into these fragments, Carlson is able to advance a number of proposals to do with important themes in Papias' writing and theology.

These essays, taken together as well as individually, demonstrate and deal with the Apostolic Fathers' unavoidable intrigue and enigma. Our hope is that readers will be not only drawn in by both the AF themselves as well as the cutting-edge scholarship provided by our authors, but will be inspired to follow the lines of research that this volume opens up.

1 The Roman Empire in the Era of the Apostolic Fathers

MICHAEL J. SVIGEL

1.1 INTRODUCTION

When considering the *terminus a quo* and *terminus ad quem* for the period of the Apostolic Fathers, we immediately face difficult and debatable decisions regarding the dating of this collection. For a few of these texts, scholarship has settled on a rather narrow range of likely dates. For example, *1 Clement* is generally dated in the 90s CE, and the epistles of Ignatius of Antioch are most commonly dated during Trajan's reign between 98 and 117, though even these have had notable exceptions. On the other hand, over the last several decades some *Didache* scholars have moved its date of composition from the second century into the late first century; others have settled on an even narrower range of 50–70 CE. Likewise, the *Epistle of Barnabas* can be reasonably situated either in the years immediately following the First Jewish Revolt (c. 75–80 CE) or those following the Bar Kokhba Revolt (c. 135–140 CE). Also, prominent scholars of the *Shepherd of Hermas* have imagined its composition or redaction spanning several decades from as early as the 90s to the 140s. And depending on one's conclusions regarding the unity of Polycarp's *Letter to the Philippians*, it could be dated anytime between about 110 to 140. Though a few have ventured to date the *Epistle to Diognetus* in the early second century, most favor a much later date, perhaps in the late second century. The same is true of the so-called *Second Epistle of Clement* and the *Martyrdom of Polycarp*.

Given the unresolvable variables with regard to dating the Apostolic Fathers, this historical survey will begin with what we might call an "establishing shot" at the widest angle – beginning briefly with the historical backdrop of the Julio-Claudian Dynasty (27 BCE–68 CE) as a possible context of the *Didache* for those who favor an early date (after 50 CE). Then I will sketch the developments of the Flavian Dynasty (c. 69–96 CE) as the possible setting for *Didache*, the probable composition of *1 Clement*, and a plausible context for *Epistle of Barnabas* and early portions of *Shepherd of Hermas*. The majority of this chapter will then zoom in on the second century, slowly panning through the "golden age" of the Roman Empire under the "Five Good Emperors" (96–180 CE). This range, known for its general stability, expansion, prosperity, and relative peace, frames the decades during which most of the writings of the Apostolic Fathers were certainly composed.

1.2 BACKDROP: THE JULIO-CLAUDIAN DYNASTY (27 BCE–68 CE)

In 27 BCE, after a long period of civil unrest following the assassination of Julius Caesar (44 BCE), the Roman Senate granted supreme power to Octavius. This launched the dynasty of Augustus or the "Julio-Claudian Dynasty." After his long, four-decade reign, Octavius died in 14 CE. His stepson, Tiberius, ruled in his place until 37 CE, when Caligula succeeded him, followed by Claudius in 41 CE. Finally, Nero began his reign in 54 CE. With regard to the writings of the Apostolic Fathers, even if *Didache* itself had not been composed during this period, at least sources like the "Two Ways" catechetical material that eventually made their way into both *Didache* and *Barnabas* were in circulation at this time.

1.2.1 The Reign of Nero (54–68)

In 58, a few years after the commencement of Nero's reign, war broke out between Parthia and Rome over the governance of Armenia (Tac. *Ann.* 13.34–41; 14.24–6; 15.1–17, 24–31; Cass. Dio *Hist. rom.* 62.19–23). Parthia had long occupied much of Mesopotamia (modern-day Iraq and Iran) rather securely. Since the first century BCE, the boundary between Parthia and Rome had been more or less settled at the Euphrates River, placing Syria and Armenia on a volatile political fault-line. However, a dispute over succession in Armenia led to open conflict between Nero's general Corbulo and the Parthian King Vologases I. When the dust finally settled in 63 after military see-sawing in which both sides could claim victory in various battles, the political situation in Armenia resolved to a state of diplomatic tension. The Parthians would continue to appoint the king of Armenia while the emperor confirmed the appointment. As before, the Roman–Parthian boundary remained at the Euphrates (Tac. *Ann.* 15.17).

Despite the positive spin placed on this political victory for Nero, his early reign was characterized by unease and distrust. Perhaps Nero's increasingly distressing reign, which was to leave significant scars on

Rome's body politic, drew attention away from the expanding presence of Christians in cities and villages. However, the emperor unleashed a major attack on the Christians in Rome in 64, sparked by a fire that destroyed much of the city (Tac. *Ann.* 15.38–41).[1] Allegedly to quell a rumor that Nero himself had started the fire, the increasingly unpopular emperor scapegoated the Christians in Rome and targeted them with brutal persecution. In this connection, both Tacitus (*Ann.* 15.44) and Suetonius (*Ner.* 16) mention the novel and superstitious beliefs of the Christians, exemplifying the pervasive negative attitude toward the new sect.[2]

After the great fire in Rome, Nero began reconstructing the city to his liking (Tac. *Ann.* 15.42–3; Suet. *Ner.* 16). But two years into this reconstruction program, Jewish unrest that had been simmering for decades boiled over into a full-scale revolt. The military success of the rebel Jewish forces in Judea was rapid but short-lived. The general, Vespasian, was dispatched to quell the revolt with the assistance of his son, Titus (Suet. *Vesp.* 4). Vespasian slowly but steadily subdued the rebel forces beginning in Galilee and progressing toward Jerusalem.

Back in Rome, Nero's legendary intemperate appetites, insatiable extravagance, and unpalatable political intrigue finally caught up with him.[3] Having been declared an enemy of the state by the Senate, Nero avoided a public and humiliating execution by ordering his own secretary to aid in his suicide before the arresting soldiers arrived (Suet. *Ner.* 49). With the death of Nero in 68, the nearly century-long Julio-Claudian dynasty came to an abrupt end.

1.2.2 The Emergence of Christianity and Its Literature

In the last few decades of the long Julio-Claudian Dynasty, Christianity emerged from the troublesome eastern borderlands of the Empire. In the days of Nero, its teachers and their texts found their way to the center of imperial power. During the reigns of Caligula (37–41 CE) and Claudius (41–54 CE), both Roman government and society seem to have been unaware of the existence of a "Christianity" distinct from "Judaism." Suetonius notes that Claudius' expulsion of the Jews from Rome

---

[1] See Edward Champlin, *Nero* (Cambridge, MA: Belknap Press, 2003), 121–5.

[2] See John Granger Cook, *Roman Attitudes toward the Christians: From Claudius to Hadrian*, WUNT 261 (Tübingen: Mohr Siebeck, 2010), 110–11.

[3] For a description of some of Nero's more questionable private and public exploits – including a discussion of doubts regarding their veracity – see Champlin, *Nero*, 145–77.

sometime after 41 was the result of a disturbance caused by one "Chrestus" (Suet. *Claud.* 25.4). Many have considered this to be a misspelling of "Christus" and the unrest a reference to conflict between Christians and Jews in Rome. In any case, Claudius failed to distinguish between the two in his expulsion (Acts 18.2).[4]

Prior to Nero, most Romans simply overlooked the advance of Christianity or only occasionally engaged it in any remarkable way. Actual persecution of Christians was localized and sporadic, not widespread and systematic. Yet with its origin in Judea and counter-cultural tenets, Christianity would have faced a priori damnation in the public eye. In a frequently referenced passage, the historian Tacitus recounts the case of one Pomponia Graecina, a "woman of high family," who was arraigned but found innocent of "alien superstition" (*superstitionis externae*) around the year 57 – during the early years of Nero's reign (54–68 CE) (Tac. *Ann.* 13.32). Whether the superstition in question was Christianity or some other religion, the incident illustrates the general negative attitude of Roman government, society, and culture toward "alien superstition" – of which Christianity was certainly a subspecies.[5]

The reign of Nero also marks the definite beginning of Christian literature. While several of the canonical writings would have been circulated during this period, many scholars of the *Didache* situate its composition as early as 50–70 CE, during the reign of Nero and the events leading up to the First Jewish War (see Chapter 13 for issues related to date of composition of the *Didache*).[6] The text itself bears no obvious witness to its political context. It seems concerned primarily with Christianity's relationship to Judaism and the general social pressures on Christian faith and witness. Perhaps the "mini-apocalypse" (*Did.* 16) comes closest to an acknowledgment of a political crisis, but the language may point the reader to an imminent eschatological trial, not to any then-current events. Yet the uncertain and tumultuous political events of the period would have created a vivid backdrop for the sense of urgency and imminence outlined in the climax of the *Didache*. In any case, the "Two Ways" didactic pattern utilized in the

---

[4] See Cook, *Roman Attitudes*, 11–28.
[5] See Stefan Krauter, *Bürgerrecht und Kultteilnahme: Politische und kultische Rechte und Pflichten in griechischen Poleis, Rom und antikem Judentum*, BZNW 127 (Berlin: de Gryuter, 2004), 279–324.
[6] See Thomas O'Loughlin, *The Didache: A Window on the Earliest Christians* (Grand Rapids, MI: Baker Academic, 2010), 26.

Apostolic Fathers (*Did.* 1.2–6.2; *Barn.* 18–20; *Herm. Mand.* 6.2) was unquestionably in use by Christians at this time.[7]

1.3 THE FLAVIAN DYNASTY (69–96 CE)

Commencing the "Flavian Dynasty," Vespasian's reign lasted nearly a decade until his death in 79. His son Titus then reigned in his place from 79 to 81, followed by another son, Domitian, who reigned the longest from 81 to 96. By the close of this period, both *Didache* and *1 Clement* were probably written. It is possible, too, that the so-called *Epistle of Barnabas* was written after the conclusion of the First Jewish War, and at least early portions of *Shepherd of Hermas* may have been known by the twilight of the Flavian Dynasty.

1.3.1 Galba, Otho, and Vitellius (69 CE)

The year 69, known as the "Year of the Four Emperors," saw a rapid succession of three short-lived rulers after Nero – Galba, Otho, and Vitellius – before Vespasian restored stability.[8] For the preceding two years, Vespasian had been carrying out the task of putting down the Jewish revolt in Judea that had begun in 66 CE. In the midst of the civil war following Nero's death in 69 CE, several armies, including those in Egypt and his own in Judea, swore allegiance to Vespasian as emperor. A broad array of supporters included even the Parthian king Vologases (Suet. *Ves.* 6). As troops secured his position in the capital city against the forces loyal to Vitellius, Vespasian left Judea for Rome. Vespasian's son and lieutenant, Titus, took command of the campaign in Judea and began his famous siege of Jerusalem in 70 (Josephus, *War* 6–7).

1.3.2 Vespasian and Titus (69–81 CE)

Both Suetonius and Tacitus assert that Vespasian's ascent from the battlefield in Judea to the throne in Rome was a fulfillment of an ancient prophecy, that the world would be ruled by leaders from Judea (Suet. *Ves.* 4; Tac. *Hist.* 5.13; cf. Josephus, *War* 6.312–13). It has been speculated that this notion of a Judean emperor was actually derived from Jewish Messianic prophecies (cf. Mic. 5:2). Suetonius says the Jews

---

[7] See M. Jack Suggs, "The Christian Two Ways Tradition: Its Antiquity, Form and Function," in *Studies in New Testament and Early Christian Literature: Essays in Honor of Allen P. Wikgren*, SUPNovT, ed. David E. Aune (Leiden: Brill, 1972), 60–74.

[8] See Martin Goodman, *The Roman World: 44 BC–AD 180*, Routledge History of the Ancient World, ed. Fergus Millar (London: Routledge, 1997), 58–63.

mistakenly applied this to themselves, provoking them to revolt. Christians at the time would no doubt have regarded both the Jewish and Roman expectations of a Judean ruler as just so much nonsense, as they regarded the crucified, resurrected, and ascended Jesus of Nazareth to be the true fulfillment of these expectations.[9]

As emperor, Vespasian immediately got to work cleaning up after Nero and restoring the glories of Rome (Suet. *Ves.* 8–9). He launched numerous building projects, including the rebuilding of the Capitol destroyed in Nero's fire and the commencement of the Colosseum in the center of the city. Regarded as a man of humility, gentleness, decency, and joviality, Vespasian was also known for his diligence in public service (Suet. *Ves.* 10–24). He enacted several decrees with the cooperation of the Senate to reform the courts and to reverse social and moral license that had taken root during Nero's negligence. He died at the age of 69, with noncontroversial instructions that his sons, Titus and Domitian, would succeed him.

For all practical purposes, Titus had been reigning together with Vespasian and reflected many of his father's virtues of leadership (*Tit.* 7). This contributed to a smooth succession in 79 CE. Tragically, at the age of 41, a mere two years after succeeding Vespasian, Titus died from an illness. According to Suetonius, Titus was "the darling and delight of the human race" (*amor ac deliciae generis humani*) (*Tit.* 1). His early death was viewed as a great loss to humanity.

In the span of time between the death of Nero and the rise of Domitian, then, the Christian churches throughout the world appear to have enjoyed a general peace and security. Though Tacitus' testimony regarding Nero's persecution reflects the general negative attitude of Romans to the Christian "superstition," he also relays that those same Romans were moved to compassion for the Christians who were brutally treated to satisfy the bloodlust of Nero (Tac. *Ann.* 15.44). In contrast, neither Suetonius nor Tacitus mentions Christian persecutions associated with the reigns of Vespasian or Titus. Suetonius even points out the justice and mercy exercised by Vespasian, noting that "he never took pleasure in the death of anyone, but even wept and sighed over those who suffered merited punishment" (Suet. *Ves.* 15).[10] It is hardly conceivable that anything like the persecutions of Nero would

---

[9] Barbara Levick, *Vespasian* (London: Routledge, 1999), 67–8.

[10] Translation from John C. Rolfe, trans., *Suetonius*, vol. 2, rev. ed., Loeb Classical Library, vol. 38, ed. Jeffrey Henderson (Cambridge, MA: Harvard University Press, 1997), 295.

have occurred at an official level in such a climate of imperial justice and restraint.

Under Vespasian and Titus, the followers of Jesus likely experienced a long summer season of growth and expansion during which they cultivated a religious and social identity distinct from their Jewish spiritual ancestors. In the aftermath of the First Jewish War (66–73), Christians would have had every motive to distinguish themselves from the Jews and their religion in the eyes of the Romans. Not only would such a distinction have distanced Christians from accusations of armed revolt, it would also have meant they avoided paying a tax levied against Jews after the Jewish War.[11] Perhaps it was during the reign of Vespasian after the First Jewish War that *Barnabas* was written.[12] The author refers to "the war" (*Barn.* 16.4) in which "the city and the temple and the people of Israel were handed over" to destruction (16.5). "This," the author notes, "came to pass, just as the Lord said" (16.5). However, the reference could also point to events surrounding the later Bar Kokhba Revolt.

1.3.3 Domitian (81–96 CE)

With the untimely death of Titus in 81 CE, his younger brother Domitian succeeded him. Domitian had commenced his public service under the reigns of Vespasian and Titus by emulating the virtue, justice, and generosity of his father and elder brother (Suet. *Dom.* 4–9). However, with greater power and responsibility, Domitian's character took a turn toward the strange and cruel. He became infamous for numerous unjust and irrational executions, often for light or non-existent offenses (*Dom.* 10–11, 15). His reasonable suspicion of disloyalty in the upper ranks led to exiles and executions of detractors and critics that deeply scarred the Senate.[13]

Eventually hated and feared by even his closest friends, not to mention by his powerful enemies, Domitian became the object of a conspiracy to assassinate him. Despite his desperate attempts at dodging his fate, the emperor was slain in his own bed chamber (Suet. *Dom.* 14, 16–17). Though the armies of Rome responded with anger at

---

[11] See Marius Heemstra, *The Fiscus Judaicus and the Parting of the Ways*, WUNT 277 (Tübingen: Mohr Siebeck, 2010).

[12] See John A.T. Robinson, *Redating the New Testament* (Philadelphia, PA: Westminster, 1976), 313–19; cf. discussion in Ferdinand-Rupert Prostmeier, *Der Barnabasbrief*, Kommentar zu den Apostolischen Vätern 8 (Göttingen: Vandenhoeck & Ruprecht, 1999), 119–30.

[13] Brian W. Jones, *The Emperor Domitian* (London: Routledge, 1992), 180–92.

the assassination of the emperor, the Senate rejoiced at his death, wasting no time in scrubbing images of Domitian from public places (Cass. Dio *Hist. rom.* 68.1; Suet. *Dom.* 23). Thus, the Flavian dynasty came to an end, having begun with nobility and virtue but ending in scandal and vice.

It is noteworthy that Domitian demanded the title "Our Lord and God" (*dominus et deus noster*) be used in oral or written address (Suet. *Dom.* 13). This, of course, would stand in direct conflict with Christian convictions (cf. Jn. 20:28; Rev. 4:11). How deep and wide Domitian's direct anti-Christian policies and practices were, however, is difficult to discern with any certainty. Portrayals of Domitian as an anti-Christian megalomaniac are almost certainly overblown. Jews were especially singled out for harsh treatment in taxation, and Suetonius' language suggests Domitian may have also imposed the same tax on Christians – "who without publicly acknowledging that faith yet lived as Jews" (Suet. *Dom.* 12).[14] Beyond this debatable possibility, neither Tacitus nor Suetonius provides any evidence of a widespread persecution targeting Christians during his reign. The later accounts of persecution directed specifically at the apostle John or others cannot be dismissed out of hand, but it is impossible to discern whether actual historical events grounding these stories represent isolated, local incidents of mistreatment or a broader policy against Christians.[15]

With regard to the Apostolic Fathers, it is hardly doubted that the epistle from the church in Rome to the church in Corinth, traditionally titled *1 Clement*, was written in the latter days of Domitian's reign.[16] Yet the epistle itself gives no clear indication of the political situation in Rome at the time. Some have suggested that Clement of Rome, perhaps a presiding elder in the city at the time, may have been related to (or even identified as) Flavius Clemens, who had been executed by Domitian for "atheism" and "Jewish" impiety. Such terms may well describe Christian convictions seen from the perspective of ill-informed outsiders (Suet. *Dom.* 15; Cass. Dio. *Hist. rom.* 67.14). This connection can be neither demonstrated nor disproved.[17] Others have interpreted the unclear phrase "sudden and successive calamities" in association with Roman Christians in *1 Clem.* 1.1 as an indirect reference to

---

[14] Rolfe, *Suetonius*, 349.
[15] Cook, *Roman Attitudes*, 136–7.
[16] Andreas Lindemann, *Die Apostolischen Väter*, vol. 1, *Die Clemensbriefe*, Handbuch zum Neuen Testament 17 (Tübingen: Mohr Siebeck, 1992), 12.
[17] Jones, *Emperor Domitian*, 115.

persecution under Domitian. If Domitian had taken actions to root out Christian superstition and impiety, this may form the political backdrop for the imagery of the canonical Apocalypse of John. It may also set the stage for the apocalyptic urgency of at least the earlier and more eschatologically dramatic visions of *Shepherd of Hermas*, which some have dated in the late first century around Domitian's reign.[18] However, a widespread official persecution of Christians under the emperor is not firmly established by historians.

1.4 THE FIVE GOOD EMPERORS (96–180 CE)

In the aftermath of the reign of Domitian and the end of the Flavian Dynasty, the Senate appointed one of their own as emperor – Nerva Cocceius. He only reigned for two years, from 96 to 98 CE, during which he adopted as his heir and successor the popular general Trajan (98–117 CE). After Trajan's death, Hadrian ruled until 138, followed by Antoninus Pius (138–161 CE), then Marcus Aurelius (161–180 CE) with Lucius Verus (161–169 CE). During this golden age of the Roman Empire, all of the writings known as the Apostolic Fathers likely had been completed. The transition from the "apostolic" teachers who were regarded with renown as associates or students of the apostles gave way to the post-apostolic age in which the memories of such first-hand witnesses of apostolic times would be available only in written records.

1.4.1 Nerva (96–98 CE) and Trajan (98–117 CE)

In the year 96 CE, the Senate appointed as Emperor the elderly and sickly senator, Nerva, who immediately began a program of reversal and restitution after the reign of Domitian. One of his reforms was to put a stop to accusations of "Jewish living" (*Ioudaikou biou*) (Cass. Dio, *Hist. rom.* 68.1). This could reasonably be interpreted as a reference to Christians who, though Gentiles, appeared to outsiders to be living by Jewish precepts. If this interpretation is correct, it slightly increases the possibility that Nerva's predecessor, Domitian, had, in fact, engaged in at least limited persecutions against Christians in Rome, which was then suspended after his death (see Eus. *Hist. eccl.* 3.20.8; 3.23.1). By all accounts, Nerva ruled peaceably, responsibly, and virtuously. As his physical strength waned, Nerva declared the adoption of the Spaniard

---

[18] Carolyn Osiek, *The Shepherd of Hermas: A Commentary*, Hermeneia (Minneapolis, MN: Fortress, 1999), 20.

governor of Germany, Trajan. After serving as emperor for one year and four months, Nerva died (Cass. Dio, *Hist. rom.* 68.3–4).

Trajan was known for justice, courage, and strength in both body and mind. Cassius Dio suggests Trajan was loved by all and feared by none but his enemies (*Hist. rom.* 68.7). He successfully waged war against the Dacians, who occupied the region of the northwest of the Black Sea, roughly coterminous with the present country of Romania. After two wars (101–2 and 105–6), Trajan secured the borderlands and expanded the boundaries of the Empire to the northeast. At the same time, the Roman governor of Syria expanded the southeastern border of the Empire into Arabia, near Petra (Cass. Dio, *Hist. rom.* 68.8–14). After 106, having subdued the Dacians, Trajan returned to Rome to carry out his administrative duties with great wisdom and skill (68.15–16). Upon his return and in celebration of the victory, Trajan hosted a number of officials from nations as far as India, and he delighted the public with gladiatorial spectacles in the arenas for four months (68.15).

It is commonly believed that on such an occasion, around 107, the governor of Syria, named Palma, arrested Ignatius of Antioch and transported him from Antioch to Rome. Having recently expanded his own borders into Arabia and thus desiring to celebrate their shared victories (Cass. Dio, *Hist. rom.* 68.14, 16), Palma offered Trajan the revered bishop of Antioch as a gift. This would place the composition of Ignatius' seven letters around 107 CE. Ignatius' arrival in Rome to fight wild beasts would have occurred at the end of a three-to-four-month journey – just near the close of Trajan's period of public spectacles around the year 108 CE (see Chapter 11 on the letters of Ignatius).

In the year 111 CE, Trajan held an illuminating correspondence with Pliny the Younger, governor of Bithynia and Pontus, regarding Christians (*Lib.* 10.96, *Plinius Traiano Imperatori* and *Lib.* 10.97, *Traianus Plinio*). In his letter to the Emperor, Pliny sought counsel concerning the prosecution and punishment of convicted members of the growing superstition of Christianity. He had personally discovered their beliefs and practices by interviewing those who had once been Christians but who had denounced the religion (10.96.6–7). This testimony he supplemented with the interrogation of two tortured female *ministrae* (ministers) who still professed Christianity. He concluded that there was nothing particularly dangerous about their absurd religion, but they were obstinate and stubborn against official Roman piety (*Lib.* 10.96.8).

Pliny's epistle provides testimony to the fact that Trajan had forbidden illicit assemblies of the Christians (10.96.7), perhaps partly in order to revive the floundering commerce of official Roman religion (96.10). Pliny also notes that the Christian superstition had already spread like a disease throughout cities and villages and was making headway in all classes of society – young and old, men and women (96.9). Even with this broad expansion, Pliny seems to have been unfamiliar with the details of Christian beliefs and practices. He had never been present at any trials of Christians and he seems not to have had direct access to any high-level officials who had (96.1–2). Thus, at least in Pliny's Bithynia and Pontus, Christianity was still seen as an obscure but growing superstition. It was illegal but not particularly dangerous. It was liable to punishment, but too new for Rome to have a well-established judicial tradition on which to lean.

In Trajan's corresponding letter, he seems to take a rather "soft" approach to the prosecution and punishment of Christians. Rather than establishing rigid guidelines, each case was to be treated individually (*Lib.* 10.97.1). The government was to spend no resources hunting down Christians, but if they were turned over to the authorities for their impiety based on credible evidence, then they should be justly punished. Nevertheless, if an accused Christian were to repent of their superstition and demonstrate loyalty to the Roman religion by invoking the gods, that one should simply be pardoned (97.2). The tenor of this approach can be read as complementary to the much later characterization of persecution described by Eusebius: sporadic, in some cities, and instigated by the populace (Eus. *Hist. eccl.* 3.32.1).

Some years later, around 114 CE, Trajan was again called to battle, this time against the perennially problematic Parthians on the eastern border (Cassius Dio, *Hist. rom.* 68.17–20). While staying in Antioch in 115 CE, a massive earthquake struck, which resulted in great damage to life and property (68.24–5). Escaping from that natural disaster, he continued eastward into Mesopotamia and reached Babylon before advancing to Ctesiphon, the capital of Parthia, then to the Red Sea (68.26–9).

It was at this time that the lands conquered by Trajan in the east began to rumble with revolt (Cass. Dio, *Hist. rom.* 68.29–33). This included numerous uprisings by Jews in various regions – Cyrene, Egypt, and Cyprus (68.32). Trajan himself fell into illness while the conquered territories of Armenia, Mesopotamia, and the Parthians slipped through the fingers of Roman armies unable to hold them. While still far from home, Trajan succumbed to his worsening sickness and died in Cilicia, west of Syria, in 117 CE.

According to a common view, Polycarp of Smyrna collected and began circulating Ignatius' correspondence within a short time after the

Antiochene bishop's brief stay in Smyrna on his way to Rome for public execution. Depending on whether one holds to one or two letters of Polycarp (see Chapter 12 on Polycarp), at least part of his extant letter to the Philippians was written during the time of Trajan, perhaps as early as 108–110 CE. About this time, Papias of Hierapolis may have begun compiling his *Expositions of the Sayings of the Lord* (Eus. *Hist. eccl.* 3.36.1–2), a project that could have extended for several decades.

It is also probable that composition, redaction, or revision on *Didache* and *Shepherd of Hermas* was occurring during this period (see Chapters 13 and 15 on these writings for introductory issues). The narrative frame of the visions, mandates, and parables of the *Shepherd* places it in Rome and its immediate environs in central Italy (*Vis.* 1.1–2; 4.1.2). Also, *Vision* 3 refers to those who were persecuted in Rome by lashings, imprisonments, great persecutions, crucifixions, and wild beasts (*Vis.* 3.2.1). The language suggests a category of faithful sufferers of the past whose example was worthy of imitating (*Vis.* 3.1.9). This indicates some period of intense local persecution in the past, but close enough to serve as a vivid example of endurance. Though the persecution under Nero had occurred decades earlier, its trauma would have lingered in the minds of Roman Christians. Perhaps the author of *Shepherd of Hermas* intended his hearers to recall the suffering under Nero. However, it is possible that the author also had in mind more recent periods of less extreme persecution during the reigns of Domitian or Trajan.

1.4.2 Hadrian (117–138 CE)

When Trajan died in Cilicia, certain less-than-scrupulous machinations by influential leaders led to the appointment of his cousin, Hadrian, governor of Syria, while he was still in Antioch (see Cass. Dio, *Hist. rom.* 69.1–2).[19] Though some took note of Hadrian's jealousy of those who seemed to surpass him in intellect and skill, he was also esteemed as generally just, wise, benevolent, affable, and attentive (69.2–4). Perhaps insecure and demanding, Hadrian could not be accurately described as cruel or capricious.

---

[19] Birley notes, "The Adoption Was, at Best, by a Dying Man and Stage-Managed by the Empress" (Anthony R. Birley, *Hadrian: The Restless Emperor* [London: Routledge, 1997], 77). Also see Michael Grant, *The Roman Emperors: A Biographical Guide to the Rulers of Imperial Rome 31 B.C.–A.D. 476* (New York: Barnes & Noble, 1985), 76–7.

Hadrian traveled far and wide throughout the empire, overseeing the organization and training of armies as well as promoting the construction of theatres, harbors, and monuments (Cass. Dio, *Hist. rom.* 69.5–11, 16). Hadrian's military preparedness prevented major wars with borderlands, and his general good will toward subjects and allies prevented revolt from his own people. However, in 133, Hadrian renamed Jerusalem "Aelia Capitolina" and constructed a new temple to Jupiter in the place of the Jewish temple that had been razed in 70 during Titus's siege. This action was regarded by Jews as an intolerable impiety and blasphemy against the one true God. It led to a major conflict known as the "Bar Kokhba Revolt" (c. 132–135), led by the messianic aspirant, Simon bar Kokhba (or ben Kosiva). Eventually the unrest and rebellion spread outside of Judea to other Jewish communities throughout the world (69.12–14).

In response to the Jewish uprising, Hadrian ordered his best generals to systematically and thoroughly break their military power, douse their burning messianic dreams of a free and independent kingdom on earth, and humiliate the Jews to such a degree that they would never think of rebelling again (69.13–15). It is difficult to exaggerate the enduring trauma affected by the Bar Kokhba Revolt on the Romans, the Jewish people, and even the Christians. Cassius Dio reports that though many Romans perished in the war, casualties among the Jews numbered 580,000, not including an inestimable number who died from the effects of famine and disease after the war (69.13–14). Rome then reorganized the regions of Syria and Judea as *Syria Palestina*, which would have been seen by Jews in the Roman Empire as a sign of utter defeat. Regarding Christians living in Judea at the time of the revolt, Justin Martyr claims that during the war, Simon Bar Kokhba unleashed violence against Christians who refused to deny Jesus as the messiah, perhaps because Bar Kokhba himself had been hailed as the long-expected messiah by his Jewish supporters (*1 Apol.* 31).

In 136 CE, when his health began to fail, Hadrian controversially adopted as heir and successor the senator Lucius (Commodus) Aelius (Cass. Dio, *Hist. rom.* 69.17). However, when Lucius died suddenly on January 1, 138 CE, Hadrian had to select a new successor. From his deathbed, in the presence of renowned senators, he adopted as heir the senator Antoninus Pius, a man deemed by Hadrian to be noble, gentle, lenient, and wise. Antoninus reluctantly accepted the appointment (69.20). Hadrian died at 62, having served as emperor for nearly 21 years.

Christian memory of Hadrian's reign was positive, as he seems to have at least upheld similar standards of justice for accused Christians as Trajan had.[20] Hadrian's reply to Minucius Fundanus, proconsul of Asia (c. 123 CE), indicates that the emperor himself had no policy of active persecution against Christians (Justin, *1 Apol.* 68; cf. Eus. *Hist. eccl.* 4.9). Yet it also demonstrates that Christians were experiencing local persecution at the hands of the general population or by Roman officials who were uncertain how to deal with the growth and expansion of the faith. The fact that the earliest Christian apologists – Quadratus, Aristides of Athens, and Justin Martyr – addressed their pleas on behalf of Christians to Hadrian or his successor, Antoninus, indicates not only the need for official imperial relief from local injustices but also the hope that their defenses might receive a favorable response from the Emperors (Eus. *Hist. eccl.* 4.3.1–2; Arist. *Apol.* 1; Justin, *1 Apol.* 1).

Though some scholars believe *Barnabas* was written sometime in the 70s after the events of the First Jewish War (see brief discussion above), most favor a later date in connection with Hadrian's reign and the Bar Kokhba Revolt. The text clearly refers to the temple in Jerusalem as a thing of the past (*Barn.* 16.1–2). Yet it also notes that though the temple was torn down by the enemies of the Jews, "now even those servants of the enemies will rebuild it" (16.4). Perhaps this rebuilding of the temple by the "servants of the enemies" of Israel refers to Hadrian's project of constructing the temple to Jupiter on the temple mount in 133 CE. If so, the use of the future tense "will rebuild" would place *Barnabas* in the early 130s – after Titus's destruction of the temple sixty years earlier but prior to the Bar Kokhba Revolt. On the other hand, the author of *Barnabas* may have simply had in mind prophecies of a future temple built in connection with the coming of the "man of lawlessness" in the last days leading to the coming of Christ (Dan. 9:26–7; 2 Thess. 2:4; cf. Iren. *Adv. Haer.* 5.25.2–4). In any case, the reign of Hadrian tends to satisfy most scholars as the *terminus ante quem* for the composition or redaction of *Barnabas*.

1.4.3 Antoninus Pius (138–161 CE)

When Antoninus assumed the throne in place of Hadrian, he proved to be a conservative force, maintaining the stability and trajectory of his predecessor. His reign was characterized by a general peace, with no major wars or upheavals and only a few relatively minor skirmishes. Perhaps most notable was the engagement and conquest of a number of British tribes in 139–140 CE by the Roman governor of Britain, Quintus

[20] Cook, *Roman Attitudes*, 279–80.

Lollius Urbicus. The three legions in Britain conquered lowland Scotland and established the border 160 kilometers farther north than Hadrian's wall. A new wall, begun in 142 CE and completed by 155 CE, marked the greatest extent of the Roman Empire in Britain. In 162 CE, however, the border was reestablished at Hadrian's Wall.

Antoninus himself was not a military leader. It is doubtful whether he ever left Italy itself, quite unlike his predecessor, Hadrian, who personally visited most of Rome's provinces. The extension of the border in Britain proved to be Antoninus' most laudable military achievement. However, the emperor was well known for his extensive projects that improved the infrastructure across the empire. Both domestically and abroad, Antoninus was respected and honored. Known as a peace-maker, he successfully negotiated disputes between subjects and cities as well as rendered financial assistance to those suffering from disasters and tragedies. Marcus Aurelius' glowing characterization of Antoninus, his adoptive father, reveals a man of gentleness, modesty, reasonableness, justice, and public and private virtues (*Med.* 1.16.1–10; 6.2–4).

Later Christian historians report that Antoninus not only exhibited good personal and noble public character, but he also showed respect and honor toward Christians. The snippets of information from later historians preserved in Xiphilinus' abridgment of Cassius Dio (*Hist. rom.* 70.1–7) read more like hagiography than history. Chronologically contemporary to Antoninus, however, are the *Apologies* of Justin Martyr. In the midst of Antoninus' reign, Justin addressed his *1 Apology* to "the Emperor Titus Aelius Hadrianus Antoninus Pius Augustus Caesar, and to his philosopher son Verissimus, and to Lucius the philosopher, Caesar's natural son and Pius's adopted son, a lover of culture, and to the Sacred Senate and all the Roman people" (Justin, *1 Apol.* 1).[21] The "philosopher son Verissimus" is none other than Marcus Aurelius, who had attended and assisted Antoninus as the emperor became increasingly enfeebled in his later years. From 156 until his death in 161, his adopted son and heir apparent, Marcus Aurelius, took on more administrative responsibilities. On his deathbed, Antoninus made it clear that his office was to be passed on to Marcus.

During Antoninus' reign, the Christians in the Roman Empire enjoyed a prolonged period of relative peace and security. However, the negative attitude toward Christianity harbored by the general

---

[21] Translation from Leslie W. Barnard, *Justin Martyr: The First and Second Apologies*, Ancient Christian Writers (Mahwah, NJ: Paulist, 1997), 23.

populace and some local governors did flare up on occasion. This is evidenced by Polycarp's public execution in Smyrna around the year 156 CE. The author of the *Martyrdom of Polycarp* suggests that with the Smyrnaean bishop's death, the persecution against the Christians in the city came to an end (*Mart. Pol.* 1.1). This is likely a reference to eleven others from Smyrna and Philadelphia who preceded Polycarp in martyrdom (cf. 19.1). Yet even this language suggests the persecution in Asia was a brief flare-up rather than a long burn. The same document also provides insight into the early Christians' policy regarding their relationship with the local authorities. Just as the policy of Trajan discouraged governors from actively pursuing the arrest of Christians, so Christians discouraged one another from actively surrendering to the authorities (*Mart. Pol.* 4).

Martyrdom provides a powerful and moving account of steadfast confession of a famous Christian leader in the face of persecution by an unjust proconsul. Yet it would probably be best to imagine that normal everyday life for Christians throughout the Empire was quiet and tranquil most of the time. With access to reliable infrastructure and secure roads, Christians would have been free and eager to travel far and wide. This would have contributed greatly to the sharing of texts, traditions, and teachers from one Christian community to another. Polycarp himself is said to have traveled from Smyrna to Rome to confer with bishop Anicetus around 154 (Eus. *Hist. eccl.* 5.24). This same environment of peace and security would also allow for the fermentation and propagation of competing documents, doctrines, and doctors. So, not only did Christians in this period compose, copy, and circulate writings like 2 *Clement* and the final form of *Shepherd of Hermas*, but other voices and viewpoints also made themselves heard. In the 140s, Marcion of Sinope planted the seeds of his alternate dualistic interpretation of Christianity in Rome. About the same time, in the same city, Valentinus' system of Christian gnosis grew in popularity. And probably shortly after Polycarp's martyrdom in the province of Asia, Montanus began his prophetic movement in nearby Phrygia, which challenged the established doctrines and leadership of the churches. Thus, with relative freedom came diversity, and with diversity came internal conflict.

1.4.4 Marcus Aurelius (161–180 CE) and Lucius Verus (161–169 CE)

When Marcus Aurelius assumed the throne as emperor according to the wishes of his adoptive father, Antoninus Pius, he appointed as co-emperor his adoptive brother Lucius Verus – natural son of Lucius

Commodus. It should be recalled that Lucius Commodus had been Hadrian's initial choice as his own successor, but Commodus' untimely death prevented it, leading to the appointment of Antoninus (Cass. Dio, *Hist. rom.* 69.17). The newly enthroned Marcus was "perhaps the most unlikely of all emperors."[22] A man of letters and deep learning, he benefitted from the military leadership of the younger Lucius Verus.

Like a lump of dough rolled too thin, the ambitious expansion of the Roman Empire during the previous century led to weak spots in the middle and instability at the edges. Marcus and Lucius inherited this situation and immediately began feeling its effects. The same year of their ascension to power, Vologases IV of Parthia rekindled a century-old conflict over the occupancy of the throne of Armenia. This led to another prolonged Parthian–Roman war between 161 and 166 CE. After devastating losses on both sides, the Roman legions achieved a hard-won victory (Cass. Dio, *Hist. rom.* 71.2). Whatever peace had been enjoyed under Antoninus Pius was lost under the brother-emperors Marcus and Lucius. Not only did the border with Parthia explode in war, but other frontiers of the Empire began to experience considerable unrest (71.3). As Roman legions focused attention on the eastern border, the northern frontier weakened. Eventually war erupted in the north-central border with the Germanic Marcomanni tribe, which raged on to 180. Other uprisings and conflicts boiled over in Syria and north Africa.[23]

After the conclusion of the Parthian War, Lucius and his armies returned to Rome with a disease – perhaps smallpox – that came to be known as the "Antonine Plague." It was this disease that likely took the life of Lucius in 169 CE. The plague continued on for another decade, killing an estimated five million people. Marcus Aurelius himself survived the plague and lived until 180 CE, when he died of natural causes. His natural son, Commodus, who had ruled with him as co-regent since 177 CE, succeeded Marcus Aurelius as Emperor. With this succession, the age of the Five Good Emperors of the Nerva–Antonine dynasty came to an end.

Though scholars believe most of the writings included in the collection of the Apostolic Fathers had been composed or redacted to their extant forms by the end of the reign of Antoninus Pius (138–161 CE), it is possible that perhaps portions of the *Epistle to Diognetus* were composed during this period, though a case could be made for an earlier date

[22] Goodman, *Roman World*, 73.
[23] Grant, *Roman Emperors*, 89–91.

(see Chapter 16 on *Epistle to Diognetus*). In that writing, the unknown author describes Christians as living in both Greek and barbarian cities, following local customs, and living virtuous lives as good citizens (*Diogn.* 5.1–5). Nevertheless, the author also describes the Christians as despised by the world, beaten up and punished simply for functioning as the conscience of the kingdoms in which they dwelled (6.1–10).

Persecutions of Christians seem to have intensified during the latter decades of the Roman Empire, as did the multiplication of competing texts, traditions, and teachers propounding versions of Christianity that challenged notions of doctrinal continuity and cohesion among the growing movement. This is probably best attributed to the general unrest and disorder fomenting throughout the Empire rather than to any deliberate, official attempt by either Marcus Aurelius or Lucius Verus to exterminate Christianity. The persecutions themselves – as well as the increasingly harsh and pointed censures against Christianity by philosophers and critics – were still localized and episodic.[24] In any case, in the midst of a local persecution targeting Christians in Rome around the year 165, Justin was executed, and Eusebius of Caesarea relays an account of brutal persecution that occurred in Vienne and Lyons in 177 CE (Eus. *Hist. eccl.* 5.1.3).

With the close of the reign of the "Five Good Emperors," the era of the Apostolic Fathers also came to an end. With the possible exception of *Epistle to Diognetus*, which may have been composed in the last decades of the second century, all of the writings in this corpus had been written. Many had been widely distributed far from their places of origin. A couple had even been occasionally quoted as Holy Scripture. From that point forward, subsequent generations would highly regard these diverse texts for their close proximity to the age of the Apostles. And today they provide invaluable insight into the history of both church and empire.

FURTHER READING

Bennett, Julian. *Trajan: Optimus Princeps.* London: Routledge, 1997.
Birley, Anthony R. *Hadrian: The Restless Emperor.* London: Routledge, 1997.
    Marcus Aurelius: A Biography. rev. ed. London: Routledge, 2013.
Cook, John Granger. *Roman Attitudes Toward the Christians: From Claudius to Hadrian.* WUNT 261. Tübingen: Mohr Siebeck, 2010.

---

[24] For a survey of Christian and non-Christian sources during this period, see Ralph Martin Novak, Jr., *Christianity and the Roman Empire: Background Texts* (Harrisburg, PA: Trinity Press International, 2001), 43–97.

Goodman, Martin, with Jane Sherwood. *The Roman World: 44 BC–AD 180*. Routledge History of the Ancient World. Ed. Fergus Millar. London: Routledge, 1997.

Grant, Michael. *The Antonines: The Roman Empire in Transition*. London: Routledge, 1994.

Jones, Brian W. *The Emperor Domitian*. London: Routledge, 1992.

Levick, Barbara. *The Government of the Roman Empire: A Sourcebook*. 2nd ed. London: Routledge, 2000.

Vespasian. London: Routledge, 1999.

Shotter, David. *Nero Caesar Augustus: Emperor of Rome*. New York: Routledge, 2014.

2 The Image of Jews and Judaism in the Apostolic Fathers

PHILIP ALEXANDER

2.1 INTRODUCTION

Christianity and Judaism as we know them today can both be traced back to the richly diverse Judaism that flourished in Palestine in late Second Temple times, but it was only after 70 CE that the two traditions began to define themselves over against each other in mutually exclusive ways. The period between the First Jewish Revolt (66–74 CE) and the Bar Kokhba war (132–135 CE) – the period in which much of the New Testament and the Apostolic Fathers was written – was crucial in this development. The aim of this study will be to throw light on this parting of the ways. It will outline briefly what we know about Rabbinic Judaism in Palestine and synagogal Judaism in the Diaspora at this time, and then read against this picture the references to Jews and Judaism in the Apostolic Fathers, especially in the Epistle of Barnabas. What Barnabas shows is a Christianity that sharply differentiates itself from Judaism, but at the same time does not want to sever all ties. It wants to hold on to the Jewish Scriptures as word of God, but through a process of allegorization to appropriate them as Christian Scripture.

2.2 THE AFTERMATH OF THE FALL OF THE TEMPLE

The defeat of the Jews in the First Revolt against Rome (66–74 CE) marks a turning point in the development of Judaism.[1] The effects would have been felt most keenly in Judea and the Galilee, the heartlands of the fighting, where devastation and disruption of economic,

---

[1] For a basic account of the war and its aftermath, see E. Schürer, *The History of the Jewish People in the Age of Jesus Christ*, rev. Geza Vermes, Fergus Millar, Matthew Black, and Martin Goodman, 3 vols. (Edinburgh: T&T Clark, 1973–86), 1.514–59; Peter Schäfer, *The History of the Jews in the Greco-Roman World* (Abingdon: Routledge, 2003), 121–62.

administrative, and social life was widespread. The Romans rounded up sizable numbers of Jews and sold them into slavery. The leadership of the Jewish community, locally and especially nationally, was severely weakened. Prior to the revolt the national leadership and the key national institutions were based in Jerusalem in or near the Temple. Now Jerusalem was laid waste, the Temple destroyed, its worship ended, and many of its priests scattered or killed. The shock-waves of the disaster rippled out into the Diaspora. Day-to-day life outside Palestine would not have been so dramatically affected, though cities such as Alexandria, where tensions between the Jewish and non-Jewish populations were high, probably witnessed a spike in anti-Jewish feeling and incidents. But the main impact on the Diaspora was emotional and theological. The Hasmoneans and the Herodians had made strenuous efforts to assume the leadership of world Jewry. They had promoted, with some success, the idea of pilgrimage to the Temple, which the Torah had enjoined on all Israelites three times a year (Exod. 34.18–23; Deut. 16.16–17). Herod's magnificent refurbishment of the building was not just an act of self-aggrandizement, but an effective way of boosting the economy of Jerusalem, a city with few natural resources or advantages, not even situated, like Mecca, close to a major international trade route. The policy was effective and many Diaspora Jews developed a strong bond with Jerusalem, and regarded it as their "mother city" (*mētropolis*: Philo, *Flacc.* 46). And, for the more reflective, there was the acute theological problem of what the end of the Temple sacrifices meant for their relationship with their God. Was the Sinai covenant broken? How would the sins of Israel be atoned for, now the sacrifices had ended?

For the events of the revolt itself we have the account of Josephus in his *Jewish War*. Despite its shortcomings this is a well-informed narrative by someone who was in the thick of the action. But Josephus tells us next-to-nothing about what happened after the war: his account effectively ends with the fall of Masada in 74 CE. The close of the first century and the first half of the second are poorly documented as far as Judaism is concerned. Little can be gleaned from Greek and Roman authors, and the archaeological and epigraphic record is meagre. We have a few apocalypses from the period, preserved by the Church, usually in translation (4 Ezra, 2 Baruch, the Apocalypse of Abraham and some of the Sybilline Oracles, e.g. Book 5), and there is the extensive Rabbinic literature, which contains some stories about these years, and the names and dicta of authorities who lived then.

2.3 THE EMERGENCE OF RABBINIC JUDAISM IN PALESTINE

It is with the last of these bodies of evidence that histories tend to start, but it is problematic in the extreme.[2] The earliest of the Rabbinic texts to touch on our period, the Mishnah, was edited around 200 CE. The rest are much later, and include traditions found not only in Palestinian sources (the Tosefta, the Midrashim, and the Talmud Yerushalmi) but in the Babylonian Talmud, compiled some 1,500 miles away from where the events were supposed to take place, and centuries after they happened. The Mishnah refers to some sixty scholars (belonging to the so-called first, second, and early third generations of Tannaim) who flourished between 70 and 150 CE, but they record little about their lives. What they give are dicta and rulings they made, and legal disputes that they had with each other. Important figures are Yoḥanan ben Zakkai, Rabban Gamaliel (the younger, grandson of the Gamaliel of Acts 5.34 and 22.3), Aqiva, Ishmael, and Eliezer ben Hyrcanus.

In the case of the more quoted Rabbis attempts have been made to cobble together some sort of biography by collecting the isolated traditions relating to a particular sage and analyzing them, but the results must be treated with caution. Though in some cases the isolated rulings, when brought together, display an impressive coherence, suggesting that they may well accurately reflect the broad legal stance of the authority in question, nothing remotely like a biography can be reconstructed. And would-be modern biographers have usually to rely on *post*-Mishnaic texts for key narrative elements – a problematic source, as I shall argue in a moment. Some scholars seek comfort in the fact that a number of the early Tannaim founded schools, and thus there was (arguably) a channel by which their sayings could be passed down through the generations, and they stress the widespread injunctions in Rabbinic literature to students to repeat faithfully the words of their teachers, but what counted as fidelity did not necessarily mean preserving the master's *ipsissima verba*. The highly formulaic structures of the Mishnah often mean that the *ipsissima verba* were *not* preserved. The substance of the ruling may have been, but not the master's actual words. Moreover, in the case of multiple attestations of the same tradition, the wording does

---

[2] For the literature, see Günter Stemberger, *Introduction to the Talmud and Midrash*, 2nd ed. (Edinburgh: T&T Clark, 1996), and for the problem of using it for historical purposes, Martin Goodman and Philip Alexander (eds.), *Rabbinic Texts and the History of Late-Roman Palestine* (Oxford: Oxford University Press, 2010).

not always agree, and the same ruling can be attributed to different authorities in different places. All this counsels caution.

A sort of Rabbinic historiography of the early Tannaitic period developed within the Rabbinic schools after the publication of the Mishnah around 200 CE. One legend that emerged has played a disproportionate role in the modern history of Judaism after 70 CE: it is the story of Yoḥanan ben Zakkai's dramatic escape from besieged Jerusalem and, with Roman permission, his founding of a House of Study (*Beit Midrash*) at Yavneh. The story is clearly offered in the ancient sources as some sort of foundation myth for the Rabbinic movement, and it has been accepted more or less at face value by many modern historians. Yoḥanan's modest school was elevated into a full-blown "Synod," which laid the foundations for the future survival of Judaism. It was credited, *inter alia*, with finally closing the canon of Scripture and sorting out the synagogue liturgy. But the story is deeply suspect. It is recorded in a variety of versions, in the Avot deRabbi Natan (both recensions A and B), in Lamentations Rabbah (to Lamentations 1.5), and in the Babylonian Talmud, Gittin 56a. The earliest of these sources probably dates to the 4th/5th century at the earliest, and many details of the story, which is told artfully and with verve, are blatantly legendary.[3]

If the evidence is so sparse and doubtful, can we say anything useful about the development of Rabbinic Judaism in the aftermath of the destruction of the Temple in 70 CE, and the catastrophic failure of the revolt? With caution, I think we can.

The subsequent course of events does strongly suggest that of the various sects and parties of Palestinian Judaism that existed before the war, the Pharisees at least successfully regrouped and began to develop a form of Judaism that addressed the realities of the post-destruction era. I see no point in questioning that the Rabbinic movement emerged out of the pre-70 Pharisees. We need to be very careful not to assume total continuity, not simply to read forward Pharisaic doctrine and practice into the Rabbinic era, nor read back Rabbinic doctrine and practice into pre-70 CE Pharisaism. The loss of the Temple and the disruption of life necessitated change, major change. But that there was *substantial* continuity in belief and practice, and that it was leading Pharisees who

---

[3] For a critical analysis, see Jacob Neusner, "The Formation of Rabbinic Judaism: Yavneh (Jamnia) from A.D. 70 to 100," *Aufstieg und Niedergang der Römischen Welt*, II 19.2 (Berlin: De Gruyter, 1979), 3–42; and Peter Schäfer, "Die Flucht Joḥanan b. Zakkais aus Jerusalem und die Gründung des 'Lehrhauses' in Jabne," *Aufstieg und Niedergang der Römischen Welt*, II 19.2 (Berlin: De Gruyter, 1979), 43–101.

founded the Rabbinic movement, is beyond reasonable doubt. Rabbinic Judaism clearly recognized Pharisaism as part of its genealogy.

The Rabbinic movement was focused on the figure of the Rabbi, and a Rabbi was an expert in the Torah. The Rabbis were not the only ones who claimed such expertise. The Torah itself entrusted the interpretation of the Torah to the priests (Lev. 10.8–11; Deut. 8.10; 21.5; Ezekiel 44.23–4), and there is no reason to think that priests both before and after 70 would not have claimed that privilege, as may other would-be Torah teachers in Israel. The Rabbis, however, posed as the *true* interpreters of the Torah. They claimed that to understand how to apply the Torah correctly you had to have studied with the right teachers in the right schools, i.e., their schools. This idea was later formalized in the doctrine of the Two Torahs: when Moses was given the Written Torah at Sinai, he was given with it an Oral Torah, which gave the definitive meaning of the Written Torah. That Oral Torah was passed down by a secure line of transmission till it was received exclusively by the Rabbinic schools.

The beating heart of the Rabbinic movement was the Rabbinic Beit Midrash (the House of Study, or school). These schools were organizationally very simple: usually, particularly at the period in question, they were little more than disciple-circles. That is to say, they comprised no more than a teacher and a small circle of students. They did not necessarily have dedicated buildings but met where they could. The Beit Midrash at Yavneh, founded by Yoḥanan ben Zakkai, may well have been, as the tradition claims, the most important of them. Disciple-circles would often have dissolved on the death of their teacher, but Yavneh seems to have persisted over several generations. Tradition has it that it was the seat of the Sanhedrin after 70 CE, but this is very doubtful. The Rabbinic movement was certainly not lacking in ambition: the Torah of Moses was the God-given constitution of Israel, and as its true custodians and interpreters the Rabbis implicitly claimed to be the true spiritual guides of Israel. But at this stage, and for many generations to come, that remained an aspiration. That Yavneh actually functioned as the supreme religious court of the Jews, in succession to the Sanhedrin that had convened in the Temple courts, is not credible.

The fact is that the Rabbinic movement that remained after 70 CE was only one of a number of movements competing for the leadership of the Jewish communities. Some accounts of early Judaism suggest that the First Revolt against Rome led to a radical simplification of Judaism.[4]

---

[4] So Schürer, *History of the Jewish People*, 1.524.

The period before 70 was one of diversity. In the period after 70 the Pharisaic–Rabbinic party seized the initiative and was effectively the only one left standing. But the situation after 70 was probably as diverse as the situation before. The Rabbis had competitors. The priestly class had received a mighty blow with the loss of the Temple. Many of them had been killed in the sack of Jerusalem. But there are signs that they regrouped in certain villages in the Galilee where they still maintained their traditional organization into "Watches" (*Mishmarot*). Pious Jews may still have supported them with tithes, so their economic viability remained reasonably secure. They would have continued to transmit and study their distinctive traditions, to teach and to adjudicate in religious matters as they had always done. They had considerable influence in the synagogues, where they were honored in various ways.

Zealotry also was probably not eradicated. The "fourth philosophy," made up of different groups of nationalists who advocated taking up arms against the Romans, had received a terrible beating, but it would be premature to assume that zealotry finally died at Masada. The problem is that we don't know to what degree Jews accepted that the destruction of the Temple marked a definitive end to the cult. There was good precedent for assuming that it would be only a temporary setback. The Jewish people had been there before! The Temple had been destroyed by the Babylonians, but it had been built again. Some upper-class Jews may have abandoned Judaism in the wake of the catastrophe, but the majority seemed to have remained true to their God. And the reason they did so was fundamentally theological. They believed in one God, the creator of the world and the Lord of history. What had happened to them must have been according to his will: he had brought it about as punishment for their sins, for their violations of the terms of his covenant with them. But that covenant was not irreparably broken, only impaired. If they repented and kept his Torah he would return to them, and with his help they would restore their Temple as before. This is the fundamental message of the apocalypses composed in the aftermath of the First Revolt. 4 Ezra by no means accepts that it is all over. It foresees imminent vengeance on Rome.

Jews, who prayed the Amidah (the Eighteen Benedictions) throughout the Talmudic period prayed daily for the restoration of the Temple. The Amidah probably goes back in some shape or form to Second Temple times, but it was clearly modified after 70, because it refers to the destruction of the Temple and the cessation of the daily service. When those modifications were introduced is uncertain but some key ones may well have been made at the end of the first century. The fast of the 9th of Av, which mourned the destruction of the first Temple, was revived. Some, such as the Qumran community, which did not recognize the legitimacy of the Jerusalem Temple, may have continued to observe the 9th of Av even when the Jerusalem Temple was gloriously functioning in a building that was one of the wonders of the ancient world, but this would have made little sense to the majority of people. However, post-70 the fast of the 9th of Av was reinstated, and became an important date in the religious calendar. But now there was a second Temple to be mourned, which tradition claimed fell on the same day as the first. But implicit in that mourning was a yearning for restoration: the fasting, the sackcloth and ashes, were meant to impress God with the sincerity of Israel's repentance and to move him to return to Zion in mercy. When this revival of the 9th of Av took place is unclear, but it would make excellent sense if it happened in the decades immediately following the destruction.[5] People needed some means to express their grief, and fasting on the anniversary of the fall of the Temple would have been an obvious way to do this. So while Rome might may have bludgeoned the Jews into submission, it did not break their spirit, their will to resist.

Nor did it take long for zealotry to raise its head again. There was a further outbreak of Jewish armed resistance to Rome in 115–117, during Trajan's reign. This mainly affected the Jewish communities in Mesopotamia and Cyrenaica: its impact in Palestine seems to have been muted, but Palestine witnessed a second full-scale revolt against Rome in 132 led by a warrior Messiah, Bar Kokhba, Son of the Star. All these uprisings were put down with great ferocity by the Romans – a ferocity that was long remembered with bitterness in Jewish tradition. Even after Bar Kokhba's defeat the Jews did not give up their messianic hopes. What they did give up, guided perhaps by the Rabbis, who came to see clearly the futility of taking on the military might of "wicked Rome," was their messianic *activism*. The Messiah would surely come, but he

---

[5] The Mishnah recognizes the 9th of Av as an important fast (Mishnah *Taᶜanit* 4.6–7), but the Rabbis were concerned about excessive mourning on this occasion. See further my essay, "Was the Ninth of Av Observed in the Second Temple Period? Reflections on the Concept of Continuing Exile in Early Judaism," in *Envisioning Judaism: Studies in Honor of Peter Schäfer on the Occasion of his Seventieth Birthday*, eds. Ra'anan S. Boustan, Klaus Herrmann, Reimund Leicht, Annette Y. Reed, and Giuseppe Veltri, 2 vols. (Tübingen: Mohr Siebeck, 2013), 1.23–38. Significantly a Greek version of Lamentations was not produced until the late 1st/early 2nd century: see my *The Targum of Lamentations* (Collegeville, MN: Liturgical Press, 2008), 46–7.

would come in God's own time. They should not try and force the redemption. What they could do was to keep the commandments and perhaps thereby move God to hasten its coming.

It is possible that two other of Josephus' Jewish sects – the Sadducees and the Essenses – also survived in some shape or form the destruction of the Temple. The evidence is circumstantial but suggestive. One thing that does seem certain is this: Rabbinic Judaism was only one form of Judaism to emerge from the debacle of 70. There were others as well – forms of Judaism that we now find it difficult to reconstruct, because, unlike Rabbinic Judaism, little or nothing of their literature has survived, and unlike Rabbinic Judaism they were not the start of a tradition that remains alive to the present day.

In the decades following the destruction of the Temple the Rabbis remained a sect within Judaism. However, what they lacked in numbers, they made up in ambition and purpose. They were on a mission to bring the Jewish community back to the rigorous observance of the Torah, as they understood it. They had to rely on persuasion, because they lacked the power to enforce their will. One institution of Jewish life that they had to influence and control was the synagogue, the importance of which rose dramatically after the loss of the Temple. The synagogue was not a Rabbinic invention: its origins predate the rise of the Rabbinism, and throughout antiquity, it retained its independence. In our period this would certainly have been the case. A synagogue would have been dominated by the leading families (socially speaking) who attended it – the families with the resources to patronize it, to pay for its maintenance and embellishment. There is evidence that the Rabbis tried to influence what went on in synagogue. For example, there is a well-known tradition that they inserted into the Amidah an additional prayer cursing the heretics – the so-called *Birkat ha-Minim*. Who these "heretics" were has been fiercely debated.[6] There is no question that the term *min* in later Rabbinic sources means "Christians," and a Palestinian version of the Amidah preserved in the Cairo Genizah actually reads "Christians" (*Notzerim*) for "heretics" (*minim*). When the additional benediction was inserted is also contested. Rabbinic tradition claims it was in the time of Gamaliel II, at the end of the first

---

[6] See Ruth Langer, *Cursing the Christians? A History of the Birkat HaMinim* (Oxford: Oxford University Press, 2011). On the term "minim," see my "Jewish Believers in Early Rabbinic Literature (2nd to 5th Centuries)," in *Jewish Believers in Jesus*, ed. Oskar Skarsaune and Reidar Hvalvik (Peabody, MA: Hendrickson Publishers, 2007), 659–709.

century (Babylonian Talmud Berakhot 28b–29a), and that makes a lot of sense. It could be seen as part of a concerted strategy to put Christians out of the synagogue, as attested in Christian sources of the period (e.g., Jn. 9.22; 12.42; 16.2; Justin Martyr, *Dialogue with Trypho* 16, 47, 93, 108, 137).

The Rabbis had also opportunity for spreading their influence within the community through the legal system. Roman law left wide scope for the day-to-day exercise of local custom, and the Rabbis could offer a service to the community by acting as arbitrators (*dayyanim*) in the disputes that inevitably arose around inheritance, land, family, and commerce. The patchwork of local courts that existed in Palestine at this period has been vividly revealed by the Babatha archive.[7] The Rabbis were experts in law, and, provided both parties accepted their authority, they could either individually or as a bench function as a law court (a *Beit Din*). And they would have adjudicated according to a Rabbinic understanding of the law. But it was above all through their teaching activities that they spread their message throughout the Jewish communities. We do not know exactly how the sermon (the *derashah*) functioned in the synagogues at this period, but that there was opportunity for an established teacher to address the congregation from time to time is highly likely, and it is equally likely that the Rabbis would have availed themselves of this chance to propagate their beliefs and values. But, as noted above, it was the Rabbinic schools that were the powerhouse of the Rabbinic movement. They would have attracted idealistic young men (the *talmidei ḥakhamim*, "disciples of the Sages"), who would have spent a time in what was in effect an intense, tight-knit religious community, learning the intricacies of Rabbinic law, and living communally the Rabbinic way of life, before returning to the community at large to rabbinize it.

2.4 SYNAGOGAL JUDAISM IN THE DIASPORA

It is important to stress that all that has been said so far relates to *Rabbinic* Judaism in *Palestine* in the period under review, and that even within Palestine Rabbinism did not dominate the Jewish communities, though it grew steadily in authority. But it would have exercised little influence *outside* Palestine, and by this time many Jews (quite probably

---

[7] See Ranon Katzoff, "Babatha," in *Encylopedia of the Dead Sea Scrolls*, ed. L.H. Schiffman and James C. VanderKam, 2 vols. (New York: Oxford University Press, 2000), 1.735.

the majority) lived abroad, their numbers swollen by refugees from the first revolt and Jewish prisoners sold in the slave-markets by the Romans. The Diaspora in our period was of long standing and very extensive, stretching from Spain in the west to Persia in the east, and taking in sizeable populations in Asia Minor, Syria, Babylonia, and Egypt. Hasmonean and Herodian policy had successfully made Jerusalem the religious capital of the Jewish world, but the destruction had broken the link, and no post-70 CE institutions or movements in the homeland had the standing or resources to project their authority much beyond their local area.

So what form of Judaism was practiced by the non-Rabbinic communities of the far-flung Diaspora in our period? Though our evidence is sparse, we can venture some modest assertions. Diaspora Judaism was based on the synagogue, in the same way as Rabbinic Judaism in Palestine was based on the Rabbinic school, and for that reason can appropriately be called "synagogal Judaism."[8] The life of the synagogue would have been dominated by the rhythm of Sabbath coming round every seven days. Jews would have stopped work and gathered in the synagogue to hear the Torah read and to say prayers. The major Torah festivals of the Jewish year would also have been observed with appropriate services. In some synagogues there was a tradition of teaching, to judge by the references to "teachers of the law" in inscriptions, though what the content of that teaching would have been is unclear. The synagogal leadership would have doubtless done its best to maintain community discipline, and may well have adjudicated disputes between members of its congregations. Personal, day-to-day life would have been dominated by some form of the dietary laws (kashrut). Circumcision seems to have been widely observed as integral to Jewish identity. Belief in one God, the Torah of Moses, and God's covenant with Israel can be assumed, though precisely what these meant in theological terms is hard to reconstruct. Beyond this sketchy outline it is hard to say more. We should not underestimate the robustness of synagogal Judaism in the Diaspora. It displayed resilience in the face of disaster, and by and large kept most Jews loyal to their faith. It seems to have been as effective in neutralizing the impact of the Christian mission on Jews, as did the Rabbinic movement in Palestine.

[8] The most ambitious attempt to reconstruct synagogual Judaism, as something distinct from Rabbinic Judaism, is Simon Claude Mimouni, *Le judaïsme ancien du VIe siècle avant notre ère au IIIe siècle de notre ère: Des prêtres aux rabbins* (Paris: Presses Universitaires de France, 2012).

2.5 THE APOSTOLIC FATHERS AND JUDAISM

It is against this picture of Judaism that we have to read the references to Jews and Judaism in the Apostolic Fathers.[9] What evidence do these writings offer of contact with the living Judaism of this period? What do they tell us about Christian views of Judaism? What light do they throw on the contested question of "the parting of the ways" between Judaism and Christianity?

Taking the corpus as a whole, several general observations are in order.

(1) First, there is less about Judaism than, perhaps, we might expect. This does not seem to be because the subjects of which many of the texts treat do not obviously raise the Jewish question. That can hardly be the whole story. The absence seems to be because the texts are written from the standpoint of a more or less established and settled *Christian* identity. Where Judaism does come into view it is presented as something sharply distinct from Christianity. This is nowhere more obvious than in Ignatius of Antioch, who would clearly have been aware of the large and influential Jewish community in his home city. He makes a very clear contrast between *Ioudaismos* and *Christianismos* – the latter possibly his own coinage on the model of *Ioudaismos* (*Magn.* 8.1–10.3; *Phild.* 6.1–2). The Epistle of Diognetus is equally confident of the difference (see especially Chapters 3–4): it sets up Christians as a "third race" – neither Jews nor pagan Greeks. Jews put in an appearance in the Martyrdom of Polycarp but only as aggressive persecutors of the Church and prime movers in the saint's death (*Mart. Pol.* 12.2; 13.1; 17.1–18.1). What this all probably indicates is that for these writers the ways had already parted.

When Christianity split from Judaism has been a topic of lively debate in recent years, and a revisionist tendency has emerged in some quarters to put the split later and later, or to deny that it was ever final.[10] There is

---

[9] In what follows I have used the Greek text and, with a few minor modifications, the English translations in Michael W. Holmes, *The Apostolic Fathers: Greek Texts and English Translations*, 3rd ed. (Grand Rapids, MI: Baker, 2007).

[10] See some of the essays in Adam H. Becker and Annette Yoshiko Reed (eds.), *The Ways that Never Parted: Jews and Christians in Late Antiquity and the Early Middle Ages* (Tübingen: Mohr Siebeck, 2003). This was a sort of "answer" to James D.G. Dunn (ed.), *Jews and Christians: The Parting of the Ways, AD 70–135* (Tübingen: Mohr Siebeck, 1992).

an element of truth in this. The separation probably moved at different speeds in different places, and was never totally final, in the sense that Judaism and Christianity continued to be locked in a dynamic symbiosis of mutual influence – right down to the present day. But for the Apostolic Fathers the separation is a thing of the past. The churches now have their own internal problems. Relations with Judaism are no longer the all-consuming issue.

(2) Second, where Judaism *is* an issue, the Christian attitude is generally dismissive and aggressive. It was in the period of the Apostolic Fathers that classic Christian anti-Judaism was forged. That aggression was to be passed down in Christian tradition with baleful results. But it has to be set in its historical context. The power relationships were reversed from those that pertained after Constantine. Where Christians lived cheek-by-jowl with Jews (in Antioch, Alexandria, and Rome, and elsewhere), the Jewish community would have been the more numerous, the wealthier, socially the more prestigious, politically the more influential. The fact that the Jews had fallen foul of the imperial power might have dented their standing, but it probably did not significantly diminish their clout at the local level. And there is reason to believe, as noted earlier, that it was at this period that Jewish communities across the Diaspora were making concerted efforts to put the Christians "out of the synagogue" – a move that the Christian leadership, though quick to complain about Jewish persecution, connived at: Christians should go to church on the Lord's day, not to synagogue on Saturday. The leadership on both sides passionately willed the divorce.

(3) Third, despite the emergence of an ever more distinctive Christian identity (institutionally, liturgically, and theologically), Christianity remained deeply indebted to Judaism. That debt was not just to the Jewish Scriptures, but also to post-biblical Jewish tradition. This can be illustrated from the Didache, which does not mention Jews or Judaism, but which, as we now have reason to think, is heavily indebted to unacknowledged Jewish sources.[11]

---

[11] The one exception is *Did.* 8.1: "But do not let your fasts coincide with those of the hypocrites. They fast on Monday and Thursday, so you must fast on Wednesday and Friday." The "hypocrites" here are clearly the Jews (cf. Mt. 23.26–8). For a discussion of the Jewish background to the *Didache*, see Huub van de Sandt and David Flusser, *The Didache: Its Jewish Sources and Its Place in Early Judaism and Christianity* (Assen/Minneapolis, MN: Royal Van Gorcum/Fortress, 2002).

Where the debt was perceived it seems to have generated anxiety, the "anxiety of influence."[12] The anxiety was born of the fact that such deep indebtedness raised acute questions of authenticity. Hadn't the Jews more right to their traditions (scriptural and non-scriptural) than the Christians had? Weren't they the natural custodians of those traditions and their true interpreters? It is this problem of authenticity that generated the recurrent judaizing tendencies in the early Church, tendencies deplored in some of the Apostolic Fathers. Judaism exerted in our period a strong gravitational pull on the nascent Christian communities. It was not just a question of its greater social cachet. There was a theological logic to judaizing as well. The strength of this pull can be measured by the aggression of the anti-Jewish language of the Christian leadership.

(4) Finally, although, as I have argued above, Judaism was diverse in our period – as diverse as it was before 70 CE – we should not overplay that diversity. It has become fashionable in some scholarship to flag the diversity by talking about "Judaisms" rather than "Judaism." The refinement is trite and explains nothing: "Judaisms" still implies a "Judaism." The fact is that there was something that could be meaningfully called "common Judaism" in our period, a Judaism to which all Jews subscribed, which allowed them to recognize each other as Jews, and be recognized as Jews by outsiders. The elements of that "common Judaism" are accurately reflected in our sources. They are: fidelity to the Torah of Moses; the observance of Shabbat and other festivals; adherence to the dietary laws; and the practice of circumcision. There are two elements, however, that are foregrounded in some of the Apostolic Fathers that cause surprise. The first is the continuing importance of the sacrifices – this at a time when, perforce, the cult had stopped, and our writers knew it. I shall return to this point in moment. Suffice to say here that one suspects that this may have had something to do with the fact that, as noted above, Jews till the time of Bar Kokhba may not have accepted that the cult had finally ceased. The cessation was only temporary. There was a widespread hope that the Temple would be rebuilt and the daily sacrifices resumed.

[12] I borrow the phrase from the literary critic Harold Bloom, without buying into his Freudian interpretation of it. See Harold Bloom, *The Anxiety of Influence: A Theory of Poetry*, 2nd ed. (New York: Oxford University Press, 1997).

The second surprising element is the prominence of fasting. There is more to this than simply the fast of Yom Kippur: that was doubtless observed but it happened only once a year. The impression from some Christian sources is that fasting was a pervasive characteristic of Jewish life, as distinctive a marker as Sabbath, circumcision, and the dietary laws (*Barn.* 3.1–6; *Ep. Diogn.* 4.1; Justin, *Tryph.* 15). There is circumstantial evidence from Jewish sources that might back this up. Such pervasive fasting is not a feature of Torah: it appears to be something new, and it is most obviously linked to the fall of the Temple. I noted earlier that the fast of the 9th of Av was probably reinstated in the post-70 CE period. We should also note penitential groups like the "Mourners for Zion," whose existence already in our period is hinted at in 2 Baruch.[13] This mourning was an expression of repentance for the sins that had brought disaster on the Jewish people, and its aim was to move God to forgive them, redeem Israel and restore his ancient Temple. For the ancient Christian writers this was all going in quite the wrong direction, and contrary to God's manifest purpose in history.

2.6 THE CASE OF THE EPISTLE OF BARNABAS

All these points are illustrated by the Epistle of Barnabas, which offers by far the most important statement in our corpus of the relationship between Christianity and Judaism. Barnabas is haunted by the looming presence of Judaism. Neither Jews nor Judaism are mentioned by name anywhere in the letter: it is always "them" as opposed to "us" (2.9; 3.6; 4.6; 5.3; 7.1; 8.7; 9.4; 10.12; 13.1; 16.1).[14] But the recipients would have had no difficulty identifying who was in view. The very obliqueness of the language conveys a sense of nearness and menace. If the Epistle was composed in Alexandria in the 90s (as some have plausibly argued), prior to the Jewish revolts under Trajan, then the church there would

---

[13] On the Mourners for Zion, see my *Targum of Lamentations*, 78–86. The Rabbis in Palestine were very ambivalent about fasting, in particular the extreme asceticism of groups like the Mourners for Zion. This comes out in their low-key treatment of the subject in Mishnah Taᶜanit. This is almost totally concerned with fasting for rain, hardly an issue for the Diaspora, which was little engaged in agriculture. Mishnah Taᶜanit is probably not an accurate reflection of the importance of fasting in the Jewish communities after 70.

[14] At 5.2, 5.8, 6.7, 11.1, and 12.5 Barnabas refers to "Israel." He presumably means by this the remnant of ancient Israel that caught the spiritual meaning of the Law and looked forward to the coming of Christ, as opposed to the "synagogues of evil men" who opposed God's anointed (5.13; 6.6). Whatever he means, I doubt he was conceding the noble title "Israel" to his Jewish opponents.

certainly have been overshadowed by a large, prosperous, and intellec-
tually vibrant Jewish community. Barnabas is worried, presumably with
good reason, by the gravitational pull of the larger body: he is afraid that
his readers might become "proselytes (epēlutoi; Latin proselyti) to the
law of those people (ekeinōn)," and so make shipwreck of their salvation
(3.6). The wording, if pressed, suggests he is not so much concerned
about Jewish Christians backsliding into Judaism as about Christianity
becoming a staging-post for gentiles into Judaism. And there is no
reason to think that the Jewish community at this period would have
rejected such proselytes. Later Judaism tended to view converts with
suspicion and to put obstacles in their way. But that may not have been
the case at this time. Indeed, the synagogue may actively have sought
converts. There may have been a clash of missions.

The anxiety (dare one say the phobia?) engendered by Judaism in
Barnabas' mind is compounded by the fact that he is deeply aware of
Christianity's debt to Judaism. There are debts to non-biblical Jewish
tradition,[15] but the debt is most obvious in his acceptance of the Jewish
Scriptures. His text is peppered with quotations and references from all
three sections of the classical Jewish canon, the Law, the Prophets, and
the Writings. He knows his Bible well. The text he uses is the
Septuagint, which he sometimes seems to quote from memory, but that
is the text that would have been circulating also in the Greek-speaking
Diaspora at that time. There are a few apparently scriptural quotations
or allusions that cannot be traced to the extant Septuagint (6.13; 7.4,8;
10.5,7; 11.10; 16.3,5,6). Whether or not these come from deviant forms
of known biblical texts or from non-canonic Jewish writings not otherwise attested is unclear, but the vast bulk of the texts quoted are from
the standard Jewish canon.[16]

Crucially Barnabas accepts the Law as word of God (Moses is a
"prophet": 6.8; 10.2; 12.2). What he rejects is the Jewish interpretation
of it. The cardinal error of the Jews was to take the ritual prescriptions
(the laws of sacrifice, kashrut, fasting, and circumcision) and apply them

---

[15] The aggadic additions to the biblical narrative at *Barn.* 7.8 (re Yom Kippur), 8.1,5 (re
the Red Heifer), 12.2 (re the defeat of Amalek at Rephidim: Exod. 17.8–13), and 12.6
(re the serpent in the wilderness) may owe something to Jewish tradition. The use of
Dan. 7.24 at 4.4 may reflect contemporary Jewish interpretation of that vision. And
the unidentified quotation (presented apparently as Scripture!) at 16.3 may have been
an oracle circulating within the Jewish community. Note also the use of a kind of
gematria at 9.7.

[16] There is a reference to "Enoch" at 4.3 (though the text is uncertain), presumably an
allusion to some part of the extensive Enochic literature.

literally in defiance of texts such as Isa. 1.11–13: "'What are the multitude of your sacrifices to me?' says the Lord. I am full of whole burnt
offerings, and I do not want the fat of lambs and blood of bulls and goats,
not even if you come to appear before me. For who demanded these
things from your hands? Do not continue to trample my court. If you
bring fine flour, it is vain; incense is detestable to me; your new moons
and sabbaths I cannot stand" (2.5). From this verse he concludes that
God "abolished (*katērgēsen*) these things, in order that the new law of
our Lord Jesus Christ, which is free from the yoke of compulsion, might
have its offering, one not made by humans" (2.6). In saying that God
"abolished" these things he seems to mean that he explicitly negated
their literal application. The idea is not that they were for a time valid in
their literal sense, but then later suspended. They were never, *ab initio*,
meant literally, and this is the message conveyed by texts such as
Isaiah 1.11–13. The same can be said of circumcision: the commandment to circumcise "is abolished (*katērgētai*)" by verses such as Jer. 4.4
(cf. Deut. 10.16; Jer. 9.26), which see the true circumcision as the
circumcision of *the heart*. They show that circumcision was never
meant literally (9.1–4). Thus, Jews had never truly fulfilled the Law,
precisely because they obeyed it literally. They never saw its spiritual
meaning because "an evil angel 'enlightened' (*esophizen*) them" (9.4).[17]
Christians who have been endowed by God with wisdom and understanding of the hidden spiritual sense of Scripture (6.10) are the true
heirs of the covenant (13.1–7).

The sin of the Golden Calf (Exod. 32.1–35), and the consequent
breaking of the tablets of the Law, signifies that the first covenant with
Israel was cancelled (4.6–8). There was, of course, a second law (Exod.
34.1–8) – the law recorded in detail in the Pentateuch – but it was never
intended for Israel. The Jews have tried to implement it, but in their
ignorance and carnality, they took it literally, whereas it was meant to
contain *spiritual* lessons for "us" (3.6; 13.1). Barnabas offers a

---

[17] Behind Barnabas is a dualism between good and evil reminiscent of the Sermon on
the Two Spirits in the Community Rule from Qumran (1QS 3.13–4.26). Barnabas has
a rich vocabulary for the Devil: the One Who is at Work (2.1); the Evil One (2.10;
21.3); the Black One (4.9; 20.1); the Evil Ruler (4.12); the Evil Angel (9.4); Satan (18.1).
Note particularly his account of the Two Ways (18.1–20.2): "There are two ways of
teaching and power, one of light and one of darkness, and there is a great difference
between these two ways. For over the one are stationed the light-giving angels of
God, but over the other are the angels of Satan. And the first is Lord from eternity to
eternity, while the latter is ruler of the present age of lawlessness." It is clear that for
Barnabas Judaism belongs to the way of darkness. The parallelism with Qumran
shows that even Barnabas' radical anti-Judaism has precedent in Jewish tradition.

hermeneutical strategy for annexing the Jewish Scriptures as Christian Scripture. The Prophets and the Psalms are relatively easy since they contain straightforward predictive prophecies of the life and death of Christ (see, e.g., 5.12–14). But significantly he affirms that the Law is also full of spiritual Christian meaning. To the Spirit-filled reader it can be seen as foreshadowing the death of Christ, as in the rituals of the Day of Atonement and the Red Heifer (7.1–8.7), or as coded moral lessons, as in the food laws. So the ban on eating pork means that we should not associate with people, who are like pigs, who "when they are well off, they forget the Lord, but when they are in need, they acknowledge the Lord, just as the pig ignores its owner when it is feeding, but when it is hungry it starts to squeal and falls silent only after being fed again" (10.3).

This approach to the Law is normally characterized as "allegorical," and the label is valid in the very broad sense that the text is taken to mean something other than what on the surface it says. But it is important to note that allegory, though widespread, was not a well-theorized hermeneutic in antiquity: it can be applied to a variety of quite different exegetical techniques that are united only by the fact that they avoid the literal sense. Barnabas himself speaks of "parables" (parabolai: 6.10; 17.2) and "types" (tupoi: 7.7,10; 8.1; 13.5), and of prophets speaking "in the spirit" (en pneumati: 9.7; 10.2; 10.9; 13.5), in the sense of, under divine guidance, intending a spiritual meaning that can be grasped only by the "spiritual" (pneumatikoi: 4.11). This approach would have cut no ice with the contemporary Rabbis of Palestine, whose every sinew was strained to implement the law literally. Rabbinic Midrash is notable for its avoidance of allegory, possibly because the Rabbis were aware of its polemical use by Christians.[18] Barnabas' approach may have been more at home in an Alexandrian Jewish setting. Philo is usually cited as an antecedent, but Philo was very careful not to allegorize the commandments in ways that might imply that they should not be literally observed, though he notes there were Alexandrian Jewish exegetes who did so (Migr. Abr. 89–93). Barnabas' basic approach may, therefore, have been borrowed from Jewish practice. Although they were turned back *against* Judaism, his exegetical tools, rather than being due to the Spirit's enlightenment,

---

[18] See my "Heraclitus's *Homeric Problems* and Midrash *Genesis Rabbah*: Comparisons and Contrasts," in *Sibyls, Scriptures, and Scrolls: John Collins at Seventy*, ed. Joel Baden, Hindy Najman, and Eibert Ticgchelaar, 2 vols. (Leiden: Brill, 2017), 1.38–67.

were in fact appropriated from Judaism – a fact that would have done little to allay in his mind the anxiety of influence.

Barnabas' knowledge of sentiment *within* his local Jewish community comes out in his eschatology. He seems to be aware of Jewish nationalism and Jewish eschatological hopes. He believes he is living in the last days (4.1–5, 9–14), but so did many Jews at the time he was writing, which coincided with a mini-revival of apocalyptic speculation within Judaism characterized by 4 Ezra, 2 Baruch, Apocalypse of Abraham, and some of the Sybilline Oracles. It may be that 16.3–4 reflects a Jewish hope for the rebuilding of the Temple: "Furthermore, again he says, 'Behold, those who tore down this Temple will build it themselves.' This is happening now. For because they went to war, it was torn down by their enemies, and now the very servants of their enemies will rebuild it." The historical context here has been hotly debated, but it would make sense to relate it to the reign of Nerva (96–98), whose abolition of the Jewish-tax (commemorated by striking the *Calumnia Sublata* coins) may have momentarily engendered "Cyrus-fever" in the Jewish community – the hope that a new Cyrus (Nerva) had arisen who would allow the rebuilding of the Temple that his forebears had destroyed some thirty years earlier.[19] Again, an Alexandrian setting for this makes good sense. If Jewish nationalism had some purchase in the Jewish communities there in the 80s and 90s, it would help explain the uprising in 115–117 CE. The prophecy that Barnabas quotes, as if it was Scripture, is from an unknown source (Isa. 49.17 is not close). Could it have been an apocalyptic oracle current in the Jewish community? For Barnabas such a restoration is unthinkable. It is absurd to imagine that the God who made heaven and earth should dwell in a building made of stone. The true Temple is the spiritual temple made up of true believers in Jesus (6.15; 16.8, 10).

Read against this background, Barnabas' interpretation of the promise of the land (6.8–10) can be seen as a pointed rejection of Jewish nationalism: "What does the other prophet say to them? 'Behold, thus says the Lord God: "Enter into the good land, which the Lord promised by oath to Abraham and Isaac and Jacob, and take possession of it as an inheritance, a land flowing with milk and honey'" (Ps. 22.17 [LXX

---

[19] See Martin Goodman, "Nerva, the Fiscus Judaicus and Jewish Identity," *Journal of Roman Studies* 79 (1989), 40–4; Goodman, "The Meaning of 'Fisci Iudaici Calumnia Sublata' on the Coinage of Nerva," in *Studies in the Varieties of Ancient Judaism: Louis H. Feldman Jubilee Volume*, ed. Shaye J.D. Cohen and Joshua J. Schwartz (Brill: Leiden, 2007), 81–9.

21.17]; Ps. 118.24 [LXX 117.24]). But now learn what knowledge has to say: set your hope upon Jesus, who is about to be revealed to you in the flesh. For a human is earth suffering, for Adam was formed out of the face of the earth. What, therefore, does 'unto the good land, a land flowing with milk and honey' mean? Blessed is our Lord, brothers, who endowed us with wisdom and understanding of his secrets. For the prophet speaks a parable concerning the Lord; who can understand it, except one who is wise and discerning and loves his Lord?" "The land flowing with milk and honey" has to be understood in a spiritual not a literal sense – as a symbol of Christ. So Jewish nationalism is emphatically rejected.

Unlike some of the other texts in the corpus of the Apostolic Fathers, the Epistle of Barnabas was influential. It was well known both in the Greek east, and, via a Latin translation, in the Latin west. It nearly made it into the New Testament canon. It was possibly known to the author of the Epistle of Diognetus. Certainly, its radical allegorizing (or something like it) has to be presupposed if we are to make sense of the attitude towards the Law and Judaism in that work. It was taken up by Clement of Alexandria and Origen, and became the classic articulation of radical supersessionism in the early church. It was not the only early Christian text to impute Christian meaning to the Jewish law through typological exegesis. About a decade before Barnabas the Epistle to the Hebrews had interpreted aspects of the sacrificial cult in an allegorical way. Like Barnabas Hebrews saw the Day of Atonement and its rituals as the heart of the Levitical system. Like Barnabas Hebrews show an interest in the obscure rituals of the Red Heifer. And it assigns to both christological significance (Heb. 9.1–22; 13.11–13).

But there the similarity ends. Hebrews sets out a more nuanced view. Barnabas paints himself into a corner by arguing that the rituals of the second law were never meant to be literally observed. The Jews in observing them *au pied de la lettre* were behaving in a typically unspiritual way, laid astray by "an evil angel." But what were they supposed to do with them? Sit for centuries and contemplate in them the foreshadowings of the work of Christ? How were they to work these out? There is a lack of common sense and realism here. In fact, says Barnabas, the Law was meant *for us*, but this is tantamount to saying it was in abeyance till Christ came, and its symbolic meaning at last became clear to the *illuminati*. For Hebrews, however, the ritual law *was* meant to be observed *literally*: it was the way God prepared his people for the coming of Christ. The Law was finally superseded by the revelation in the Son, but it provided the categories – the God-given categories – by which the Christ-event was to be understood, and those categories remain valid for the Church, even though it is no longer obliged to *keep* the Law. This is surely a more nuanced and defensible position than Barnabas' supersessionism (whether in the radical inflection of Barnabas, or the moderate inflection of Hebrews) has had a bad press in recent Christian thought, and Barnabas in particular has come in for harsh criticism. But it should be remembered that when Barnabas wrote the power-relations between the Jewish and Christian communities were reversed, that the small and beleaguered Christian churches were trying to forge an independent identity in the shadow of a self-confident and dominant synagogue, which was prepared to make life difficult for them; that the allegorical reading of Scripture they employed to do so was actually borrowed from Judaism; and that reading Scripture in this way allowed Christians, unlike the Gnostics, to hold on to the Jewish Scriptures as word of God – to the enrichment of the later Church.

FURTHER READING

Alexander, Philip. "The Rabbis and Their Rivals in the Second Century CE," in *Christianity in the Second Century: Themes and Developments*, ed. James Carleton Paget and Judith Lieu. Cambridge: Cambridge University Press, 2017, 57–70.

Barclay, John M.G. *Jews in the Mediterranean Diaspora from Alexander to Trajan (323 BCE–117 CE)*. Edinburgh: T&T Clark, 1996.

Dunn, James D.G. (ed.). *Jews and Christians: The Parting of the Ways, AD 70–135*. Tübingen: Mohr Siebeck, 1992.

Goodman, Martin. *Rome and Jerusalem: The Clash of Ancient Civilizations*. London: Allen Lane, 2007.

Hezser, Catherine. *The Social Structure of the Rabbinic Movement in Roman Palestine*. Tübingen: Mohr Siebeck, 1997.

Horbury, William. "Jewish–Christian Relations in Barnabas and Justin Martyr," in William Horbury, *Jews and Christians in Contact and Controversy*. Edinburgh: T&T Clark, 1998, 127–61.

Jewish War under Trajan and Hadrian. Cambridge: Cambridge University Press, 2014.

Katz, Steven T. (ed.). *The Cambridge History of Judaism. Volume 4: The Late Roman-Rabbinic Period*. Cambridge: Cambridge University Press, 2006.

Levine, Lee I. *The Ancient Synagogue: The First Thousand Years* (New Haven, CT: Yale University Press, 2000).

Lieu, Judith. *Image and Reality: The Jews in the World of the Christians in the Second Century*. Edinburgh: T&T Clark, 1996.

Mimouni, Simon Claude. *Le judaïsme ancien du VIe siècle avant notre ère au IIIe siècle de notre ère: Des prêtres aux rabbins.* Paris: Presses Universitaires de France, 2012.

Paget, James Carleton. *Jews, Christians and Jewish Christians in Antiquity.* Tübingen: Mohr Siebeck, 2010.

Rosenfeld, Ben-Zion. *Torah Centres and Rabbinic Activity in Palestine 70–400 CE: History and Geography.* Brill: Leiden and Boston, MA, 2010.

3 Second-Century Diversity

DAVID E. WILHITE

3.1 KINDS OF DIVERSITY

When discussing diversity among early Christians, one can point to both geographic dispersion and to doctrinal difference. The first kind, geographic diversity, can be treated briefly, since its contours have been catalogued in detail by other scholars.[1] The larger task for this essay is to reassess various doctrinally distinct groups in light of recent scholarly debates to see what conclusions can be drawn for the second century, with special reference to the corpus known as the Apostolic Fathers.

In terms of geographical diversity, the opening and close of the second century hint at a widespread movement. There are first-century indications that Paul may have reached as far as the Iberian Peninsula (Rom. 15.24–8; *1 Clem.* 5.7), and although they likely do not constitute independent verification of this supposed journey, later sources accepted this tradition.[2] A Christian community was already well established among the Gauls by the time Irenaeus arrives there in the second half of the second century, and numerous Christian communities are spread throughout Africa by the year 200 CE.[3] A generation after him,

---

[1] Adolf von Harnack, *Die Mission und Ausbreitung des Christentums in den ersten drei Jahrhunderten* (ET = *The Mission and Expansion of Christianity in the First Three Centuries* (1905 orig.; 4th ed., 2 vols., 1924), is still a valuable introduction; see esp. vol. 2/book 4 = "The Spread of the Christian Religion." More recent studies include Roderic L. Mullen, *The Expansion of Christianity: A Gazetteer of Its First Three Centuries*, SuppVigChrs (Leiden: Brill, 2004); and Frank Trombley, "Overview: The Geographical Spread of Christianity," in *The Cambridge History of Christianity, Vol. 1: Origins to Constantine*, ed. Margaret M. Mitchell and Frances M. Young (Cambridge: Cambridge University Press, 2006), 302–13. For the geographic diversity in the first Christian century, see E.J. Schnabel, *Urchristliche Mission* (Brockhaus, 2002; = *Early Christian Mission* [Downers Grove, IL: 2004]).

[2] E.g., Acts of Peter 1.6; Martyrdom of Peter and Paul 1.

[3] See John Behr, *Irenaeus of Lyons: Identifying Christianity* (Oxford: Oxford University Press, 2013); and David E. Wilhite, *Ancient African Christianity: An Introduction to a Unique Context and Tradition* (London: Routledge, 2017).

Tertullian claims that Christianity has been embraced by all (known) peoples of the (Mediterranean) world, and because of its specific details, it is a passage worth citing in full. He boasts,

> In fact, in whom else have the clans of the world believed if not in the Christ who has come already? For in whom have the other clans (the Parthians, Medes, Elamites and those who inhabit Mesopotamia, Armenia, Cappadocia, those dwelling in Pontus and Asia, Phrygia and Pamphylia, those remaining in Egypt and those inhabiting parts of Africa beyond Cyrene, Romans and foreign residents, then also Jews in Jerusalem) and the remaining clans (as now the various Gaetulians and the many territories of the Moors, all within the boundaries of both Spains, the diverse tribes of the Gauls, and the region of the Britons that is inaccessible to the Romans but subject to Christ, and the Sarmatians, Dacians, Germans, Scythians, and the many concealed clans and provinces and islands unknown to us that we are less able to count) believed?[4]

While Tertullian's rhetorical intent to show the superiority of Christianity to Judaism makes his claims in this passage suspect, his general geographic scope can be confirmed by the Abercius Inscription (dated before 216 CE), in which the Christian bishop of Hieropolis in Phrygia claims to have visited Christian communities from Rome to Syria and even some beyond the Euphrates. Eusebius reports that Pantaenus, the Alexandrian Christian teacher from the late second century, traveled further east to India, and there he found Christians reading the Gospel of Matthew in Hebrew.[5] The mid-second-century text the *Epistle of Diognetes* describes Christianity as saturating the whole world by way of the body/soul analogy: "The soul is dispersed through all the members of the body, and Christians throughout the cities of the world."[6] Again, this is theological doxology, and not documented ethnography. Nevertheless, such a claim can only be made if there is some semblance of reality. Christians by the second half of the second century believed that their communities were spread throughout the known world, and so the Jesus followers must have extended to enough cities and villages that they could expect to find a community of believers wherever they went.

---

[4] *Adv. Iud.* 7.4 (trans. Geoffrey D. Dunn, *Tertullian* [London: Routledge, 2004], 79).
[5] *Hist. eccl.* 5.10.2–3.
[6] *Ep. Diogn.* 6.2 (text/trans. Michael W. Holmes, *The Apostolic Fathers*, 3rd ed. [Grand Rapids, MI: Baker, 2007], 702–5).

The rapidity and breadth of this dispersion is bewildering to say the least, for the faith and practice of a small band of disciples whose leader had been crucified covered much of the Roman Empire and even transcended its boundaries within the span of less than two hundred years.[7] The expansion of Christianity includes the growth of this movement from primarily (but not exclusively) lower classes into (by at least the late third century) a collection of individuals from all levels of society.[8]

In addition to this geographic and social expansion one also finds a wide breadth of surviving sources from the first three centuries. Collections and copies of bodies of literature, such as Paul's letters and such as writings known as the Apostolic Fathers, are well known. But even here it is worth cataloguing the various genres known from the second century. The list includes letters, various doctrinal, polemical, and apologetic treatises, various ("apocryphal") accounts of Jesus and the apostles, apocalyptic treatises, martyr accounts, confessional statements, sermons, hymns, and then various fragments from second-century Christians only preserved in quotations from later authors. Some of the manuscripts themselves, namely papyri from Egypt, can be dated to the second century.[9] It should also be noted how many second-century texts were known by later authors, but which have been entirely lost to history.[10] In addition to these literary sources, we could turn to inscriptions (some of which may be as early as the second century), and other kinds of material remains, such as Christian graffiti, frescoes, mosaics, sarcophagi, and even some church buildings.[11]

Of course, not all sources carry the same weight, when it comes to assisting the historian in assessing the geographic and doctrinal

---

[7] For an attempt to provide population statistics for this growth, see Rodney Stark, *The Rise of Christianity: A Sociologist Reconsiders History* (Princeton, NJ: Princeton University Press, 1996), 7.

[8] See the treatments of this question in Todd D. Still and David G. Horrell (eds.), *After the First Urban Christians: The Social Scientific Study of Pauline Christianity Twenty-Five Years Later* (London: T&T Clark, 2009); and Alexander Weiß, *Soziale Elite und Christentum: Studien zu ordo-Angehörigen unter den frühen Christen*, Millenium Studies 52 (Berlin: De Gruyter, 2015).

[9] For recent discussions, see Larry Hurtado, *Texts and Artifacts: Selected Essays on Textual Criticism and Early Christian Manuscripts* (London: Bloomsbury/T&T Clark, 2017). For details on specific manuscripts, see J.K. Elliott, *A Bibliography of Greek New Testament Manuscripts*, NovTSupp 160 (Leiden: Brill, 2015).

[10] E.g., see those listed in Andrew Carriker, *The Library of Eusebius of Caesarea*, SuppVigChr 67 (Leiden: Brill, 2003).

[11] For an introduction, see Graydon F. Snyder and Ante Pacem: *Archaeological Evidence of Church Life before Constantine*, rev. ed. (Macon, GA: Mercer University Press, 2003).

diversity in the second century. For example, the *Epistle to Diognetus* is only known from one manuscript, in the Codex Argentoratensis Graecus IX found in Constantinople in 1436. The text is cited by no other extant Christian writer. Therefore, the text, while valuable in many ways, is not necessarily representative of the state of Christianity in the second century writ large, but it can only indicate the view of one anonymous author who likely wrote sometime in this early period. Similarly, some texts from Nag Hammadi are otherwise unknown altogether, and so while they are invaluable documents in one sense, in another sense it is difficult to know how widespread the views in them would have been known or upheld by other Christians. At the same time, other texts in this collection were known from other sources, and so they may give us a glimpse of a more widespread expression of Christianity.

At the other end of the spectrum are letters associated with martyrs like Ignatius and Polycarp or with early Christian leaders like Barnabas and Clement of Rome. These can be found in manuscripts, lists, and citations from numerous later sources, and these later sources often represent various parts or regions of the Mediterranean. Sometimes, the reception and dispersion of these texts may be little more than accidents of history, or even intentional manipulation of textual traditions by propagandists attempting to promote certain forms of Christianity over others.[12]

The *Didache* is an interesting case study, because – like the *Epistle to Diognetus* – it is only known from one manuscript, Codex Hierosolymitanus found in Constantinople in 1873.[13] In this case, however, the text is also known in several other ancient sources, most of which come from Alexandria[14] and Antioch.[15] Not only was it widely known, but it was highly revered: many of the witnesses to this text count it as scripture, and Eusebius of Caesarea claims it was "widely used" as such.[16] The *Shepherd of Hermas* is a similar case in that it was widely received, and in some instances classified as scripture. This web of reception of texts from various cities like Alexandria, Antioch, and

---

[12] See the compelling argument about Justin's promotion of the *Syntagma* over other heresiological texts made by Geoffrey Smith, *Guilt by Association: Heresy Catalogues in Early Christianity* (Oxford: Oxford University Press, 2015).

[13] Also, some verses have been found in papyri from Oxyrynchus.

[14] E.g., Clement of Alexandria, Origen, Didymos the Blind, and Athanasius.

[15] E.g., *Didascalia Apostolorum*, *Doctrina Apostolorum*, and *The Apostolic Constitutions*; cf. *Constitutio Ecclesiastica Apostolorum*.

[16] *Hist. eccl.* 3.25.

Rome among various regions like Africa, Syria, Asia Minor, and Italy reflects some sort of network of Christian communities. A remaining question for scholars is whether or not this network of Christians who shared their literature represents "Christianity" or simply one stream of Christianity, or – to put it more controversially – one of many Christianities. This question requires us to explain some recent shifts in scholarly paradigms before returning to the matter of doctrinal diversity among early Christians, because one's understanding of what constitutes Christianity and who counts as a Christian is now disputed.

3.2 SCHOLARLY PARADIGMS

At the beginning of the twentieth century, church historians like Harnack continued to use the central paradigm found in ancient writers like Irenaeus of Lyon: heretics were deviant Christian groups who had turned away from orthodox teaching and recruited followers from the Christian churches into their sects.[17] Since this model has been so dominant for so long, it is worth outlining how Christianity in the second century looked from this vantage point before explaining one major shift in scholarship.

In the traditional way of looking at the evidence, heretics could be easily categorized. What follows is a brief list of the five main heretic groups from this time period and their primary tenets as (mis-) understood in the traditionalist view.

First, Ebionites were Jewish Christians who continued in many non-Christian, Jewish practices, unlike the rest of the church, which accepted their freedom from the Law. In addition to these practices, they held to an adoptionist Christology in which Jesus was a messianic prophet who became God's son – only not ontologically speaking. Second, the Gnostics rejected the goodness of creation, teaching that lesser deities produced this fallen world. Their Christology in turn was docetic, meaning that the heavenly Savior could not take on real flesh, but must instead merely appear to do so. Similarly, and third, Marcion and the Marcionites rejected the Christian canon, especially the Old Testament, which meant that only a few New Testament texts could be retained, and even then they had to be significantly censored. Fourth, the Montanist sect represented a group whose attachment to scripture was also suspect, because they promoted the teachings of ecstatic

---

[17] Harnack, *The Mission and Expansion of Christianity*, 2.308.

prophets over the Bible and the church's teachings. Finally, in the later second century the Sabellians embraced a view of God that is monarchianist, which denies the doctrine of the Trinity by positing God as one person who simply appeared in different modes at different times. In this sense Jesus is really the Father God in the form of a son who suffered and died on the cross, a teaching known as patripassianism.

This list represents an oversimplification to be sure, for no one scholar agreed to these caricatures for all of these heretical groups. Even so, it summarizes the standard depictions of this group by traditionalist scholars, and so for the sake of space we can leave behind former scholarship that remained uncritical in its acceptance of how these so-called heretics were depicted by their opponents, the orthodox. From this point on, the revisionist view can be explained.

The details in this standard view have been questioned by numerous scholars, but the overall depiction was challenged most completely by Walter Bauer in 1934. In his book, *Rechtgläubigkeit und Ketzerei im ältesten Christentum/Orthodoxy and Heresy in Earliest Christianity*, Bauer claimed that the prior paradigm is wrong.[18] Instead of a preexisting orthodoxy, from which heretics deviated, scholars should instead assume that some groups that later became known as heretics were simply practicing Christianity in one of its various expressions. Bauer himself stated this tentatively and cautiously,[19] but his claim has in more recent decades become axiomatic for many scholars. The notion that all heretical groups began as an intentional rejection of and deviation from a clearly established orthodoxy cannot be supported by the evidence from the primary sources themselves. This can best be illustrated by returning to the above list of second-century groups and comparing what can be known about them when read in this revisionist view.

3.3 DIVERSE CHRISTIAN COMMUNITIES

When looking at specific Christian "heresies" as distinct Christian communities, and not as evil troublemakers who intentionally deviated from the truth, one reads the data differently. To begin with the

---

[18] English trans. = *Orthodoxy and Heresy in Earliest Christianity*, ed. Robert A. Kraft and Gerhard Kroedel (Philadelphia, PA: Fortress Press, 1979).

[19] *Orthodoxy and Heresy*, xxii, "Perhaps – I repeat, perhaps – certain manifestations of Christian life that the authors of the church renounce as 'heresies' originally had not been such at all, but, at least here and there, were the only form of the new religion – that is, for those regions they were simply 'Christianity.'"

Ebionites, despite the claims of some later heresiologists,[20] the
Ebionites clearly were not founded by a man named "Ebion." These
later defenders of orthodoxy assumed that all heretical sects had a
founder after whom they are named. The fact that earlier authors did
not know of an individual named Ebion, and that authors most likely to
have contact with this group also know of no such person, makes the
later claim suspect.[21] The word *ebion* comes from the Aramaic word for
"poor," and this group likely understood themselves as in solidarity
with those in need (cf. Mt. 5.3//Lk. 6.20). Furthermore, the claim that
this group is a Jewish Christian group that retained certain practices is a
gross oversimplification of how the church and synagogue emerged in
the aftermath of the Jewish Wars and the destruction of the Ttemple.
The vast majority of early Christians were "Jewish Christians," and
when later, fourth-century, gentile Christians came into contact with
Christian groups that still identified as Jewish and retained Jewish
customs, they were quick to see this group as the "Ebionites" spoken
of by earlier heresiologists.

It is worth noting that none of the texts from the Apostolic Fathers
collection knows of Ebionites or any adoptionist Christology.[22]
Furthermore, this group is never even named before Irenaeus (c. 190
CE), and so the attempts by some modern scholars to link the Ebionites
to the original Jerusalem church are difficult to defend.[23] Even further
uncertainty arises when one attempts to ascertain what Gospel text this
group used, for it could have been the *Gospel according to Matthew*, the
Gospel according to the Hebrews, or their own *Gospel according to*

---

[20] Tertullian, *Prae. Haer.* 10, 33; *Carn.* 14, 18, 24; *Vir.* 6. See also Pseudo-Hippolytus,
Ref. Haer. 7; Pseudo-Tertullian, *Haer.* 3.3.

[21] cf. Irenaeus, *Adv. Haer.* 1.26.2; Origen, *Princ.* 4.3.8; Eusebius, *Hist. eccl.* 3.27.1;
3.27.6; *Eccl. theol.* 1.14. Epiphanius speaks of Ebion (*Pan.* 30), and also claims to
have first-hand knowledge of Ebionites (*Pan.* 30.15.4; 30.18.7–9). However,
Epiphanius in fact speaks of a different group altogether (cf. the Elkasaites in *Pan.*
30.3.1), who are nevertheless "Christian Jews," and so must be dubbed Ebionites
according to Epiphanius' sources (esp. Irenaeus and Origen).

[22] The one possible exception would be *The Shepherd of Hermas* 59.5–7/*Sim.* 5.6.5–7.
However, this passage is as likely to speak of Christ as preexistent (apart from his
"flesh"), or at least of the/a preexistent S/spirit who created the world and then later
dwelt in Christ (at some point).

[23] The view of Bauer, *Orthodoxy and Heresy*, which was followed by many notable
scholars, such as James D.G. Dunn, *Unity and Diversity in the New Testament: An
Inquiry into the Character of Earliest Christianity* (Philadelphia, PA: Westminster,
1977), 244. See other examples in Petri Luomanen, "Ebionites and Nazarenes," in
Jewish Christianity Reconsidered: Rethinking Ancient Groups and Texts, ed. Matt
Jackson-McCabe (Minneapolis, MN: Fortress Press, 2007), 81–118.

the Ebionites.[24] Similarly, this group's alleged adoptionist Christology wherein they viewed Jesus as merely a human (i.e., psilanthropism) is not substantiated by the sources, for their view is more akin to the teaching that a heavenly power possessed the earthly Jesus (i.e., dynamic monarchianism), a view normally associated with gnostic groups.[25] In sum, very little can be known about the Ebionites when employing a more critical reading of the sources, other than to say that their opponents only notice them in the late second and third century.[26]

More certain answers can be given for the Marcionites in this revisionist approach, for the newer understanding is a significant rethinking of Marcion himself. To begin with his canon, it is now widely recognized that Marcion did not reject the Old Testament and then reduce the New Testament,[27] especially since this Christian canon was far from fixed by the time of Marcion's arrival in Rome (c. 140).[28] In all likelihood, he only knew some already shortened form of Luke and Paul's letters, since no consistent editorial agenda can be found in what is known of his version of these works.[29] Because of this, some scholars

[24] Cf. Irenaeus, *Adv. Haer.* 1.26.2; Eusebius, *Eccl. hist.* 3.27.4; 6.17; and Epiphanius, *Pan.* 30.3.7.

[25] *Adv. Haer.* 1.26.1–2; Epiphanius, *Pan.* 30.14.5; 30.16.4–5. The later sources speak of two kinds of Ebionites, with one holding to orthodox Christology while the other does not (cf. Origen, *Contr. Cels.* 5.61; Eusebius, *Eccl. hist.* 3.27.3). Epiphanius is the first to mention the "Nazoreans" or "Nazarenes" (*Pan.* 29), but since later authors like Jerome continue to speak of Ebionites and Nazarenes as synonymous, it seems that Epiphanius has attempted to differentiate Origen's two kinds of Ebionites, labeling the Christologically orthodox group as Nazoreans.

[26] See further discussion in Sakari Häkkinen, "Ebionites," in *A Companion to Second-Century Christian "Heretics,"* ed. Antti Marjanen and Petri Luomanen (Leiden: Brill, 2005), 247–78; and Wilhite, *The Gospel According to the Heretics* (Grand Rapids. MI: Baker, 2015), 41–60.

[27] Irenaeus, *Adv. Haer.* 1.27.2, claims Marcion "circumcised" the scriptures. Tertullian, *Prescript Against the Heretics* 38.9, says he edited "with a sword instead of a stylus" (cf. *Against Marcion* 5.2.7).

[28] The fragmented text known as the Muratorian Canon is possibly dated to the late second century, but there are serious questions about this text; see Clare K. Rothschild, "The Muratorian Fragment as a Roman Fake," *Novum Testamentum* 60 (2018): 55–82. Even so, its list is a fair representation of texts widely attested in the late second century. For the first half of the second century, there is no attestation for a fourfold Gospel collection, a complete corpus of Paul's letters, or a collection of Catholic Epistles.

[29] Some "Old Testament" material can still be found in Marcion's version of Luke and Paul's letters; see bibliography and discussion in Dieter T. Roth, *The Text of Marcion's Gospel* (Leiden: Brill, 2015), 7–28; and Judith M. Lieu, *Marcion and the Making of a Heretic: God and Scripture in the Second Century* (Cambridge: Cambridge University Press, 2015), 183–269.

have argued that Marcion's versions represent original forms of these documents.[30] However, this view has its own problems, such as explaining the widespread reception of the final form of Luke and Paul's letters.[31] A more plausible explanation can be offered in light of Marcion's context and the context of some of the texts from the Apostolic Fathers.

Marcion came from Pontus, where the evidence for Jewish communities is slim.[32] The wider region of Asia Minor with a lower percentage of its population consisting of Jews (than say Alexandria, Antioch and even Rome; cf. Josephus, *Ant.* 14.7.2) produced forms of Christianity less familiar with and less certain of the Jewish scriptures. Comparison with some of the Apostolic Fathers texts is also telling. Sometime in the first half of the second century, Ignatius of Antioch traveled through Asia Minor on his way to Rome. When in Marcion's region, Ignatius knows but does not use (at least not explicitly) the Jewish scriptures in his seven letters. Either he does not know them, or he chose not to cite them, perhaps because he knew that these Jewish texts were unfamiliar to gentile Christians in this area. Similarly, Polycarp's only known letters – also in Asia Minor – make no use of Jewish scriptures.[33] Additionally, in the immediate aftermath of the Jewish revolts (66–140 CE) wherein Jews were ultimately expelled from Jerusalem and Judea, there would be additional incentive, when proselytizing gentiles, to provide an abridged (that is, de-Judaized) set of scriptures. Marcion arrives in Rome and "rejects" the Jewish scriptures as antithetical to the God he knows in Christ.

---

[30] E.g., Joseph Tyson, *Marcion and Luke-Acts: A Defining Struggle* (Columbia: University of South Carolina Press, 2006); Matthias Klinghardt, "Markion vs. Lukas: Plädoyer für die Wiederaufnahme eines alten Falles," *NTS* 52 (2006): 213–32; Klinghardt, "'Gesetz' bei Markion und Lukas," in *Das Gesetz im Neuen Testament und im Frühen Christentum*, ed. M. Konradt and D. Sänger, NTOA 57 (Göttingen: Vandenhoeck & Ruprecht, 2006), 102–3; and Klinghardt, "The Marcionite Gospel and the Synoptic Problem: A New Suggestion," *NovT* 50 (2008): 1–27.

[31] See further discussion in Christopher M. Hayes, "M. vs. the 'Plädoyer' of Matthias Klinghardt," *ZNW* 99 (2008): 213–32; and Dieter T. Roth, "Marcion's Gospel and Luke: The History of Research in Current Debate," *JBL* 3 (2008): 513–27.

[32] See Acts 18.2; 1 Pet. 1.1; and the convert to Judaism, Aquila of Sinope. For further discussion, see Heikki Räisänen, "Marcion," in *A Companion to Second-Century Christian "Heretics,"* ed. Antti Marjanen and Petri Luomanen (Leiden: Brill, 2005), 102.

[33] Charles M. Nielsen, "Polycarp and Marcion: A Note," *Theological Studies* 47 (1986): 297–9.

In view of the wider regional dynamics, we can appreciate how the writings of the Apostolic Fathers were later preserved by anti-Marcionite Christians, but not because they offer proof of pre-Marcion positive usage of the Old Testament (only the *Didache*, *1 Clement*, and *2 Clement* do so),[34] nor because they offer proof of pre-Marcionite positive identification of Israel (*Barnabas*, Ignatius, *Letter to the Magnesians*, and *The Epistle of Diognetus* explicitly denigrate the Old Testament "Jews").[35] These texts were preserved not because they directly addressed Marcionism, but because – among other things – they offer statements about Christ and his positive identification with the Creator God of Israel's scriptures,[36] a preemptive strike against Marcion.[37]

With this revised view of Marcion, scholars have reconsidered much of the claims against him as rhetorical.[38] The various attacks against his hatred of all things created, including human bodies and procreation, are likely deduced from his "rejection" of the Old Testament and from the Marcionites' tendency to insist on bodily asceticism (as was common among various early Christian groups). Even Marcion's alleged docetism

---

[34] *1 Clem.* 29.2–30.1, even assumes that Christians are the "Israel" chosen by God.

[35] Ign.*Magn.* 10.3 states, "It is utterly absurd to profess Jesus Christ and to practice Judaism. For Christianity did not believe in Judaism, but Judaism in Christianity, in which every tongue believed and was brought together to God" (Holmes 209: *atapon estin, Iēsoun Christon lalein kai ioydaizein. Ho gar kristianismos ouk eis Xristianismon, Hō pasa glōssa pisteusasa eis Theon sunēchthē*). Also, the Jews are blamed for Polycarp's trial in *Mart. Pol.* 13.1; 17.2; however, this could be part of the rhetorical strategy to depict Polycarp as like Jesus in his death.

[36] E.g., *1 Clem.* 20.11; 26.1; 33.2; *Ep. Diogn.* 7.2.

[37] Few, if any, statements found in the Apostolic Fathers' corpus could be directly anti-Marcionite. Pol. *Phil.* 7.1, attacks docetists, but this need not be Marcion (see below; and Paul Hartog, *Polycarp's Epistle to the Philippians and the Martyrdom of Polycarp: Introduction, Text, and Commentary* [Oxford: Oxford University Press, 2013], 35–6). There is a later account recorded by Irenaeus where Polycarp encountered Marcion and called him the "Firstborn of Satan" (*Adv. Haer.* 3.3.4), which appears dubious (cf. Epiphanius, *Pan.* 30.24.5). The same account is found in the ending to the Moscow manuscript of *The Martyrdom of Polycarp*; the *Martyrdom* itself shows signs of third-century editing; see Candida Moss, "On the Dating of Polycarp: Rethinking the Place of the *Martyrdom of Polycarp* in the History of Christianity," *Early Christianity* 1 (2010): 539–74.

[38] E.g., Pseudo-Tertullian, *Haer.* 6.2, claims Marcion raped a virgin in his hometown of Sinope and was then excommunicated by his father, the bishop. However, this information was not known to earlier writers like Justin Martyr, Clement of Alexandria, or Tertullian, who certainly would have capitalized on it (see where Tertullian makes similar claims against Apelles in *Praer. Haer.* 30). See further elaboration in Paul Foster, "Marcion: His Life, Works, Beliefs, and Impact," *ExpT* 121.6 (2010): 269–80; and Wilhite, *The Gospel According to Heresy*, 21–40.

can now be seen to be a charge laid against him, and not a teaching of his found in the reliable sources themselves.[39] Marcion's Christ simply descended or "went down" to Capernaum, where his version of Luke begins (in 4.31), and then he ministers, dies, resurrects, and ascends. This is not necessarily a rejection of "real flesh" in the incarnation; it is likely a common view from antiquity in which deities are mutable – metamorphosis as needed. In sum, Marcion looks more like a product of Gentile Christianity completely unmoored from Judaism, rather than a heresy that intentionally deviated from a preestablished orthodox set of texts and teachings. A similar conclusion is often given now for the phenomenon known as Gnosticism.

Scholarly opinion about the gnostics has changed more than any other group from early Christianity. In the late second century Irenaeus catalogued the genealogy of gnostics, starting with Simon Magus and his successors, such as Menander, Saturninus, and Basilides, each of whom elaborated their predecessors' teachings.[40] Other groups sprang from these early teachers, such as the Sethians, and then from them Valentinus and his students further deviated and expanded the heretical doctrines. Each development offered more elaborate theogonies and cosmogonies. Irenaeus' claims about these groups, while often proven reliable in specific details, give the impression that there is one general group, the Gnostics, and each sub-group is somehow related. This general claim, however, has now been rejected by many scholars.

The category of "Gnosticism" itself has been largely rejected because it is used to cover a wide range of Christian sources, but these sources witness to communities with little to no internal relationship and who have few if any common characteristics.[41] Even when admitting to this problem, many will continue referring to these Christian groups as "Gnosticism," or "Gnostics" (or, perhaps better, "gnostic"), only with qualifications about how this category is a construct of their opponents.[42] The revisionist approach to "Gnosticism" has been

---

[39] David Wilhite, "Was Marcion a Docetist? The Body of Evidence vs. Tertullian's Argument," *VigChr* 70 (2016): 1–36.

[40] *Adv. Haer.* 1.23–4.

[41] Michael A. Williams, *Rethinking "Gnosticism": An Argument for Dismantling a Dubious Category* (Princeton, NJ: Princeton University Press, 1996). See also Karen King, *What Is Gnosticism?* (Cambridge, MA: Belknap Press, 2003); and Ismo Dunderberg, *Beyond Gnosticism: Myth, Lifestyle, and Society in the School of Valentinus* (New York: Columbia University Press, 2008).

[42] See the helpful studies of Christoph Markschies, *Gnosis: An Introduction*, trans. John Bowden (London: T&T Clark, 2003); Antti Marjanen, "Gnosticism," in *Oxford Handbook of Early Christian Studies* (Oxford: Oxford University Press, 2008),

bolstered by the discovery of codices at Nag Hammadi, which are texts representing a diverse range of genres and topics. Many consist of the first-hand teachings of those attacked by the "orthodox" writers, and so now the "heretics" can be heard on their own terms.[43]

Admitting that any given source on Gnosticism must be read critically and on a case-by-case basis, scholars still tend to list gnostic "characteristics" – only then they often must note all of the exceptions to sources or groups that do not exhibit this characteristic. One frequent tenet shared by virtually all gnostic sources is the teaching that a Demiurge, or some lesser deity or heavenly being (or beings), created the world.[44] Corresponding to this negative view of the creator-deity, gnostic thinking often denigrates the created order, including human bodies. On this point, however, it must be admitted that there is a range of nuance when it comes to speaking of the cosmos as evil: some texts may be thinking merely in terms of being imperfect or fallen,[45] and sometimes "the world" in view is the political realm.[46]

The identity of Christ among gnostic thinkers also involves for a range of views. Irenaeus outlined various cosmogonies in which "Christ" is one of many aeons or emanations from the ultimate Father, and the bishop of Lyon bemoaned the fact that these groups deceptively confess "one Christ Jesus" but secretly continue to believe

203–20; David Brakke, *The Gnostics: Myth, Ritual, and Diversity in Early Christianity* (Cambridge, MA: Harvard University Press, 2010). Also, see the recent treatments by Karen L. King, "'The Gnostic Myth': How Does Its Demise Impact Twenty-first Century Historiography of Christianity's Second Century?," in *Christianity in the Second Century: Themes and Developments*, ed. James Carleton Padget and Judith Lieu (Cambridge: Cambridge University Press, 2017), 122–36; and Mark Edwards, "The Gnostic Myth," in *Christianity in the Second Century: Themes and Developments* (Cambridge: Cambridge University Press, 2017), 137–50.

[43] The categories now became doubly problematic because many Gnostics saw themselves simply as "orthodox" Christians, and they in turn attacked "heretics." E.g., *The Apocalypse of Peter; The Testimony of Truth;* and *The Concept of Our Great Power.*

[44] Exceptions include the *Dialogue of the Savior,* in which the "Logos" makes the world; see discussion in Pierre Létourneau, "The Dialogue of the Savior as a Witness to the Late Valentinian Tradition," *VigChr* 65 (2011): 74–98. Also, cf. *Gospel of Mary* 9.

[45] Comparing texts from Nag Hammadi with other possibly gnostic traditions, as found for example in apocryphal acts of the apostles, is illuminating on this point.

[46] Michael A. Williams, "Life and Happiness in the 'Platonic Underworld,'" in *Gnosticism, Platonism, and the Late Ancient World: Essays in Honour of John D. Turner,* ed. Kevin Corrigan and Tuomas Rasimus (Leiden: Brill, 2013), 497–523

in various entities in a chain of being.[47] In the gnostic sources themselves, this claim is sometimes verified, while at other times the distinction between "Jesus" and the heavenly being who indwells him may simply be an attempt to distinguish Christ's divine and human natures.[48] Along with the alleged denial of Christ's "true flesh" (however defined), the gnostics are then accused of denigrating the flesh and acts done in the flesh, and so they are said to be libertines who may even deny the goodness of martyrdom. These claims, however, must be false accusations, exaggerations, or applicable only to a few gnostic communities because the gnostics are also accused of the opposite: some gnostics are labeled encratites, which is to say that they prohibit marriage, meat, and other forms of fleshly pleasure. Of course, the label encratite belongs to a number of second-century Christians other than gnostics, such as Tatian and his followers, and therefore this accusation seems to require close scrutiny, given the widespread emphasis in the second century on celibacy and asceticism.[49]

As to gnostic origins, not only Irenaeus but even some modern Gnostic specialists think this movement or at least some in this group can trace their views back to the first century. The difference is that Irenaeus, and the traditionalist view that continued after him, and the revisionist view disagree about the sources of this first-century heritage. Irenaeus thinks the gnostics all descend in their own unholy form of apostolic succession, wherein each generation deviates further from the previous and creates its own school or faction.[50] The revisionist view suspects that Simon Magus (cf. Acts 8.9–25) is a fictional character, or at least a ghost of the past used to represent any rival power to a group trying to claim orthodoxy. Jesus' teaching, in this view, spread to groups who held to various cultural thought-worlds.[51] Any given gnostic text, therefore, should be read, not as intentionally disagreeing with a pre-established orthodox doctrine, but as a witness to an early Christian community holding to what it views as orthodoxy. For example, the *Gospel of Thomas* has much material that parallels the canonical Gospels, and so the question is whether the differences and differing

---

[47] See *Adv. Haer.* 3.16.1, for a concise report, but the lengthier descriptions are throughout book 1 of his work.

[48] E.g., *Apocalypse of Peter; Letter of Peter to Philip;* and *First Apocalypse of James.*

[49] Compare, for example, *The Acts of Paul and Thecla.*

[50] *Adv. Haer.* 1.23.4.

[51] In contrast to his depiction of an unbroken line of succession of gnostic teachers, Irenaeus elsewhere concedes that the gnostics are more like "mushroom" that emerge sporadically (*Adv. Haer.* 1.29.1).

content are a matter of intentional change or alternative tradition.[52] So with other material from Nag Hammadi: the manuscripts themselves are late, but many texts belong to the second century, and the default assumption in revisionist circles is that these bear equal witness to earlier Christian expressions as texts found in the Apostolic Fathers.[53]

Because the gnostics are now understood to be such a disparate form of Christians, it is difficult to isolate passages from the Apostolic Fathers that could be in response to them.[54] Ignatius is concerned with those "teach strange doctrines (*heterodidaskalountes*)" (*Poly.* 3.1), and he may know some of the Valentinian theogonies (cf. *Magn.* 8.2), but the details are severely lacking. Ignatius and others are also concerned with some form of docetism, denouncing anyone who denies that Christ has come in the flesh.[55] There are also responses about the resurrected body as composed of true flesh; this was once thought to be denied by gnostics, but perhaps merely a widespread view of the new "spiritual body" (cf. 1 Cor. 15.44).[56] Aside from these somewhat oblique references, there is a surprising silence about any specific gnostic teachers or teachings among the Apostolic Fathers.

The same silence falls on the last two heresies to be covered here. Traditionally speaking, Montanism began in 170 CE when the prophets

---

[52] See the introduction and notes in April D. DeConick (ed./trans.), *The Original Gospel of Thomas in Translation*, JSNTS 287 (Edinburgh: T&T Clark, 2006).

[53] Possible second-century texts from Nag Hammadi include *The Acts of Peter and the Twelve Apostles*, *The Apocryphon of John*, *The Apocalypse of Paul*, *The Apocalypse of Peter*, *First Apocalypse of James*, *Second Apocalypse of James*, *Gospel of the Egyptians*, *Gospel of Mary*, *Gospel of Philip*, *Gospel of Truth*, *Sophia of Jesus Christ*, and *Letter of Peter to Philip*. Other gnostic texts that possibly date from the second century include *The Apocalypse of Thomas*; *Excerpts from Theodotus* (apud Clement of Alexandria); Ptolemy, *Letter to Flora* (apud Epiphanius, *Pan.* 33.3–8); *Gospel of Judas*; and *Gospel of the Savior*.

[54] 2 *Clement* has been read as directed against the gnostics (see *Praedestinatus* 1.14). Alternatively, the *Epistle of Diognetus* may itself be gnostic. For bibliography, see Michael F. Bird, "The Reception of Paul in the *Epistle to Diognetus*," in *Paul and the Second Century*, ed. Michael F. Bird and Joseph R. Dodson (London: T&T Clark, 2011), 89–90. In both instances, the argument depends on one's definition of gnostic.

[55] E.g., Ign. *Magn.* 1.2; *Trall.* 9.1; 10; *Rom.* 6.1; *Smyrn.* 4.2; Pol. *Phil.* 7.1–2.

[56] Ign. *Smyrn.* 3.1 insists on the real flesh of Christ, "even after the resurrection (καὶ μετὰ τὴν ἀνάστασιν)." Ignatius then cites Jesus in a statement close to that of Lk. 24.39, but which more closely corresponds to the saying found in the *Gospel of the Hebrews* and the *Teachings of Peter*: "Take hold of me; handle me and see that I am not a disembodied demon' (*Smyrn.* 3.2 [Holmes 250–1: *Labete, psēlaphēsate me kai idete, hoti ouk eimi daimonion asōmaton*]). Similarly, 2 *Clem.* 9.1–5 knows that some claim that the flesh does not rise, but "Clement" insists that it does, as proven that "Christ the Lord became flesh even though he was originally spirit" (2 *Clem.* 9.5 [Holmes 148–9: *Christos, Ho Kurios ho sōsas hēmas, ōn men to proton pneuma*]).

Montanus, Priscilla, and Maximilla broke from the catholic church and began uttering ecstatic teachings that diverged from the scriptures and the official teachings of the bishops.[57] In the revisionist approach, however, the category itself is problematic, since this group referred to their group as "the New Prophecy"[58] – or perhaps even, those who believe in "new prophecies" and ongoing prophecy since the inauguration of the new covenant.[59] This shift in thinking results in the "Montanists" belonging to a wider trend in second-century Christianity wherein pious acts like fasting, celibacy, ecstatic states, and martyrdom are championed.[60] The actual prophets from Phrygia (this heresy was called Kataphrygian or even Phrygian before it was labeled Montanist) did seem to teach a specific form of chiliasm (which in general is common in this era) wherein the heavenly Jerusalem would descend in their region to the cities of Pepuza and Tymion.[61]

Given the common dating of the writings collected in the Apostolic Fathers corpus, it is no surprise that there is virtually nothing said in them about Montanism. The *Shepherd of Hermas* is often compared with Montanism because of the ongoing visions that seem to be normative to its community.[62] The other possible reference is from the

---

[57] See Eusebius, *Eccl. hist.* 5.14–19. For additional primary sources, see Pierre de Labriolle, *Les sources de l'histoire du montanisme* (Fribourg: Librairie de l'Université, 1913); Ronald E. Heine, *The Montanist Oracles and Testimonia*, Patristic Monograph Series 14 (Macon, GA: Mercer University Press, 1989); and William Tabbernee, *Montanist Inscriptions and Testimonia: Epigraphic Sources Illustrating the History of Montanism* (Macon, GA: Mercer University Press, 1997).

[58] Christine Trevett, *Montanism: Gender, Authority and the New Prophecy* (Cambridge: Cambridge University Press, 1996); Alistair Stewart-Sykes, "The Original Condemnation of Asian Montanism," *JEH* 50 (1999): 1–22; Nicola Denzey, "What Did the Montanists Read?," *HTR* 94 (2001): 427–48; William Tabbernee, "'Will the Real Paraclete Please Speak Forth!': The Catholic–Montanist Conflict over Pneumatology," in *Advents of the Spirit: An Introduction to the Current Study of Pneumatology*, ed. Bradford E. Hinze and D. Lyle Dabney (Milwaukee, WI: Marquette University Press, 2001), 197–218.

[59] Cf. Tertullian, *Prax.* 30.5; 31.1.

[60] Laura Nasrallah, *An Ecstasy of Folly: Prophecy and Authority in Early Christianity*, Harvard Theological Studies 52 (Cambridge, MA: Harvard University Press, 2003); and Nasrallah, "Prophecy, the Periodization of History, and Early Christian Identity: A Case from the So-Called Montanist Controversy," in *Religious Identity in Late Antiquity*, ed. Robert M. Frakes and Elizabeth DePalma Digeser (Toronto: Edgar Kent, 2006), 13–35, 246–50.

[61] For a careful sifting of the evidence, see William Tabbernee, *Fake Prophecy and Polluted Sacraments: Ecclesiastical and Imperial Reactions to Montanism* (Leiden: Brill, 2007).

[62] E.g., Rex D. Butler, *The New Prophecy and "New Visions": Evidence of Montanism in The Passion of Perpetua and Felicitas*, Patristic Monograph Series 18 (Washington,

Martyrdom of Polycarp, which again begs the question of dating for this text. A certain Phrygian named Quintus led people to volunteer themselves for martyrdom, but he in fact apostasized when threatened with beasts.[63] Montanists were accused of being enthusiasts when it came to martyrdom, and so this could possibly be an anti-Montanist episode, but it is also the case that many early Christians were eager to be martyred.[64] In short, there are no explicit interactions with a sect of Montanists in the Apostolic Fathers, but there are commonalities of ideas, such as belief in ongoing visions.[65]

The last second-century heresy to be addressed here is Sabellianism. Sabellius was a bishop from Pentapolis who was condemned around 220 CE.[66] Though later than our scope, the teachings associated with his name can be found earlier in writers like Noetus, who came to Rome around 190 from Smyrna.[67] This heresy entailed a form of monotheism that identified the Father and the Son as the same person, only appearing in different modes (i.e., modalism). According to this teaching, the Father incarnate, known as a son born to Mary, suffered and died (i.e., patripassianism).[68] Suffice it to say that Sabellianism is now not understood as a sect or even an intentional deviation from prior dogma, but as an attempt by several ancient Christians to retain a strict form of monotheism.[69]

There are no interactions with Sabellianism found within the Apostolic Fathers corpus. There is, however, an interesting case found in one of Ignatius' letters. Because he spoke of "the blood of God" in response to docetic teachings, a later copyist feared that the bishop of Antioch would be misunderstood as a Sabellian, and so (in what is called the Long Recension) his text was changed to "the blood of Christ."[70] It is clear from the rest of Ignatius' letters that he differentiates between God the Father and Christ, who is also "God" or "divine." Therefore,

---

DC: The Catholic University of America Press, 2006), frequently speaks of this text as if it were Montanist in order to compare Montanism with wider phenomena.

[63] *Mart. Pol.* 4.

[64] Cf. *Mart. Pol.* 3.1; Ign. *Rom.* 1.2; 4.1; 5.2. See discussion in Hartog, *Polycarp's Epistle to the Philippians and the Martyrdom of Polycarp*, 221–6.

[65] Also see *Mart. Pol.* 5.2.

[66] Basil of Caesarea, *Ep.* 125; Eusebius, *Eccl. hist.* 7.6.

[67] Hippolytus, *Against Noetus*.

[68] Tertullian attacked a certain "Praxeas" for "crucifying the Father (*patrem crucifixit)*" (*Prax.* 1.5). This same Praxeas also denied "new prophecy" and so he also "put to flight the Paraclete (*Paracletum fugavit*)."

[69] See Wilhite, *Gospel According to Heretics*, 87–104.

[70] *Eph.* 1.1.

his statement does not at all endorse patripassionism, but it does illustrate how easily monotheistic Christians could speak in ways that sound modalist.[71]

3.4 ASSESSING THE DIVERSITY

Given the doctrinal diversity found in these various groups (formerly known as heresies), it is notable that our survey of their teachings in the Apostolic Fathers has found surprisingly few interactions with them. The only explicit candidate is some form of docetism, and even then no teacher or heretic is named. That being said, the writers in this collection know of schism, heresy, and doctrinal diversity, and a few examples of their statements on factionalism can help illuminate further their own concern with doctrinal diversity. For instance, the author of *1 Clement* mentions the "detestable and unholy schism, so alien and strange to those chosen by God, which a few reckless and arrogant persons have kindled" among the Corinthian Christians.[72] In other words, the rupture that has taken place in Corinth is portrayed as rare and done by a small minority. But if this is the case, how were such a small and novel group able to oust presbyters in Corinth? Furthermore, the author admits in the very next paragraph that schisms were more common: "Every faction and every schism was abominable to you."[73] What remains unclear is whether or not these schisms represent substantive doctrinal diversity or factionalism along some other lines; the reference may even be to the problem known from Paul's letter (1 Cor. 1.10–12), and so arguably particular practices like eating meat offered to idols are in view.

Several instances occur in the letters of Ignatius, where the bishop explicitly speaks about factions. Ignatius claims that in Ephesus "no heresy has found a home" because the Ephesian Christians "do not so much as listen to anyone unless he speaks truthfully about Jesus Christ."[74] Of course, this suggests that there were "heretical" teachers in Ephesus to be avoided, but how many and of what kind of following

---

[71] It is worth noting that Ignatius has connections with Polycarp of Smyrna, and both Noetus and Praxeas are said to be from this area.

[72] *1 Clem.* 1.1 (Holmes 44–5: *allotrias kai ksenēs tois eklektois tou Theou, miaras kai anosiou staseōs hē oliga prosōpa propetē*).

[73] *1 Clem.* 2.6 (Holmes 46–7: *pasa stasis kai pan schism bdelukton ēn hymin*).

[74] *Eph.* 6.2 (Holmes 188–9: *oudemia airesis katoikei ... oude akouete tinos pleon, ē peri Iēsou Christou lalountos en alētheia*).

they had is not apparent.[75] Elsewhere, Ignatius mentions "some" who acknowledge the bishop (Damas of Magnesia) but meet apart from him in what Ignatius believes is an unsanctioned and invalid meeting.[76] But no further details are given about the size of what appears to be a small faction, or even a house-church continuing its traditions while still acknowledging the bishop. Without seeming to know much of the details, he warns the Trallian Christians to "keep away" from heresy, which may be a general kind of warning, implying that there are "heretical" factions of Christians in virtually every city.[77] There is a curious case in his letter to the Philadelphian Christians. He applauds them for their unity: "Not that I found any division among you: instead, I found that there had been a purification."[78] What or who had been purged is unclear. The statement is complicated by next mentioning a "schismatic (schizonti)" (3.3), and then later speaking of "the division (ton merismon)" among the Philadelphian Christians (7.2). Evidently, this "purification" of people from the church in Philadelphia was a schism of some sort.

What can be concluded about these divisions and schisms? From the previous review of the instances when texts from the corpus of the Apostolic Fathers directly responded to second-century "heresies," it was seen that the only explicit instances were in response to the gnostic views of Christ's flesh – and even this could have been about his (and believers') resurrected body in particular. Otherwise, there is surprisingly little devoted to what would be labeled today as doctrinal diversity. There is certainly no concern with low Christology, apocryphal scriptures, millennial expectations, or other central tenets of the faith normally thought to be contested among various "Christianities." If these matters were so contested at this time, then why do they not show up in the Apostolic Fathers? The only other stated debates in the Apostolic Fathers centered on matters of ecclesiological structure, church officers, and how Christians relate to one another across geographical distances. Perhaps, the Ebionites, Valentinans, Marcionites, and other groups – or at least groups with similar teachings – should be

---

[75] More description of the false teachers can be found in *Eph.* 7.1; they seem to be docetic. Also, in *Eph.* 9.1 Ignatius describes these teachers as transitory.

[76] *Magn.* 4.1.

[77] *Trall.* 6.1. Similarly, in *Smyrn.* 8.1–2, Ignatius argues that no gathering without the bishop is valid, in particular not a Eucharist or baptismal service. The need to make this argument, however, implies that there were Christian gatherings without the bishop.

[78] *Phil.* 3.1 (Holmes 238–9: *ouch hoti par hymin merismon heuron, all apodiulismon*).

understood to be lingering in the background of the Apostolic Fathers, but the authors of these texts failed to mention them explicitly. This is certainly possible, but there is no evidence to support such speculation.

Even if the scope of doctrinal diversity is more limited than is sometimes acknowledged, the sources from the second century do indicate doctrinal diversity along the lines of practice. There was no centralized Christian power structure within any given city, and much less between cities, for most of the second century.[79] This lack of centralized authority coupled with a desire (at least on the part of some) to be in fellowship and harmony with one another sometimes brought to light the diversity of practice. This can be seen in middle of the second century during the quartodeciman controversy: Christians from Asia Minor continued to use the Jewish calendar for calculating the celebration of Easter, whereas Christians in Rome believed their practice of always celebrating on the first day of the week should be normative.[80] Sometime later, Irenaeus reminded the bishop of Rome, Victor, how his predecessor, Anicetus, had met with Polycarp: though the two differed in regard to this practice, they continued to recognize one another's validity. In short, despite some differences, these late second-century Christian communities continued to understand themselves as belonging to the "catholic church."[81] This is likely because these communities have defined themselves over against other various sects, which are seen to be smaller factions. Irenaeus describes how the heretics demean "the multitude (*multitudinem*)" of Christians as "common (*communes*)," in order to try to seduce some to join their sect.[82] In sum, many Christians that will later be accepted as "orthodox," insist that their heretical opponents consist of small factions. Interestingly, when looking to the sources written by groups Irenaeus would call heretics, we find examples of the exact same understanding of the demographics.

In the sources normally considered to be gnostic, there are several instances where the authors write with a self-understanding of being a

---

[79] Helpful studies of this question include Benjamin L. Merkle, *The Elders and the Overseer: One Office in the Early Church*, SBL 57 (New York: Lang, 2003); Alistair C. Stewart, *The Original Bishops: Office and Order in the First Christian Communities* (Grand Rapids, MI: Baker, 2014).

[80] Eusebius, *Eccl. hist.* 5.23–4.

[81] It is worth noting that this phrase occasionally appears in the writings of the Apostolic Fathers: *Mart. Pol.* pref.; 8.1; 16.2; 19.2; cf. Ign. *Smyrn.* 8.2. The use and dating, however, should be taking into account.

[82] *Adv. Haer.* 3.15.2.

part of a minority group, one that is set apart from the larger Christian network of churches. One example is found in the *Gospel of Judas*, where it reads, "[The disciples] said, "We have seen a great house with a large altar in it, and twelve men – we would say they are the priests – and a name."[83] After hearing this vision, Jesus responds, "they have shamefully planted trees without fruit in my name."[84] In other words, this text represents a community that distinguishes itself from the larger bodies of Jesus' disciples, which stems from the twelve but which is thought to be spiritually fruitless. A similar idea is likely found in the *Gospel of Thomas*: Jesus calls Thomas aside to teach him; when the other disciples asked what Jesus had said, Thomas answers, "If I tell you one of the things which he told me, you will pick up stones and throw them at me.'[85] This seems to be the explanation of why the rest of the disciples did not teach what is found in Thomas's *Gospel*, and it predicts that the rest of the Christians would reject the teaching therein. Another example of this can be found in the *Gospel of Mary*, where Andrew and Peter (who are clearly meant to represent the Christian groups who claim these apostles) doubt that the Savior would have shared such "strange teachings" with Mary (who clearly represents the teachings of the community from which this text derives). In response, Mary exclaims, "My brother Peter, what are you thinking? Do you think that I have thought up these things alone in my heart or that I am telling lies about the Savior?"[86] The obvious answer to this rhetorical question is... yes!, the rest of the followers of Jesus do think you are lying. The fact that this text even has to address this question shows an awareness that the author believed others said so about his or her community. Similarly, the Nag Hammadi text *The Second Treatise of the Great Seth* bemoans how believers are "hated and persecuted, not only by those who are ignorant, but by those who think that they are advancing the name of Christ."[87] In other words, this texts reflects a community that knows of others who bear the name Christ and are in a

---

[83] *Gospel of Judas* 38 (Bart D. Ehrman and Zlatko Pleše, *The Apocryphal Gospels: Texts and Translations* [Oxford: Oxford University Press, 2011], 396–7).

[84] *Gospel of Judas* 39 (Ehrman and Pleše, *The Apocryphal Gospels*, 398–9). Also, cf. *Gospel of Judas* 44–5, "Judas said to [Jesus], 'I saw myself in the vision as the twelve disciples threw stones at me and persecuted me zealously'" (Ehrman and Pleše, *The Apocryphal Gospels*, 400–1).

[85] *Gospel of Thomas* 13/II.35.10–14 (James N. Robinson, *The Coptic Gnostic Library* [Leiden: Brill, 2000], 2.XXXIII).

[86] *Gospel of Mary* 18 (Ehrman and Pleše, *The Apocryphal Gospels*, 596–9).

[87] *The Treatise of the Great Seth* VII.59.22–6 (Robinson, *The Coptic Gnostic Library* 4. XXX).

position of strength, probably a majority, who can somehow "persecute" this small group that differs in its views.

In sum, these examples show that (a) there is doctrinal diversity, (b)
that both sides claim to be heirs of apostolic teachings, and (c) that at
least some of the communities who hold to some form of gnostic
Christianity acknowledge that they are a smaller faction when compared to the rest of the heirs to Jesus' disciples. With the possible
exception of the *Gospel of Thomas*, these texts stem from the late
second century, and so their claims to represent the original Jesus
community is, at the least, dubious.

At this point the debate between the traditionalist and revisionist
scholars can be revisited and assessed in light of the current findings. In
a recent study, Lewis Ayres addressed the current climate of studying
early Christian development.[88] He begins by noting two ways to "narrate continuities and discontinuities" in early Christianity: one way
sees the core of what will become the New Testament already written
by the end of the first century; this core represents a central orthodoxy
that can be summarized in "quasi-creedal statements (the rules or
canons of faith or truth)," which was guarded by monepiscopal guard-
ians of this orthodoxy protecting the widespread Christian movement
from heresy.[89] The other is to see the many "lost Christianities" as an
array of numerous expressions of reactions to Jesus' teachings and
which should all be understood equally as valid expressions, even if
"proto-orthodoxy" eventually suppressed the other forms.[90] Ayres does
not wish to return to the "naïve" expressions of the first option, but he
does argue against the second to say "when we narrate the development
of Christianity during this period, we *can* legitimately begin by emphasizing fundamental continuities between the discursive space of our
earliest Christian texts – say in the period between 60 and 120 CE –
and the discursive space of proto-orthodox writers in the period between
180 and 220 CE."[91] Ayres follows Rowan Williams's use of "tradition"
and pairs it with "discursive space" as defined by Foucault, Habermas,

---

[88] Lewis Ayres, "Continuity and Change in Second-Century Christianity: A Narrative
Against the Trend," in *Christianity in the Second Century: Themes and
Developments*, ed. James Carleton Paget and Judith Lieu (Cambridge: Cambridge
University Press, 2017), 106–21.

[89] Ayres, "Continuity and Change," 106.

[90] In particular, he cites the following studies: Brakke, *The Gnostics*; Bart D. Ehrman,
Lost Christianities: The Battles for Scriptures and the Faith We Never Knew (Oxford:
Oxford University Press, 2003); and King, *What Is Gnosticism?*

[91] Ayres, "Continuity and Change," 107.

and MacIntyre in order to speak of "discursive tradition."[92] He then contends that the proto-orthodox writers represent a faithful discursive tradition to first-century Christianity, something that cannot be said for the later developments found in gnostic myths. He ends by asserting, "The claim by an Irenaeus or a Tertullian to have maintained the faith of the apostles of course needs much nuance, but dismissing it as naive or as deceitful rhetoric is not good history."[93]

Ayres, as the title of his essay indicates, feels the need to "go against the trend" of current scholarship, or what has been labeled here as revisionist scholarship. Ayres, however, only offers a preliminary and brief response to this trend. When speaking in general terms, his point may be valid that not enough attention is paid to the larger claims to the authentic claims to the tradition of the original Jesus community. Even so, when working with specific sources and groups labeled heretical, Ayres could do more to acknowledge that some history needs revising.[94]

In the ongoing work of scholars who are trying to understand ancient sources on their own terms, and not anachronistically deem them "heretical" by using later standards, there is much to be gained by the revisionist approach. At the same time, more work also needs to be done to assess how much any given source can be understood to reflect the larger landscape of second-century Christianity. The survey of geographical and doctrinal diversity offered here is meant to help supplement current discussions. Most of the clear evidence for distinct groups and teachings that would later be labeled heretical turns out to belong to the second half of the second century, and the earlier surviving texts of the Apostolic Fathers show little to know interest in these factions. Furthermore, the data from both the Apostolic Fathers and the surviving gnostic texts indicate that groups labeled gnostics were small factions in comparison with the larger network of Christian communities. That being said, this larger network had almost no centralization, and there was no standardized sets of dogma that later groups knowingly rejected or revised.

---

[92] Ibid., 108 n.5.
[93] Ibid., 119.
[94] For a balanced view of "diversity" and "plurality," which still belong to a single Christian "identity," see Christoph Markschies, *Kaiserzeitliche christliche Theologie und ihre Institutionen Prolegomena zu einer Geschichte der antiken christlichen Theologie* (Tubingen: Mohr Siebeck, 2007); now in English translation: *Christian Theology and Its Institutions in the Early Roman Empire*, trans. Wayne Coppins (Waco, TX: Baylor University Press, 2015).

In sum, the doctrinal diversity found in the second century may not be as diverse as has sometimes been claimed, and at the same time the ecclesial communion and unity may not have been as unified as has often been believed. There were clear ties by some groups to the first-century Christian communities, whereas other groups' claims appears to be forced explanations as to why they developed so differently from the majority of Christians. Just how much each side developed and to what extent any group can claim to be legitimate heirs to the earlier tradition remains an open question for further studies.

FURTHER READING

Berzon, Todd S. *Classifying Christians: Ethnography, Heresiology, and the Limits of Knowledge in Late Antiquity.* Oakland, CA: University of California Press, 2016.

Bingham, D. Jeffrey, and Clayton N. Jefford (eds.). *Intertextuality in the Second Century.* Leiden: Brill, 2016.

Marjanen, Antti, and Petri Luomanen (eds.). *A Companion to Second-Century Christian "Heretics."* Leiden: Brill, 2005.

Markschies, Christoph. *Christian Theology and Its Institutions in the Early Roman Empire,* trans. Wayne Coppins. Waco, TX: Baylor University Press, 2015.

Paget, James Carleton, and Judith Lieu (eds.). *Christianity in the Second Century: Themes and Developments.* Cambridge: Cambridge University Press, 2017.

Smith, Geoffrey. *Guilt by Association: Heresy Catalogues in Early Christianity.* Oxford: Oxford University Press, 2015.

Wilhite, David. *The Gospel According to the Heretics.* Grand Rapids, MI: Baker, 2015.

4 The Jesus Tradition in the Apostolic Fathers

STEPHEN E. YOUNG

4.1 INTRODUCTION

This essay will analyze the Jesus tradition in the Apostolic Fathers in light of recent debates on the relationship between orality and textuality in antiquity. Specifically, it will analyze the Jesus tradition in the Apostolic Fathers *as oral tradition*, given that it almost certainly derived from an oral-traditional source.[1] This approach reflects a scholarly paradigm-shift that has been gaining momentum over the last three decades in studying the interplay of orality and textuality in early Christian circles. Prior to this paradigm-shift one could say with Werner H. Kelber that historical biblical scholarship was "empowered by an inadequate theory of the art of communication in the ancient world."[2] The paradigm-shift involves taking seriously that early Christianity arose and spread within societies that were predominantly oral. Not that attention to oral tradition is something new; New Testament scholars appealed to it for centuries, for example, in debating the sources and historical reliability of the canonical Gospels.[3] Relatively recent, however, are the many insights into the inner workings of oral tradition in antiquity provided by a newer generation of

---

[1] With the possible exception of *2 Clement* (c. 120–150 CE), which may mark the beginning of the appeal to written sources; the evidence, however, is inconclusive. The present chapter is an updated and revised treatment of ideas developed in greater detail (with extensive bibliography) in my book *Jesus Tradition in the Apostolic Fathers: Their Explicit Appeals to the Words of Jesus in Light of Orality Studies*, WUNT 2.311 (Tübingen: Mohr Siebeck, 2011), used with permission from Mohr Siebeck Tübingen.

[2] W.H. Kelber, *The Oral and the Written Gospel: The Hermeneutics of Speaking and Writing in the Synoptic Tradition, Mark, Paul, and Q*, repr. with a new intro. by the author and a foreword by W.J. Ong (Bloomington and Indianapolis: Indiana University Press, 1997), xxviii.

[3] Appeal traceable, e.g., through the works of Gotthold Lessing (1729–1781), Johann Gottfried Herder (1744–1803), Johann Gieseler (1792–1854), and Brooke Foss Westcott (1825–1901).

scholars,[4] many of whom built upon the pioneering work of Milman Parry and Albert Lord.[5] These new insights are reshaping our understanding of the role of oral Jesus tradition in the early Christian community, and causing us to rethink the impact of orality and textuality upon early Christian writings and their sources.

Analyzing the Jesus tradition in the Apostolic Fathers from the perspective of this paradigm-shift implies altering our default setting, to use an idea popularized by James Dunn: the modern Western scholarly "default setting" is literary, so that literary answers are naturally proposed for problems in early Christianity that may be addressed better from the perspective of orality.[6] When one encounters variations between the Jesus tradition as contained in the Apostolic Fathers and its parallels in other documents (including the Gospels), these are best analyzed not from the perspective of modern literary considerations such as an author's redactional choices, but from the perspective of how orality interacted with textuality in antiquity.[7] One would expect, for example, that the Jesus tradition contained in the Apostolic Fathers would reflect the traditionists' need to give a mnemonic shape to their tradition, and that it would share the fixity within flexibility, or stability within diversity, characteristic of oral tradition in their cultural milieu.

4.2 ORALITY AND JESUS TRADITION

What do we mean by "oral Jesus tradition"? One could define it as discourse material either attributed to Jesus or about him, which arose

---

[4] As representative of many others, see J.M. Foley, *The Singer of Tales in Performance*, VPT (Bloomington and Indianapolis: Indiana University Press, 1995); J.R. Goody, *The Interface between the Written and the Oral*, SLFCS (Cambridge: Cambridge University Press, 1987); E.A. Havelock, *The Muse Learns to Write: Reflections on Orality and Literacy from Antiquity to the Present* (New Haven, CT and London: Yale University Press, 1986); W.J. Ong, *Orality and Literacy: The Technologizing of the Word*, New Accents (London and New York: Methuen, 1982); J. Vansina, *Oral Tradition as History* (Madison: University of Wisconsin Press and London: Currey, 1985). The journal *Oral Tradition* (journal.oraltradition.org/; accessed April 5, 2019) is a good entry point to the field.

[5] See, e.g., M. Parry, *The Making of Homeric Verse: The Collected Papers of Milman Parry*, ed. A. Parry (Oxford: Clarendon, 1971); A. Lord, *The Singer of Tales*, HSCL 24 (Cambridge, MA: Harvard University Press, 1960).

[6] James D.G. Dunn, *The Oral Gospel Tradition* (Grand Rapids, MI: Eerdmans, 2013), 43.

[7] Kelber's *Oral and the Written Gospel* (1983; repr. 1997) provided the catalyst for much work from this perspective on early Christian texts; for a bibliography, see Young, *Jesus Tradition*, 295–347.

in a spoken venue and was transmitted from the past via the spoken word, and was shared by the members of the first- and second-century Jesus movement. Oral Jesus tradition, then, includes not only traditions containing Jesus' words but also those that describe his actions. It is "oral" because it originated and was transmitted (primarily) via speaking and hearing, and any written notes functioned as aids to memorization rather than vessels of tradition. It is "tradition" because it was performed repeatedly over time, by more than one traditionist, in more than one context, maintaining a tie to the past and to the Christian community distinct from the individuality of its performers. Because it was shared by the members of the Jesus community, it shaped that community, as essential to its proclamation and didactic activity, and it also was shaped by it, as the community interpreted it in its retelling so as to apply it in ever new situations. This kept it a *living* tradition, relevant to the community's present.

In its use of oral tradition, the Christian community reflected the wider society of its time, which was "predominantly oral": i.e., its members made little use of literacy, and functioned primarily on the basis of orality. Literacy rates varied depending on a number of factors (region; urban vs. rural; gender)[8] but was around 10–15 percent for the general population,[9] and for Palestinian Jews probably not much higher than 3 percent.[10] These low literacy levels were not a detriment, however, within societies in which people would have preferred the spoken word over the written. Various contexts (occupational, socioeconomic, or geographical, among others) required various levels of literacy:[11] e.g., farmers and members of rural communities would have needed it little, using the spoken word for the majority of their activities. For activities that demanded writing (letters, contracts) they would have hired a scribe, usually in the islands of literacy provided by urban centers. In urban centers even those who could read and write did not always do so, but relied on orality for functions that would seem to invite the skills of

---

[8] "Literacy" here is understood (with W.V. Harris, *Ancient Literacy* [Cambridge, MA: Harvard University Press, 1989], 3–5), to exclude rates calculated on the basis of people's ability only to sign their name or to read but not write.

[9] Harris, *Ancient Literacy*, 327–30; similarly H.Y. Gamble, *Books and Readers in the Early Church: A History of Early Christian Texts* (New Haven, CT: Yale University Press, 1995), 2–10.

[10] Meir Bar-Ilan, "Illiteracy in the Land of Israel in the First Centuries C.E.," in *Essays in the Social Scientific Study of Judaism and Jewish Society*, ed. S. Fishbane, S. Schoenfeld, and A. Goldschläger (Hoboken, NJ: KTAV, 1992), 46–61.

[11] Harris, *Ancient Literacy*, 25–42, 66–115, 142–3, 190–3, 248–59, 289–306.

literacy; for example, Greek and Roman elites accustomed to dictate letters rather than personally write them, or have a slave read a text aloud rather than read it themselves.[12] Within this context it is best to view those who did not read and write not as literacy-deficient, but as orality-proficient, and those who *did* have literacy skills as no less proficient in orality.

This interplay between orality and literacy spilled over into the use of written texts: texts were spoken and heard. In composing a text, it was common for authors to speak it aloud while writing it themselves or dictating it to a scribe. Similarly, readers usually *vocalized* texts, even if reading them to themselves.[13] The cultural ideal was for traditionists and orators to memorize the contents of written texts and deliver them from memory, so that the written text need not be physically present during the process of its delivery.[14] Texts served as intermediaries between spoken word and spoken word.

4.3 JESUS TRADITION IN THE APOSTOLIC FATHERS

That the writings from the Apostolic Fathers that will be considered in the present essay all date from before the mid-second century is a key factor in considering the Jesus tradition they contain: they were at home in the predominantly oral social context described above, characterized by the interplay between literacy and orality.[15] Whereas today one may read these texts silently and in isolation, their writers were immersed in a social web of literacy and orality without clearly defined boundaries.

---

[12] Ibid., 35–6.

[13] See P.J. Achtemeier, "*Omne Verbum Sonat*: The New Testament and the Oral Environment of Late Western Antiquity," *JBL* 109 (1990), 14–15; Martin S. Jaffee, *Torah in the Mouth: Writing and Oral Tradition in Palestinian Judaism 200 BCE–400 CE* (Oxford: Oxford University Press, 2001), 17–18.

[14] Whitney Shiner, *Proclaiming the Gospel: First Century Performance of Mark* (Harrisburg, PA: Trinity Press International, 2003), 103–25. For a more recent, alternative view on the role of writings in first-century Christian communities, see B.J. Wright, *Communal Reading in the Time of Jesus: A Window into Early Christian Reading Practices* (Minneapolis, MN: Augsburg Fortress, 2017).

[15] The texts known as the "Apostolic Fathers" were probably gathered into one corpus based on the double criteria of their early date (roughly between the late first and the mid-second centuries) and the view that their authors either knew one of the Twelve Apostles or were taught by somebody who had. The phrase "Apostolic Fathers" may have entered common usage following how seventeenth- and eighteenth-century booksellers and librarians handled a 1672 work by J.B. Cotelier; see David Lincicum, "The Paratextual Invention of the Term 'Apostolic Fathers,'" *JTS* 66 (2015): 139–48.

During this time the oral tradition that made its way into the canonical Gospels and other writings was still widely used among the churches.[16] It was not yet standard practice for writers to appeal to the written canonical Gospels, something that became characteristic only after the time of Irenaeus (c. 130/40–after 198).

The following analysis will seek to tease out evidence of the interplay between literacy and orality within the Jesus tradition contained in the Apostolic Fathers, and suggest some implications. Since the scope of this essay does not allow for a detailed treatment of all the relevant material, it will focus on four of the most important texts in which the Apostolic Fathers explicitly quote Jesus tradition: *1 Clement* 13.1c–2, Polycarp's *Epistle to the Philippians* 2.3, the Lord's Prayer in *Didache* 8.2, and Papias fragment 1.1b–5 (preserved in Iren. *Adv. Haer.* 5.33.3–4).

4.3.1 *First Clement* 13.1c–2 and Poly. *Phil.* 2.3

The Jesus tradition preserved in *1 Clement* 13.1c–2 and Polycarp's *Philippians* 2.3 is a good place to begin, as the complexity of its parallels will allow us to address many issues involved in this kind of analysis. The accompanying synopsis lists the texts in the order they appear in *1 Clement*, and identifies each segment by a letter (a–h, though saying "h" in Polycarp has no parallel in *1 Clement*) to facilitate discussion. Translations are rendered rather woodenly at times in order to capture differences in Greek wording:[17]

a) *1 Clem.* 13.2a	show mercy, so that you may be shown mercy
Poly. *Phil.* 2.3c	show mercy, so that you may be shown mercy
Mt. 5.7	blessed are the merciful, for they will receive mercy
Lk. 6.36	be compassionate, just as your Father is compassionate
b) *1 Clem.* 13.2b	forgive, in order that it may be forgiven you
Poly. *Phil.* 2.3b	forgive, and it will be forgiven you
Mt. 6.14	for if you forgive people their wrongdoings
	your heavenly Father will also forgive you
Mk. 11.25	forgive, if you hold anything against anyone
	so that your Father in heaven may also forgive you your wrongdoings
Lk. 6.37c	release [forgive], and you will be released [forgiven]

---

[16] For a classic treatment, see H. von Campenhausen, *The Formation of the Christian Bible*, trans. J.A. Baker (Philadelphia, PA: Fortress Press, 1972), 121.

[17] Though slightly revised for this purpose, unless otherwise indicated all citations from the Apostolic Fathers are from Bart D. Ehrman, *The Apostolic Fathers*, LCL 24, 25; 2 vols. (Cambridge, MA.: Harvard University Press, 2003); translations from the Gospels are my own.

c) *1 Clem.* 13.2c   as you do, so it will be done to you

   Mt. 7.12   In all things, as you wish people do to you so also you should do to them

   Lk. 6.31   just as you wish people do to you,   do the same to them

d) *1 Clem.* 13.2d   as you give, so it will be given to you

   Lk. 6.38a   give,   and it will be given to you

e) *1 Clem.* 13.2e   as you judge, so you will be judged

   Poly. *Phil.* 2.3a   do not judge, so that you may not be judged

   Mt. 7.1   do not judge, so that you may not be judged

   Mt. 7.2a   for with the judgment you judge you will be judged

   Lk. 6.37a   do not judge, and you yourselves may not be judged

   Lk. 6.37b   do not condemn, and you yourselves may not be condemned

f) *1 Clem.* 13.2f   as you show kindness, so will kindness be shown to you

   Lk. 6.35   love those who hate you, do good, and lend expecting nothing in return,
                     and your reward will be great, and you will be children of the Most High;
                     for he is good to the ungrateful and the evil

g) *1 Clem.* 13.2g   what measure you measure out, the same will be measured out to you

   Poly. *Phil.* 2.3d   what measure you measure out   will be measured in return to you

   Mt. 7.2b   with what measure you measure out   it will be measured out to you

   Mk. 4.24   with what measure you measure out   it will be measured out to you
                        and still more will be given you

   Lk. 6.38c   for what measure you measure out   will be measured in return to you

h) Poly. *Phil.* 2.3e   blessed are the poor and those being persecuted for righteousness' sake
                        because to them belongs the kingdom of God

   Mt. 5.3   blessed are the poor in spirit
                        because to them belongs the kingdom of Heaven

   Mt. 5.10   blessed are   those   persecuted for righteousness' sake[18]
                        because to them belongs the kingdom of Heaven

   Lk. 6.20b   blessed are the poor
                        because to you   belongs the kingdom of God

Focusing first on the parallels between *1 Clement* and the Gospels, it is easy to see why most scholars hold that there is no literary relationship between them. None of them are verbatim parallels, and some are only parallel at the level of ideas, not in wording. Even with parallels that are closer in wording, such as *d*, *e*, and *g* in which the form of the verbs in *1 Clem.* matches at least one of the Gospels,[19] there are other

---

[18] The passive participle "persecuted" (*diōkō*) is in the present tense in Polycarp, but in the perfect tense in Matthew.

[19] Clement's *didote* ("give") and *dothēsetai* ("given") in saying *d* are found in Lk. 6:38; his *krinete* ("judge") in saying *e* is found in Mt. 7.1 and Lk. 6.37a, and both *krinete* and *krithēsthe* ("be judged") in Mt. 7.2a; and all of *hō metro metreite* ...

significant differences: for example, while saying *e* in Clement is a positive construction ("as you judge, so you will be judged"), Matthew and Luke phrase it in the negative ("do not judge" with "so that you may not be judged/and you yourselves may not be judged"), and Matthew appends extra material ("for with the judgment you judge you will be judged"). All of the parallels also contain many differences in adverbs, conjunctions, and prepositions. In sum, there is little reason to posit a literary relationship between them.

So if Clement did not derive these sayings from the Gospels, where did they come from? Though it is possible that they came from an unknown gospel, or some form of written or oral catechism or sayings collection (as suggested by various authors), given the cultural milieu within which *1 Clement* was written there is no need to posit any source other than the oral tradition that circulated among the churches.[20] In oral tradition one would *expect* to find the kind of stability within variability evident in these sayings when compared to their Gospel parallels: an essential stability in content (meaning, certain catch-words), with variability in form (such as differences in order, in adverbs, conjunctions, prepositions, verb forms).

In comparing Poly. *Phil.* 2.3 to its parallels in *1 Clem.* 13.2 some of the same dynamics recur: only saying *a* ("show mercy, so that you may be shown mercy") is exactly the same in both texts. The other sayings reflect the same type of variability within stability that we found when comparing *1 Clement* to the Gospels: essential stability in meaning, but a range of variability in adverbs, conjunctions, prepositions, and verb forms. In addition, three sayings in *1 Clem.* 13.2 are not found in Pol. *Phil.* 2.3 (*c, d,* and *f*), and all the sayings are in a different order: in *1 Clem.* 13.2 the order is *a–b–c–d–e–f–g*, while in Pol. *Phil.* 2.3 it is *e–b–a–g–h*. Though from other considerations it is clear that Polycarp knew *1 Clement*,[21] given all of the above there is little reason to hold that *1 Clem.* 13.2 was the source of the Jesus tradition in Pol. *Phil.* 2.3.

As for the relationship between Poly. *Phil.* 2.3 and the Gospels, much of what has been said regarding *1 Clem.* 13.2 in relation to its

---

metrēthēsetai hymin ("what measure you measure out ... will be measured out to you") of saying *g* is also found in Mt. 7.2b and Mk. 4.24c.

[20] See Donald A. Hagner, *The Use of the Old and New Testaments in Clement of Rome*, NovTSup 34 (Leiden: Brill, 1973), 145–51.

[21] A majority of scholars have accepted the conclusions drawn by J.B. Lightfoot; see his *The Apostolic Fathers: Clement, Ignatius, and Polycarp: Revised Texts with Introductions, Notes, Dissertations, and Translations*, 2nd ed., 2 parts in 5 vols. (London: Macmillan, 1889–90), 1.1.149–52.

Gospel parallels also holds true here. Three sayings, however, may point
to a closer proximity between Polycarp and its Gospel parallels: saying
e is identical in Polycarp and in Mt. 7.1, "do not judge, so that you may
not be judged" (*mē krinete hina mē krithēte*). The same holds true
for saying *g* in Polycarp and Lk. 6.38c, "what measure you measure
out will be measured in return to you" (*hō [gar] metro metreite anti-
metrēthēsetai hymin*).[22] In addition, saying *h*, found in Polycarp but not
in *1 Clement*, is closely paralleled by Mt. 5.10: "blessed are the poor and
those being persecuted for righteousness' sake because to them belongs
the kingdom of God" (Poly. *Phil.* 2.3e); "blessed are those persecuted for
righteousness' sake because to them belongs the kingdom of Heaven."
Could this indicate that Polycarp's *Philippians* is dependent on
Matthew and/or Luke?

As we consider this possibility, we begin by noting that Polycarp
divides the material in Poly. *Phil.* 2.3 into two parts, the first made up
of sayings *e*, *b*, *a*, and *g*, introduced by "remembering what the Lord
said when he taught," the second by saying *h* introduced by "and
that" (implying "he also said"). A majority of scholars holds that the
first block of four sayings in Pol. *Phil.* 2.3 is dependent on *1 Clem.*
2.3, but that Polycarp corrected some of the sayings in order to bring
them into a closer alignment with either Matthew or Luke.[23] For
these scholars it naturally follows that Polycarp derived saying *h* also
from Matthew. A minority of scholars holds that Polycarp derived all
of the sayings from a different source such as an early catechism[24] or
oral tradition.[25]

Space does not allow for a discussion of the evidence for and against
the dependence of each saying upon either Matthew or Luke, but it is
instructive to take a step back and look at the form of the material in the
first block of sayings as a whole. Here is a transliteration of Polycarp's
Greek text:

---

[22] The *gar* found only in Lk. 6.38c, being postpositive, does not break up the symmetry
of the sayings.

[23] E.g., Paul Hartog, *Polycarp and the New Testament: The Occasion, Rhetoric,
Theme, and Unity of the Epistle to the Philippians an its Allusions to New
Testament Literature*, WUNT 2.134 (Tübingen: Mohr Siebeck, 2002), 180–1, 191,
195.

[24] E.g., Édouard Massaux, *The Influence of the Gospel of Saint Matthew on Christian
Literature before Saint Irenaeus*, 3 vols. Trans. by N.J. Belval and S. Hecht; ed. A.J.
Bellinzoni; New Gospel Studies 5 (Leuven: Peeters/Macon, GA: Mercer University
Press, 1990–3), 2.29–30.

[25] E.g., Hagner, *Clement of Rome*, 142–3, 279, 306–7.

Mē krinete hina mē krithēthe	do not judge, so that you may not be judged
aphiete kai aphethēsetai humin	forgive, and it will be forgiven you
eleate hina eleēthēte	show mercy, so that you may be shown mercy
hō metro metreite	what measure you measure out
antimetrēthēsetai humin	will be measured in return to you

The cadence, rhythm and rhyme of this block of tradition in the Greek suggest that Pol. *Phil.* 2.3 was given this particular shape to facilitate memorization. This in turn suggests that Polycarp incorporated this block of sayings into his text as a whole from an oral traditional source, and not from either *1 Clement* or a mixture of different Gospel sources.

Something similar can be said of the material in *1 Clem.* 13.2; the rhythmic, echoing structure of its Greek also evinces a mnemotechnic approach (best appreciated when reading the following transliteration out loud):

	... *te, hina*	... *thēte*
	... *te, hina*	... *thē hymin*
hōs	... *te, houtō*	... *tai hymin*
hōs	... *te, houtōs*	... *tai hymin*
hōs	... *te, houtōs*	... *tai hymin*
hōs	... *te, houtōs*	... *sthe*
hōs	... *sthe, houtōs*	... *tai hymin*
hō	... *te, en autō*	... *tai hymin*

Given that both Clement and Polycarp wrote within a society and for an audience that was far more proficient in orality than in textuality, when one considers the origin of *mnemonically constructed materials* one should default in favor of an oral rather than a written source. This in turn highlights the futility of arguing over minute differences between Jesus tradition in these texts and their parallels: if each traditionist in passing on this material superimposed a mnemonic structure upon it, selecting a particular array of conjunctions, pronouns, and adverbs so as to attain a certain rhythm and cadence to aid memorization and transmission, then one can dispense with arguments over whether these details point to dependence upon other written texts.

The most likely scenario, then, that accounts for the array of similarities and differences between *1 Clem.* 13.2, Pol. *Phil.* 2.3, and portions of Matthew and Luke, is that their authors all had access to the same oral traditional source. Dale Allison has identified just such a cohesive block of tradition that circulated fairly widely within the early Christian community. Allison mounts a convincing argument that this block of tradition stands behind *1 Clem.* 13.2 and Poly. *Phil.* 2.2–3

(as well as *Did.* 1.3–5 and several texts in Paul[26]) and also was incorporated into Q, the hypothetical document that many scholars believe
both Matthew and Luke used as a source for their Gospels
(Q 6:27–38).[27] The similarities and differences between the texts we
are considering are probably due to their dependence upon this block
of tradition in its oral form (whether or not it became part of a
written Q).[28]

What if, however (for the sake of argument), one were able to show
conclusively that the Jesus tradition in either *1 Clem.* 13.2 or Poly. *Phil.*
2.2–3 contained an element that originated without question from the
redactional activity of a Gospel writer? What if, for example, Polycarp
did revise Jesus' sayings to cohere at times with Matthew and at times
with Luke, in spite of the above arguments to the contrary? In this case,
given the above considerations regarding the mnemotechnical shape of
the tradition as found in Polycarp, one would have to view the material
as evidence of the re-oralization of written tradition. In this case a likely
scenario would be that a traditionist, upon witnessing the oral
performance of one of the Gospels, then adopted part of this material
by incorporating it into the oral tradition that he or she had already
mastered. In passing it on, they then would have treated this re-oralized
tradition in the same way they treated oral tradition more generally,
making it indistinguishable from tradition that had never been given
written form.

While one may never know for certain whether Clement and
Polycarp derived their sayings from an oral Q, pre-Q oral tradition, or
a stream of oral tradition that ran parallel to Q, the very quest for
certitude in sources betrays a bias toward textuality. In comparing
written sources one might hope to arrive at *the* original source, but

---

[26] Rom. 2:1; 12:14, 17, 21; 1 Cor. 4:12; 1 Thess. 4:12.

[27] Dale Allison, *The Jesus Tradition in Q* (Harrisburg, PA: Trinity Press International,
1997), 80–92. Scholars use "Q" as part of a hypothesis regarding the origins of the
Synoptic Gospels, which holds that Mark was written first and was used as a source
by both Matthew and Luke. Within this hypothesis, Q refers to a reconstructed (no
longer extant) text believed to have provided much of the material held in common
by Matthew and Luke but not found in Mark; "Q" is short for the German *Quelle*, or
"Source" (see further G.N. Stanton and N. Perrin, "Q," in *Dictionary of Jesus and the
Gospels*, ed. J.B. Green, J.K. Brown, and N. Perrin, 2nd ed. [Downers Grove, IL:
InterVarsity Press, 2013], 711–18).

[28] The argument behind this statement is complex; for a detailed discussion, see
Young, *Jesus Tradition*, 120–46, 165–8. On Q and orality, see Richard A. Horsley
and Jonathan A. Draper, *Whoever Hears You Hears Me: Prophets, Performance, and
Tradition in Q* (Harrisburg, PA: Trinity Press International, 1999).

with oral tradition there is no "original performance" or "original text" against which to compare tradition in any given document. With oral tradition one might think instead of the image of a river, something that is flowing and active, from which not only Clement and Polycarp but also Matthew and Luke (and others) have drawn. In drawing from this same river different writers may end up with versions of a saying that are similar in meaning but not in wording or form, or contain similar words that are structured differently or given a different emphasis. This reflects the context within which the tradition was transmitted, which called for mnemotechnical devices that both shaped the details of the material and enabled traditionists to faithfully recall and transmit its essential content.

Before moving on, it is worth highlighting an insight that can be gathered from the above material: the commands to be merciful, not judge, not condemn, forgive, and give generously found in the pre-Q block of tradition identified by Allison, in Luke are applied to the daily realities of the oppression of the poor by the rich (Lk. 6.20–35). In *1 Clem.* 13.2, however, these commands are applied to a situation of jealousy and envy over leadership that has led to inner-church schism (*1 Clem.* 1.1–6.4). The similar material in Poly. *Phil.* 2.3 is applied in turn to what will bring about righteousness in the readers (Poly. *Phil.* 3.1). All of this provides an example of one of the hallmarks of *living* oral tradition: oral tradition remains alive insofar as it remains relevant to the ever-changing needs of the community that preserves it.

4.3.2 The Lord's Prayer in *Didache* 8.2

The *Didache* contains many parallels to the Synoptic Gospels, but only two are identified explicitly as Jesus tradition: an isolated proverb in 9.5 ("For also the Lord has said about this, 'Do not give what is holy to the dogs'"), and the Lord's Prayer in 8.2, which will be the topic of the discussion below.

The following synopsis displays the Lord's Prayer as found in the *Didache* with its parallels in Matthew and Luke:

| *Did.* 8.2 | Nor should you pray | like the hypocrites |
| *Mt.* 6.5 | and whenever you pray do not be like the hypocrites | |

Did. 8.2	but as the Lord commanded in his gospel, you should pray as follows
Mt. 6.9	you pray then as follows
Lk. 11.2	whenever you pray say

Did. 8.2	Our Father in the heaven, may your name be kept holy
Mt. 6.9	Our Father in the heavens, may your name be kept holy
Lk. 11.2	Father may your name be kept holy

Did. 8.2	may your kingdom come, may your will be done on earth as in heaven
Mt. 6.10	may your kingdom come, may your will be done on earth as in heaven
Lk. 11.2	may your kingdom come

Did. 8.2	give us today our daily bread
Mt. 6.11	give us today our daily bread
Lk. 11.3	give us each day our daily bread

Did. 8.2	and forgive us our debt
Mt. 6.12a	and forgive us our debts
Lk. 11.4	and forgive us our sins

Did. 8.2	as we forgive our debtors
Mt. 6.12b	as we forgave our debtors
Lk. 11.4	for we also forgive all those who sin against us

Did. 8.2	and do not bring us into temptation but deliver us from the evil one
Mt. 6.13	and do not bring us into temptation but deliver us from the evil one
Lk. 11.4	and do not bring us into temptation

| *Did.* 8.2 | for the   power and the glory are yours forever |

In some later MSS only:

| *Mt.* 6.13x | [for the kingdom and the power and the glory are yours forever] |

Immediately striking upon perusing this synopsis is the almost verbatim similarity between the prayer in the *Didache* and in Matthew. In
contrast, Luke's version is considerably shorter and differs at times in
wording. Understandably, most scholarly attention has focused on the
relationship between the *Didache* and the First Gospel.

Though it might seem obvious at first reading that the *Didache* is
dependent on Matthew, certain factors complicate the matter. First,
there is no consensus on the order in which these documents were
written; if the *Didache* was written before Matthew, then the direction
of any dependence would be reversed.[29] A second consideration, however, is even more fundamental: if the *Didache* and Matthew originated

---

[29] The *Didache* may date from the middle of the first century; see A. Milavec, *The
Didache: Faith, Hope, and Life of the Earliest Christian Communities, 50–70 C.E.*
(Mahwah, NJ: Newman, 2003), xii–xiii.

within a closely related milieu,[30] in which the Lord's Prayer was recited regularly from memory ("pray like this three times a day"; *Did.* 8.3), then why would either writer need to turn to the writings of the other for the text of the prayer? Here again, when dealing with texts produced within a culture that was proficient in orality, one's default setting should be to opt for an oral source over a written one. This is especially true of the source of a key element within the Christian liturgy such as the Lord's Prayer; even in today's primarily *literate* cultures millions can recite the Lord's Prayer from memory, so why look for literary dependence in a primarily *oral* culture, such as the one out of which these texts arose?

The oral-liturgical use of the Lord's Prayer in its early Christian setting explains some details from the above synopsis that otherwise seem puzzling. First, it accounts for the small differences between the *Didache* and Matthew: neither the Didachist nor Matthew corrected the text of the other, but each used the form of the liturgy current within their own community. The survival of minor differences in the *Didache*'s form of the prayer even after Matthew became an authoritative Gospel attests to the persistence of oral tradition within liturgical settings. Second, a liturgical use explains why *Did.* 8.2 concludes with a doxology ("for the power and the glory are yours forever") but the original text of Matthew's prayer does not: the *Didache* is an instrument of the liturgy, so one would expect the inclusion of a doxology at the conclusion of this prayer as with its other liturgical prayers.[31] Matthew belongs to a different genre, so its prayer did not originally include a doxology. The prayer's liturgical use impacted the history of Matthew's text of the prayer, however, via the addition of a variety of doxologies to early manuscripts of the Gospel.[32]

---

[30] See the essays in H. van de Sandt, ed., *Matthew and the Didache: Two Documents from the Same Jewish–Christian Milieu?* (Assen: Van Gorcum/Philadelphia, PA: Fortress, 2005); H. van de Sandt and Jürgen K. Zangenberg, eds., *Matthew, James, and Didache: Three Related Documents in Their Jewish and Christian Settings*, SBL Symposium Series 45 (Atlanta, GA: Society of Biblical Literature, 2008); J.A. Draper and C.N. Jefford, eds., *The Didache: A Missing Piece of the Puzzle in Early Christianity*, SBL Early Christianity and Its Literature 14 (Atlanta, GA: Society of Biblical Literature, 2015).

[31] E.g., "To you be the glory forever" (9.2, 3; 10.2, 4); "for the glory and the power are yours through Jesus Christ forever"(9.4); "For yours is the power and the glory forever" (10.5).

[32] On the textual history of the doxology, see David C. Parker, *The Living Text of the Gospels* (Cambridge: Cambridge University Press, 1997), 54–60.

Oral-liturgical tradition such as that found in *Did.* 8.2 functioned a little differently than the tradition examined above from *1 Clement* and Polycarp's *Philippians* within the Christian community. In a liturgical context, tradition is ritually repeated in a carefully guarded and therefore relatively fixed form, so that variability is minimized and stability becomes the norm.

4.3.3 The Fragments of Papias

In light of Papias' preference for "a living and abiding voice" over "what came out of books" (Eusebius, *Hist. Eccl.*, 3.39.4), one would think that his writings would offer many insights into the inner workings of oral Jesus tradition. It is difficult, however, to say anything with confidence about the Jesus tradition in Papias, because of the fragmentary nature of the material and how it is handled in the sources in which it is preserved. It is not even clear if all the material traditionally included among the "fragments of Papias" actually qualifies as such. Take, for example, fragment 1.1b–5b preserved in Iren. *Adv. Haer.*, 5.33, 3–4:

> Thus the elders who saw John, the disciple of the Lord, remembered hearing him say how the Lord used to teach about those times, saying: [2] "The days are coming when the vines will come forth, each with ten thousand boughs; and on a single bough will be ten thousand branches. And indeed, on a single branch will be ten thousand shoots and on every shoot ten thousand clusters; and in every cluster will be ten thousand grapes, and every grape, when pressed, will yield twenty-five measures of wine. [3] And when any of the saints grabs hold of a cluster, another will cry out, 'I am better, take me; bless the Lord through me.' So too a grain of wheat will produce ten thousand heads and every head will have ten thousand grains and every grain will yield ten pounds of pure, exceptionally fine flour. So too the remaining fruits and seeds and vegetation will produce in similar proportions. And all the animals who eat this food drawn from the earth will come to be at peace and harmony with one another, yielding in complete submission to humans." [4] Papias as well, an ancient man – the one who heard John and was a companion of Polycarp – gives a written account of these things in the fourth of his books. For he wrote five books. And in addition he says: [5] "These things can be believed by those who believe. And the betrayer Judas," he said, "did not believe, but asked, 'How then can the Lord bring forth such produce?' The Lord then replied, 'Those who come into those times will see.'"

In a straightforward reading, Irenaeus cites "the elders who saw John" in vv. 2–3 and appeals to Papias' writings to support their words in v. 4, citing Papias only in v. 5; i.e., Irenaeus does not say that the Jesus tradition in vv. 2–3 derives from Papias.[33]

Supposing one were able to show, however, that vv. 2–3 came from Papias – from where did Papias himself derive this material? The promise of plenty described in verses 2–3 appears to be an elaboration of similar Jewish apocalyptic imagery found in texts such as *1 Enoch* 10.19 (middle to end of 3rd century BCE) and *2 Baruch* 29.5 (roughly contemporary with Papias).[34] The parallel in *2 Bar.* 29.5, for example, reads "The earth will also yield fruits ten thousandfold. And on one vine will be a thousand branches, and one branch will produce a thousand clusters, and one cluster will produce a thousand grapes, and one grape will produce a cor of wine."[35] The later *Apocalypse of Paul* (mid-third to late fourth century) pushes the eschatological abundance to a level similar to that found in Papias, but without attributing the words to Jesus:

> And the trees were full of fruit from root (up) to tree-top. From the root of each tree up to its heart there were ten thousand branches with tens of thousands of clusters [and there were ten thousand clusters on each branch] and there were ten thousand dates in each cluster. And it was the same with the vines. Each vine had ten thousand branches, and each branch had on it ten thousand bunches of grapes, and each bunch had ten thousand grapes. And there were other trees there, myriads of myriads of them, and their fruit was in the same proportion. (*Apoc. Paul*, 22)[36]

Given a trio of considerations – that it is paralleled in a number of Jewish and Christian sources, that it is nowhere else attested in the Jesus tradition, and that a close parallel to it in a later Christian

---

[33] See the detailed argument along these lines by Richard Bauckham, "Intertextual Relationships of Papias' Gospel Traditions: The Case of *Irenaeus, Haer.* 5.33.3-4," in *Intertextuality in the Second Century*, eds. D. Jeffrey Bingham and Clayton N. Jefford, The Bible in Ancient Christianity 11 (Leiden: Brill, 2016), 38–9.

[34] See W.R. Schoedel, *Polycarp, Martyrdom of Polycarp, Fragments of Papias*, The Apostolic Fathers 5 (Camden, NJ: Thomas Nelson & Sons, 1967), 94–6.

[35] Trans. by A.F.J. Klijn in "2 (Syriac Apocalypse of) Baruch: A New Translation and Introduction," in *The Old Testament Pseudepigrapha*, ed. J.H. Charlesworth, 2 vols. (New York: Doubleday, 1983, 1985), 1.630.

[36] Trans. by H. Duensing and A. de Santos Otero, "Apocalypse of Paul," in *New Testament Apocrypha*, ed. Wilhelm Schneemelcher, Vol. 2: *Writings Relating to the Apostles: Apocalypses and Related Subjects*, rev. ed. (Cambridge: James Clarke/Louisville, KY: Westminster/John Knox, 1992), 2.726.

document does not attribute it to Jesus – it is likely that this saying from Papias did not originate in the Jesus tradition but was a foreign element incorporated into it. In light of Papias' preference for oral over written sources, one must further consider that his source might have been oral rather than written. Taking all of this into consideration, it may be that this saying came to Papias through the process of re-oralization: it may have originated from the adaptation of a written source that was taken up and assimilated into oral tradition, from whence he incorporated it into his writings.

It is important for our purposes here, however, to emphasize that only v. 5 can be held with any confidence to have come from Papias: "These things can be believed by those who believe. And the betrayer Judas ... did not believe, but asked, 'How then can the Lord bring forth such produce?' The Lord then replied, 'Those who come into those times will see.'" Papias fragment 4.2–3 (from Apollinaris of Laodicea, 4th cent.) contains other material about Judas, which is clearly apocryphal:

> But Judas went about in this world as a great model of impurity. He became so bloated in the flesh that he could not pass through a place that was easily wide enough for a wagon – not even his swollen head could fit. They say that his eyelids swelled to such an extent that he could not see the light at all; and a doctor could not see his eyes even with an optical device, so deeply sunken they were in the surrounding flesh. And his genitals became more disgusting and larger than anyone's; simply by relieving himself, to his wanton shame, he emitted pus and worms that flowed through his entire body. And they say that after he suffered numerous torments and punishments, he died on his own land, and that land has been, until now, desolate and uninhabited because of the stench. Indeed, even to this day no one can pass by the place without holding his nose. This was how great an outpouring he made from his flesh on the ground.

This gossip-like material – harmonizing Mt. 27.3–10 in which Judas hangs himself with Acts 1.18 in which he falls and bursts open so that his bowels gushed out[37] – is worthless in terms of its historicity. It is valuable, however, in witnessing to a certain type of Judas-related tradition in Papias: both of these texts (Papias 1.5 and 4.2–3) have to do with

---

[37] Schoedel, *Polycarp, Martyrdom of Polycarp, Fragments of Papias*, 111.

Judas as the ultimate nonbeliever, as one who had been one of the Twelve Disciples and yet betrayed the Lord, and one who would not "come into those times" (1.5).

This material provides an example of the basic truth that not all oral tradition is treated equally. Material central to the identity of the community of Jesus-followers, such as the Jesus tradition we considered earlier from *1 Clement*, Polycarp, and the *Didache*, was guarded carefully in its transmission. The type of oral tradition in both the above Papias fragments on Judas, which was only tangentially related, if at all, to the self-understanding of the Jesus-community (as portraying the ultimate nonbeliever), was not subject to such control.

4.4 CONCLUSIONS

It may be easy for readers today to picture Clement, Polycarp, the Didachist, or Papias sitting at their desks with copies of Matthew and Luke open beside them as they wrote. Though this scenario is *possible*, it is probably an anachronism arising from the default setting of today's literate worldview, and does not accurately reflect ancient realities. In a culture that highly valued orality, it is more likely that these authors used orally transmitted tradition immediately available in their minds as they wrote.

This study has approached the Jesus tradition in the Apostolic Fathers using the default-setting of orality. We have sought to answer the question, "What can one learn from the Jesus tradition in the Apostolic Fathers by analyzing it as deriving from *oral* tradition?" We are now in the position to offer some general conclusions.

As became clear in our analysis of *1 Clem.* 13. 2 and Poly. *Phil.* 2.3, in the case of orally transmitted tradition one should not expect verbatim similarity, as one might in the copying of written texts, but rather variability within stability; consistency in meaning within variability of form. Both the variability and the stability are important for understanding the role of oral tradition within a community. The variability points to the shaping of the tradition in any given performance so as to address the specific current needs of a community, leaving out certain elements and emphasizing others, or leaving implicit in some performances what in others might be made explicit. Within this process originality is not expressed via the invention of new materials, but in the adaptation of the tradition to the current life experience of the community. This variability is what gives *life* to oral tradition, maintaining its relevance to ever-changing situations. Variability also points to the needs of the traditionists, who were free to apply mnemonic techniques to the tradition so as to facilitate its faithful recall in performance (e.g., rhyme, rhythm, the linking of material with similar themes). Stability is found in the fact that variable elements – particles, adverbs, verb tenses, particles, synonymous rather than identical terms, word order, and order of sayings – did not compromise the essential meaning of the content. In short, the oral tradition that was taken up into the writings of Clement and Polycarp was stable because it was living *tradition*, a tradition with an ongoing role within the community that preserved it and which therefore had good reason to protect its integrity; it was variable because it was *living oral* tradition, and the very dynamic nature of its oral use enabled its application to ever new situations in life.

Variability within stability is not a given of oral tradition, but rather a reflection of its context of use. This can be seen in the other materials analyzed above from the *Didache* and the fragments of Papias. The variability within the tradition decreased almost to the point of disappearing in the case of the Lord's Prayer in *Did.* 8.2, as is to be expected: liturgical traditions are guarded closely as central to the self-identity of a religious community, so that stability becomes the norm. In contrast, given that it held no importance for the community's self-identity, the Christian community had no reason to protect the integrity of the gossip-type tradition regarding Judas preserved in the above Papias fragments.

FURTHER READING

Dewey, Joanna, ed. *Orality and Textuality in Early Christian Literature.* SBL Semeia 65. Atlanta, GA: Society of Biblical Literature/Scholars, 1994.

Dunn, James D.G. *The Oral Gospel Tradition.* Grand Rapids, MI: Eerdmans, 2013.

Gregory, Andrew F., and Christopher M. Tuckett, eds. *The Reception of the New Testament in the Apostolic Fathers.* The New Testament and the Apostolic Fathers 1. Oxford: Oxford University Press, 2005.

Horsley, Richard A., Jonathan A. Draper, and John Miles Foley, eds. *Performing the Gospel: Orality, Memory, and Mark: Essays Dedicated to Werner Kelber.* Minneapolis, MN: Fortress, 2006.

Kelber, Werner H. *The Oral and the Written Gospel: The Hermeneutics of Speaking and Writing in the Synoptic Tradition, Mark, Paul, and Q.* Philadelphia: Fortress, 1982. Repr. with a new introduction by the author and a foreword by Walter J. Ong. Bloomington and Indianapolis: Indiana University Press, 1997.

Kelber, Werner H., and Samuel Byrskog, eds. *Jesus in Memory: Traditions in Oral and Scribal Practices.* Waco, TX: Baylor University Press, 2009.

Kirk, Alan, and Tom Thatcher, eds. *Memory, Tradition, and Text: Uses of the Past in Early Christianity.* SBL Semeia Studies 52. Atlanta, GA: Society of Biblical Literature, 2005.

Thatcher, Tom, ed. *Jesus, the Voice, and the Text: Beyond The Oral and the Written Gospel.* Waco, TX: Baylor University Press, 2008.

Wansbrough, Henry, ed. *Jesus and the Oral Gospel Tradition.* JSNTSup 64. Sheffield: JSOT Press, 1991.

Young, Stephen E. *Jesus Tradition in the Apostolic Fathers: Their Explicit Appeals to the Words of Jesus in Light of Orality Studies.* WUNT 2.311. Tübingen: Mohr Siebeck, 2011.

5 The Text of the New Testament in the Apostolic Fathers

PAUL FOSTER

5.1 INTRODUCTION

If the term "the text of the New Testament" refers to the continuous text of any one or several of the Greek writings that constitute the twenty-seven-document collection that became known as the New Testament, then the writings of the Apostolic Fathers are of virtually no use in reconstructing any significant portion of any one of those writings. Indeed, there appear to be only three sources that may assist with that task. In turn these are the first continuous-text manuscripts of New Testament writings that survive in full or in fragmentary form of which to date there are 133 catalogued papyrus fragments, 323 majuscule manuscripts, and 2,936 minuscule manuscripts.[1] Secondly, there are numerous lectionary texts, the majority of which are manuscripts of the Gospels arranged for liturgical use. To date 2,465 Greek manuscripts of this type have been catalogued. Thirdly, there are commentaries on the Greek text where the text is often broken into lines before exposition of the text is provided. The relative importance of these three witnesses to the text of the New Testament follows the order in which the categories have been listed: that is, continuous Greek manuscripts, lectionaries, and then commentaries.

A fourth category, related to the third group, is that of citation in the works of early Christian writers. The difference between this fourth group and the third category is that commentators tend to provide the entire text of a New Testament writing, although broken into small sense units.[2] By contrast, other early Christian texts refer to phrases from the New Testament, in an ad hoc fashion, and often employing the

---

[1] These figure are derived from the *kurzgefasste liste* hosted by the INTF, http://ntvmr .uni-muenster.de/liste/, accessed December 10, 2018.

[2] One example of the commentary tradition is Theodore of Mopsuestia, *Commentary on the Minor Pauline Epistles*, ed. and trans. R.A. Greer, Writings from the Greco-Roman World 26 (Atlanta, GA: Soxiety of Biblical Literature, 2010).

relevant text in a free manner, or sometimes adapting the wording to fit the argument at hand. It is into this last category that the fleeting references or snippets of phraseology from the New Testament that are found among the writings known as the Apostolic Fathers are to be placed. Within this artificial collection of somewhat disparate texts, when the New Testament is referenced the allusion or citation typically involves a few words or perhaps a single verse. One of the most significant exceptions occurs with the citation of the Matthean version of the Lord's Prayer, as it occurs in the *Didache*.

> Neither pray as the hypocrites; but as the Lord commanded in His Gospel, thus pray: Our Father who art in heaven, hallowed be Thy name. Thy kingdom come. Thy will be done, as in heaven, so on earth. Give us today our daily (needful) bread, and forgive us our debt as we also forgive our debtors. And bring us not into temptation, but deliver us from the evil one (or, evil); for Thine is the power and the glory for ever. (*Did.* 8.2)

Here there is a close reproduction of four verses of Matthean text (Mt. 6.9–13). However, this example raises the larger question of whether the text of the New Testament is being consulted directly and copied, or whether another transmission process is being employed – such as recalling from memory material that was used repeatedly in a liturgical context.

So in exploring the text of the New Testament in the Apostolic Fathers it is not possible to reconstruct the text of any canonical writing on the basis of the textual citations contained in that later corpus. It may be possible to find a reading that provides a variant reading of the citation drawn from the New Testament. However, unless the textual variation is also attested in the continuous-manuscript tradition it is difficult to determine whether the alternate reading contained in the writings of the Apostolic Fathers is a textual variant that originates in a text of the New Testament, or whether it is a textual adaptation by the author of the later text. Therefore, when one speaks of the text of the New Testament in the writings of the Apostolic Fathers a narrower, more specific enquiry is being carried out. Namely, the investigation is seeking to determine which writings, that were later collected to form the New Testament, can be shown to have been used by the authors of the texts that form the collection that became known as the Apostolic Fathers. For those who are seeking clear indications about the form of the New Testament text prior to the third century the data from the various writings of the Apostolic Fathers offers meagre results. This is because, as has been stated elsewhere, "the loose 'citations' of the NT text that have been detected provide no conclusive evidence for identifying the forms of the text of the NT which may have been in circulation in the second century."[3]

5.2 THE TEXTS UNDER CONSIDERATION

The collection of texts known as the Apostolic Fathers is largely a modern scholarly construct. It is the case that certain of these texts circulated in combination with others that are found in modern editions. Examples of this include: the *Shepherd of Hermas* and the *Epistle of Barnabas* found in Codex Sinaiticus dating to the fourth century[4]; *1 Clement* and *2 Clement* in Codex Alexandrinus dating to the fifth century[5]; and in the eleventh-century Bryennios Codex the *Epistle of Barnabas*, *1 Clement*, *2 Clement*, the *Didache*, and the long recension of the thirteen Greek letter collection of the Epistles of Ignatius.[6] By contrast, modern printed editions from the seventeenth century onwards contain anywhere between five and eleven writings (taking the letters of Ignatius as a single textual unit). Recent editions tend to be maximalist, typically including ten or eleven writings in the collection. The first published collection, issued by J.-B. Cotelier in 1672, contained seven texts, including Ignatius' letters, *Barnabas*, *1 & 2 Clement*, the *Epistle of Polycarp*, the *Martyrdom of Polycarp*, and the *Shepherd of Hermas*. More recent editions, such as the volume edited by Michael Holmes,[7] have tended to supplement this collection with additional texts including the *Didache*, the *Letter of Diognetus*, the

---

[3] See P. Foster, "The Text of the New Testament in the Apostolic Fathers," in *The Early Text of the New Testament*, ed. Charles E. Hill and Michael J. Kruger (Oxford: Oxford University Press, 2012), 300.

[4] For this standard date for Codex Sinaiticus, see Barbara and Kurt Aland, Johannes Karavidopoulos, Carlo M. Martini, Bruce M. Metzger, and the Institute for New Testament Textual Research under the direction of Holger Strutwolf (eds.), *Novum Testamentum Graece* (Based on the work of Eberhard and Erwin Nestle), 28th ed. (Leipzig: Deustsche Bibelgesellschaft, 2012), 799.

[5] Ibid., 799.

[6] A colophon in the manuscript is dated June 11, 1056 and ascribes the codex to a scribe named Leo. The manuscript was rediscovered at the monastery of the Church of the Holy Sepulchre in Istanbul in 1873, and published in 1883. It is now housed in the Greek Orthodox Library in Jerusalem.

[7] M.W. Holmes, *The Apostolic Fathers: Greek Texts with English Translations*, 3rd ed. (Grand Rapids, MI: Baker, 2007).

fragments of Papias, and the fragment of the *Apology of Quadratus*.[8] It is difficult to determine why some equally early texts, such as the *Apology of Arisitides*, have not been included in the collection. However, a convention appears to have been established where the maximal corpus includes eleven texts: *Didache, Barnabas, 1 Clement, 2 Clement,* the Letters of Ignatius, the *Epistle of Polycarp,* the *Martyrdom of Polycarp,* the *Shepherd of Hermas,* the *Letter of Diognetus,* the fragments of Papias, and the fragment of the *Apology of Quadratus.*

Among these eleven texts in a small number the New Testament is not cited or used as the source for obvious allusions. Within this corpus, texts that show little or no use of the New Testament include the *Martyrdom of Polycarp,* the *Letter of Diognetus,* the fragments of Papias, and the fragment of the *Apology of Quadratus.* The fragments of Papias form a special case, since what can be reconstructed of this text is a collection of excerpts from authors who wrote several centuries later. It is frequently difficult to determine where the citation of Papias begins and ends in these later literary works, and where the comments of the later writer (such as Eusebius, Jerome, Philip of Side, and so on) commence. Papias appeared to know of Mark and Matthew as evangelists. Later writers accuse Papias of holding a chiliastic view (the view that Christ will return to earth and reign with the righteous on earth for a thousand years). Such a view may indicate that Papias knew the text of Revelation. However, there are no clear citations of the New Testament that are clearly attributable to Papias in the later fragments embedded in the literary works of other authors, composed several centuries after Papias. Therefore, the fragments of Papias will not be used in the following discussion.

The remaining seven texts – *Didache, Barnabas, 1 Clement, 2 Clement,* the Letters of Ignatius, the *Epistle of Polycarp,* and the *Shepherd of Hermas* – potentially contain material that may be drawn from the New Testament, but the level of dependence varies considerably. Rather than treat these seven texts in order, the approach here is different. The discussion will consider which New Testament writings are represented by citation or possible allusion within the corpus of the Apostolic Fathers. This will be undertaken by considering in turn the four sub-collections in which the manuscripts of New Testament

---

[8] See the discussion of the contents of various editions of the Apostolic Fathers in W. Pratscher (ed.), *The Apostolic Fathers: An Introduction* (Waco, TX: Baylor University Press, 2010), 2–6.

writings typically circulated: the Gospels; the Pauline letters; the Apostolos (Acts and the Catholic Letters); and Revelation.

5.3 THE GOSPELS IN THE WRITINGS OF THE APOSTOLIC FATHERS

Of the earliest surviving manuscripts of the New Testament, that is, those classified as papyri or majuscules, the majority are manuscripts of the Gospels rather than the other portions of the New Testament.[9] This preponderance of Gospel manuscripts may attest to the wider use of Gospel manuscripts in comparison with other New Testament texts. The writings of the Apostolic Fathers could potentially contribute either negatively or positively to this hypothesis concerning the higher use of Gospel writings relative to other New Testament texts. However, one of the chief difficulties that besets the identification of a specific Gospel by a later writer arises from the level of parallelism and borrowing among the Synoptic Gospels. Thus it is sometimes possible to argue that Gospel tradition is being used, while it is simultaneously not possible to determine which specific Synoptic Gospel is the source of the tradition.

5.3.1 The Gospel of Matthew

In two of the texts that form the corpus of the writings of the Apostolic Fathers, the Gospel of Matthew is almost certainly employed as a source text. In the Letters of Ignatius there are two examples where material found in Ignatius' writings parallels Synoptic tradition that is unique to Matthew's Gospel. The first instance occurs in the *Letter to the Smyrnaeans*, where Ignatius presents a creed-like list of events marking the life of Jesus. Among these affirmations, he states that the Lord was "baptized by John in order that all righteousness might be fulfilled by him" (Ign. *Smyrn.* 1.1). This parallels the explanatory phrase found only

---

[9] Of the current (as of March 17, 2017) 131 items classified in the *kurzgefasste liste* as papyri a number of these have been identified as fragments of the same Manuscript; e.g. P^{11} and P^{14}; P^{13} and P^{58}; P^{64} and P^{67}. This results in 128 unique texts (although a couple of these may have been amulets rather than continuous manuscript). Among these 128 manuscripts 52 contain texts of one or more of the four Gospels, or approximately 41 percent. This outstrips the number of manuscripts of the Apostolos Acts and Catholic letters), the Pauline epistles, or the book of Revelation. Similarly, with the 323 items in the list of majuscules (although some have been removed from the list) around 182 contain text of portions of the Gospels. So a conservative estimate would be 56 percent of majuscule manuscripts represent Gospel texts.

in Matthew's Gospel where after John declares that Jesus has no need to undergo baptism, Jesus counters with the explanation that although John is correct at one level, the Baptist is, in the Matthean Jesus' words, instructed "to permit it now for thus it is fitting for us to fulfil all righteousness" (Mt. 3.15). While there is not perfect correspondence in the phraseology, Ignatius reveals knowledge of an explanation that is found solely in Matthew's account. Both parallels in Greek share three words in the same order "fulfil," "all," and "righteousness," although admittedly in different verbal forms or different cases. These three terms are used in connection with the story of Jesus' baptism by John. Thirdly, the term "righteousness" is one of Matthew's favourite concepts, being used by Matthew on seven occasions. By contrast, Ignatius uses the term only once, which is in this context. Therefore, given that it is a term favoured by Matthew, but not by Ignatius, it is likely that it was derived through a knowledge of the text of Matthew and not coincidentally, or from another source for the baptismal stories. Notwithstanding this, the way Ignatius deploys this tradition in a sequence of "events" from the life of Jesus and with differences in phraseology, it would appear that he was not directly consulting the text of Matthew to look up this material. Rather, it would be a reasonable supposition that while Ignatius was in custody being transported to his execution he did not have copies of the scriptures with him but recalled familiar phrases from his memory.

This is not the only example of Ignatius' knowledge of unique Matthean material. In his Letter to Polycarp, bishop of Smyrna, Ignatius counsels his episcopal counterpart to "be shrewd as a serpent in all circumstances, yet always innocent as a dove" (Ign. *Pol.* 2.2). A highly similar sentiment is found in the first Gospel when Jesus addresses his disciples prior to sending them to spread his message. He states, "Behold I send you out as sheep in the midst of wolves; therefore be shrewd as serpents and innocent as doves" (Mt. 10.16). While the first half of the Gospel saying is paralleled elsewhere in the Synoptic tradition (cf. Lk. 10.3), the serpents/doves element is unique to Matthew among the canonical Gospels. There is, however, also a version of this saying in the *Gospel of Thomas*: "be as wise as serpents, and innocent of doves" (*G. Thom.* 39.3//P. Oxy. 655, lines 47–9). Since this saying is more widespread than just Matthew and Ignatius, there is a possibility that this tradition came to Ignatius independently of Matthew's Gospel. However, given that the example of the tradition about the baptism "fulfilling all righteous" points to Ignatius' knowledge of the first Gospel, the more likely source for Ignatius' version of the serpent–dove saying is also Matthew's Gospel. Moreover, despite varied opinions in scholarship, it appears more likely that the *Gospel of Thomas* was likewise dependent on Matthew.[10] It should be noted that Ignatius' version of the saying refers to "serpent" and "dove" in the singular, in contrast to Matthew's plural forms. This may lend further weight to the supposition that Ignatius is drawing upon Gospel traditions from memory, rather than through directly consulting a written text.

The second text among the Apostolic Fathers that probably demonstrates dependence on Matthew's Gospel is the *Didache*. There are significant scholarly debates concerning whether Matthew is earlier than the *Didache*, or the *Didache* earlier than Matthew, or even if there was a form of the *Didache* or the traditions it contains that predate both Matthew's Gospel and the final form of the *Didache*, which perhaps both texts drew on independently.[11] None of the examples drawn from the *Didache* that will be discussed below provide extensive verbatim parallels to material that is unique to Matthew. There are, however, also examples where the parallels involve cases where the material is contained in two or three of the Synoptic Gospels, but an individual work or phrase is closer to the Matthean form of the tradition. The lack of extensive verbatim agreement is at one level unsurprising, since the author of the *Didache* was not a scribe replicating any one of the Gospels, but an individual aiming to compose a new work to be read in a certain context. In what follows, examples will be selected that most strongly suggest the *Didache*'s knowledge of traditions is drawn from Matthew, even if those traditions come to the author of the *Didache* through a process that does not involve direct consultation and copying of a written text of the Gospel of Matthew.

The composition of the *Didache* is complex and would appear to have taken place in a number of stages. In particular, a section (*Did.* 1.3–2.1) of the so-called Two Ways material, which has a number of parallels with material in the Sermon on the Mount, is often seen as a later expansion. While this needs to be acknowledged, for the sake of the discussion here the final form of the *Didache* will be analyzed when attempting to detect its dependence on Matthew's Gospel. In the

---

[10] In particular, see S. Gathercole, *The Composition of the Gospel of Thomas: Original Language and Influences*, SNTSMS 151 (Cambridge: Cambridge University Press, 2012), 168–84.

[11] See H. van de Sandt (ed.), *Matthew and the Didache: Two Documents from the Same Jewish-Christian Milieu?* (Assen/Minneapolis, MN: Royal Van Gorcum/Fortress, 2005); J. Draper, "The Didache," in *The Writings of the Apostolic Fathers*, ed. P. Foster (London: T&T Clark, 2007), 15.

Didache readers are informed "if you are able to bear the whole yoke of the Lord, you will be perfect" (*Did.* 6.2). The theme of perfection is prominent in Matthew's Sermon on the Mount, with the injunction "Be therefore perfect as your heavenly father is perfect" (Mt. 5.48). The theme of perfection is prominent elsewhere in Matthew's Gospel (Mt. 19.21), but the Greek term *teleios* "perfect" does not occur in the other canonical Gospels. Similarly, the notion of the "yoke of the Lord" only find a parallel in Matthew's Gospel, where Jesus calls upon his hears to "take my yoke" since "my yoke is easy" (Mt. 11.29–30). Thus in *Did.* 6.2 a number of Matthean themes and concerns coalesce. This suggests some knowledge of Matthean ideas and terminology, in ways highly reminiscent of the way the first evangelist deploys these concepts and words.

5.3.2 The Gospel of Mark

Finding traces of the Gospel of Mark in early Christian writings is difficult. This is not simply because Mark's Gospel is not widely cited, since it is overshadowed by the use of Matthew. The larger problem is that when a tradition occurs in the writings of the Apostolic Fathers that has a parallel with material in Mark's Gospel that material often has a parallel also with material in Luke, or more frequently Matthew. Therefore, it becomes problematic to determine whether Mark is the source of the tradition, because the majority of Mark's Gospel was used as source material in Matthew and Luke.[12]

The strongest potential example of the use of Mark in the Apostolic Fathers occurs in the *Shepherd of Hermas*. In the *Mandates* section, a request is issued for permission to address "a few more words, since I do not understand anything and my heart has been hardened by my previous deeds" (*Mand.* 4.2.1). There is some similarity with Jesus' words addressed to the disciples in the boat after he had come to them walking on the water. Mark explains the disciples' astonished lack of perception, with the following editorial gloss: "for they did not understand about the loaves, but their hearts were hardened" (Mk. 6.52). While both passages contain the description of hardened hearts, in the singular in the *Shepherd of Hermas* and the plural in Mark's Gospel, it must be acknowledged that the point of contact is slight, the metaphor not

---

[12] One of the earliest Christian writings outside of the New Testament to show clear dependence on the Gospel of Mark is the Gospel of Peter, typically dated to the second half of the second century. See P. Foster, *The Gospel of Peter: Introduction, Critical Edition and Commentary* (Leiden: Brill, 2010), 139–42.

uncommon, and the respective contexts are fundamentally different. This means that very little can be concluded from this example of partial shared terminology.

Given that this is the strongest potential example and that it is unpersuasive, there appears to be no convincing case of the writings of the Apostolic Fathers employing the Gospel of Mark. Even the example from *Mand.* 4.2.1 is extremely weak, and it is either due to the use of a common metaphor or maybe due to coincidence.

5.3.3 The Gospel of Luke

The third Gospel, unlike Mark's Gospel, does contain a significant amount of material that is distinctive. Therefore, at least theoretically, there is a much higher chance of being able to detect material from Luke's Gospel in a later text. Despite this theoretical possibility, even adopting a maximalist approach, there are at best only possibly slight traces of the use of Luke's Gospel in the writings of the Apostolic Fathers.

The *Didache* offers enigmatic and fleeting points of contact with the third Gospel. However, on most occasions where there are parallels between the *Didache* and Luke's Gospel, these involve Gospel tradition that are also paralleled in Matthew's Gospel. This makes it hard to determine whether the source of the tradition in Matthew, Luke, or even some independent (perhaps pre-Synoptic) source. Perhaps the strongest example involves the "love your enemies' saying. The parallel may be set out in tabular form:

Did. 1.3	Mt. 5.44	Lk. 6.27–8
Bless those who curse you, and pray on behalf of your enemies and fast on behalf of those who persecute you.	Love you enemies and pray on behalf of those who persecute you.	Love your enemies, Do good to those who hate you. Bless those who curse you, Pray concerning those who mistreat you.

To further complexify this example, there is a further partial parallel in Paul's writings: "bless those who persecute you, bless and do not curse" (Rom. 12.14). The phrase "bless those who curse you" is shared by the *Didache* with Luke (but not with Matthew), although the English translation masks the fact that the final pronoun "you" occurs in different cases in Greek. However, the final phrase, "on behalf of those who persecute you" is unique to Matthew and the *Didache*, and is identical in the four Greek words that comprise this phrase, *hyper tōn diōkontōn hymas*. The evidence for direct knowledge of Luke's Gospel is inconclusive in this example. By contrast, the use of the verb "to persecute," *diōkō*, which is a term that Matthew editorially introduces into his Gospel on a number of occasions, may offer some slightly stronger evidence for the knowledge of the Matthean form of the saying by the author of the *Didache*.

There is also a tradition in Ignatius' *Letter to the Smyrnaeans* that some have seen as forming a parallel in some way to unique Lukan material. Ignatius rebuffs a docetic tendency by stating that Jesus remained in the flesh after his resurrection. Thus he recalls concerning Jesus that "when he came to Peter and to those with him, he said to them 'Take hold of me; handle me and see that I am not a disembodied demon.'" (Ign. *Smyrn*. 3.2). This is similar both in idea and in some of its wording to the Lukan resurrection tradition where Jesus declares "touch me and see, because a spirit does not have flesh and blood, just as you see I have" (Lk. 24.39). Notwithstanding the fact that both traditions recount the same scene, it must be noted that they do so in markedly different ways, and with some startlingly divergent choices of vocabulary (perhaps none more so than the choice between "demon" or "spirit"). Several explanations have been offered to account for the divergence: (i) Ignatius is a witness to the original Lukan wording; (ii) Ignatius knows a variant (but not necessarily the original) reading of Lk. 24.39; (iii) each independently draws on the same source, or presents a parallel or distinct tradition.[13] Again, the example is partial and inconclusive. Moreover, there is no reason to support the idea of direct dependence on the third Gospel, and several stronger reasons to see both authors utilizing shared or parallel traditions.

Therefore, there is no strong evidence for the use of the third Gospel in the corpus of writings that form the Apostolic Fathers. This aligns with Gregory's larger finding that "there is extant relatively little unambiguous and compelling evidence to demonstrate the extensive use of *Luke* in the period before Tatian and Irenaeus."[14]

---

[13] A. Gregory, *The Reception of Luke and Acts in the Period before Irenaeus*, WUNT 2.169 (Tübingen: Mohr Siebeck, 2003), 69–75.

[14] Ibid., 293.

5.3.4 The Gospel of John

The use of the fourth Gospel by the Apostolic Fathers has divided scholars into highly divergent positions. The letters of Ignatius have been particularly contentious in the assessment of whether their author knew and used John's Gospel. In his commentary on the Ignatian epistles, Schoedel stated baldly but dispassionately that it is "unlikely that Ignatius was acquainted with the Gospel of John."[15] By contrast, after analysis of various passages from Ignatius' letters, Hill states equally straightforwardly that "Ignatius' knowledge of John can be taken as proven."[16] In a somewhat more medial position, Munier summarises the tendency among recent scholars who tend "to exclude a relation of direct dependence between Ignatius and the Fourth Gospel … but to recognize so much the more firmly that the two writings belong to the same doctrinal milieu, use the same religious language and witness to incontestable spiritual affinities."[17] In effect, Munier is stating what scholars now believe in distinction from previously articulated positions. Early Christian communities were not as oppositional as once thought, and that there was a circulation of ideas and linguistic expressions. However, the basic problem remains concerning the competing views regarding Ignatius' knowledge of the fourth Gospel. In large part, the problem arises owing to differing interpretations of what is considered sufficient or satisfactory evidence to postulate direct knowledge and use of one literary source by a later writing.

While this division of viewpoints is likely to remain in place, it is worthwhile considering some of the evidence typically discussed to see why scholars take such divergent views. One of the most regularly discussed examples is taken from Ignatius' *Letter to the Romans*, where he states:

> My love has been crucified, and there is no matter-loving fire in me; but water living and speaking in me, saying to me inwardly, Come to the Father. I have no delight in corruptible food, nor in the pleasures of this life. I desire the bread of God, the heavenly bread, the bread of life, which is the flesh of Jesus Christ, who is from the seed of David; and I desire the drink of God, namely His blood, which is incorruptible love. (Ign. *Rom.* 7.2b–3)

---

[15] W.R. Schoedel, *Ignatius of Antioch*, Hermeneia (Philadelphia, PA: Fortress, 1985), 9.

[16] C.E. Hill, *The Johannine Corpus in the Early Church* (Oxford: Oxford University Press, 2004), 442.

[17] C. Munier, "Où en est la question d'Ignace d'Antioch? Bilan d'un siècle de recherches 1970–1988," *ANRW* 2.27.1 (Berlin: de Gruyter, 1993), 395.

In this passage there are certain terms that recall phraseology found in the fourth Gospel. For instance, Ignatius' reference to "water living and speaking in me" is reminiscent of the "living water" described in conversation with the Samaritan woman (Jn. 4.10, 14), or of Jesus' statement at the feast of the tabernacles "out of his inner parts will flow living water" (Jn. 7.38). Similarly, the reference to "the heavenly bread, bread of life" recalls the following Johannine statements: "I am the bread of life" (Jn 6.48); "I am the living bread that came down out of heaven" (Jn 6.51). Whatever these verbal similarities may be, they are certainly not referenced or extended citations of material drawn from the fourth Gospel. At most they are fragments of shared phraseology, and consequently the relationship between John's Gospel and Ignatius' *Letter to the Romans* remains ambiguous at this point. Other examples of broadly the same type can be multiplied. These shared images of partially paralleled phrases are fascinating, but one may ask what is possible to conclude from these fleeting resemblances. Perhaps no more than that at some stages removed, the fourth Gospel has informed the thought and wording used in a few places in Ignatius' writing. However, the strong evidence of extended verbatim agreement between John and Ignatius is lacking. Therefore, one is left far short of establishing the direct literary dependence of Ignatius on the fourth Gospel, or even of Ignatius' direct knowledge of the fourth Gospel.

Certain sections of Polycarp's *Epistle to the Philippians* survive only in Latin. One key phrase, *fraternitatis amatores*, "lovers of brotherhood" (Pol. *Phil.* 10.1) has been seen as a loose repackaging of the Johannine command to love one another (Jn. 13.34). Not only does the brevity of the parallel tell against drawing a strong conclusion, but the lack of terminological equivalence (even when the translational challenges have been taken into account) mediates against seeing this as an example of literary borrowing. Hill sees Polycarp's statement concerning Jesus' words "just as he promised to us to raise us from the dead" (Pol. *Phil.* 5.2) as recalling Jesus' statement in the fourth Gospel "I will raise him up on the last day" (Jn. 6.40, 44, 54). From these points of contact with the fourth Gospel, Hill concludes that "Polycarp indeed knew and valued the Fourth Gospel by the time he wrote his letter to the Philippians probably just before but in any case not long after AD 110."[18] Given that resurrection belief was not unique to John's Gospel, and that the phraseology between the two texts is quite distant in terms of close correspondence, the degree of certainty concerning Polycarp's

---

[18] Hill, *The Johannine Corpus in the Early Church*, 420.

knowledge of the John's Gospel appears to go beyond the bounds of the available evidence.

5.4 THE APOSTOLOS IN THE WRITINGS OF THE APOSTOLIC FATHERS

The texts that comprise the Apostolos are Acts and the Catholic Epistles. The use of these texts are not particularly prominent in the first half of the second century. In fact, specifically in relation to 2 Peter, various scholars would argue that the text was written after many of the writings that form the corpus of the Apostolic Fathers.[19]

5.4.1 The Acts of the Apostles

Like its literary counterpart, the Gospel of Luke, evidence for the use of the Acts of the Apostles by any of the authors of the writings that form the Apostolic Fathers collection is both meagre and not strong. Very few potential parallels have been proposed. Two of the most frequently considered examples occur in *1 Clement* and Polycarp's *Letter to the Philippians*. The first example from *1 Clement* is seen as forming a partial parallel to material in Acts 13.22. Within the context of providing examples of humility based upon that of biblical characters the author of *1 Clement* turns to the figure of David. According to *1 Clement*, speaking in regard to David, God said, "I have found a man after my own heart, David the son of Jesse; I have anointed him with eternal mercy" (*1 Clem.* 18.1b). In similar language, while described as addressing the synagogue at Pisidian Antioch, in Acts Paul states that God testified concerning David that "I have David the son of Jesse a man after my heart, who will do all my will" (Acts 13.22b). This case is complicated by the parallels in the Septuagint: "and the Lord will seek for himself a man after his heart" (LXX 1 Sam. 13.14), and "I found David my servant, with holy oil I have anointed him" (LXX Ps. 89.21). There are points of commonality between *1 Clement* and Acts, against the two LXX texts, most notably that both describe David as "the son of Jesse" and that both combine phrases from the two LXX texts. However, the differences between *1 Clement* and Acts must also be taken into account. As its final statement, Acts concludes with the non-biblical phrase "who will do all my will," while *1 Clement* draws upon, but

---

[19] For instance, see W. Grünstäudl, *Petrus Alexandrinus: Studien zum historischen und theologischen Ort des zweiten Petrusbriefes*, WUNT II.353 (Tübingen: Mohr Siebeck, 2014), 206–26, 293.

modifies the text from LXX Psalm 89 "with holy oil I have anointed him" by adapting it to "I have anointed him with eternal mercy" (*1 Clem.* 18.1b). This overlapping textual data does not readily support the idea that *1 Clement* drew on Acts 13.22b at this point. The precise mechanism by which these scriptural citations came to the authors of Acts and *1 Clement* is no longer known, but the complex and repeated use of certain texts from the Jewish scriptures in early Christian writings militates against postulating direct dependence between *1 Clement* and Acts at this point.

The second case may be slightly stronger, owing to a lower probability of thoroughgoing dependence on material drawn from the Jewish scriptures. Polycarp, speaking of Jesus, states that he is the one "whom God raised up, having loosed the pains of Hades" (Pol. *Phil.* 1.2c). In similar terms, reporting Peter's Pentecost speech, Acts has Peter state that Jesus was the one "whom God raised up having loosed the pains of death" (Acts 2.24). The key phrase that occurs in Acts 2.24 is "pains of death." This expression, however, occurs on a number of occasions in the Jewish scriptures: LXX 2 Kgs. 22.6; Ps. 114.3. The related phrase "pains of Hades" occurs in LXX Ps. 17.6. To further complicate matters, among Greek witnesses there is a variant reading of Acts 2.24 found in D 05 (Codex Bezae) that reads "pains of Hades," rather than the variant "pains of death" that is found in the majority of manuscripts. The phrase "whom God raised up" or similar expressions are commonplace in the NT (Acts 3.15; 4.10; 5.30; 13.30; 13.33–4; 17.31; 1 Cor. 6.14; 2 Cor. 4.14; Gal. 1.1; Eph. 1.20; 1 Thess. 1.10; 1 Pet. 1.20). This reveals that the correspondence between *1 Clement* and Acts at this point is plausibly not due to direct literary dependence. Therefore, there is little textual basis on which to establish the use of Acts by any of the authors contained in the Apostolic Fathers.

5.4.2 The Catholic Epistles

The Catholic Epistles, James, 1 & 2 Peter, 1, 2, 3 John and Jude, gain little prominence in the Apostolic Fathers. In fact some commentators regard 2 Peter as having been written in the second half of the second century, and therefore after the composition of many of the texts that constitute the corpus of the Apostolic Fathers.[20] One of the reasons for

[20] While there is no consensus on the dating of 2 Peter, for a recent defence of a late dating of this letter, see the commentary of Jörg Frey who postulates a date in the middle of the second century (14–160 CE). J. Frey, *Der Brief des Judas und der zweite Brief des Petrus*, THzNT 15/II (Leipzig: Evangelische Verlagsanstalt, 2015), 186–7.

positing a late date for this text is the fact that 2 Peter is not cited by early Christian authors in the first half of the second century. Other texts among the Catholic Epistles that have left no discernible trace on the writings of the Apostolic Fathers include 2 and 3 John and Jude. Consequently, only James, 1 Peter and 1 John have been suggested as potentially being used in the writings of the Apostolic Fathers. However, most of these cases are highly questionable. In relation to 1 John, there are two brief passages in *1 Clement* that contain a slight verbal parallel to 1 John. These two putative parallels occur in close succession. On two occasions the author of *1 Clement* makes reference to those "who were perfected in love" (*1 Clem.* 49.5; 50.3). This is verbally similar to the statement "the one who fears has not been perfected in love" (1 Jn. 4.18). While there is some terminological correspondence the striking difference is that *1 Clement* offers two positive statements whereas 1 John makes a negative statement speaking of those who are not perfected in love. This striking difference in meaning and purpose militates against seeing an example of literary dependence in this proposed parallel. The second example of the possible use of 1 John is far more compelling. It occurs in a passage in Polycarp's *Letter to the Philippians*, which appears to conflate a couple of passages from 1 John.

Pol. *Phil.* 7.1	1 Jn. 4.2b–3a; 3.8
For whosoever does not confess that Jesus Christ has come in the flesh, is antichrist"; and whosoever does not confess the testimony of the cross, is of the devil;	every spirit which confesses that Jesus Christ has come in the flesh is of God, and every spirit that does not confess Jesus is not from God; and this is the antichrist, the one who practices sin is of the devil

While this does not constitute a direct citation, the language Polycarp uses is reminiscent of the way the polemical accusations are formulated in 1 John. Moreover, there are numerous points of verbal contact, and both texts are written in order to refute those accused of denying the reality of Christ having come in the flesh. The use of language characteristic of 1 John, which is employed in a manner that makes the same type of argument, is therefore highly suggestive of some level of literary dependence.

The case for the literary dependence of the Apostolic Fathers on James primarily involves the *Shepherd of Hermas*. In *Mandate* 9 there are some striking examples of similarity of terminology in about half a dozen cases. Both Jas. 1.7 and *Mand.* 9 tackle the theme of the double-minded person. In particular, *Mand.* 9.6 states, "those who are complete in faith make all requests trusting in the Lord." The terminology is paralleled to some extent in James: "the testing of your faith produces endurance. And let endurance have a perfect result, in order that you might be perfect and complete, lacking in nothing" (Jas. 1.3–4). Both passages use the same terms for "faith" and for being "complete." Also, there is perhaps a shared conceptual idea in "making all requests" and "lacking in nothing." Yet despite these tantalizing similarities, the differences are far greater than the points of contact. Precisely what this implies is difficult to determine. It is not possible to determine whether there is some literary connection even at a secondary level, or whether the connection is looser, with the similarity of language attesting to both authors inhabiting related linguistic communities, or even if the shared language is no more than due to the coincidence of early Christian authors addressing the same broad topic. These uncertainties mean that one must refrain from advancing any firm conclusion about direct literary dependence, while at the same time noting the intriguing common selection of a range of lexical items, albeit used in different orders and often with notably differing expressions of thought.

In the case of 1 Peter, Polycarp in his *Letter to the Philippians* appears to demonstrate a knowledge and use of several passages from that New Testament letter. Addressing the Philippians, Polycarp declares, "though you have not seen him, you believe in him with an inexpressible and glorious joy" (Pol. *Phil.* 1.3). In very similar terms and at the start of his letter, the author of 1 Peter tells his recipients "though you have not seen him, and while not seeing him you believe in him, rejoicing with an inexpressible and glorious joy" (1 Pet. 1.8). While Polycarp presents a slightly shortened form of the statement from 1 Peter, the level of verbal correspondence is high, the shared terms occurring in the same order and the meaning of the two passages aligning. This is not the only example where there is close correspondence. There is marked similarity between Pol. *Phil.* 8.1–2 and 1 Pet. 2.21–4. Polycarp again offers a slightly shorter form of the parallel, and here some of the elements are transposed. Some key examples are the following parallels in phrasing: "who bore our sins in his own body on the tree" (Pol. *Phil.* 8.1) and "he himself bore our sins in his body on the cross" (1 Pet. 2.24); and especially the phrase "who committed no sin, also no deceit was found in his mouth" (Pol. *Phil.* 8.1), where there is a correspondence with the same string of eleven identical words in Greek in 1 Pet. 2.22. Furthermore, there appears to be a direct citation of 1 Pet. 2.12 in Pol. *Phil.* 10.2, although the complication here is that Polycarp's letter survives in Latin rather than Greek at this point, so it is not possible to establish verbatim agreement in the original language.

5.5 THE PAULINE LETTERS

In this section it will not be possible to provide a comprehensive assessment of the all the proposed parallels between passages in the Apostolic Fathers that might potentially draw upon the corpus of Paul's letters. Only the most compelling cases will be discussed. As has been mentioned, Hebrews typically circulated with the Pauline letters in the antique period, and therefore will be considered in this section.

5.5.1 Romans

Among the writings of the Apostolic Fathers, *1 Clement, Polycarp,* and *Barnabas* appear to demonstrate reasonably secure knowledge of Paul's letter to the Romans. By contrast, Ignatius has some suggestive phraseology, but the case is not compelling. While the parallel is not identical, *1 Clement* presents a vice list that is remarkably similar to the one found in the opening chapter of Romans.

1 Clem. 35.5–6	Rom. 1.29–30, 32
casting away from us all unrighteousness and lawlessness, greed, strife, malice, deceit, gossip, and slander, hatred of God, arrogance and boasting, vainglory and ambition. For they that do such things are hateful to God; and not only they that do them, but also those that take pleasure in them that do them.	being filled with all unrighteousness, wickedness, greed, evil; full of envy, murder, strife, deceit, malice; *they are* gossips, slanderers, haters of God, insolent, arrogant, boastful, inventors of evil, disobedient to parents, and, although they know the ordinance of God, that those who practice such things are worthy of death, they not only do the same, but also give hearty approval to those who practice them.

While the two lists do not correspond precisely in contents or order, the overwhelming similarity is striking. Furthermore, the manner in which the closing reflections on the vice lists coincide in both Romans and *1 Clement* lends strong support to the suggestion that the latter is dependent on Romans for its own vice list and interpretation of it. Also there is a further significant agreement between *1 Clem.* 32.1 and Rom. 6.1, again reinforcing the case for *1 Clement*'s knowledge of Romans.

In the Epistle of Barnabas, the author recalls the figure of Abraham in much the same manner as Paul does in Romans. The complicating factor is that both authors also draw upon the same texts from Genesis (Gen. 15.6; 17.4) as part of their respective arguments. However, the introductory phrases are similarly close, "What then does he say to Abraham" (*Barn.* 13.7) and "For what does scripture say, 'Abraham believed God . . .'" (Rom. 4.3). While not as compelling as the example from *1 Clement*, there is still reasonable ground for supposing Barnabas is indebted to Rom. 4.3 at this point.

The example from Polycarp's letter is stronger than the previous case from *Barnabas*. Polycarp warns the Philippians that "we must all stand before the judgment seat of Christ, and each one must account for his own actions" (Pol. *Phil.* 7.2). This is close in wording and sentiment to Romans: "for all will stand before the judgment seat of God [variant reading "Christ' ²א C² L P Ψ 048 0209 33 81 104 365 1175 1241 1505 1881], . . . so then each one of us will give account of himself to God" (Rom. 14.10, 12). Here it appears that Polycarp has drawn on the wording of Romans.

Ignatius' possible use of Romans is less certain. He refers to Christ as "the seed of David" (Ign. *Rom.* 7.3). This is partially reminiscent of the statement in the opening of Paul's letter to the Romans that "the son" was "from the seed of David according to the flesh" (Rom. 1.3). Reference to Christ's Davidic descent occurs multiple times in the writings of Ignatius, alternating between references to "David's seed" (Ign. *Eph.* 18.2; *Rom.* 7.3) and his "race" (Ign. *Eph.* 20.2; *Trall.* 9.1; *Smyrn.* 1.1). Given that these statements concerning Davidic descent are embedded in Ignatius' creed-like affirmations it is uncertain whether these partial parallels to Rom. 1.3 are necessarily derived directly from Rom. 1.3, or whether this tradition has come to Ignatius by some other mechanism.

5.5.2 1 Corinthians

Among the writings of the Apostolic Fathers, 1 Corinthians is the most widely and accurately cited of all the Pauline letters. The trio of *1 Clement*, Ignatius, and Polycarp each draw upon 1 Corinthians in a fairly clear and direct manner. Moreover, there is a strong probability that the *Shepherd of Hermas* appears to be dependent on this Pauline epistle. In the case of *1 Clement*, also addressed to the believers in Corinth, Clement's letter refers directly to 1 Corinthians: "Take up the epistle of the blessed Paul the apostle. What did he first write to you in the beginning of the gospel? Truly he wrote to you in the Spirit about himself and Cephas and Apollos, because even then you had split into factions" (*1 Clem.* 47.1–3). Combined with this, *1 Clement* reformulates the Paul body metaphor for the church (1 Cor. 12.12–24// *1 Clem.* 37.5–38.1). Clement also draws heavily on the discussion of love contained in 1 Cor. 13, when he writes, "love endures all things, is patient in all things" (*1 Clem.* 49.5).

For Ignatius, 1 Corinthians is the section of the New Testament that he draws upon most extensively. The reality of Ignatius' circumstances must be held in mind. As a convict, undergoing transportation to death in Rome, it is unlikely that he was carrying any written documents with him. For this reason, it is unsurprising that the phrases from 1 Corinthians that are paralleled in his writing do not exhibit exact agreement with Paul's wording. Notwithstanding this, the volume of use and the close correspondence suggest that much of the content of 1 Corinthians may have been committed to Ignatius' memory. A couple of examples will suffice to illustrate this. Ignatius draws upon the phraseology of 1 Corinthians when he writes, "do not be misled my brothers, those who corrupt houses will not inherit the kingdom of God" (Ign. *Eph.* 18.1). This utilizes the Pauline statement "or do you not know that the unrighteous will not inherit the kingdom of God. Do not be misled ..." (1 Cor. 6.9). Here Ignatius uses Pauline language in a similar, but not identical manner to that found in 1 Corinthians. Ignatius describes the cross as a stumbling block to unbelievers, but as salvation and life to believers (Ign. *Eph.* 16.1). Again while the language is not identical, the metaphor is broadly the same as that found in 1 Cor 1.18.

The most striking example from Polycarp's epistle to the Philippians occurs in a portion of the text extant in Latin, but where he directly attributes his statement to Paul: "or do we not know that the saints will judge the world, as Paul teaches?" (Pol. *Phil.* 11.2). The underlying Greek is almost certainly in verbatim agreement with 1 Corinthians: "or do you not know that the saints will judge the world?" (1 Cor. 6.2). A further example involves a shorter form of material drawn from 1 Cor. 6.9, where Polycarp agrees in listing three categories of people who will not inherit the kingdom of God (Pol. *Phil.* 5.3).

5.5.3 2 Corinthians

There is a much narrower evidential base for establishing the use of 2 Corinthians. The only plausible example of dependence on 2 Corinthians occurs in Polycarp's letter. Polycarp writes, "the one who raised him from the dead will also raise us" (Pol. *Phil.* 2.2). In 2 Corinthians, Paul writes, "knowing that the one who raised the Lord Jesus, will also raise us with Jesus" (2 Cor. 4.14). While there is undoubtedly some level of parallelism it is not exact correspondence. Moreover, the subject matter is widely discussed in early Christian writers. Hence, while it is plausible that Polycarp was dependent in some way on 2 Corinthians, that is not the only possible explanation for the similarity of expression.

5.5.4 Galatians

Again, Polycarp's letter is the only plausible example of dependence on Galatians. The one consideration is the brevity of the shared parallel. Addressing the Galatians, Paul writes in angry tones, "Do not be deceived, God is not mocked" (Gal. 6.7). Polycarp utilizes this saying, introducing it in the following manner: "knowing therefore that God is not mocked' (Pol. *Phil.* 5.1). The verb of "knowing" that introduces this quotation is a formula designed to point to information already in the possession of the recipients of the letter. Furthermore, the expression "God is not mocked" is not found outside of Galatians prior to Polycarp's use of the same expression. While the common phrase is brief, here Polycarp almost certainly draws on Galatians.

5.5.5 Ephesians

Ignatius, Polycarp, and perhaps the *Shepherd of Hermas* all present material that is likely to draw upon Paul's letter to the Ephesians. Interestingly, the opening of Ignatius' letter to the Ephesians imitates the opening of the Pauline letter to the Ephesians. This does not comprise of exact repetition, but rather a selection of key expressions drawn from Eph. 1.3–14, and redeployed to construct Ignatius' own letter opening addressed to recipients in the same city. Ignatius writes that the Ephesians are

> blessed with greatness and through the fulness of God the Father, and predestined before the ages for lasting and unchangeable glory for ever, being united and elect through genuine suffering by the will of the Father, and Jesus Christ, our God, to the church worthy

of blessing which is in Ephesus of Asia, fullest greetings in Jesus Christ and in blameless joy. (Ign. *Eph.* inscript.)

Features such as the opening blessing, reference to God as Father, being elect, predestined, blameless, God's will, and "the fulness," are all key points of terminological correspondence. In writing to Polycarp, Ignatius instructs him to inform "the brothers" to "love their wives as the Lord loves the church" (Ign. *Pol.* 5.1). This appears to replicate the instruction to husbands in the household code in Ephesians, "love your wives as Christ also loved the church" (Eph. 5.25). The degree of similarity may be magnified in English translation. The Greek text uses different words for wives in each context, and Ignatius does not repeat the verb "to love" as is the case in Ephesians, although it is implied in the second clause. Notwithstanding these differences, the similarities remain striking.

The case of the *Shepherd of Hermas* is not as strong. The examples of parallel phrasing are not as extensive and the level of verbal correspondence is not as close. First, in *Similitude* 9.13 those who believe are told on two occasions that they will become "one spirit and one body" (*Sim.* 9.13.5, 7). This expression is reminiscent of the phrase "there is one body and one spirit" (Eph. 4.4). Several sections later in the same *Similitude* the author writes, "the church of God will be one body, one thought, one mind, one faith, one love" (*Sim.* 9.18.4). Although Eph. 4.3–6 does not explicitly refer to the church, the passage in Ephesians appears to have an ecclesial outlook in mind, and it does make reference to "one faith." So at this point the text of the *Shepherd of Hermas* is suggestive of some potential link with the ideas in Eph. 4.3–6, but the lack of close correspondence limits the case for literary dependence being mounted in any strong form. Similarly, the statement that "grief crushes the holy spirit and saves again" (*Mand.* 10.2.1) is not dissimilar to the instruction in Ephesians, "do not grieve the holy spirit, in whom you were sealed for the day of redemption" (Eph. 4.30). Here, once again, the connection is intriguing, but falls short of establishing literary dependence.

Therefore, there is relatively strong evidence for concluding that Ephesians was known and used by both Polycarp and Ignatius. The case for the *Shepherd of Hermas* using Ephesians is less compelling.

5.5.6 Philippians

Only one of the writings in the corpus of the Apostolic Fathers provides evidence for the likely literary use of Philippians. It is perhaps unsurprising that the text in question is Polycarp's *Letter to the Philippians* – addressed to the same geographic location as Paul's letter to the Philippians. Polycarp recalls those believers who have died for their faith, informing the Philippians that "all these did not run in vain" (Pol. *Phil.* 9.2). In this phrase there is a string of four Greek words that is identical to Paul's phraseology when he tells the Philippians "I did not run in vain" (Phil. 2.16). This parallel is likely due to some recollection of the text of Philippians. There are also a couple of other lighter resemblances such as the Latin expression for "enemies of the cross" (*inimicis cruces*; Pol. *Phil.* 12.3), which parallels the same striking phrase that Paul uses (Phil. 3.18). These two examples support the argument that Polycarp utilized Paul's letter to the Philippians in his own letter to the believers of a later generation in the same city.

5.5.7 2 Thessalonians

There is only one plausible example of the possible use of 2 Thessalonians, again occurring in Polycarp's *Letter to the Philippians*. In the introductory thanksgiving section, Paul tells the Thessalonians, "we ourselves boast about you among the churches of God" (2 Thess 1.4). Polycarp, addressing the Philippians makes direct reference to one of Paul's written comments, stating that "in whose midst the blessed Paul laboured, and who are praised at the beginning of his letter. For he boasts about you in all the churches ..." (Pol. *Phil.* 11.3). There seems to be some confusion here on the part of Polycarp in relation to the addressees of the passage he quotes from Paul. As Benecke observed, "The context shows that Polycarp supposes himself to be quoting words addressed to the Philippians (cf. *etenim*). Similar words actually only occur in 2 Thessalonians, and Epistle addressed to another Macedonian Church, which Polycarp might easily have thought of, by a lapse of memory, as sent to the Philippians."[21] Despite this misunderstanding, Polycarp presents the reference to Paul as the one who "boasts about you in all the churches" as material drawn from the apostle's writings. Since this phrase only occurs in 2 Thessalonians, this provides evidence of the citation of that letter even if Polycarp has misremembered the correct addressees.

---

[21] P.V.M. Benecke, "The Epistle of Polycarp," in *The New Testament in the Apostolic Fathers*, eds. A Committee of the Oxford Society of Historical Theology (Oxford: Clarendon, 1905), 95.

5.5.8 1 & 2 Timothy

The two letters to Timothy may potentially have been known to Ignatius and Polycarp. The parallels provide evidence that is far from conclusive, but the repeated points of contact may suggest that the balance of probability is slightly in favour of both authors knowing the letters addressed to Timothy. The strongest parallel found in Ignatius' writings involves a series of allusions which parallel passages in 1 Tim. 1.3–5.

Ign. *Magn.* 8.1; Ign. *Eph.* 20.1; 14.1	1 Tim. 1.3–5
Do not be deceived by strange doctrines or ancient myths which are worthless. I will make clear to you what I begun to speak about, the administration The beginning is faith, the end is love.	As I urged you upon my departure for Macedonia, remain on at Ephesus so that you may instruct certain men not to teach strange doctrines, nor to pay attention to myths and endless genealogies, which give rise to mere speculation rather than the administration of God which is by faith. But the goal of our instruction is love from a pure heart and a good conscience and a sincere faith.

The strongest point of contact is with the combination of "strange doctrines" and "myths' found in Ign. *Magn.* 8.1 and 1 Tim. 1.3–4. While the whole passage is not a direct citation, the shared phrasing is reminiscent of the language in 1 Timothy. The potential use of 2 Tim. 1.16 in Ign. *Eph.* 2.1 (and maybe also in Ign. *Smyrn.* 10.2) involves the same type of correspondence: the shared use of slightly uncommon terminology. In both passages from his writings Ignatius speaks of figures who have "refreshed" him during his transportation to Rome, in a similar vein to the manner in which Paul describes Onesiphorus who "often refreshed me, and was not ashamed of me chains" (2 Tim. 1.16). Ignatius' self-presentation of his journey as imitating Paul's journey to Rome lends further weight to the suggestion that the choice of language is intentional to create a parallel with Paul's expressions.

The parallels between Polycarp's *Letter to the Philippians* and the letters to Timothy are even stronger. The most obvious point of contact occurs when Polycarp appears to conflate two statements from 1 Timothy.

Pol. *Phil.* 4.1	1 Tim. 6.10a, 7
But the love of money is the beginning of all troubles.	For the love of love money is a root of all evils ...
Knowing therefore, that we brought nothing into world and can take nothing out ...	For we brought nothing into the world so we can take nothing out.

The second part of the statement in Pol. *Phil.* 4.1 forms the stronger parallel. In Greek there is a string of eight words where the only difference is the choice of the conjunction. This provides strong evidence of literary dependence. The opening clause is also similar to 1 Tim. 6.10a, although admittedly not with quite the same level of verbatim agreement. When, however, it is recognized that the two parallels are drawn from the same section of 1 Timothy this increases the probability that Polycarp's "love of money" is likewise literarily dependent on the material from 1 Timothy. There are also a number of potential parallels with 2 Timothy. The strongest of these is Polycarp's statement about Ignatius, Zosimus, Rufus, and others that "they did not love the present world," and the statement in 2 Timothy that describes Demas as a deserter "having loved the present world" (2 Tim. 4.10). While Polycarp supplies a negative particle (thus making the statement a positive affirmation), given that the reference to "the present age" among the New Testament writings only occurs in the Pastoral Epistles this makes it more likely that there is some kind of dependence on 2 Tim. 4.10 for Polycarp's wording.

5.5.9 Hebrews

Since Hebrews circulated with manuscripts of the Pauline letters it is appropriate to treat it with this corpus of New Testament writings. There is only one passage in the writings of the Apostolic Fathers for which dependence on Hebrews may be plausibly suggested. The parallel is between *1 Clem.* 36 and Heb. 1. For A.J. Carlyle the parallelism was deemed to be of such strength that he could state, "There can be practically no doubt that in this passage we have a reminiscence of the first chapter of Hebrews."[22] Clement quotes Pss. 2.7; 104.4; and 110.1 in common with Heb. 1, although there are differences in terms of

---

[22] A.J. Carlyle, "First Clement," in *The New Testament in the Apostolic Fathers*, eds. A Committee of the Oxford Society of Historical Theology (Oxford: Clarendon, 1905), 46.

the textual citations in *1 Clem.* 36 and Heb. 1. The more striking parallel is the material that the two passages share when they are not citing traditions from the Jewish scriptures. *1 Clement* states of Christ, "he, being the radiance of his majesty, is as much superior to angels as the name he has inherited is more excellent" (*1 Clem.* 36.2). This is an abbreviated form of material found in Hebrews, the relevant passages reading: "he is the radiance of his glory . . . having become as much better than the angels, as he has inherited a more excellent name than they" (Heb. 1.3a, 4). The correspondence is not perfect, but it indicates some type of relationship between the two passages. Some have not been as confident as Carlyle concerning the strength of the relationship, noting that this may just show dependence on an excerpted passage from *1 Clement*, or even the possibility of a common source.[23] However, given the cumulative weight of three common citations from the Jewish scriptures, and the similarity of wording with Heb. 1.3–4 where earlier material is not being cited, this appears to be a reasonably strong example for establishing the dependence of *1 Clement* on Hebrews.

5.5.10 Colossians, 1 Thessalonians, Titus, Philemon

While there have been occasional suggestions of an allusion to the four Pauline letters, Colossians, 1 Thessalonians, Titus, and Philemon, in the writings of the Apostolic Fathers the parallels are extremely tenuous. It is of course impossible to say that none of the authors of the writings that constitute the Apostolic Fathers knew these four letters. However, it is possible to state that from their surviving literary works that no conclusive evidence exists that would demonstrate the knowledge and use of these four epistles.

5.6 REVELATION

It is difficult to detect any reception of Revelation prior to the mid second century. The earliest reference might be found in Justin's *Dialogue with Trypho*, where he states "there will be a resurrection of the dead, and a thousand years in Jerusalem, which will be built, adorned and enlarged" (Justin, *Dial.* 80). This chiliastic expectation of a resurrection for the faithful dead and their thousand-year reign with Christ on earth finds its antecedent in Rev. 20. In the writings of the Apostolic Fathers, however, there is no obvious reference to or use of the text of Revelation.

---

[23] A. Lindemann, *Die Clementsbriefe*, HNT 17 (Tübingen: Mohr Siebeck, 1992), 122.

5.7 CONCLUSIONS

The results of the foregoing investigation can be summarized and tabulated. The accompanying table presents the total number of Apostolic Fathers who cite a particular New Testament writing, and the number of New Testament writings cited by each of the Apostolic Fathers.

Cases of Plausible Literary Dependence of an Apostlic Father on a New Testament Writing

	1 Clement	2 Clement	Ignatius	Pol. Phil.	Barnabas	Hermas	Didache	Total
Matthew			•				•	2
Mark								0
Luke								0
John				○				0
Acts								0.5
Romans	•			•	•			3
1 Corinthians	•		•	•		○		3.5
2 Corinthians				○				0.5
Galatians				•				1
Ephesians			•	•		○		2.5
Philippians				•				1
Colossians								0
1 Thess								0
2 Thess				•				1
1 Timothy			•	•				2
2 Timothy			•	•				2
Titus								0
Philemon								0
Hebrews	•							1
James						○		0.5
1 Peter				•				1
2 Peter								0
1 John				•				1
2 John								0
3 John								0
Jude								0
Revelation								0
Total	3	0	5	11	1	1.5	1	

From this data it is possible to see that *1 Clement*, Ignatius, and Polycarp's *Letter to the Philippians* show knowledge of the greatest range of New Testament texts, with Polycarp's *Letter to the Philippians* demonstrating a fairly certain knowledge of ten of the New Testament writings, and a possible knowledge of two others. It is interesting that the sub-collection of New Testament writings that have the greatest use among the Apostolic Fathers is the Pauline Epistles. The reason for this is not entirely certain. Paul's letters may have been particularly useful for the didactic purposes of the authors who cite them. Alternatively, perhaps a collection of Pauline letters was in circulation earlier than the Gospel texts.[24] While such hypotheses are beyond proof, the possible reasons are intriguing. What is certain is that none of the authors who constitute the collection known as the Apostolic Fathers cites the documents that would become the New Testament in an extensive manner. However, the range of material cited (even in the form of short phrases and similar formulations) suggests these texts were valued and seen as a source of ideas and shared beliefs.

FURTHER READING

Foster, P. "The Text of the New Testament in the Apostolic Fathers," in *The Early Text of the New Testament*, ed. Charles E. Hill and Michael J. Kruger. Oxford: Oxford University Press, 2012, 282–301.

Foster, P. (ed.). *The Writings of the Apostolic Fathers*. London: T&T Clark, 2007.

Gregory, A. *The Reception of Luke and Acts in the Period before Irenaeus*. WUNT 2.169. Tübingen: Mohr Siebeck, 2003.

Gregory, A.F., and Tuckett, C.M. (eds.). *The Reception of the New Testament in the Apostolic Fathers*. Oxford: Oxford University Press, 2005.

Holmes, M.W. *The Apostolic Fathers: Greek Texts with English Translations*. 3rd ed. Grand Rapids, MI: Baker, 2007.

Lightfoot, J.B. *The Apostolic Fathers, parts 1 & 2, Ignatius and Polycarp*. 5 vols. London: Macmillan, 1885–90.

Köster, H. *Synoptische Überlieferung bei den Apostolischen Vätern*. TU 65. Berlin: Akademie Verlag, 1957.

Pratscher, W. (ed.). *The Apostolic Fathers: An Introduction*. Waco, TX: Baylor University Press, 2010.

Schoedel, W.R. *Ignatius of Antioch*, Hermeneia. Philadelphia, PA: Fortress, 1985.

---

[24] For the idea of an early collection of Pauline letters, see D. Trobisch, *The First Edition of the New Testament* (Oxford: Oxford University Press, 2000), 58, 60–2.

6 The Reception of Paul, Peter, and James in the Apostolic Fathers

BENJAMIN EDSALL

6.1 INTRODUCTION

Within the early Christian communities, according to the documents that bear witness to them, the figures of Paul, Peter, and James the brother of Jesus loom large. Already in Paul's letter to the Galatians, Peter (Cephas) and James are noted as "pillars" of the church (Gal. 2.9) and are the only two apostles Paul deemed it necessary to meet during his first trip to Jerusalem (1.18–19).[1] In subsequent decades and centuries, the importance of all three figures was continually reaffirmed through communal memory, traditions, and writings about them or attributed to them. Limited to the writings that comprise the Apostolic Fathers, however, their representation is somewhat sparser. Of the eleven authors now conventionally included among the Apostolic Fathers, five do not explicitly mention Paul, Peter or James at all.[2] Considered individually, appeals to these figures are not evenly distributed: Peter and Paul appear variously while James is entirely absent, with the possible exception of one fragment from Papias, discussed below. Even within the letters of Ignatius, whose seven-letter corpus contains the majority of appeals to Peter and Paul in the Apostolic Fathers, only three or four of the seven mention Peter or Paul.[3] All this amounts to the fact that roughly half of the authors or

---

[1] On the question of identifying Peter and Cephas, see further below.

[2] These are the *Didache*, the *Shepherd of Hermas*, *The Epistle of Barnabas*, the *Martyrdom of Polycarp* or the *Apology of Quadratus*, of which we have only fragments.

[3] These include *Ephesians, Smyrneans, Romans*, and perhaps *Trallians*. Notably, the longer recensions of Ignatius' letters include added appeals to all three apostles. See the recent discussion of this recension in relation to Paul in L. Stephanie Cobb, "Neither 'Pure Evangelic Manna' Nor 'Tainted Scraps': Reflections on the Study of Pseudo-Ignatius," in *The Apostolic Fathers and Paul*, ed. Todd D. Still and David E. Wilhite, Pauline and Patristic Scholars in Debate (London: Bloomsbury, 2017), 181–202.

writings of the Apostolic Fathers do not feel the need to appeal explicitly to any of these apostolic figures in the course of their arguments, however much they may be indebted to them on the level of broader early Christian discourse. This is no doubt due, at least in part, to the artificial and somewhat arbitrary nature of the textual corpus labeled the "Apostolic Fathers," which arose in the seventeenth century and whose textual contents were not fixed in convention until after the publication of the *Didache* in 1883.[4] It is perhaps also a function of the nature of the works included in the collection: the occasional nature of the Ignatian letters, the appropriation of apocalyptic discourse in *The Shepherd of Hermas*, the presumption of many shared, and therefore unstated, traditions in all texts, etc.

The present discussion will focus principally on the reception of the apostolic figures Paul, Peter, and James, rather than on the presence of citations or allusions, a task that would in any case apply chiefly to Paul's letters and has been more thoroughly covered elsewhere than would be possible here. Of course, where explicit appeals to these figures are absent, more subtle appeals to their legacies, textually or orally transmitted, may be at work. Even so, this study focuses on the ways in which these apostles are explicitly presented and appropriated by the Apostolic Fathers. To minimize repetition as much as possible, Peter and Paul will be treated together under three themes that recur across the various appeals to them: their link with authoritative teaching; the theme of their death; and their place among a network of other apostles. The notably minor presence of James will be addressed in its own section before drawing the discussion together in the conclusion.

6.2 PAUL, PETER, AND AUTHORITATIVE TEACHING

It is perhaps unsurprising that Paul and Peter were remembered and appealed to as authoritative teachers. What may be surprising in the case of Paul the "blessed apostle,"[5] however, is that his teaching

---

[4] See Chapter 5 in this volume for further discussion and references about the development of the Apostolic Fathers. On the title "Apostolic Fathers," see David Lincicum, "The Paratextual Invention of the Term 'Apostolic Fathers,'" *JTS* 66.1 (2015): 139–48, and now Clare K. Rothschild, *New Essays on the Apostolic Fathers*, WUNT 375 (Tübingen: Mohr Siebeck, 2017), 7–33; Rothschild's "Appendix B" provides the contents for Cotelier's first edition, which lacked the *Epistle to Diognetus*, the *Apology of Quadratus*, Papias and, of course, the *Didache* while including a large selection of other Pseudo-Clementine texts.

[5] *1 Clem.* 47.1; see also "the blessed and glorified Paul" in Polycarp, *Phil.* 3.2.

authority was not principally, and certainly not exclusively, rooted in his letters. For both, their status as "apostles" appears to guarantee them a certain authoritative status, which is inflected differently between the two, shaped by memories or traditions of their ministries. These commonalities and divergences appear, notably, within the writings of a single author, namely Ignatius of Antioch.

Writing to the Roman Christians, Ignatius begs his readers not to be "inopportunely well-intentioned" toward him but rather to let him face the beasts and so attain to God (Ign. *Rom.* 4.1). While asking them to pray to Christ for his impending "sacrifice," Ignatius distances himself from apostolic authority.

> I do not command you like Peter and Paul. They are apostles, I am condemned. They are free, I am even still a slave. But if I suffer I will become a freedman of Jesus Christ, and I shall rise in him free. Now, by being bound, I learn not to desire anything. (Ign. *Rom.* 4.3)

While scholars often muse over this passage in relation to historical questions, concerning the presence of Peter in Rome, for instance, what interests us here is the rhetorical presentation of the apostles.[6] On that level, appealing to these two in his letter to the Romans may well indicate an attempt to tap into traditions about the apostles' presence in Rome, a sort of *captatio benevolentiae* through noting the church's apostolic connections.[7] For Ignatius, both figures had authority as apostles to issue orders, to provide authoritative instruction to the Roman Christian community, in a way that exceeded his own authority as erstwhile bishop of Antioch (*Rom* 2.2).[8] Elsewhere, Ignatius indicates that, in the hierarchy of Christian authority, the apostles inhabit a place just below Christ, allowing them a kind of universal Christian

---

[6] For different sides of the debate about whether Peter ever went to Rome, see Markus N.A. Bockmuehl, *The Remembered Peter: In Ancient Reception and Modern Debate*, WUNT 262 (Tübingen: Mohr Siebeck, 2010), 114–32, and Otto Zwierlein, *Petrus in Rom, die literarischen Zeugnisse: mit einer kritischen Edition der Martyrien des Petrus und Paulus auf neuer handschriftlicher Grundlage*, UALG 96 (Berlin: De Gruyter, 2009), among others.

[7] This is argued in different ways by William R. Schoedel, *Ignatius of Antioch: A Commentary on the Letters of Ignatius of Antioch*, ed. Helmut Koester, Hermeneia (Philadelphia, PA: Fortress, 1985), 176–7, and Markus N.A. Bockmuehl, *Simon Peter in Scripture and Memory: The New Testament Apostle in the Early Church* (Grand Rapids, MI: Baker Academic, 2012), 48.

[8] So also Andreas Lindemann, *Paulus im ältesten Christentum: d. Bild d. Apostels u. d. Rezeption d. paulin. Theologie in d. frühchristl. Literatur bis Marcion*, BHT 58 (Tübingen: Mohr Siebeck, 1979), 86.

authority that Ignatius cannot claim (*Trall.* 2.1–3.3).[9] Elsewhere in his letters, however, the way in which their apostolic cachet is cashed out differs in ways representative of their reception among the other Apostolic Fathers.

Paul's authority to instruct Christians is filled out with reference to his relation to Christian initiation and his post-mortem status in Ignatius' letter to the Ephesians.[10] Paul's letter writing is also brought up as a matter of fact, but is not appealed to as such here for its authority. The bishop casts his readers as "fellow initiates of Paul," drawing on the language of mystery cults prevalent throughout the Roman empire (*Eph.* 12.2).[11] As "fellow initiate," Paul stands alongside the Ephesians in their initiation into the divine mysteries. Unlike the Ephesians, however, Paul is one of "those who have been taken up to God" already: he is sanctified (*hēgiasmenos*), he has been approved (*memartyrēmenos*), and he is worthy of blessing (*axiomakaristos*). Paul's example is decisive, for Ignatius: it is Paul's footsteps in which the bishop hopes to be found.[12] The authority of the Apostle for instruction, then, does not end with issuing orders but extends to his very life and death as an example for Ignatius and the Ephesians – and, by extension, for all Christians. While Paul's letters are not cited for their authoritative teaching or exhortation by Ignatius here, his mention of

---

[9] Cf. the comments in Alexander N. Kirk, *The Departure of an Apostle: Paul's Death Anticipated and Remembered*, WUNT II/406 (Tübingen: Mohr Siebeck, 2015), 81, and Schoedel, *Ignatius of Antioch*, 176–7 and 144 (on *Mag.* 6.1, which also apply here). Whether the order Peter–Paul reflects historical order or a Pauline climax (Andreas Lindemann, *Die apostolischen Väter I: Die Clemensbriefe*, HNT 17 (Tübingen: Mohr Siebeck, 1992), 37) is difficult: see further 2.2 below.

[10] For general considerations about Paul's influence on Ignatius, see e.g., Carl B. Smith, "Ministry, Martyrdom, and Other Mysteries: Pauline Influence on Ignatius of Antioch," in *Paul and the Second Century*, ed. Michael F. Bird and Joseph R. Dodson, LNTS 412 (London: T& T Clark, 2011), 37–56 and the earlier comments in Henning Paulsen, *Studien zur Theologie des Ignatius von Antiochien*, FKD 29 (Göttingen: Vandenhoeck & Ruprecht, 1978), 44.

[11] On the various mystery cults and their initiation practices, see now esp. Jan N. Bremmer, *Initiation into the Mysteries of the Ancient World*, MVAW 1 (Berlin: De Gruyter, 2014), but note the strong argument in T.J. Lang, *Mystery and the Making of a Christian Historical Consciousness: From Paul to the Second Century*, BZNW 219 (Berlin: De Gruyter, 2015), 132–47 that Ignatius' mystery language as a whole is more closely related to his discussion of revelation than to themes of initiation.

[12] On Ignatius' Pauline patterning of his death, see Alexander N. Kirk, "Ignatius' Statements of Self-Sacrifice: Imitations of an Atoning Death or Expressions of Exemplary Suffering?," *JTS* 64.1 (2013): 66–88; David L. Eastman, "Paul as Martyr in the Apostolic Fathers," in *The Apostolic Fathers and Paul*, ed. Todd D. Still and David E. Wilhite, Pauline and Patristic Scholars in Debate (London: Bloomsbury, 2017), 8–14.

"every letter" from the apostle (12.2) points toward the high regard in which Ignatius no doubt held them.[13]

Peter's authority, on the other hand, has a different set of connections for Ignatius. Writing to the Smyrneans, in his attempt to oppose certain docetic tendencies present among that community, the bishop appeals to traditions about Jesus appearing "in the flesh" after his resurrection (*Smyrn.* 2–3). This took place, he recounts, "when he came to those around Peter" and "he said to them, 'receive and touch me and see that I am not a bodiless daemon.' And immediately they touched him and believed" (3.2). In this tradition about Jesus, Peter appears as a named guarantor: he stands for and among the other disciples. As in the middle ending of Mk. 16.8, where the otherwise silent women make a report to those *peri ton Petron*, and similar to the singling out of Peter in Lk. 9.32 ("Peter and those with him"; *ho de Petros kai oi syn autō*), Peter is the central disciple.[14]

Elsewhere in the Apostolic Fathers, these particular traits of Pauline and Petrine appeals continue in a similar vein. Paul is remembered in relation to his ministry of teaching/exhortation as well as his authoritative legacy in his letters, while Peter is associated with the maintenance and transmission of traditions about Jesus. It will suffice to survey these briefly here.

6.2.1 Paul, His Ministry and His Letters

When one turns to Polycarp's letter to the Philippians, one finds a greater concentration of explicit citations of and appeals to Paul than elsewhere among the Apostolic Fathers.[15] For Polycarp, Paul's authoritative teaching, proclaiming true "righteousness" (*dikaiosunē*), spanned

---

[13] On the difficult phrase in *Eph.* 12:2 and its implications for Ignatius' Pauline corpus, see esp. the summary and evaluation in Paul Foster, "The Epistles of Ignatius of Antioch and the Writings that Later Formed the New Testament," in *The Reception of the New Testament in the Apostolic Fathers*, ed. Andrew F. Gregory and Christopher M. Tuckett (Oxford; New York: Oxford University Press, 2005), 162–72.

[14] See the discussion in Bockmuehl, *The Remembered Peter*, 87–90 and cf. Todd D. Still, "Images of Peter in the Apostolic Fathers," in *Peter in Early Christianity*, ed. Helen K. Bond and Larry W. Hurtado (Grand Rapids, MI: Eerdmans, 2015), 164. Schoedel, *Ignatius of Antioch*, 226 notes the affinities of this passage with Lk. 24.39. Of course, the authority of this tradition is not derived from a link with the Gospel of Luke (a link Schoedel doubts in any case) but rather from the witness of the disciples, whose representative is Peter.

[15] Annette Merz, *Die fiktive Selbstauslegung des Paulus: intertextuelle Studien zur Intention und Rezeption der Pastoralbriefe*, NTOA/SUNT 52 (Göttingen: Vandenhoeck & Ruprecht; Fribourg: Academic Press, 2004), 114, 131 refers to the

his missionary and his letter-writing activities.[16] Writing to a community among whom Paul had worked and to whom he had also addressed a letter, Polycarp twice makes use of a present/absent schema, itself likely indebted to Paul (cf. 1 Cor. 5.3; 2 Cor. 10.11 etc.), which emphasizes the "blessed and glorified" apostle's work among the Philippians: "When he was among you, face to face with those then alive, he taught the true word. And when he was absent he wrote letters to you and if you carefully examine them you will be able to build up the faith given to you" (*Phil.* 3.2). The question of how many letters Polycarp thinks Paul wrote to the Philippians is difficult but rather beside the point, both for the present discussion and for Polycarp.[17] What matters to the Bishop of Smyrna is that Paul's teaching on righteousness was first personally experienced by the forbears of the Philippian Christians and that Paul's message continues to instruct the *current* Philippian believers through study of his letters. Later in his letter, Polycarp appeals to Paul's teaching on judgment as the authoritative word on the matter, even borrowing the Apostle's use of rhetorical questions in the process: "Or do we not know that 'the saints will judge the world'? So Paul teaches" (11.2). He goes on to note that the "blessed Paul labored among" the Philippians, calling attention again to the missionary activity of Paul, which goes hand-in-hand with his letter writing. As he spoke, so he wrote.

The authority of Paul's letters is also emphasized in *1 Clement*.[18] Writing to a Corinthian community recently wracked with internal divisions, the author of *1 Clement* turns to 1 Corinthians: "Take up the letter of the blessed Paul the Apostle. What did he write you at first in the beginning of the gospel? Truly he sent you a letter in the Spirit about himself and Cephas and Apollos, on account of the fact that even

---

letter as "a highly intertextual document" and argues that "Polycarp anchors his faith and his teaching in Pauline tradition."

[16] Cf. the comments in Kirk, *Departure*, 92–3; Michael W. Holmes, "Paul and Polycarp," in *Paul and the Second Century*, ed. Michael F. Bird and Joseph R. Dodson, LNTS 412 (London: T&T Clark, 2011), 64

[17] On this question, see esp. Kenneth Berding, *Polycarp and Paul: An Analysis of Their Literary & Theological Relationship in Light of Polycarp's Use of Biblical & Extrabiblical Literature*, VC Sup 62 (Leiden: Brill, 2002), 63, and Paul Hartog, *Polycarp's Epistle to the Philippians and the Martyrdom of Polycarp: Introduction, Text, and Commentary*, OAF (Oxford: Oxford University Press, 2013), 113–14.

[18] Regarding the pervasive influence of Paul on *1 Clement*, see Paul Hartog, "Peter in Paul's Churches: The Early Reception of Peter in *1 Clement* and in Polycarp's *Philippians*," in *Peter in Early Christianity*, ed. Helen K. Bond and Larry W. Hurtado (Grand Rapids, MI: Eerdmans, 2015), 168.

then you were behaving in a partisan fashion" (*1 Clem* 47.1–3). We will return to this passage below in relation to Paul's position among other apostles. The value of this passage for the present discussion, however, is that here Paul's first (extant) letter to Corinth is assumed to be available both to Clement in Rome as well as to the Corinthians. Paul's authority and message, moreover, continues to be mediated through this letter, here establishing just how far the factions Clement addresses have fallen from the ideal of unity.

The final passage in the Apostolic Fathers that appeals to Paul's authority does so without naming Paul as such. In his retelling of the story of the tree of life and tree of knowledge in Paradise, the author of the *Epistle to Diognetus* states that it is not the tree of knowledge itself that killed, but the disobedience that led to the eating (*Ep. Diog.* 12.1–2).[19] Rather, the tree of knowledge and the tree of life in Paradise symbolize the fact that "life" is revealed "through knowledge" (12.3); each needs the other. This unity of knowledge with "the true commandment leading to life," the author argues, is what Paul was concerned with when he states "Knowledge puffs up, but love edifies" (12.5; citing 1 Cor. 8.1). Paul's theological (and implicitly exegetical) authority offers the author an apostolic foundation upon which to base his retelling of Paradise and his final exhortation concerning the knowledge transmitted in the letter as a whole.[20]

6.2.2 Peter and Traditions about Jesus

In the somewhat inappropriately named "Clement's Second Letter to the Corinthians" (*2 Clement*), the writer offers a sort of homiletical address on the coming judgment and the importance of repentance.[21] Amidst a variety of appeals to Gospel material that resembles the

---

[19] The well-known and intractable question around the relation of chapters 1–10 to chapters 11–12 in this work need not detain us her; note the discussion in the introduction of Clayton N. Jefford, *The Epistle to Diognetus (with the Fragment of Quadratus): Introduction, Text, and Commentary* (Oxford: Oxford University Press, 2013). The difficulties of the date and composition of the *Epistle* only underscore the problems involved in considering the Apostolic Fathers as a unified corpus.

[20] See the discussion in Horacio E. Lona, *An Diognet: Übersetzt und erklärt*, KfA 8 (Freiburg: Herder, 2001), 343–5, who highlights certain remaining tensions in the author's appropriation of Paul, such as the rather underdeveloped role of "love" in the citation; cf. also the brief treatment in Michael F. Bird, "The Reception of Paul in the *Epistle to Diognetus*," in *Paul and the Second Century*, ed. Michael F. Bird and Joseph R. Dodson, LNTS 412 (London: T&T Clark, 2011), 75.

[21] On the difficult question of the "genre" of the work, see esp. James A. Kelhofer, "If *Second Clement* Really Were a 'Sermon,' How Would We Know and Why Would We Care? Prolegomena to Analyses of the Writing's Genre and Community," in *Early*

Synoptic Gospels, toward the beginning of the address the author brings Peter into the discussion. The exhortation, that Christians should not fear "going out from this world," is grounded in Jesus' teaching.

> For the Lord said, "You shall be like sheep in the midst of wolves." And Peter answered him, "What if the wolves tear the sheep apart?" But Jesus said to Peter, "The sheep should not fear the wolves after they are dead. You too should not fear those who kill you and then no longer have power over you. But you should fear the one who, after you die, has authority over your soul and body to throw them into fiery hell." (2 Clem. 5.2–4)

Aside from the theme of "death" that will be picked up below, it is notable that Peter is the only disciple or apostle mentioned in 2 Clement. His presence is notably minor here and his role as representative disciple may well be indebted to general tendencies in Synoptic-like material that underlie the work as a whole. In this case, however, the Synoptic parallels (Mt. 10.16, 28 and Lk.10.3; 12:4–7) do not include Peter's answer. Wilhelm Pratscher takes this passage as an instance of "a specific Peter-tradition" to which the author had access.[22] What is particularly interesting for the present argument is that Peter's presence suggests a specific and personal point of contact between Jesus' revelatory teaching and the apostolic church recently made manifest, of which the writer considers himself a part.[23]

If this mark of Peter as an authorizing figure in relation to Jesus traditions is fairly light, this role is considerably more pronounced in the fragments of Papias.[24]

Christian Communities between Ideal and Reality, ed. Mark Grundeken and Joseph Verheyden, WUNT 342 (Tübingen: Mohr Siebeck, 2015), 83–108.

[22] Wilhelm Pratscher, Der zweite Clemensbrief: Übersetzt und erklärt, KAV 3 (Göttingen: Vandenhoeck und Ruprecht, 2007), 101–2.

[23] See the comments in 2 Clem. 14.2–3 – "the books and the apostles [say that] the church is not new but is from above [or 'is recurring anew'; Gk. anōthen]. For it is spiritual as is our Jesus too. Now, he was made manifest in the last days so that he might save us. The church, being spiritual, was made manifest in the flesh of Christ…"

[24] The enumeration of Papias' fragments is difficult, and there are several competing reference systems. I follow here the most recent edition of Stephen C. Carlson, The Fragments of Papias of Hierapolis: Studies in the Receptions of a Second-Century Commentator, OECT (Oxford: Oxford University Press, 2021), who includes cross references between his Testimonia/Fragment numbering and previous reference systems.

According to Papias, an unnamed presbyter (perhaps the "presbyter" John mentioned previously in F6),[25] passed on to him that

> Mark, being an interpreter of Peter, wrote accurately (though not at all in order) whatever he [*viz.* Peter] recalled about the things said or done by the Lord. For he did not hear the Lord nor follow him but later, as I said, he followed Peter who presented his teaching according to his needs and not making something like a ordered account of the Lord's sayings.[26]

Mark's non-chronological presentation of Jesus' sayings and actions, then, were not an error ("Mark was not in error"; *ouden hēmarten Markos*) but reflected the testimony of Peter, who had heard and followed Jesus, unlike Mark. No doubt this contributed to Papias' view that Peter was among the most important "teachers of the truth" (*tois talēthē didaskousin*) about whom he sought information whenever a traveler chanced to visit Hierapolis.[27]

The link between Peter's continuing status as an authoritative teacher and handing on Jesus traditions is hardly surprising, especially among the so-called Apostolic Fathers, a collection that was first compiled by a theologically conscientious scholar in the seventeenth century. What is perhaps more interesting is that, even well beyond the boundaries of the churches represented in this collection, Peter's authority in mediating Jesus traditions is also recognized, even if variously portrayed and contested.[28] In this respect, then, the Apostolic Fathers collection turns out not to be as idiosyncratic as might otherwise have been expected.

6.3 PAUL, PETER, AND DEATH

As ubiquitous as are appeals to their teaching authority, almost as common is the link drawn between Paul, Peter, and death. Perhaps

---

[25] See the discussion of this point in Enrico Norelli, *Papia di Hierapolis, Esposizione Degli Oracoli del Signore: I frammenti*, Letture Christiane del primo millennio 36 (Milan: Figlie di San Paolo, 2005), 292–4, who thinks the identification is possible.

[26] This is Papias F4, preserved in Eusebius, *Hist. eccl.* 3.39.15–16.

[27] Papias F6, preserved in Eusebius, *Hist. eccl.* 3.39.3–4.

[28] See the discussions in Wilhelm Pratscher, "Die Bedeutung des Petrus in gnostischen Texten," *SNTU.A* 37 (2012): 111–50; Tobias Nicklas, "'Gnostic' Perspectives on Peter" and Paul Foster, "Peter in Noncanonical Traditions," in *Peter in Early Christianity*, ed. Helen K. Bond and Larry W. Hurtado (Grand Rapids, MI: Eerdmans, 2015), 196–221, 222–62.

the most famous passage on this topic among the so-called Apostolic
Fathers is found in *1 Clem.* 5. Following on from the examples of
suffering and death due to jealousy, the author of *1 Clement* turns here
to the "noble examples from our generation" (5.1) and begins with "the
good apostles" (5.3), that is, Peter and Paul.[29]

> There is Peter, who because of unjust jealousy bore up under
> hardships not just once or twice, but many times; having thus
> borne his witness he exited into the glorious place he earned.
> Because of jealousy and strife Paul displayed the prize for
> endurance. Seven times he bore chains; he was sent into exile and
> stoned; he served as a herald in both the East and the West; and he
> received the noble reputation for his faith. He taught righteousness
> to the whole world and when he came to the limits of the West he
> bore witness to the rulers, and so he was released from the world
> and taken up into the holy place, the greatest example of
> endurance.[30]

The "good apostles" faithfully endured jealousy and physical hardship
and in that way attained their holy or glorious place. While this passage
could have been discussed in the previous section, Clement's emphasis
here is on their death.[31] Or, perhaps more accurately, the author is
concerned not about their death as such but about their *escape* through
death to their appointed places: Peter "exits" and Paul is "released from
the world and taken up." Even so, the link between their faithful
teaching work – Peter "bore witness" and Paul "taught righteousness"
and "bore witness" – and their death is fundamental to the author's
exhortation. If factionalism and jealousy are community-destroying
vices, the correct response is to bear up under such injustice and
complete one's athletic competition (cf. *1 Clem* 5.1).

---

[29] Both Richard J. Bauckham, "The Martyrdom of Peter in Early Christian Literature,"
ANRW 26.1 (1992): 556, and Hermut Löhr, "Zur Paulus-Notiz in 1 Clem 5,5–7," in
Das Ende des Paulus: Historische, theologische und literaturgeschichtliche Aspekte,
ed. F.W. Horn, BZNW 106 (Berlin: De Gruyter, 2001), 199–200 argue for a double
pattern of seven martyrs, with the first set based on scriptural examples and the
second set coming from "our generation."

[30] *1 Clem.* 5.1–7 (trans. modified from Ehrman, *The Apostolic Fathers,* 1.43, 45).

[31] The impact of this has led some to view the term *martyreō* here as already serving as
a technical term for martyrdom (e.g., Bauckham, "Martyrdom of Peter," 559), though
the majority of scholars argue that such a technical use is a later development (a
point that applies in the case of Ignatius as well); see Eastman, "Paul as Martyr," 3;
Löhr, "Paulus-Notiz," 209; Horacio E. Lona, *Der erste Clemensbrief: Übersetzt und
erklärt,* KAV 2 (Göttingen: Vandenhoeck & Ruprecht, 1998), 160.

Beyond *1 Clement*, the theme of death accompanies both Peter and Paul throughout the rest of the Apostolic Fathers who appeal to them. In fact, this link is so close that the passages surveyed here have already been covered above, almost without exception. In Ignatius' letter to the Ephesians, Paul is one who has already been "taken up into God" after being "approved" (*memartyrēmenos; Eph.* 12.2).[32] In his letter to the Smyrneans, the Syrian bishop relates that Jesus' appearance in the flesh led the apostles – represented by Peter –to "despise" death because "they were beyond death."[33] As noted earlier, Peter also stands for the disciples of Jesus in *2 Clem.* 5, where the theme of death arises again: Peter engages with Jesus in a short dialogue about fear of suffering and death.[34]

If Peter can stand for the other disciples in their stance toward death for Ignatius, for Polycarp it is Paul who holds this paradigmatic place.[35] Paul's ability to instruct the Philippians does not end, for Polycarp, with his ministry and letters, but includes his death among other martyrs. Offering examples of patient endurance (*hypomenein*), the Smyrnean bishop begins with his contemporaries – Ignatius, Zosimus and Rufus – and culminates with "Paul himself and the rest of the apostles" (*Phil.* 9.1). Their example shows that such endurance is not empty but is ultimately rewarded by attaining one's "earned place" (9.2). For Polycarp, Paul teaches and exhorts in his ministry while present, in his letters while absent, and through his death itself in his ultimate absence.

6.4 PAUL AND PETER AMONG THE OTHER APOSTLES

A recurrent aspect of the Pauline and Petrine profile in the passages discussed above is the fact that each apostle is enmeshed in a network of other apostles. Peter and Paul appear together in Ign. *Rom.* 4 and *1 Clem.* 5. Peter is among "the other apostles" and Paul with "the rest

---

[32] Ign., *Eph.* 12.2.

[33] Ign. *Smyrn.* 3.2. While the "freedom" of Peter and Paul in Ign. *Rom.* 4 may refer to their deaths (so Eastman, "Paul as Martyr," 10; Kirk, *Departure*, 82, and Smith, "Ministry, Martyrdom," 38–9), others consider it a reference to their apostolic freedom (e.g., Bauckham, "Martyrdom of Peter," 566 and Schoedel, *Ignatius of Antioch*, 176–7).

[34] Pratscher, *Clemensbrief*, 100 argues that martyrdom is not at issue in this passage but rather death *simpliciter*. The context of fearing "wolves," however, suggests at least a context of possible persecution and martyrdom, even if the relevance of the passage is not limited to that context.

[35] So Lindemann, *Paulus im ältesten Christentum*, 89.

of the apostles" in Ign. *Smryn.* 3 and Poly. *Phil.* 9, respectively. Paul also appears among "approved apostles" in *1 Clem.* 47. This point stands in some contrast with many contemporary presentations of Paul, in which his evident conflict with Peter in Antioch (cf. Gal 2, linked, moreover, with "certain people from James") and potentially non- (even anti-) Pauline threads in Matthew or James signify a deep and abiding conflict between the Apostle and the Gentiles and other early Christian leaders. For these early Christian writers, however, even if Paul is "the (blessed) apostle," he is not so to the point of critique or rejection of other apostles.[36] The same goes, *mutatis mutandis*, for Peter in these texts.

There remains, however, a difficult question about the relation of Peter and Paul in *1 Clem.* 47, namely, whether the passage includes a reference to Peter at all. Insofar as that passage relies on the opening chapters of 1 Corinthians, it would seem obvious that "Cephas" should be identified as "Peter" and that, therefore, he features among the "approved apostles."[37] What is less clear is whether the author of *1 Clement* took such a view. A variety of early Christian writers certainly did not do so. Clement of Alexandria, for instance, identified Cephas with one of the seventy disciples rather than Peter.[38] The second-century *Epistula Apostolorum* also distinguishes between the two figures among the apostles.[39] The author of *1 Clement* does not clearly identify Cephas as Peter, nor does he clearly distinguish them one from the other. Given that other early Christians considered Cephas a separate apostolic figure, it may be the case that *1 Clem.* 47 provides a false positive for the emerging profile of Peter in the early church, at least insofar as it does not necessarily constitute an

---

[36] For an extended discussion of the difference between an ecclesially integrated and a conflictual portrayal of Paul, with consideration of their exegetical foundations, see Benjamin A. Edsall, *The Reception of Paul and Early Christian Initiation: History and Hermeneutics* (Cambridge: Cambridge University Press, 2019), 201–250.

[37] This majority view of scholars, suggested by the evidence of 1 Cor. 15.5 and Gal. 1–2 and by the traditions preserved in Mt. 16.18 and Jn. 1.42; e.g., Lindemann, *Clemensbriefe*, 139. The counter-reading offered in Bart D. Ehrman, "Cephas and Peter," *JBL* 109 (1990): 463–74 is less than compelling, though his collection of early Christian texts that distinguish between Cephas and Peter is useful.

[38] From book five of Clement's lost *Hypotyposes*; Eusebius, *Hist. eccl.* 1.12.2. (ed. Gustave Bardy, *Eusèbe de Césarée: Histoire ecclésiastique*, SC 31, 41, 55 [Paris: Cerf, 1952–8]).

[39] *Ep. apost.* 2.1 (according to the enumeration in Francis Watson, *An Apostolic Gospel: The 'Epistula Apostolorum' in Literary Context*, SNTSMS 179 (Cambridge: Cambridge University Press, 2020). Note the examples gathered in Ehrman, "Cephas and Peter," 463–6.

intentional reference to him. Even so, Paul would still stand with an (admittedly different) apostle in *1 Clem.* 47, approving Apollos as a non-apostolic teacher.

Within the Apostolic Fathers, Peter and Paul are representative apostles among a larger group. They are, moreover, viewed as exemplars of the pastoral and theological views of the authors who appeal to them. While this may seem hardly surprising, it is worth remembering that neither Peter nor Paul escaped criticism from other early Christian sources.[40] At least for the authors of *1 Clement* and the *Epistle to Diognetus*, Ignatius, and Polycarp, though, Paul and Peter were unproblematically *their* apostles, and their appeals to them are not evidently tainted by a concern over his use by other conflicting early Christian groups.

6.5 THE DEARTH OF JAMES IN THE APOSTOLIC FATHERS

In view of the relative (if limited) popularity of Paul and Peter among the Apostolic Fathers, the absence of James the brother of Jesus stands in stark relief. As indicated earlier, this omission is not at all matched by a broader account of second-century Christian literature. The possible mentions of James in the Apostolic Fathers are found in the fragments of Papias, which present their own difficulties. The first fragment, discussed earlier with respect to Peter, mentions a certain "James" among the other figures about whom Papias would seek information from passers-through in Hierapolis. As Eusebius preserves it, Papias wrote,

> Whenever someone arrived who had been a companion of one of the elders, I would carefully inquire after their words, what Andrew or Peter had said, or what Philip or what Thomas had said, or James or John or Matthew or any of the other disciples of the Lord, and what things Ariston and the elder John, disciples of the Lord, were saying.[41]

---

[40] Other early Christian writers variously value, critique, or reject Peter and or Paul; e.g., in the critique of Peter at the end of the *Gospel of Mary* (cf. the Petrine-critical readings discussed in Pratscher, "Bedeutung," 113–28) or the possible identification of Paul with Simon Magus in the Pseudo-Clementine literature, though that reading has been strongly contested by Bockmuehl, *The Remembered Peter*, 94–113.

[41] Papias F6.4 in Eusebius, *Hist. eccl.*. 3.39.3–4.

In the context of Eusebius' citation, he is trying to dissociate Papias from the *apostolic* figure of John – against Irenaeus' account in *Adv. haer.* 5.33.4 – in an effort to delegitimize Papias' millenarian eschatology. Hence the distinction between the two different Johannine figures.[42] What is unclear, however, is the identity of various of these other figures. While they look to parallel various lists of apostles elsewhere in early Christianity, the term "apostle" does not occur in the extant Papian fragments, and it is difficult to know exactly how these specific figures dovetail with his (apparent) overarching concern to establish his own testimony as founded on the "living and lasting voice." If the parallels with other apostolic lists are relevant, especially as extant in the four now-canonical Gospels, the juxtaposition of James with John may well suggest that the former is James the son of Zebedee.[43] On the other hand, it is unclear what sort of traditions James the brother of John would have left behind, given his early death reported in Acts 12.2, that a Christian in the early second century would still be interested in gathering. By contrast, James the brother of Jesus long held an influential position in the Jerusalem community, whose profile generated a large amount of literature and whose death was noted by Josephus (*Ant.* 20.197–203). The identity of "James" in this fragment, then, is uncertain.[44]

The question remains: why does James not feature significantly in the Apostolic Fathers?[45] There are perhaps two partial answers. The first is that, as noted above, the Apostolic Fathers is a fairly arbitrary collection of early Christian writings, a modern scholarly construct

---

[42] I am indebted to Stephen Carlson for this general point. On the significance of the aorist ("said") and present tense (saying) of *legō* in this fragment, see esp. the arguments of Stephen C. Carlson, "Papias's Appeal to the 'Living and Lasting Voice' over Books," in *Rise of the Early Christian Intellectual*, ed. Lewis O. Ayres and Clifton Ward, AZK (Berlin: De Gruyter, 2020).

[43] This is the connection and conclusion drawn by Norelli, for example; Norelli, *Papia*, 269–70; cf. also Körtner, *Papias*, 177.

[44] The "James" in Papias F7, preserved by Philip of Side, is from an epitome of Eusebius' *Ecclesiastical History*, but there James is explicitly identified as the "brother of John." Carlson considers this a dubious fragment, owing to its introduction of certain differences to Eusebius' account, on which it is clearly dependent, from some other unknown source; see Carlson, *Fragments of Papias*, ad loc. Earlier editions of Papias included a further excerpt that explicitly mentions James the brother of Jesus, but it is from a medieval lexicographer by the same name; cf. Norelli, *Papia*, 26 n. 24.

[45] Notably the survey of James's early Christian profile in John Painter, *Just James: The Brother of Jesus in History and Tradition* (Columbia: University of South Carolina Press, 2004), which does not mention the Apostolic Fathers.

from the start.[46] While the works now conventionally included involve a certain cross-section of genre and theological emphases, they are not ultimately representative of the breadth of early Christianity. Moreover, and as a second partial answer, early on James was associated with Jewish-Christian groups, as seen in Acts, the Pseudo-Clementines and even as early as Galatians.[47] The clear non- or even anti-Judaic bent of some of these writers – for instance, in the case of *The Epistle of Barnabas* and Ignatius – may be related to their omission of any concern for James. That said, James was by no means *exclusively* associated with Jewish-Christian tendencies, a fact that perhaps limits the impact of this second explanation. Indeed, the *Gospel of Thomas*, not known for its affinities with Judaism, famously identifies "James the Just" as a centrally important leader among the apostles (*GThom* 12.2) even while implicitly criticizing Peter for his ignorance (114.1–3).[48] Ultimately, however one decides the matter, the lack of appeals to James in the Apostolic Fathers remains something of an anomaly in an account of early Christian writings.

6.6 CONCLUSION

The collection of the so-called Apostolic Fathers, then, offer a perspective on Paul, Peter, and James that is at once in keeping with certain broader early Christian trends – especially with respect to the former two – and also idiosyncratic in its almost complete omission of James. For Ignatius, Polycarp, *1* and *2 Clement*, the *Epistle to Diognetus*, and for Papias, Peter and/or Paul offer examples in their apostolic teaching authority, in their bold approach to death and attaining their allotted place thereafter, and in their relation to other apostolic and non-apostolic leadership figures. For other texts in the Apostolic Fathers, however, even Paul and Peter are absent. At this stage in the development of early Christianity – roughly, the first half of the second

---

[46] See the comments and references in n. 6 above.

[47] One may think here also of the figure of James in the *Protoevangelium of James*. The term "Jewish Christian" is not without its problems. There is no space here to develop an alternative, but see esp. the discussion in James Carleton Paget, *Jews, Christians and Jewish Christians in Antiquity*, WUNT 251 (Tübingen: Mohr Siebeck, 2010), 289–320.

[48] The authoritative role of James is also present in several (other) texts discovered at Nag Hammadi, e.g., *Apocryphon of James* (NHC I,2: 1,1–16,30) or the two sequential works simply entitled *The Apocalypse of James* (NHC V,3: 24,10–44,10; NHC V,4: 44,11–63,32).

century – it appears, then, that appeals even to such "pillars" as these were not always deemed necessary. An ambiguous result for an ambiguous scholarly collection, as one might expect, after all.

FURTHER READING

Bockmuehl, Markus N.A. *Simon Peter in Scripture and Memory: The New Testament Apostle in the Early Church.* Grand Rapids, MI: Baker Academic, 2012.

Gregory, Andrew F., and Christopher M. Tuckett, ed. *The Reception of the New Testament in the Apostolic Fathers.* Oxford; New York: Oxford University Press, 2005.

Hartog, Paul. *Polycarp and the New Testament: The Occasion, Rhetoric, Theme, and Unity of the Epistle to the Philippians and its Allusions to New Testament Literature.* WUNT II/134. Tübingen: J.C.B. Mohr, 2002.

Kirk, Alexander N. *The Departure of an Apostle: Paul's Death Anticipated and Remembered.* WUNT II/406. Tübingen: Mohr Siebeck, 2015.

Lindemann, Andreas. *Paulus im ältesten Christentum: d. Bild d. Apostels u. d. Rezeption d. paulin. Theologie in d. frühchristl. Literatur bis Marcion.* BHT 58. Tübingen: Mohr Siebeck, 1979.

Marguerat, Daniel. "Paul after Paul: A (Hi)story of Reception," in *Paul in Acts and Paul in his Letters.* WUNT 310. Tübingen: Mohr Siebeck, 2013, 1–21.

Nicklas, Tobias. "'Gnostic' Perspectives on Peter," in *Peter in Early Christianity*, ed. Helen K. Bond and Larry W. Hurtado. Grand Rapids, MI: Eerdmans, 2015, 196–221.

Painter, John. *Just James: The Brother of Jesus in History and Tradition.* 2nd ed. Columbia: University of South Carolina Press, 2004.

Pervo, Richard I. *The Making of Paul: Constructions of the Apostle in Early Christianity.* Minneapolis, MN: Fortress Press, 2010.

7 Between Ekklēsia and State: The Apostolic Fathers and the Roman Empire

ANDREW GREGORY

7.1 INTRODUCTION

The discrete texts known collectively as the Apostolic Fathers may each be dated somewhere between the end of the first century CE and the end of the second century, with the majority written in the first half of the second century, variously in Rome or in Roman provinces around the eastern Mediterranean.

This means that these texts are all products of the High Roman Empire.[1] It is therefore possible to place them in a shared social and political context, broadly understood, provided that we recognize that the Roman Empire operated and was experienced in different ways both at different times and in different parts of the broad territories over which it ruled. As the Roman Empire extended around the eastern Mediterranean it subsumed regions with their own traditions and customs, but which had been Hellenized by Alexander the Great and his successors. Thus Greek served as a *lingua franca*, and there were already ruler cults that honoured the reigning king with forms of veneration that paved the way for the spread of the Roman imperial cult from the first century CE, which in turn helped to establish a sense of Roman rule and order that accommodated allowed local traditions and customs within an overarching Roman framework.

Roman armies stationed around the Empire and a system of rule by officials sent from Rome helped to maintain stability and order, and good roads and a sea kept free of pirates facilitated communication and trade. Political and religious stability went hand in hand, and networks of patronage that extended from the Emperor and his court to individual households across the Empire helped to preserve and disseminate

[1] Brief introductions include C. Kelly, *The Roman Empire: A Very Short Introduction* (Oxford: Oxford University Press, 2006), and H.-J. Klauck, "The Roman Empire," in *Cambridge History of Christianity: Origins to Constantine*, ed. M.M. Mitchell and F.M. Young (Cambridge: Cambridge University Press, 2006), 69–83.

Roman ideals of *Romanitas* ("Roman cultural identity and values") and *pietas* (which may be defined as "the typical Roman attitude of dutiful respect towards gods, fatherland, and parents and other kinsmen").[2] All subjects of the Empire were expected to conform to such ideals (although clearly there was never a time when all of them did), or at least to coexist peaceably within this framework, and Roman officials moved quickly when they sensed that order and peace might be threatened. Broadly speaking, this is the second-century imperial setting for the Apostolic Fathers, all of which were written in a Greek-speaking Roman Empire.

Moving beyond this very general and outline picture, it is possible to identify two types of evidence that each shed light on the political context of the communities in and for which these texts were written. The first are non-Christian sources that show how some elite Roman authors and officials viewed followers of Jesus, and how they responded when they encountered them. The second is a range of evidence from Christian sources that may antedate the Apostolic Fathers, or that are approximately contemporary with or even slightly later than them. Both sets of evidence are discussed below, before we turn to the texts of the Apostolic Fathers themselves.

7.2 NON-CHRISTIAN SOURCES

Christians followed a leader who had died by crucifixion on the authority of the Roman governor of the Roman province of Judea. This was a form of execution reserved for those who were not Roman citizens, and that was considered particularly brutal and degrading. Early Christian sources try to apportion responsibility more to jealous Jewish rivals than to the Roman authorities, and the fact that Jesus' followers were not executed alongside him raises questions about whether he was really seen as a threat to Roman order and stability. But neither of these factors detracts from the fact that any Greek or Roman polytheists who knew anything about the practices or beliefs of those who followed Jesus were likely aware that Christians followed a man who had been put to death by a Roman official. It seems difficult to overestimate the importance of this point; it need not follow that all Romans in positions

---

[2] So W.C. Greene and J. Scheid, who provide a useful brief discussion in their entry on *"pietas"* in *The Oxford Classical Dictionary*, 1148. At greater length, see T.C. Hoklotubbe, *Civilized Piety: The Rhetoric of Pietas in the Pastoral Epistles and the Roman Empire* (Waco, TX: Baylor University Press, 2017).

of authority will have seen all followers of Jesus as politically suspect or subversive, but the manner of Jesus' death likely raised questions for those who encountered his followers in official contexts or as neighbors in the places where they lived or worked.

Some accounts of the relationship between early Christians and the Roman state present the former as an oppressed group whom the Roman authorities sought out and persecuted on a frequent or regular basis. Yet most scholars now agree that there is virtually no evidence to suggest that second-century Roman emperors or their representatives were involved in the systematic persecution of Christians.

One Roman author who provides evidence of one instance of persecution is the Roman historian Tacitus, who was writing c. 115 CE, toward the beginning of the period when some of the Apostolic Fathers may be dated. In his *Annals*, which cover the period 14–68 CE, he refers to an instance in 64 CE when the Emperor Nero tortured and executed an "immense multitude" of Christians (*Ann.* 15.44). But it is important to note that he presents this not as an example of any systematic persecution of Christians but as act of expediency on the part of a cruel and capricious emperor who picked on an unpopular group in order to divert attention from reports that he was himself responsible for the Great Fire of Rome, which caused widespread destruction in the city.

Also significant is Tacitus' testimony to a general dislike for Christians, whom he describes as hated for their abominations, and who he says were convicted not for the crime of arson, but for hatred of the human race. Such statements show that Christians were widely disliked, and Tacitus does not question this view, since he refers to Christians as criminals who deserved extreme and exemplary punishment. Yet he also notes their non-Roman origins, which may suggest that he saw them less as a movement that was significant in its own right, than yet another example of a foreign group who brought trouble to Rome, and he describes them as a "deadly *superstitio*" – a pejorative term used of those who did not conform to the norms of the civic ideal of *pietas* and socially expected ways of honoring the gods,[3] and that Tacitus also used in an earlier work, his *Histories*, to describe Jewish customs and beliefs (*Hist.* 5.8.3, 5.13.1).

---

[3] For a brief discussion, see the entry on *"superstitio"* by J. Scheid in *The Oxford Classical Dictionary*, 1413. Longer discussions include D.B. Martin, *Inventing Superstition: From the Hippocratics to the Christians* (Cambridge, MA: Harvard University Press, 2004).

A second piece of evidence relating to Nero's treatment of the Christians may be found in a biography of Nero written by the Roman author Suetonius, who also wrote in the early second century, and had served as a Roman provincial official in the eastern part of the Empire. As does Tacitus, Suetonius refers to Christians by that name and says that they received punishment under Nero; he adds that they were "a class of men given to a new and wicked *superstitio*" (*Ner.* 16.2). Once again there is no evidence to suggest any systematic persecution of Christians, and they are said to hold a *superstitio* (on which see above, and note 3).

The third and most extensive source of evidence for how Roman officials viewed Christians is found in a letter written by Pliny the Younger to the Emperor Trajan (*Ep.* 10.96), and in the reply from Trajan (or from one of his court officials, writing in his name; Pliny, *Ep.* 10.97). Pliny writes as Governor of the Roman province of Bithynia, and his letter may be dated to 112 CE. He explains that he has never taken part in any investigation of Christians (which may imply that others had), for which reason he asks the Emperor's advice on what to do. Yet Pliny (who wrote his letters with a view to their publication) has not been idle in the meantime; he has already executed some people who refused to deny that they were Christians and ordered others who were not only similarly stubborn but also Roman citizens to be sent to Rome, and he has released others who denied that they were Christians and agreed to pray to the gods, to worship their statues, and to partici-pate in the imperial cult – things that, he believed, Christians could not be made to do. Thus he notes that what he describes as their "perverse and extravagant *superstitio*" prevented Christians from participating in civil religion, and claims that their refusal to do so had been sufficiently widespread to have an economic impact on those who had struggled to sell animals for sacrifice, at least until Pliny had intervened. As did Tacitus, Pliny also referred to this *superstitio* of the Christians as contagious; it threatens not only the economy but also Roman order, and is something harmful from which the body politic needs to be protected.

Pliny's letter reveals not only acquaintance with various Christian practices and beliefs, which he recounts to the Emperor, but also that he was not aware of any policy about how they were to be treated. Trajan's reply, which Pliny published in his collection of his own letters, con-firms that no such policy existed – and that although Christians were not to be sought out, they should be punished if they are accused and convicted, presumably on the charge of being Christians. Yet those who deny that they are Christians, and worship the gods, are not to be punished, regardless of how they may have conducted themselves in the past. Thus Trajan suggests that the issue at stake is Christian refusal to participate in civic religion, which is what might draw them to the attention of Roman officials; the refusal of Christians to supplicate to the Roman gods, as Trajan required them to do, put them outside the bounds of acceptable religious practice, and outside the bounds of what the society in which they lived could tolerate, since the refusal of Christians to participate in the imperial cult and civic religion was a form of disloyalty or even treason. Once again there is no evidence of any official or systematic persecution – which remains the case until the persecutions ordered by the Emperor Decius in the mid-third century CE – but it is easy to see why Christians may nevertheless have been aware that they were vulnerable to local and sporadic attack because of their refusal to engage with important aspects of public life, with consequences for non-citizens that were both summary and swift.

7.3 CHRISTIAN SOURCES

A number of Christian sources may also help to illuminate the political and social context of the Apostolic Fathers, since they too were written at a similar time and in a similar setting. These include a number of texts that came to be included in the New Testament, some of which may be earlier than or contemporary with some of the Apostolic Fathers. Also relevant are two other bodies of Christian literature that postdate the New Testament and shed further light on the imperial setting of the Apostolic Fathers and on answers to questions about how some Christians understood their place in society. One consists of a number of writings about apostles and other Christians who came to prominence in different ways, including both apocryphal acts and early martyrdom accounts. The others are the texts referred to as the work of the Christian Apologists. These may be dated from the mid-second century onwards, so they may postdate most or all of the Apostolic Fathers, but may nevertheless contribute to our understanding of their context in the Roman Empire.

7.3.1 The New Testament
Of particular interest is the Acts of the Apostles, which offers our earliest narrative account of the growth and spread of the early Jesus movement from Jerusalem and Judea westward through parts of the Eastern Empire and eventually to Rome. Although traditionally dated

to the late first century it reflects a number of interests found in the Apostolic Fathers, and a growing number of scholars are arguing that it should be dated to the early second century.[4] Acts was written to continue the account that begins in the Gospel according to Luke, so it presupposes the death of Jesus, which is part of the message that his early followers proclaim. It also includes an account of the death of Stephen, usually regarded as the first Christian martyr, as well as other incidents in which followers of Jesus face trial or arrest.

However, the opposition to followers of Jesus that Luke portrays comes not from Roman officials but from Jewish leaders in Jerusalem and elsewhere, so Acts provides a very different perspective from Tacitus, Pliny, and Suetonius on questions about whether and why followers of Jesus may have faced violent opposition or persecution. Roman officials, in fact, are presented as generally not hostile to followers of Jesus. When Paul is accused of taking away trade from temples not only in Ephesus but elsewhere in the province of Asia Minor, a Roman official intervenes to support him, in sharp contrast to the response of Pliny in similar circumstances (Acts 19.21–41). Another Roman official, apparently favorable to what he has heard from Paul, refers to his beliefs as matters of *desdaimonia*, the Greek word that corresponds to the Latin word *superstitio*, but suggests that differences between Paul and his opponents reflect different types of Jewish belief, rather than the emergence of anything new (Acts 23.19). Here, as elsewhere, Roman officials are portrayed as witnesses to the belief that the Roman Empire has nothing to fear from the followers of Jesus (Acts 18.12–15, 19.40, 23.29, 25.18–19, 26.31–2, 28.18), whose leader was himself an innocent man (*dikaios*, Lk. 24.47). Thus Acts foregrounds claims about the political innocence of the followers of Jesus, despite their leader having been executed by a Roman official, and reflects early Christian anxieties about opposition that they faced from Jews, against whom and in distinction from whom they may have wished to differentiate themselves. The book ends with Paul having traveled to Rome, under a Roman guard, as would also Ignatius of Antioch.

It is possible that a fear of Roman persecution lies behind the Revelation to John, since apocalyptic texts often reflect times of uncertainty and oppression. But while its apocalyptic imagery and depiction of cosmic conflict point to a Christian self-understanding and identity that is rooted in opposition to the world, Revelation includes no clear or

---

[4] See especially Richard Pervo, *Dating Acts: Between the Evangelists and the Apologists* (Santa Rosa, CA: Polebridge Press, 2006).

unambiguous evidence for any historical persecution from Rome, but does appear to reflect conflict between followers of Jesus and other Jews (Rev. 2.9).

Concerns about Jewish persecution are also reflected in sayings of Jesus in the Gospels (e.g. Mt. 5.10–11; Mk. 13.11–13; Lk. 12.51–3; Jn. 15.18–20) and in a number of letters included in the New Testament. Thus we may note not only references to Jewish persecution in 1 Thessalonians, often thought to be the earliest of Paul's letters, but also in texts that are usually dated later, including 1 Peter, the Pastoral Letters and perhaps the Letter to the Hebrews. Questions may be asked about the extent to which such references reflect external realities or the anxieties and rhetorical construction of their authors. However, as with the threat of Roman persecution, we may note that even one or two instances of violent opposition may have cast a long and anxious shadow over members of a movement that believed themselves to be both vulnerable and liable to persecution by others.

Yet references to suffering or persecution are not the only way in which these writings reflect a sense that followers of Jesus were part of a distinct movement that differentiated itself not only from Greek and Roman polytheists but also from Jews, from whom the first followers of Jesus emerged, and from whom some of his later followers sought to differentiate themselves so that Jews and Christians became increasingly recogniable as two different groups – the former as a religion rooted in an ethnic identity and the later as a group based on practice and belief but consisting of adherents from different ethnic groups.

7.3.2 Apocryphal Acts and Martyrdoms

Apocryphal acts are often treated alongside other texts also described as Early Christian Apocrypha or New Testament Apocrypha, whereas martyrdoms are treated as early forms of hagiography, or writings about the saints. Yet both types of literature feature Christians who testify publicly to their faith, and some of the acts include accounts of the martyrdoms of their protagonists, so it seems reasonable to treat them together. Five texts are often referred to as the major apocryphal acts, and are dated variously to the late second or the early third century. This means that they are each almost certainly later than most or all of the Apostolic Fathers, but they may nevertheless help to illuminate their political and social context insofar as they may point to issues that may have been current already in the period before they were written.

One feature that is found in a number of these texts, and may be illustrated from the *Acts of Paul* (which may be dated to the late second century, or possibly before, and is often considered the earliest of the apocryphal acts), is the way in which Roman emperors or other officials are portrayed in a negative light, in contrast to their often positive portrayal in the Acts of the Apostles. Their weakness may be seen, for example, in their inability to control women who are converted by the teaching of the apostles and who then either refuse to marry men to whom they are betrothed or refuse to continue sexual relations with their husbands or with other men. The most prominent example in the *Acts of Paul* is that of Thecla (in *Acts of Paul* 3, also known as the *Acts of Paul and Thecla*), who comes to faith through the preaching of Paul and refuses to marry Thamyris, a leading figure in Iconium, to whom she was betrothed. That this should be seen as a challenge to the social order of the city, and not just as a personal affront to Thamyris is seen in his decision to bring the matter to the Roman governor Castellius, who condemns Thecla to be burned, but is prevented from doing so when God sends rain and hail that extinguishes the funeral pyre on which she was condemned to die. Thus both Thamyris and Castellius are frustrated, and Thecla is able to follow Paul, proclaim the gospel, and resist further threats to her chastity and maintain her autonomy until she dies. A similar threat to domestic and social order may be seen in the text's account of Artemilla and Eubula in Ephesus (*Acts of Paul* 7), whose devotion to Paul leads them to defy their husbands, who out of jealousy try to have Paul killed, only to be thwarted. Once again, allegiance to Christ or to his representative challenges the institution of the household and through it the wider social and political order in which wives obeyed their husbands; the contrast between the portrayal of independently minded women like Thecla, Artemilla, and Eubula and the submissive wives presupposed in or prescribed by household codes and similar texts is very stark.

Also noteworthy in the *Acts of Paul*, in the section that deals with Paul's martyrdom (*Acts of Paul* 11, also known as the *Martyrdom of Paul*), is its account of an encounter between Paul, Nero, and Patroclus the emperor's cupbearer. Paul raises Patroclus from the dead, and when Nero learns that he is alive he summons his slave and asks who has made him alive. Patroclus replies that it was Jesus Christ, the king of the ages, who destroys all kingdoms under heaven and for whom Patroclus will now serve as a soldier, since he raised him from the dead. These words, spoken by a member of the emperor's household, challenge both the emperor and the whole imperial order, and lead to the death of Paul, who like Patroclus presents Jesus as a king greater than Nero. Here we see an explicit challenge to the imperial order, coupled with a negative portrait of an emperor lacking in self-control, whom his own officials had to stop from killing Christians without a proper trial.

Similar accounts are also found in texts that focus entirely on the martyrdom of their subject or subjects. Among them is the *Martyrdom of Polycarp*, which is included among the Apostolic Fathers, and has therefore been more widely read than other less well-known accounts, often known as martyr acts. They may be compared not only to accounts of martyrdoms found in apocryphal acts but also to the work of the Apologists, and are influenced by earlier Jewish and pagan accounts as well as by Christian texts. Those that may be dated to the middle of the second century witness not only to the sporadic persecution that they depict but to the long and pervasive shadow that it cast over the developing church and those who in their writings helped to develop and to shape Christian self-understanding and identity in the different forms that it took.

7.3.3 The Apologists

The final Christian texts to be noted as potential evidence for the political and social context of the Apostolic Fathers are those written by Apologists, authors who presented defences of Christianity that were addressed to Roman officials or other non-Christian readers, even if their most likely readers were Christians. They include Aristides, Justin Martyr, Tatian, Theophilus of Antioch, Melito, and Athenagoras, as well as the author of the *Epistle of Diognetus* and Quadratus, each of whom is often included among the Apostolic Fathers.

The most relevant for our purposes is Justin Martyr, author of the *Dialogue with Trypho* and of one or two apologies, because he may be reliably dated to the mid-second century, and because some of his work survives. His *1 Apology*, addressed to the Emperor Antoninus Pius and his sons Marcus Aurelius and Lucius Verus, the Senate and all the Roman people, may be dated c. 151–155 CE and his *2 Apology*, probably written as an appendix or supplement to the *1 Apology*, slightly later. Relevant themes include a response to charges or slanders against Christians (*1 Apol.* 3–12), and the demand that Christians should not be punished simply for "the name" (i.e., for being Christians), but only if they are tried and found guilty of particular offences (*1 Apol.* 4). Justin also argues that Christians are not atheists, but worship the one true God (*1 Apol.* 6–10, 13), and that they are loyal to the emperor, and are his helpers and allies in the cause of peace, which is consistent with their desire for the kingdom of God (*1 Apol.* 11–12). He also addresses a specific instance of persecution arising from the case of a woman who became a Christian and divorced her husband (*2 Apol.* 1–2).

7.4 THE APOSTOLIC FATHERS

It is difficult to reach firm views on questions about where and when many of the writings of the Apostolic Fathers were written. I make no attempt to do so here, but instead arrange the texts by reference to how much they seem to say about the relationship between the community that they address, or in which they were written, and the wider world, with particular reference to the Roman Empire. I begin with those that say little or nothing, and progress to those that address more explicitly questions about how the emerging Christian community reflected or addressed in the text might engage with its social environment and political context.[5] None was written to address this question in the way that this chapter seeks to ask it, so it should come as no surprise that some of these texts address it only obliquely or not at all.

7.4.1 The *Didache*

The *Didache*, in which we find both ethical instruction and a concern for church order, appears to have been written to addressees who were very Jewish in outlook, although they also wished to differentiate themselves from Jews in at least some respects (8.1–2). The community whose concerns its author or complier addresses is identified as the church (*ekklēsia*, 4.14), met together on the Lord's Day (14.1) and had recognized leaders and teachers (10.7–13.7, 15.1–2). At one point the author draws on traditional "Two Ways" material that refers to outsiders as Gentiles or pagans (*ethnē*), and he enjoins those whom he addresses to avoid evil behavior including sexual immorality and idolatry (5.1), which in some Jewish traditions were seen as distinctively Gentile vices. There is little other reference to life outside the bounds of the community (imagined or real), although in traditional material the author appears to instruct his audience to go for two miles when forced to go one (1.4, cf. Mt. 5.41), which is usually interpreted as a command to cooperate or collaborate willingly with Roman soldiers who compel others to do their bidding. Thus the author appear to be aware of the

---

[5] I omit the fragments of Papias, since none address these questions.

presence of the Roman authorities in ways that could impinge on the daily life of his community, even if he refers to them only obliquely, and his text (which may draw on a range of sources) appears to reflect a community that already had a clear sense of its own identity, or was written in order to help to create such a sense.

Yet even if the *Didache* is largely inward-looking, its author or compiler recognizes that there is more to life than the present, for eschatological judgment is yet to come (16.4–8). This claim provides motivation for ethical living in the present, and reminds the community that its allegiance is to the Lord who will come upon the clouds of heaven (16.8). His coming will bring to an end the rule of "the deceiver of the world" into whose hands the whole world will be delivered (16.4), but the text does not allow us to identify who this figure is; the author makes no explicit reference to or rejection of Roman rule, and it seems difficult to know whether any such anti-imperial critique is implied.

7.4.2 The *Letter of Barnabas*

The *Letter of Barnabas* appears to be addressed to a community whose self-understanding is constructed or developed in contrast to Judaism, which some of its members appear to find very attractive. As does the *Didache*, *Barnabas* draws on a "Two Ways" tradition as part of its moral instruction, and it reflects a thoroughgoing ethical concern that it presents within an apocalyptic eschatological perspective. Like the *Didache*, it instructs readers living in the present (which its author characterizes as the present evil age, 2.1, 4.1, 4.9) to live in such a way that they are prepared for the arrival of the age to come (4.1) and the judgment that it brings (4.12, 5.7, 15.5, 21.6). Thus followers of Jesus, who the author distinguishes sharply from Jews (whether actual historical figures, or a literary foil) owe their ultimate allegiance to no earthly power or ruler, but there is no explicit rejection of or antipathy toward Roman rule.

It is possible that there is an anti-imperial edge to the reference to "one who is at work who has power" in the context of these evil days (4.1), and that some of the letter's polemic against sacrifices might have an anti-pagan or anti-Roman as well as an anti-Jewish reference (or might be understood in that way in the event that a pagan ever heard or read this text, e.g., 2.4–10). Yet it is clear that most of its anti-sacrificial polemic is explicitly anti-Jewish (e.g. 7.3–8.7) and that its real animus seems directed at Jews (e.g., 9–10, and passim). Its author's use of Daniel (4.5) might perhaps suggest a wider political horizon, since the passage quoted appears to refer to a pagan enemy of God's people,

Antiochus Epiphanes, but in its context here it may be understood more easily as anti-Jewish polemic (of a kind that appears particularly distasteful today) rather than as anti-Roman. Like the author of the *Didache*, the author of *Barnabas* urges those whom he addresses to live together as a community and to support each other in the last days (4.9–14). But both the kingdom to which they belong and the evil ruler who opposes them appear to belong to another world (4.13), rather than to a worldly power that he presents as being a rival to Rome.

7.4.3 The *Shepherd of Hermas*

The *Shepherd of Hermas* is by some way the longest of the texts included among the Apostolic Fathers.[6] It appears to have been written in Rome, in the early to mid-second century, and focuses mainly on the internal affairs of the church in Rome, whose leaders it sometimes directly addresses (*Vis.* 2.2.6, 2.4.3). Its author assumes clear boundaries between those inside the church and those outside (*Vis.* 1.3.4). His views on marriage and remarriage after divorce (*Vis.* 2.2.3, *Vis.* 1.1.1; *Sim.* 9.11.3; *Man.* 4.1.5–10, *Man.* 4.4.2) are quite different from Roman norms and represent a challenge to them, and he displays a negative approach to outsiders, from whose practices insiders should distance themselves (*Vis.* 1.18). He also teaches insiders that the world is like a foreign land and a city distant from their own city (*Sim.* 1.5.1), although members of the church seek to share their faith with others (*Vis.* 3.5.4, 3.7.3).

The location of the author and the community that he addresses in Rome make it likely that they will have been aware of the persecution of Christians under Nero, although – unlike the author of *1 Clement* – he makes no explicit reference to them. However the author's awareness of a social and religious separation between his community and the wider world inevitably has a political dimension, as when he notes that God's servants live in the present world as if in a foreign place, with its own Lord and its own laws (*Sim.* 1). For although he recognizes that the Lord of this world expects everyone to follow its laws (*Sim.* 1.1.4), and that God has placed his creation under human dominion (*Man.* 12.4.2), nevertheless believers who come into conflict with the authorities should leave their land (*Sim.* 1.5–6). This suggests that he shares the view found elsewhere that obedience to God is more important than obedience to the authorities, but it is not clear whether the other land to

---

[6] In my discussion of Hermas I draw heavily on the careful and perceptive analysis of Mark Grundeken, *Community Building in the Shepherd of Hermas: A Critical Study of Some Key Aspects*, SuppVC 131 (Leiden: Brill, 2005), 69–97.

which he refers is Rome in particular or the world in general. Nor is it clear whether the movement of believers implies past or present clashes with the Roman authorities, or is to be taken to refer to an eschatological change of place.

Fear of persecution may lie behind references to those who have suffered for the name through severe persecutions, including crosses and wild beasts (*Vis.* 3.1.9, 3.2.1), and the author's belief that imperial power is subordinate to God (*Sim.* 5.7.3, 9.23.4; *Vis.* 3.3.5) who will being to an end the whole of the current order (*Vis.* 1.3.4) and replace it with his own kingdom (*Sim.* 9.12.3–5.8, 9.13.2, 9.15.2–3, 9.16.2–4, 9.20.2–3, 9.29.2, 9.31.2) certainly reflects eschatological beliefs that the Roman authorities could hardly fail to perceive as hostile. Yet although his theological beliefs challenge and undermine imperial ideology, and would appear to rule out veneration of the emperor, nowhere does he explicitly address participation in the imperial cult, unless rejection of the cult is implicit in his rejection of idolatry in general (*Sim.* 9.21; *Man.* 4.1.9). As Grundeken observes, "Hermas' attitudes towards the authorities is not so much characterized by hostility as by indifference,"[7] which may be explained quite plausibly by the likelihood that "for the author, who belongs to a small Christian minority and to the lower social classes of society, any revolutionary ideas are out of the question."[8]

7.4.4 2 *Clement*

2 *Clement* is often said to be a homily or a sermon, and its anonymous author refers to it as exhortation (19.1). It is addressed to followers of Jesus who have a clear sense of what differentiates them from those outside their community (3.1) and who wish to be part of the preexistent church (14.1) with its own leaders (17.3) that will go on to find future salvation in the coming kingdom (5.6). Thus the author reminds those whom he addresses that while on earth they are resident aliens (5.1), not full members or citizens of the wider society in which they live, and that their time in this world is transient (5.5). They are therefore to live as members of a community that acknowledges God and honours him in word and deed (3–4), recognizing that what matters is the prize of salvation in the world to come, to which the present age is the enemy (6–7, 5.2–4). Thus the focus of the letter is on ethical living, motivated by a clear belief in God as judge of the living and the dead (1.1, 8–9).

---

[7] Ibid., 90.
[8] Ibid., 93, 97.

The author's references to the world outside the community that he addresses are not only negative but also few, and they appear to serve more to strengthen the sense of Christian identity that he shares with them than to say very much about outsiders. Certainly he condemns pagan worship, which he describes as idolatry (1.6), and he makes no explicit reference to anyone being pressurized or compelled to participate in the imperial cult or in any other form of civic religion. However that could be implied in his exhortation for followers of Jesus not to belittle him (1.2) and in his reminder of how much suffering Jesus endured for their sake (1.2), or in his reference to the righteous who endured torments (17.7), rather vague though that statement is. When he does refer to opponents, they appear to be within the church (10.5). His eschatological framework and clear distinction between the importance of striving to attain the prize of eternal life in the world to come and his downplaying of the significance of the transient life of the present world certainly suggests not only indifference but also antipathy to the world outside the church. Yet it is difficult to point to any clear evidence for particular antipathy to the Roman state in particular rather than to the world in general. It would seem very likely that the community whom he addressed would have had to engage with questions about how to respond to the norms of the world around them, and how the claims of Caesar may have competed with those of Christ, but the author of 2 *Clement* does not explicitly address them.

7.4.5 *1 Clement*

The author of *1 Clement* begins his letter with a greeting from one group of Christians who are "resident aliens" or "sojourners" to another (inscr.). Thus he distinguishes followers of Jesus who live in Rome, the imperial capital, from the citizen population of that city, just as he distinguishes followers of Jesus in Corinth, a Roman colony (and possibly in his time the capital city of the Roman province of Achaea), from the citizen population there. In so doing he assumes, or seeks to create, a clear sense of a distinctive identity for the Christian community (the *ekklēsia*) that is distinct from others around them, has its own leaders (44.1–6), and has its citizenship not in any earthly city but in heaven (54.4).

The author uses politically charged language when he refers to sedition (*stasis*, 1.1, 3.2, 46.5, 57.1; cf. 2.6) in Corinth, and for the need for peace and harmony to be restored. But the threat that such sedition brings has arisen within the church, almost certainly as the result of an intergenerational revolt in which some young members have overthrown their elders (3.3), not as the result of any external pressures or forces in Corinth. The author makes no reference to any difficulties between the Corinthians Christians and either non-Christian neighbors or any Roman officials, and his emphasis on the need for order and harmony within the Christian community (14.1–15.7, 21.6–22.5, 38.3–4, 41.1–53.4) coheres with his belief in the importance of the order that he sees in the natural world (20.1–12, 33.2–8, 60.1). This belief in the importance of divinely created cosmic order in turn underscores the need for order and stability in society at large, which means that Christians should obey those in positions of political authority because God has put them there (60.4–61.1). Thus Christians should both obey their rulers and governors on earth (60.4), and also pray for them that they may administer the government that God has given to them (61.1–2).

The author is aware of the past persecution of Christians, including Peter and Paul to whom he refers by name (5.4–7), as well as many others (6.1–2). He also speaks of certain "sudden and repeated misfortunes and reverses" (1.1) that have happened to the church in Rome, and have delayed him from writing, but it is not clear to what this vague language refers, and there is no evidence of any current hostility to Christians in Rome, unless it is implied in his references to past persecution. He is at home using military imagery (37.3), referring to Christians as soldiers and to their leaders as generals, and gives little reason to suppose that there was any necessary conflict between the followers of Jesus and the Roman authorities in either Corinth or in Rome.

7.4.6 Polycarp, Letter to the Philippians

Polycarp was Bishop of Smyrna in Asia Minor. His letter to the Philippians variously addresses their request for a discussion of righteousness (3.1–10.3), comments on the issue of a presbyter, Valens (11.1–4), and refers to the plight of Ignatius of Antioch. Polycarp thanks the Philippians for having helped Ignatius and his companions as they passed through Philippi on their way to Rome (1.1) and appeals to the example of Ignatius and others (including some from among the Philippians) and also Paul and the rest of the apostles for enduring suffering, so that they are now with the Lord whose suffering they shared (9.1–2). Polycarp also refers to letters from Ignatius, which he is sending to the Philippians at their request (13.1–2).

Polycarp's reference to the suffering and endurance of Ignatius, Paul and others shows that he can be in no doubt of what can happen when followers of Jesus clash with Roman authorities. Yet either despite this, or because of it, he writes very little about how followers of Jesus might relate to the Roman authorities in Philippi, a Roman colony in the Roman province of Macedonia. Two passages may be noted in which he perhaps addresses the issue obliquely. The first is when he refers to God as the one who has raised Jesus from the dead, and has subjected all things to him. Thus, he claims, Jesus will come as judge of the living and the dead, and God will hold responsible for his blood those who disobey him (2.2). Here all human authority is said to be subject to God, and Polycarp's appeal to eschatological judgment may be considered a comment on the status of imperial authorities intended to encourage his readers, as well as an incentive for followers of Jesus to live a righteous life. The second is when Polycarp exhorts the Philippians to maintain an irreproachable standard of conflict among the Gentiles, so that the Lord is not blasphemed (10.2). This coheres with his ethical instruction about righteous living, which appears to mean following Roman norms with regard to many aspects of social life, although not to sexual ethics where his views reflect Jewish rather than Greek or Roman assumptions.

It is possible that Polycarp's concern that the Lord not be blasphemed may reflect the sort of situation where followers of Jesus were punished for no reason other than being Christians (cf. Pliny, etc.), but it is not possible to be sure. Certainly Polycarp has a strong sense of a church community that lives as non-citizens of Philippi (inscr.) and that has both its own structures and also clear boundaries between those within and those outside (10.2). Yet his letter does not provide direct or unambiguous instruction about how followers of Jesus should relate to state authorities.

7.4.7 Ignatius of Antioch

Ignatius of Antioch was the author of seven surviving letters, all written as he was escorted under Roman guard (*Rom.* 5.1) from Antioch to Rome, where he expected to die a martyr's death (*Rom.* 4.1). Thus his letters testify to what could happen when a Christian leader was arrested by the Roman authorities. Yet we do not know why Ignatius was arrested, or whether any other Christian in Antioch was arrested with him; there is no evidence that he traveled with other Christians as prisoners, nor that any other Christians were dealt with in Antioch without any need to be sent to Rome. Whether because of his circumstances, or despite them, Ignatius says little about how followers of Jesus in general should relate to the Roman authorities, although he is very clear that he wishes to face execution, and that he does not want any of those to whom he writes to try to prevent this (*Rom.* 4.1, 7.1).

The way in which Ignatius refers to the church in Antioch suggests that it had a clear sense of its own identity, and in his letters to communities elsewhere he addresses them each as a church, and refers very frequently to the leadership of bishops, elders or councils of leaders, and deacons (*Eph.* 1.3, 2.1–2; *Mag.* 2–4; *Trall.* 2–3, etc.). Insofar as he is concerned about threats to the wellbeing of these churches his concerns seem to relate to internal dissension in Antioch (before he learned that peace had been restored, whatever exactly that might mean; *Phld.* 10.1; *Smyrn.* 11.2; *Pol.* 7.1) rather than external pressure. Ignatius appears to have been more concerned by the threat of false teaching within churches (*Eph.* 6.2; *Trall.* 6.1) rather than of threats from outside, despite the situation in which he found himself.

Ignatius' references to Roman authorities are historic, as when he names Pontius Pilate (and Herod) in order to date the life, death, and resurrection of Jesus (*Magn.* 11; *Smyrn.* 1.2) but his only clear reference to contemporary representatives of Rome is to the soldiers (*Rom.* 5.1) who bring him in chains (*Eph.* 1.2, 3.1. 11.2, 21.2; *Magn.* 1.12; *Trall.* 5.2, etc.) from Antioch to Rome. When writing to believers in Rome he writes of Christianity being opposed to the world (*Rom.* 3.2, cf. 2.2, 4.2, 6.1–2) and exhorts the Romans not to talk about Jesus Christ while they desire the world (*Rom.* 7.1). Yet elsewhere he seems to encourage followers of Jesus to seek good relationships with those outside the church. He is aware that they meet with hostility from outsiders (*Eph.* 10.2) but they are to respond positively, praying for all humanity (*Eph.* 10.1) and proving themselves brothers to unbelievers (*Eph.* 10.3), and giving pagans no cause for offence and no grounds on which to criticize the church (*Trall.* 8.2). He insists that he will die for God of his own free will (*Rom.* 4.1), and is concerned that the ruler of this age (who here appears to be a non-human figure, not a reference to Roman authority) does not take him captive and corrupt his godly intentions (*Rom.* 7.1), which seems to mean preventing him from dying a martyr's death. Thus, from Ignatius' perspective, the Roman authorities play only a minor role in the events that will lead to his death. This implies that his theological framework meant that he was skeptical about the reality of Roman power in comparison to the sovereignty of God, but it is possible that his awareness of the ability of Roman officials to treat others as they treated him made him reticent from any obviously hostile comments.

7.4.8 The *Martyrdom of Polycarp*

The *Martyrdom of Polycarp* is usually dated *c.* 155–160 CE, although some scholars have argued for a later date. The text is in the form of a letter, from the church of God that lives as non-citizens or aliens in Smyrna to those that live as non-citizens or aliens in Philomelium and elsewhere (inscr.). Its author writes about the martyrdom of twelve Christians but focuses on the death of Polycarp, whose martyrdom is said to be in accord with the gospel (1.1, 19.1). The subject matter can leave his readers in no doubt of what can happen when there is a clash between the power of Rome and Christians' allegiance to their faith. Yet even martyrdom is said to take place according to the will of God, who has power over all things (2.1, cf. 1.1) – so even when the Roman authorities persecute Christians, they do so only because God permits them (cf. Jn. 19.11). Thus the events that the text records are said to have taken place during the proconsulship of Statius Quadratus, "but while Jesus was reigning as king forever" (21).

Even in this situation of persecution Polycarp is said to have told the proconsul that Christians were taught by God to pay proper respect to rulers and authorities, so long as it did them no harm (10.2), but he will not do what the proconsul demands – either to sacrifice, or to provide a defence before the assembled people. Thus the author asserts the supremacy of God, far above Roman rule, and the need for his people to put God before any human allegiance. He also points to a great difference between unbelievers and the Christian elect (16.1), and while those outside the Christian community may describe them as destroyers of the gods, because of their refusal to participate in public sacrifice or civic religion (12.2), Polycarp is confident of the coming judgment of God and that eternal punishment is reserved for the ungodly (11.2).

The difference between the church and the rest of society is clear, unambiguous and stark: on one side are those who follow the way of Christ in accordance with the gospel, although others call them atheists (3.2, 9.2). On the other are the Roman authorities (3.1, 4, 6.2, 7.1, 9.2–12.1, 17.2) and people (10.2, 13.1), abetted by the Jews (12.2, 13.1, 17.2, 18.1). Those who persecute the followers of Jesus are agents of the devil (2.4) or the evil one (17.1).

7.4.9 The *Epistle to Diognetus* and the Fragment of Quadratus

Unlike the other Apostolic Fathers, the *Epistle to Diognetus* and the fragment of Quadratus are both directed to non-Christians, which explains in part why some scholars prefer to associate them with the writings of the Apologists. According to the fourth-century Christian author Eusebius of Caesarea, who preserves one short excerpt from it, Quadratus' text was an apology addressed to the emperor Hadrian, "because some evil men were trying to trouble the Christians" (*Hist. eccl.*, 4.3.1–2).

More can be said of the *Epistle to Diognetus*, the author of which states that he sets out to address three questions: about Christian belief and worship, and how it differs from that of Greeks and Jews; about the love that they have for each other; and why they came into the world at this particular time. He refers to Christians as a new race or way of life (1), emphasizes the difference between them and the rest of humanity (5.1), and sets out at length what it means for them to live as aliens or foreigners in the world (5.1–17), whose citizenship is in heaven (5.9). He refers to persecution (5.11,17), but does not dwell on it, although his early reference to Christians as those who disregard the word and despise death (1) might suggest that a wish to respond to persecution was part of what motivated the author, and he claims that they are assaulted by Jews and persecuted by Greeks, "yet those who hate them are unable to give a reason for their hostility" (5.17). The author is frank in his critique of Greek and Roman pagan religion, which he terms idolatry, in polemic that draws on themes familiar from Jewish sources.

7.5 CONCLUSION

With the possible exceptions of the *Epistle to Diognetus* and the fragment of Quadratus, all the other texts included among the Apostolic Fathers are written by followers of Jesus to communities who shared their faith. Thus, as James Carleton Paget has observed, their concerns – all of which, in different ways, are very specific responses to the situations of those whom they address – arise within the internal life of "tightly-knit communities, intent upon the promotion of unity and the maintenance of an identity which finds much of its inspiration from a particular moral vision of what it is to be a Christian."[9]

It is therefore not surprising that these texts give only glimpses of what their authors and those whom they addressed believed about how they should relate to those outside their own communities, and that they pay little explicit attention to political questions arising in their Roman imperial context, and the civic and religious structures that

[9] J.M. Carleton Paget, "The Vision of the Church in the Apostolic Fathers," in *A Vision for the Church*, ed. M. Bockmuehl and M. Thompson (Edinburgh: T&T Clark, 1997), 205.

helped to bind together the different parts of the Roman Empire and Roman society. For none of these communities had the numbers or resources to enter into active resistance or rebellion against Rome, even if they were inclined to do so. Yet, as we have seen, followers of Jesus understood and responded to the rule of the Emperor and his officials, and also the social structures that sustained them, in a range of different ways, and those different ways may be reflected variously and implicitly (and occasionally explicitly) in the writings of the Apostolic Fathers. None called for open rebellion against the Emperor, but most may be read in such a way as to conclude that the exclusive allegiance of followers of Jesus to their Lord and to the God of whom they read in their Scriptures should have some significance for how and whether they engaged with civic religion, or how they behaved in other contexts that might draw them to the attention of Roman officials or others outside the Christian communities to which they belonged.

As the followers of Jesus developed from a Jewish sectarian move-ment into a wider movement that was not based on ethnic identity but included both Jews and pagans their worship of Jesus as both crucified and resurrected set them apart from the religious practice and from many of the cultural norms of the Roman Empire. It also set them on a path that was opposed to or different from much of the world around them, even as they found ways of living in the long term as aliens and exiles, while looking forward to life in a kingdom that was yet to come.

That a Roman emperor, Constantine, could later identify Christianity as having the potential to help him to hold together the Empire, by closely aligning church and state, reminds us of how the political context of Christianity came to shape the church, just as Christianity came to shape the exercise of power in the Roman Empire and beyond. But this was hardly a foreseeable or even likely outcome in the second century, which has been described as the labora-tory[10] of early Christianity because experiments conducted then, on the basis of trial and error, might have led to very different outcomes.

FURTHER READING

Cook, J.G. *Roman Attitudes towards the Christians: From Claudius to Hadrian.* WUNT 2.261. Tübingen: Mohr Siebeck, 2010.

---

[10] See, for further discussion, J. Lieu, "Modelling the Second Century as the Age of the Laboratory," in *Christianity in the Second Century: Themes and Developments*, ed. J. Carleton Paget and J. Lieu (Cambridge: Cambridge University Press, 2017), 294–308.

Dunning, B.H. *Aliens and Sojourners: Self as Other in Early Christianity. Divinations.* Philadelphia: University of Pennsylvania Press, 2009.

Hurtado, L.M. *Destroyer of the Gods: Early Christian Distinctiveness in the Roman World.* Waco, TX: Baylor University Press, 2016.

Jefford, C.M. *The Apostolic Fathers and the New Testament.* Peabody, MA: Hendrickson, 2006.

Kruger, M.J. *Christianity at the Crossroads: How the Second Century Shaped the Future of the Church.* London: SPCK, 2017.

Moss, C. "Roman Imperialism: The Political Context of Early Christian Apocrypha," in *The Oxford Handbook of Early Christian Apocrypha*, ed. A. Gregory and C. Tuckett. Oxford: Oxford University Press, 2015, 378–88.

Rhee, H. *Early Christian Literature: Christ and Culture in the Second and Third Centuries.* London: Routledge, 2005.

8 Church, Church Ministry, and Church Order

DAVID J. DOWNS

8.1 INTRODUCTION

The title of this essay assumes that "church" was an operative category for those second-century Christian authors whose writings are included in the collection called "the Apostolic Fathers."[1] Such an assumption is valid, provided that it is accompanied with the caveat that the Greek noun *ekklēsia*, which is typically rendered with the English word "church," is but one image among many used to describe communities of Christ-followers in these writings, even as *ekklēsia* is of particular importance because it is found as a designation for these groups in each of the documents under consideration in this essay. Another necessary qualification is that statements about and reflections on Christ-following *ekklēsiai* ("churches, assemblies") in the writings of the Apostolic Fathers are contingent and not systematic. The modern theological discipline of "ecclesiology" tends to frame its considerations of the identity and mission of the church in conversation with Scripture (especially the New Testament) and tradition.[2] Yet the second-century writings known as the Apostolic Fathers were penned before there was a New Testament as such and at a time when Christian tradition was yet in its infancy. Thus, we find in these important nascent witnesses snapshots of early Christ-followers debating and defining the identity, mission, and organization of their groups. In order to manage the disparate available evidence from *1 Clement*, *2 Clement*, the Letters of Ignatius, the *Letter of Polycarp to the Philippians*, the *Martyrdom of Polycarp*, the *Didache*, the *Epistle of Barnabas*, the *Shepherd of Hermas*, and the *Epistle to Diognetus*, this essay concentrates on three

---

[1] Unless otherwise noted, all translations are from M.W. Holmes, *The Apostolic Fathers: Greek Texts with English Translations*, 3rd ed. (Grand Rapids, MI: Baker Academic, 2007).

[2] See P. Avis, "Introduction to Ecclesiology," in *The Oxford Handbook of Ecclesiology*, ed. P. Avis (Oxford: Oxford University Press, 2018), 1–37.

separate but related questions: (1) How is the identity of the church presented? (2) What is the work of the church? (3) What, if anything, is said about the ordering and structures of the church?[3]

8.2 *1 CLEMENT*

The letter known as *1 Clement*, sent by the church of Rome to the church of Corinth, attempts to resolve an ecclesiastical conflict among the Corinthian Christ-followers. The missive is occasioned by a schism in Corinth, a conflict that involved the removal of certain elders from their leadership positions (44.1–6; 47.6). Thus, the letter assumes the disruption of a particular form of church order in Corinth and argues for the restoration of those Corinthian elders who had been deposed.

Given the letter's focus on the issue of ecclesiastical schism, it will be helpful to begin with a discussion of the nature of the conflict in Corinth, including the particular form of church order presupposed in *1 Clement*. Early in the letter the Roman authors offer a brief description of the conflict. Framing the situation in Corinth as the fulfillment of Deut. 32.15 ("My beloved ate and drank and was enlarged and grew fat and kicked"), the authors assert, "From this came jealousy and envy, strife and sedition, persecution and anarchy, war and captivity. So people were stirred up: those without honor against the honored, those of no repute against the highly reputed, the foolish against the wise, the young against the old" (3.1–3). While the precise nature of this division is unclear, taken at face value this statement would appear to suggest intergenerational conflict between younger men and their elders within the Corinthian *ekklēsia* (3.3).[4] It is not until ch. 44, however, that the Roman church alludes to more specific details regarding the conflict in Corinth:

> Our apostles likewise knew, through our Lord Jesus Christ, that there would be strife over the bishop's office. For this reason, therefore, having received complete foreknowledge, they appointed the leaders mentioned earlier and afterwards they gave the offices a permanent character; that is, if they should die, other approved men should succeed to their ministry. These, therefore, who were appointed by them or, later on, by other reputable men

---

[3] The *Fragment of Quadratus* and the *Fragments of Papias* are also included in modern editions of the Apostolic Fathers, but they are omitted from discussion here.

[4] See L.L. Welborn, *The Young against the Old: Generational Conflict in First Clement* (Lanham, MD: Lexington/Fortress Academic, 2018).

with the consent of the whole church, and who have ministered to
the flock of Christ blamelessly, humbly, peaceably, and unselfishly,
and for a long time have been well-spoken of by all – these we
consider to be unjustly removed from their ministry. For it will be
no small sin for us if we depose from the bishop's office those who
have offered the gifts blamelessly and in holiness. Blessed are those
elders[5] who have gone on ahead, who took their departure at a
mature and fruitful age, for they need no longer fear that someone
may remove them from their established place. For we see that you
have removed certain people, their good conduct notwithstanding,
from the ministry that had been held in honor by them blamelessly.

Several important conclusions about church order in Corinth can be
drawn from these statements, if indeed they represent an accurate
characterization of the situation that obtained in Corinth. First, the
object of the conflict among the Corinthians was "the bishop's office"
(tou onomatos tēs episkopēs; 44.1). Second, and importantly, unlike the
view reflected in the writings of Ignatius of Antioch (see below), there is
no indication in 1 Clement that a singular bishop led the Christ-
following community in either Corinth or Rome.[6] Instead, the authors
of 1 Clement indicate that those unjustly removed from the bishop's
office are the very elders who "have ministered to the flock of Christ
blamelessly, humbly, peaceably, and unselfishly" (44.3). That is, in 1
Clement an episkopos and a presbyteros are synonymous (or inter-
changeable), with an ecclesiastical leadership structure consisting of a
college of elders who together served in the "bishop's office," rather
than a singular bishop leading elders and deacons (as in Ignatius'
letters).[7] Third, the proper solution to the schism in Corinth, according

---

[5] The Greek here is presbyteroi, which Holmes translates "presbyters." Both for the
sake of consistency of translation in other documents in the Apostolic Fathers and as
a way to acknowledge the connections between the office of presbyteros and the
status of those who held it, throughout this essay presbyteros will be rendered "elder"
rather than "presbyter."

[6] As in the letters of Ignatius, however, 1 Clem 42.4–5 does refer to the ministry of
"deacons": "So, preaching both in the country and in the towns, [the apostles]
appointed their first fruits, when they had tested them by the Spirit, to be bishops
and deacons for the future believers. And this was no new thing they did, for indeed
something had been written about bishops and deacons many years ago; for
somewhere thus says the scripture, 'I will appoint their bishops in righteousness
and their deacons in faith'" (LXX Isa 60.17).

[7] For a different view – one that argues that episkopos and presbyteros in early
Christian texts are "perionymns" and not synonyms, with the implication that
presbyteroi is a collective term used when individual household leaders (i.e.,

to the letter from the Roman church, is for the deposed elders to be restored to their positions (cf. 54.1–4). Later, the Roman authors write, "You, therefore, who laid the foundation of the revolt must submit to the elders and accept the discipline leading to repentance, bending the knees of your heart" (57.1). Fourth, the bishops/elders are characterized as those who have "ministered to the flock of Christ" (44.3) and who have "offered the gifts blamelessly and in holiness" (44.4). It is not clear exactly what this service entailed, however. Fifth, and finally, there is an allusion to an appointment process for bishops/elders that allows for "the consent of the whole church" (44.3), although nothing more is said about the selection of these leaders.

1 Clement does not offer much dedicated reflection on the identity of the church. The epistle's opening address frames the authors as "the church of God that sojourns in Rome" and the addresses as "the church of God that sojourns in Corinth" (inscr.). The language of "sojourning" evokes the trope of Christ-followers as "strangers and aliens," a motif found in a number of other early Christian texts (e.g., 1 Pet. 2.9–12; Heb. 11.13; 13.13; *Herm.* 50; *Diogn.* 5.1–6.10; *Mart. Pol.* inscr.). Yet this image is not developed in any detail in the body of *1 Clement.*[8] Interestingly, the authors encourage the Corinthian readers to "take up the epistle of the blessed Paul the apostle," referring to Paul's treatment of factionalism in 1 Corinthians (47.1–4). In making this connection, the Roman authors state that their Corinthian contemporaries are part of "the ancient church of the Corinthians" (47.6). Also likely with reference to 1 Corinthians, the authors of *1 Clement* develop the Pauline image of the *ekklēsia* as a body (37.5–38.1; 46.7), an image that is evoked to promote harmony, mutual subjection, and a reciprocal exchange between the rich and the poor in which the rich provide material support and the poor respond with respect and thanksgiving (38.1–2).

Aside from its primary aim to promote "peace and concord" (65.1) among the Corinthian Christ-followers, *1 Clement* does not offer much information about communal practices in Corinth or Rome. There is a possible allusion to the Eucharist in 7.4 ("Let us fix our eyes on the blood of Christ"), and the authors are concerned about how the

---

episkopoi) of Christian communities met as a collective – see A.C. Stewart, *The Original Bishops: Office and Order in the First Christian Communities* (Grand Rapids, MI: Baker Academic, 2014).

[8] On the resident alien trope in early Christian texts, see B.H. Dunning, *Aliens and Sojourners: Selfs as Other in Early Christianity*, Divinations (Philadelphia: University of Pennsylvania Press, 2009).

schismatic behavior of the Corinthians might compromise the church's witness to outsiders (47.7; cf. 5.3–7; 30.7). Finally, there is a rather remarkable reference to "many among us" imprisoning themselves in order to ransom others and selling themselves into slavery in order to feed others with the price received for their bodies (55.2).

8.3 2 CLEMENT

The homily called 2 Clement is primarily concerned to exhort its audience toward repentance and virtuous living (8.1–3; 9.8; 13.1; 16.1; 17.1; 19.1). Although the terminology and concept of an ekklēsia is present in 2 Clement, little is said about its practices and organization. At one point the author implies that his audience has gathered together away from their homes to be admonished by "elders" (presbyteroi) and that the hearers will return home after the instruction (17.3; cf. 19.2). Who these "elders" may have been, and even whether the author of 2 Clement was included among this group, is unclear, however.

Yet the author of 2 Clement does offer one of the more distinctive, if not perplexing, second-century visions of the church. An initial mention of the ekklēsia comes in an exposition of Isa. 54.1 near the beginning of the document, where the author of 2 Clement asserts that Isaiah's barren woman is "us, for our church was barren before children were given to it" (2.1). More expansive is the reflection on the ekklēsia in ch. 14, worth citing in full:

> So then, brothers and sisters, if we do the will of God our Father we will belong to the first church, the spiritual one, which was created before the sun and moon. But if we do not do the will of the Lord, we will belong to those of whom the scripture says, "My house has become a robbers' den." So let us choose, therefore, to belong to the church of life, in order that we may be saved. Now I do not suppose that you are ignorant of the fact that the living church is the body of Christ, for the scripture says, "God created humankind male and female." The male is Christ; the female is the church. Moreover, the books and the apostles declare that the church not only exists now but has been in existence from the beginning. For she was spiritual, as was also our Jesus, but was revealed in the last days in order that she might save us. Now the church, being spiritual, was revealed in the flesh of Christ, thereby showing us that any of us who guard her in the flesh and do not corrupt her will receive her back again in the Holy Spirit. For this flesh is a copy of the Spirit.

No one, therefore, who corrupts the copy will share in the original. This, therefore, is what he means, brothers and sisters: guard the flesh, in order that you may receive the Spirit. Now if we say that the flesh is the church and the Spirit is Christ, then the one who abuses the flesh abuses the church. Consequently such a person will not receive the Spirit, which is Christ. So great is the life and immortality that this flesh is able to receive, if the Holy Spirit is closely joined with it, so that no one is able to proclaim or tell what things the Lord has prepared for his chosen one. (14.1–5)

In line with the author's overall purpose, this reflection on the church aims to promote proper behavior in the present so that readers might receive "life and immortality" in the future. The ecclesiology of 2 Clem. 14.1–5, therefore, needs to be situated in this rhetorical context of moral exhortation. Yet the church is imaged in unique ways in 2 Clement. The author indicates that the "spiritual" (pneumatikos) church is preexistent, a point said to be confirmed by "the books and the apostles" (14.1–2). As is the case in the Pauline writings, the church in 2 Clement is described as "the body of Christ" (14.2; cf. Rom. 12.5; 1 Cor. 10.16–17; 12.27; Eph. 1.22; 4.4–16; 5.21–33; Col. 1.18, 24). But the use of Gen. 1.27 ("God created humankind male and female") to assert that humankind consists of the male Christ and the female ekklēsia is puzzling and may reflect the author's attempt to take up but also redefine ideas from the second-century Gnostic teacher Valentinus and his followers.[9] Moreover, in presumably continuing the image of the church as the body of Christ in 14.2, the author declares that the church was "revealed in the flesh of Christ," with the implication and exhortation that "the flesh" should be guarded (14.3–5). That is, the author's ecclesiology is closely integrated with the ethical vision of the homily.

8.4 THE LETTERS OF IGNATIUS

Nowhere else among the Apostolic Fathers is there found such a developed, influential, and debated vision of the organizational structure of the church as in the letters of Ignatius of Antioch. Ignatius himself was bishop (episkopos) of the church in Syrian Antioch before his arrest and deportation to martyrdom in Rome, the occasion upon

---

[9] So C. Tuckett, 2 Clement: Introduction, Text, and Commentary, OAF (Oxford: Oxford University Press, 2012), 252.

which he sent letters to five churches in Asia Minor, one to the church
in Rome, and one to his friend and fellow bishop, Polycarp of Smyrna.
Ignatius' ecclesiology has been controversial in large part because, at
least since the Reformation period, competing views of his understanding of church order have factored in disputes about church government
in various Christian traditions.[10] For that reason, it may be helpful to
begin with what Ignatius says about the ordering and structures of
the church.

Ignatius is clear in his conviction that the church should be organized according to a threefold office of a bishop (*episkopos*), elders (*presbyteroi*), and deacons (*diakonoi*). Among these leaders, the role of the
bishop, who appears to preside over a council of elders, is paramount.
Thus, Ignatius is an important early advocate of what has been called
the monepiscopacy, namely, a system of church governance with a
singular bishop given ultimate authority over a local congregation (or,
later, multiple congregations). According to Ignatius, the bishop and the
elders must be obeyed (*Eph.* 2.2; 20.2; *Magn.* 13.2; *Trall.* 2.1) and the
bishop should be regarded as the Lord himself (*Eph.* 6.1; cf. *Magn.* 3.2).
Unity with the bishop is a sign that readers belong to God and Jesus
Christ (*Phld.* 3.2). Indeed, as Ignatius says in his letter to the
Smyrnaeans:

> You must all follow the bishop as Jesus Christ followed the Father,
> and follow the council of elders as you would the apostles; respect
> the deacons as the commandment of God. Let no one do anything
> that has to do with the church without the bishop. Only that
> Eucharist which is under the authority of the bishop (or
> whomever he himself designates) is to be considered valid.
> Wherever the bishop appears, there let the congregation be; just as
> wherever Jesus Christ is, there is the catholic church. It is not
> permissible either to baptize or to hold a love feast without the
> bishop. But whatever he approves is also pleasing to God, in order
> that everything you do may be trustworthy and valid.
>
> (*Smyrn.* 8.1–2; cf. *Trall.* 2.2; *Phld.* 7.2)

It is an open question how widely the ecclesiastical structure pro-
pounded by Ignatius was embraced by other Christ-followers in the
second century. Yet the fact that Ignatius assumes rather than argues
for this threefold office in the letters he writes to churches in Asia

---

[10] See A. Brent, *Ignatius of Antioch: A Martyr Bishop and the Origin of the Episcopacy*
(London: T&T Clark, 2007).

Minor, and indeed names both bishops and elders in his letters (*Eph.* 1.3; *Magn.* 2.1; 15.1; *Trall.* 1.1; *Phld.* 1.1; Ign. *Pol.* inscr.), should be taken as an indication that some version of this structure was adopted, or at least known, outside of Ignatius' own region.[11]

In light of the importance for the church's identity that Ignatius ascribes to bishops, elders, and deacons, it is not surprising that Ignatius frames the work of the church largely in terms of the functions of these leaders. The bishop, who is imaged as a household manager (*Eph.* 6.1), presides over the Eucharist or designates others to fulfill this role on his behalf (*Smyrn.* 8.1). The bishop leads the church in prayer during corporate gatherings (*Eph.* 5.1–3), provides consent for marriages (Ign. *Pol.* 5.2), and in his letter to Polycarp Ignatius implies that preaching is a duty of the bishop (Ign. *Pol.* 5.1). Ignatius holds it impermissible "either to baptize or to hold a love feast without the bishop"; yet whatever the bishop "approves is also pleasing to God" (*Smyrn.* 8.2).

The nature of the work of elders and deacons, according to Ignatius, is less clear. Elders, who are called "God's council" and equated with the council of the apostles (*Trall.* 3.1; cf. *Magn.* 6.1; 7.1; *Trall.* 2.2; *Smryn.* 8.1), serve with and in submission to the bishop, and are exhorted to encourage the bishop (*Trall.* 12.2). Deacons, similarly, must obey the bishop (and elders; *Magn.* 2.2). Ignatius also requests that a deacon from the Philadelphian church be appointed as an ambassador on a mission to his own city of Antioch (*Phld.* 10.1), and there is a hint that deacons are tasked with serving food and drink, although they are also "ministers of God's church" (*Trall.* 2.3).

The notion of "unity" (*enotēs*) is a key theological concept for Ignatius, who identifies himself as "a man set on unity" (*Phld.* 8.1). As Ignatius writes to the Ephesians, the unity of a church with its bishop parallels the unity of the church with Jesus Christ and Jesus Christ's unity with the Father, "so that all things may be harmonious in unity" (*Eph.* 5.1). Thus, ecclesiological unity – in the sense of submission to the bishop and his authoritative teaching – brings Christ-followers into union with God: "all those who repent and enter into the unity of the church will belong to God, so that they may be living in accordance with Jesus Christ" (*Phld.* 3.2).

Ignatius commonly uses the noun *ekklēsia* to refer to a local church (*Eph.* inscr.; 5.2; 8.1; 21.2; *Magn.* inscr.; 14.1 [3x]; *Trall.* inscr.; 3.1; 13.1;

---

[11] It is curious that Ignatius identifies himself as the bishop of Syria in his letter to the Romans (2.2; cf. 9.1) but says nothing about a bishop in Rome and does not refer to elders or deacons in the epistle.

Rom. inscr.; 9.1; *Phld.* inscr.; 10.1; *Smyrn.* inscr.; 8.1; 11.1, 2; Ign. *Pol.*
inscr.; 7.1) or a collection of local churches (*Magn.* 1.2; 15.1; *Trall.* 12.1;
Rom. 4.1; 9.3; *Phld.* 10.2; Ign. *Pol.* 8.1 [2x]). Yet Ignatius does also speak
of "the church" (*Eph.* 5.1; 17.1; *Phld.* 3.2; 9.1; *Smyrn.* 1.2; Ign. *Pol.* 5.1) or
"God's church" (*Trall.* 2.3; cf. *Phld.* 10.1) in a more global sense, even
asserting that "wherever Jesus Christ is, there is the catholic [i.e.,
"universal," *katholikē*] church" (*Smyrn.* 8.2).

In addition to the noun *ekklēsia*, Ignatius employs a variety of
images to refer to the people of God. Two are particularly noteworthy.
The first is God's people as a temple. In his letter to the Ephesians, for
example, Ignatius employs a proto-Trinitarian formulation in the context of an architectural metaphor, characterizing readers as "stones of a
temple": "You covered up your ears in order to avoid receiving the
things being sown by [people teaching evil doctrine], because you are
stones of a temple, prepared beforehand for the building of God the
Father, hoisted up to the heights by the crane of Jesus Christ, which is
the cross, using as a rope the Holy Spirit" (*Eph.* 9.1). Later in the same
letter, Ignatius utilizes temple imagery to speak of the indwelling of the
Lord with believers: "Therefore let us do everything with the knowledge
that [the Lord] dwells in us, in order that we may be his temples, and he
may be in us as our God" (*Eph.* 15.3; cf. *Phil.* 7.2). Moreover, like the
apostle Paul, whom Ignatius mentions twice by name (*Eph.* 12.2; *Rom.*
4.3), the bishop from Antioch characterizes the *ekklēsia* as "one body"
(*Smyrn.* 1.2).

8.5 POLYCARP: *THE LETTER OF POLYCARP TO THE PHILIPPIANS* AND *THE MARTYRDOM OF POLYCARP*

Polycarp's *Letter to the Philippians* and the account of Polycarp's
martyrdom may be treated together. Neither document offers detailed
ecclesiological reflection, yet each provides intriguing clues about the
nature of the church in one strand of Christianity in Asia Minor in the
second century.

Polycarp does not describe himself as the bishop (*episkopos*) of the
Christ-following community in Smyrna, although he is so identified in
other contemporary sources (Ign. *Pol.* inscr.; cf. Ign. *Magn.* 15; *Mart. Pol.*
16.2). Instead, the greeting in Polycarp's epistle begins, "Polycarp and
the elders (*presbyteroi*) with him, to the church of God that sojourns at
Philippi" (inscr.). That Polycarp indicates that he is writing to the
Philippians at their request (3.1) points to some kind of relationship
between the churches of Smyrna and Philippi (cf. 13.1), although more

information about this connection is not available. The prayer in 12.2–3 reveals Polycarp's conviction that the Philippians are part of a larger community of all the saints "under heaven."

While Polycarp does not promote the threefold office of bishop, elders, and deacons – unlike his friend and fellow *episkopos*, Ignatius – he does refer to the work of deacons and elders. In the body of the letter, Polycarp provides a "congregational duty code" that offers instruction to various groups within the *ekklēsia*, including wives, widows, deacons, young men, young women, and elders (4.2–6.2). Deacons are to be "servants of God and Christ and not of people" (5.2). In addition to requisite virtues, elders (*presbyteroi*) are charged with visiting the sick, caring for widows, orphans, and the poor, and avoiding all love of money, duties that suggest that elders exercised some financial responsibility within and on behalf of the congregation. Polycarp also expresses his grief regarding the case of Valens, formerly an elder among the Philippian *ekklēsia* who, perhaps along with his wife, appears to have committed some fiscal transgression (11.1-4). Polycarp also writes about the work of apostles, "who preached the gospel to us" (6.3) and among whom is included the apostle Paul (9.1).

Through its narration of the aged Polycarp's death as "a martyrdom in accord with the gospel" (*Mart. Pol.* 1.1; 19.1), the letter known as the *Martyrdom of Polycarp* bears witness to the connections and activities of churches in Asia Minor. The account is framed as a letter from the *ekklēsia* that sojourns at Smyrna to that of Philomelium "and to all the communities of the holy and catholic church sojourning in every place" (inscr.). The concept of the "catholic" church in the sense of a world-wide community of believers is reflected a several points in the *Martyrdom of Polycarp* (cf. 5.1; 8.1; 16.2; 19.2), and the request in 20.1 that the Philomelians "send the letter on to the brothers and sisters who are farther away" testifies to the networks of shared information among communities of Christ-followers across a wide geographical distribution.

In the *Martyrdom of Polycarp*, it is said that Polycarp "proved to be an apostolic and prophetic teacher in our own time, bishop of the catholic church in Smyrna" (16.2). It is not entirely clear whether Polycarp's "apostolic" identity here marks him as a prophetic teacher of apostolic truth (cf. Eusebius, *Hist. eccl.* 5.20.7, where Polycarp is called a "blessed and apostolic elder" in Irenaeus' "Letter to Florinus") or as a companion of the apostles (Eusebius, *Hist. eccl.* 3.36.1), but both senses may be in play. Polycarp is also "bishop of the catholic church in Smyrna," an interesting formulation that may implicitly contrast

Polycarp's leadership of a doctrinally sound *ekklēsia* with heretical communities in Smyrna or elsewhere.

The *Martyrdom of Polycarp* uses the designation "Christians" (*christianoi*) to refer to Jesus-followers: the crowds that witness the death of Germanicus are said to marvel "at the bravery of the God-loving and God-fearing race of Christians" (3.2; cf. the designation "the race of the righteous" in 14.1 and 17.1). Unsurprisingly given the nature of the stories it recounts, the *Martyrdom of Polycarp* highlights conflict between "unbelievers and the elect" (16.1).

8.6 THE *DIDACHE*

Since its initial publication in 1883, the *Didache* has been at the center of debates about ecclesiastical organization within the nascent Christian movement. The influential Adolph von Harnack, for example, interpreted references to various church leaders in *Did.* 15.1–2 as an indication that, at the time of the document's composition, the earliest threefold ministry of traveling apostles, prophets, and teachers was in the process of being replaced by non-itinerant bishops and deacons, a sign of the increasing institutionalization of the second-century church.[12] Others have cautioned, however, that evidence from the *Didache* cannot be used to construct a singular narrative of ecclesiastical organization that moves from charismatic leadership to settled offices.[13] The relationship of various functionaries mentioned in the *Didache* is complicated by the fact that the final form of the text was likely subjected to various levels of redactional activity.

The *Didache* offers instruction about "the way of life" to those who are to be baptized "in the name of the Father and of the Son and of the Holy Spirit" (7.1). As such, the *Didache* is a kind of manual for those who follow the teaching of the Lord, covering communal church practices such as the sharing of material resources (4.2–8), confession of sin (4.14), baptism (7.1–4), fasting (8.1), prayer (8.2–3), the Eucharist (9.1–10.7), support for teachers, apostles, and prophets (4.1; 11.1–14.7),

---

[12] A. von Harnack, *Die Lehre der zwolf Apostel nebst Untersuchungen zur iiltesten Geschichte der Kirchenverfassung und des Kirchenrechts*, TU 211-2 (Leipzig: Hinrichs, 1884).

[13] See, e.g., J.A. Draper, "Apostles, Teachers, and Evangelists: Stability and Movement of Functionaries in Matthew, James, and the Didache," in *Matthew, James, and Didache: Three Related Documents in Their Jewish and Christian Settings*, ed. H. van de Sandt and J.K. Zangenberg, SBL SmyS 45 (Atlanta, GA: Society of Biblical Literature, 2008), 139–76.

gatherings on the Lord's Day (14.1–3), and the appointment of bishops and deacons (15.1–2), in addition to more general moral instruction (1.1–6.2; 15.3–16.8), much of it reflecting traditions similar to those found in the Gospel of Matthew. Thus, the *Didache* is especially concerned with the practices of the Christ-following community, a group called the *ekklēsia* at several points in the text (4.14; 9.4; 10.5; 11.11).

The *Didache* assumes but does not articulate in detail, nor does it always harmonize, an organizational structure for the *ekklēsia* that includes teachers, apostles, prophets, bishops, and deacons. Already the title identifies the work as "Teaching of the Twelve Apostles."[14] A brief discussion of "apostles and prophets" later in the document suggests that apostles – a group ostensibly not limited to twelve men – are itinerant visitors to be welcomed as representatives of the Lord (11.4). Yet restrictions are also placed on the amount of time that visiting apostles may stay with the community (11.5) and what material support they may receive during their sojourn (11.6).

The relationship or differences between "apostles" and "prophets" in this section of the *Didache* is unclear. If an apostle stays longer than three days or requests money, he is labeled a "false prophet" (11.5, 6), an association that appears to suggest an overlap in these two offices. Yet the discussion of prophets in the *Didache* extends beyond what is said of apostles, and differences in statements about prophets between *Did.* 11 and *Did.* 13 may suggest different layers of redactional activity. In *Did.* 11, for example, a warning is given against testing the spirit-inspired words of a prophet (11.7), although the prophet is also to be judged on the basis of his conduct (11.8). A false prophet will partake of a meal that he has ordered in the spirit (11.9) and not practice what he teaches (11.10). Genuine prophets may engage in symbolic action in order to deliver spiritual truth (11.11), and they may request that assistance be given to others (11.12b), but they may not ask for money or material goods for themselves (11.12a). The instruction in *Did.* 11,

---

[14] This is the short title that stands at the beginning of the eleventh-century manuscript (H) published by Bryennios in 1883. There follows a longer title, or perhaps the beginning text of H: "The teaching of the Lord to the Gentiles *by the twelve apostles.*" The question of the original title of the *Didache* is quite complex. It may be the case that neither the short nor the long appellation of H is original, not least because the document itself, although it refers to apostles (11.3, 4, 6), never claims apostolic authorization (see K. Niederwimmer, *The Didache: A Commentary*, Hermeneia [Minneapolis, MN: Fortress, 1998], 56–7).

therefore, implies that prophets are itinerants. Yet in 13.1–7 prophets are allowed to settle within the community and to receive the first fruits of the community's agricultural produce, as well as money and clothes. In 13.2 there is reference to a teacher (*didaskalos*) as someone who is also worthy of food from the community.

Near the end of the document, identical qualifications for "bishops" and "deacons" are given (cf. *Phil.* 1.1): they are to be "men who are humble and not avaricious and true and approved" (15.1), characteristics that might suggest the administration of finances was a key responsibility. The local community is instructed to appoint these leaders, so they are not itinerants, yet bishops and deacons also conduct the ministry of the prophets and teachers within the local community, and therefore bishops and deacons should not be despised but honored, along with prophets and teachers (15.2). As in *1 Clement*, the plurality of bishops in the *Didache* is different from Ignatius' monepiscopacy, although the *Didache* does not equate *episcopoi* with *presbyteroi*.

8.7 THE *EPISTLE OF BARNABAS*

The *Epistle of Barnabas* aims to minister to "sons and daughters" by imparting a brief note that will lead them to "perfect knowledge" (1.5). The document is initially framed as instruction about three "doctrines" (*dogmata*; 1.6), and much of the letter consists of a polemic against those (Israelites) whom the author believes have forfeited their covenant with God, with the goal of exhorting Christ-followers to avoid the same fate (2.4–17.2, esp. 4.6–9 and 13.1–7).

Outside of a possible citation of LXX Ps 21.23 in 6.16, the noun *ekklēsia* occurs in *Barn.* only in 7.11. There, in a typological reading of the scapegoat ritual of Leviticus 16, the author interprets the placement of "wool in the midst of the thorns" as a "type (*typos*) of Jesus, set forth for the church, because whoever desires to take away the scarlet wool must suffer greatly, since the thorns are so terrible, and can only gain possession of it through affliction." The use of the noun *ekklēsia* to describe the recipient of this typological connection is unique within Barnabas; yet the notion that rituals, events, or people from Israel's past apply to a group whom the author consistently denotes as "we/us" lies at the heart of the document's scriptural exegesis. As the author states at the beginning of a christological reading of Isa. 53.5, 7: "For the scripture concerning him relates partly to Israel and partly to us" (5.2).

Throughout the document, the author develops an oppositional identity for himself and his readers through rhetoric that pits "us" against "them/those people." For example, the image of the author and his readers as a temple is a dominant metaphor for the Christ-following community in the document. Early in the letter, the author exhorts readers, "Let us become spiritual; let us become a perfect temple for God" (4.11). Temple imagery is then connected with the noun *ekklēsia* in an allegorical reflection on God's promise to Abraham, Isaac, and Jacob of the inheritance of a land flowing with milk and honey (6.8–19). Interpreting Ezek. 11.19 ("I will take away from these their stony hearts, and put in hearts of flesh") as a reference to Christ's manifestation in the flesh and his dwelling "in us," the author states, "For the dwelling place of our heart, my brothers and sisters, is a holy temple dedicated to the Lord" (6.14–15). The author then glosses this statement with a citation or paraphrase of material that resembles LXX Ps 21.23: "I will confess you in the congregation [*ekklēsia*] of my brothers and sisters, and I will sing to you in the midst of the congregation [*ekklēsias*] of the saints" (6.16). The author's conclusion: "Therefore we are the ones whom he brought into the good land" (6.16).

In ch. 16, the author offers a characteristically polemical discourse about the Jerusalem temple. In a first move, the author critiques "those wretched people [who] went astray and set their hope on the building, as though it were God's house, and not on their God who created them" (16.1). According to the author, the destruction of the temple in Jerusalem is a sign that "the people of Israel were destined to be handed over" (16.5). The author then insists that "there is in fact a temple of God" (16.6). What the author calls "the spiritual temple that is being built for the Lord" (16.10) involves God dwelling within those who have received forgiveness of sins and set their hope on the name of God (16.8).

Little is said in *Barnabas* about the ordering of the church and its practices. Twice the author eschews the title of "teacher" (1.8; 4.9); he writes "not as a teacher but as one of you" (1.8). As a feature of the oppositional identity developed in *Barnabas*, some practices – such as offering cultic sacrifices (2.4–10) or fasting (3.1–6) – are rejected "in order that we might not shipwreck ourselves as proselytes to their law" (3.6). The author of Barnabas does encourage the practice of gathering together and seeking out the common good (4.10). In a section that offers an allegorical interpretation of scriptural teaching on the Sabbath and a polemical denunciation of Sabbath observance, the author indicates that his community spends "the eighth day in celebration (i.e., Sunday), the day on which Jesus both arose from the dead and, after appearing again, ascended into heaven" (15.9). Finally, the "two ways" tradition at the end of the document (18.1–20.1) supplies pragmatic wisdom for those who want to walk in the way of light, including caring for the needy (19.8–11).

8.8 THE *SHEPHERD OF HERMAS*

The *Shepherd of Hermas* is a deeply ecclesiological document.[15] Aside from the lexeme *ekklēsia*, which occurs sixteen times in the document (although not in the Mandates), *Hermas* employs a variety of terms to denote Christ-followers: saints (*hagioi*, 9x), elect ones (*eklektoi*, 9x), the righteous (*dikaioi*, 22x), servants (*douloi*, 53x), and the people (of God) (*laos*, 10x).[16] *Hermas* speaks of the universal church as "the church of God" as "one body, one thought, one mind, one faith, one love" (95.2–4). Yet church in the *Shepherd of Hermas* first appears not as a social institution, nor as a theological concept, but rather in the form of an elderly woman who shares with Hermas a message of reproof and comfort and then reads to him from a book that communicates terrifying words about the glories of God (2.1–3.4). Hermas initially supposes this woman is the Sibyl, but he is later corrected in a dream in which a handsome young man reveals that the elderly woman is the church (*hē ekklēsia*). She is elderly, Hermas is told, "because she was created before all things; therefore she is elderly, and for her sake the world was formed" (8.1). In her second and third appearances to Hermas the woman church becomes increasingly youthful and beautiful (18.3–6), a transformation that a young man, an angelic messenger, interprets as the result of Hermas's own spiritual renewal and movement toward repentance (19.1–21.4). In *Hermas*, therefore, the church is both an agent of revelation and the subject of much of what is revealed to Hermas, and both Hermas and the church are changed as a result of what is disclosed.[17] While there has often been a tendency to draw a

---

[15] See M. Grundeken, *Community Building in the Shepherd of Hermas: A Critical Study of Some Key Aspects*, VCSup 131 (Leiden: Brill, 2015).

[16] See the thorough catalog and discussion in D. Hellholm, "The Shepherd of Hermas," in *The Apostolic Fathers: An Introduction*, ed. W. Pratscher (Waco, TX: Baylor University Press, 2010), 220–1, from which these numbers are adopted.

[17] At the beginning of the parable of the twelve mountains, the angel of repentance indicates that the holy spirit (*to pneuma to hagion*) spoke with Hermas in the form of the church, "for that spirit is the Son of God" (78.1). This equation of the spirit with God's Son is perplexing. One solution is to view the claim that the Son of God is the

sharp distinction in *Hermas* between the idealized, heavenly church and the empirical, earthly church, it is important to recognize that in the account of *Hermas* the preexistent holy church appears to Hermas – as a woman, in the image of the tower – with the aim of teaching the sinful and often-confused Hermas, and through him others, the way of repentance that leads to life (3.2).

As an example of early Christian apocalyptic literature, the *Shepherd of Hermas* presents the church in a number of symbolic images. Four images are especially noteworthy: the tower (10.4–18.10; 79.1–86.7; 89.1–93.7; 107.1–108.6), the elm tree and the vine (51.1–10), the willow tree (67.1–77.5), and the twelve mountains (78.1–10; 94.1–106.4).[18] As Osiek comments, "Each image serves as a symbol with its own integrity, yet each points in the same direction: there are different kinds of people, both more and less holy, who inhabit the church."[19] The image of the tower is central to *Hermas*, both in terms of the extent of the symbol and its importance for the moral transformation advocated by the document. Indeed, the final words of revelation to Hermas in the narrative, spoken to him by the angel, capture well the themes of conversion and eschatological judgment so closely tied to the image of the church as a tower: "Do good works, therefore, you who have received from the Lord, lest while you put off doing them the building of the tower is completed. For it is on your account that the work of building has been suspended. So unless you act quickly to do right, the tower will be completed, and you will be excluded" (114.4).

In one sense, the work of the church according to the *Shepherd of Hermas* is deceptively simple. The people of God are called to purity and repentance: "Only continue to be humble and to serve the Lord with a pure heart, with your children and your household, and walk in my commandments that I give you, and it will be possible for your repentance to be strong and pure" (66.6). Repentance (*metanoia*) in *Hermas* is not to be equated with an institutionalized system of penitence. Instead, *metanoia* in the narrative evokes notions of spiritual and moral renewal, a transformation of the heart and mind that might even be labeled a "conversion"(see, e.g., 30.2–4; 33.7).

---

holy spirit in light of early Jewish and Christians of angelomorphism in which *pneuma* can designate angelic figures (see Bogdan Bucur, "The Son of God and the Angelomorphic Holy Spirit: A Reading of the *Shepherd's* Christology," *ZNW* 98 (2007): 120–42).

[18] See C. Osiek, *Shepherd of Hermas: A Commentary*, Hermeneia (Minneapolis, MN: Fortress, 1999), 36–7.

[19] Ibid., 37.

At the same time, *Hermas* assumes, alludes to, or advocates a vision of embodied communal life that includes practices such as baptism (10.9; 11.5; 15.3; 31.1; 72.3; 93.1–7; 108.1), community meals (17.1–10), hospitality and the provision of material support to the needy (14.6–7; 17.2–6; 27.4–7; 38.10; 50.8–11; 51.4–10; 55.9; 56.7–9; 97.2; 101.2; 104.2; 107.5; 114.2–4), fasting (6.1; 9.2; 18.6–7; 54.1–56.8), prayer (1.3–4, 9; 5.2–3; 6.1; 9.2, 6–7; 11.2; 18.6–7; 22.3; 25.1; 33.6; 43.9), prophecy (43.1–21; 94.4), and perhaps even singing and dancing (88.4–6).[20]

When the woman church appears to Hermas in a vision early in the narrative, his exchange with her reveals some intriguing information about the church at Rome. The elderly woman tells Hermas to add words to a book she had given him:

> So when I finish all the words, they will be made known to all the elect through you. Therefore you will write two little books, and you will send one to Clement and one to Grapte. Then Clement will send it to the cities abroad, because that is his job. But Grapte will instruct widows and orphans. But you yourself will read it to this city, along with the elders who preside over the church. (8.2–3)

Not only does this dialogue suggest that the church at Rome had an individual commissioned to disseminate written materials beyond the city and a woman (Grapte) to share the message with widows and orphans in Rome; the exchange also intimates that the Roman church was governed by "elders" (*presbyteroi*). Outside of 8.2–3, however, the term *presbyteros* is not used in *Hermas* to denote ruling elders; instead, other terms are employed, including apostles (*apostoloi*: 13.1; 92.4; 93.5; 94.1; 102.2), bishops (*episkopoi*: 13.1; 104.2), teachers (*didaskaloi*: 13.1; 31.1; 92.4; 93.5; 99.2; 102.2; cf. "teachers of evil" in 96.2), and deacons (*diakonoi*: 13.1; 92.4; 103.2).

8.9 THE *EPISTLE TO DIOGNETUS*

As a text addressed to an outsider ostensibly interested in "the religion of the Christians" (1.1), the author of the *Epistle to Diognetus* frames Christians as residents of earthly cities but citizens of heaven (5.1–17). Christians "live as strangers amid perishable things, while waiting for the imperishable in heaven" (6.8). Given its apologetic aims, the *Epistle to Diognetus* does not dwell much on the identity, work, and

---

[20] This list of practices is taken from Grundeken's excellent study.

organization of the *ekklēsia* in its first ten chapters. The letter's construction of a distinctively "Christian" identity is oppositional, opening with an extended contrast of the beliefs and practices of the "new race" (1.1) of *Christianoi* with those of pagans and Jews (1.1–6.10).

The final two chapters of the *Epistle to Diognetus* offer more focused, if brief, comments on the church. It is questionable, however, whether chs. 11–12 represent the original ending of the document. Yet as the text was preserved in the one extant manuscript of it (until that thirteenth- or fourteenth-century manuscript was destroyed during the Franco-Prussian War in 1870), chs. 11–12 are presented as part of the larger document, and so will be treated here.

At the beginning of the concluding meditation on "the Word," a section that has some parallels with the *logos* Christology of the Gospel of John, the author claims to have been "a disciple of apostles" and to have become "a teacher of the Gentiles" (11.1; for second reference to apostles, see 12.9; cf. 12.5, where the citation of 1 Cor. 8.1 must mean that "the apostle" is Paul). The author envisions a transmission of the truth that runs from the Word to disciples to outsiders (11.1–3). The Word, the Eternal One and God's son, is the one "through whom the church is enriched and grace is unfolded and multiplied among the saints" (11.5). Then, in what may be a nod the *ekklēsia*'s communal practices of singing, preaching, and reading (Christian) Scripture, the author notes that when the Word's grace is given "the reverence of the law is praised in song, and the grace of the prophets is recognized and the faith of the gospels is established, and the tradition of the apostles is preserved, and the joy of the church exults" (11.6). Similarly, the letter concludes with a summary statement about what happens when God's people bear fruit from the tree of knowledge, "[S]alvation is made known, and apostles are instructed, and the Passover of the Lord goes forward, and the congregations (*sunagontai*) are gathered together, and all things are arranged in order, and the Word rejoices as he teaches the saints, the Word through whom the Father is glorified" (12.9).

FURTHER READING

Bakke, Odd Magne. "The Episcopal Ministry and the Unity of the Church from the Apostolic Fathers to Cyprian," in *The Formation of the Early Church*, ed. Jostein Ådna. WUNT 183. Tübingen: Mohr Siebeck, 2005, 379–408.

Callam, Daniel. "Bishops and Presbyters in the Apostolic Fathers," *Studia Patristica* 31 (1997): 107–11.

Giles, Kevin. *Patterns of Ministry among the First Christians*. 2nd ed. Eugene, OR: Cascade, 2017.

Paget, James Carleton. "The Vision of the Church in the Apostolic Fathers," in *A Vision for the Church: Studies in Early Christian Ecclesiology*, ed. Markus Bockmuehl and Michael B. Thompson. Edinburgh: T&T Clark, 1997, 193–206

Stewart, Alistair C. *The Original Bishops: Office and Order in the First Christian Communities*. Grand Rapids, MI: Baker Academic, 2014.

9 The Apostolic Mothers

CLARE K. ROTHSCHILD

9.1 INTRODUCTION

In a debate with Origen over the interpretation of Paul's invitation to fools (not the wise) to join the Christian movement, Celsus argues that Christianity is a religion of the *stulti* – women, children, and slaves (*Cels.* 3.44). Origen counters that the statement is a faulty generalization, jumping to a conclusion about all reached on the basis of just a few. Conversely, the history of early Christianity frequently emphasizes the history of men and male authors, without sufficient attention drawn to the role and significance of women in the early church. This short essay focuses on Christian women of the first four centuries either named as apostles, or playing the same role as apostles, or remembered as having done so, in a direct line of succession to the companions or early followers of Jesus.[1] The title "Apostolic Mothers" is based, of course, on the title, "Apostolic Fathers" – not a group of writers, but a collection of texts, some undoubtedly pseudonymous. According to new research, the question of who devised the title "Apostolic Fathers" is debated, coming down to a choice between bookbinders[2] and librarians.[3] The collection includes writings attributed to figures including Barnabas, Clement of Rome, Diognetus, Hermas, Ignatius, and Polycarp. These writings seem to have been clustered, not because their authors were "apostles" (although the historical Barnabas was contemporaneous with the apostles), but because they were regarded

---

[1] Definitions of apostleship: literally: *apostolos* < *apostellein*, "to send" 1. James's and Peter's definition: baptized by John the Baptist, commissioned by Jesus; 2. Paul's definition: commissioned by Christ; 3. Acts' definition (1.22): baptized by John the Baptist, commissioned by Jesus, and witness to his resurrection.

[2] David Lincicum, "The Paratextual Invention of the Term 'Apostolic Fathers,'" *JTS* 66.1 (2015): 139–48.

[3] C.K. Rothschild, *New Essays on the Apostolic Fathers*, WUNT I/375 (Tübingen: Mohr Siebeck, 2017).

as *post*-apostolic, i.e., in a direct line of succession from Jesus' apostles.[4] That said, not all "apostolic fathers" fit a single definition of "apostolic." It is thus impossible to feminize the definition ("apostolic mothers") without additional clarification. In this essay, the title is employed to refer to named female leaders of the church: (1) not referred to as "apostle" in the NT, but acting in a parallel fashion to the apostles, irrespective of their dominant NT role or the tradition about their role; (2) in a direct line of succession (real or fabricated) from Jesus' apostles; and (3) contemporaneous with the purported authors of the "apostolic fathers" (i.e., first and second century CE).[5] While both martyrs (e.g., Ignatius, Polycarp) and teachers (e.g., Diognetus) figure among the apostolic fathers, I have excluded women in these roles if we lack evidence for their even fictional succession to the apostles of Jesus. Thus, the martyrs Perpetua and Felicity are not considered here, nor for the same reason are the following writers: Faltonia Betitia Proba, 320–370 CE; Marcella, 327–410 CE; Macrina the Younger, 330–379 CE; Melania the Elder, 340–410 CE; Paula, 347–404 CE; Egeria, 380s CE and Aelia Eudocia Augusta, 400–460 CE.[6] Likewise, prophetesses, such as Prisca and Maximilla (Montanism) and nameless female leaders in catacomb art such as the third-century fresco *Fractio Panis* have been excluded.[7]

Although some women in early Christian writings, such as those whom Paul greets in the undisputed letters, were certainly historical personages, others were, or are developed in the extant writings as, mere stereotypes and legends. Those covered below (roughly chronological), thus, will reflect a hybrid group of real and invented figures. Most

---

[4] E.g., Barnabas: Gal. 2.1, 9–13; 1 Cor. 9.6, 12; Acts 4.36; 11.24; 14.14; 15.2, 35–8; Hermas: Rom. 16.14; Clement: Phil. 4.3.

[5] Recent work that redates certain texts among the Apostolic Fathers significantly lengthens the period in which these texts were written, giving us a range of the first four centuries CE. Yet the definition of "apostolic" sets a constraint of the first two centuries CE on the women to be considered because after that time ostensible ties to Jesus' apostles disappear. See Candida Moss, *Other Christs: Imitating Jesus in Ancient Christian Ideologies of Martyrdom* (New York: Oxford University Press, 2010); Rothschild, *New Essays*; and C.K. Rothschild, "Down the Rabbit Hole with Barnabas: Rewriting Moses in Ep. Barn. 10," *NTS* 64 (2018): 410–34.

[6] *Handbook of Women Biblical Interpreters*, ed. Marion Ann Taylor et al. (Grand Rapids, MI: Baker Academic, 2012), 557.

[7] According to Nicola Denzey-Lewis, *Fractio Panis* (a third-century catacomb fresco) depicts six women receiving Eucharist – with one woman acting as priest. If we could trace the priestess in particular in a line of succession to Jesus' followers, her role of leadership would qualify her as an apostolic mother. Nicola Denzey-Lewis, *The Bone Gatherers: The Lost Worlds of Early Christian Women* (Boston, MA: Beacon, 2007).

women in these texts – real, fictive, or some combination of two – are highly fetishized (i.e., the fact that they are women is their most important quality).[8] This fact does not exclude them as apostolic mothers, it only points to the compromised quality of the extant texts. Utilizing the criteria outlined above, the apostolic women are: Mary the mother of Jesus, Mary of Magdala, Phoebe, Prisca, Mary, Junia, Persis, Tryphaena, Tryphosa, Phillip's daughters, Thecla, Maximilla, Flora, Zenaida, and Philonella. Naturally there were many more apostolic mothers of the church. Here I focus on those for whom text and tradition retains more than just their name.

9.2 INDIVIDUAL EXEMPLARS

9.2.1 Gospels

9.2.1.1 Mary the Mother of Jesus

Mary is the name of as many as seven different women in the NT, and even more if we include non-canonical reports. Because it is difficult to ascertain which of these accounts refers to the mother of Jesus, a distinct picture eludes us. Furthermore, many of her traits represent typologies of female Jewish biblical figures. In Acts 1.14, however, Jesus' mother and brothers are mentioned in the company of the apostles gathered in the upper room after the ascension: "All these were constantly devoting themselves to prayer, together with certain women, including Mary the mother of Jesus, as well as his brothers." In this vignette, Mary resides alongside the apostles praying with them, implying her role as an apostle. Eventually Justin Martyr and Irenaeus present Mary as instrumental in Christian redemption. According to these apologists, as Christ reverses the disobedience of Adam, Mary reverses the disobedience of Eve: "virginal disobedience" overturned by "virginal obedience" (Haer. 5.19.1; cf. Justin Dial. 100).[9] Later centuries elevate her status yet further (e.g., mother of God, perpetual virgin, assumption, immaculate conception). Although (like Barnabas) Mary is not referred to as an "apostle," she acts in a parallel fashion to the apostles, irrespective of her dominant NT role as the mother of Jesus, and thus qualifies as the first apostolic mother.

---

[8] Sarah Parkhouse, "The Fetishization of Female Exempla: Mary, Thecla, Perpetua, and Felicitas," NTS 63 (2017): 567–87. Fictional women are in many ways as useful as the real ones, in terms of what they tell us about ideals of femininity in discipleship and the kinds of challenges such women confronted in the real world.

[9] Cf. Christ–Adam model in 1 Cor. 15.22.

9.2.1.2 Mary of Magdala

Many scholars argue that Mary of Magdala is the protagonist of the Gospel of Mary (Berlin Codex BG 8502).[10] The extant text begins *in media res* with Jesus ("the Savior") fielding questions from his disciples (7.1–8.11). Next, he issues instructions and sends them out to preach (8.12–9.4). When the disciples express fear, Mary consoles them (9.5–20), prompting Peter to exclaim that the Savior loves her more than all other women (10:2–3). On Peter's instigation, she narrates one of her visions of the Lord (10.10–13), after which some disciples dispute its credibility (17.7 *al fin*). The text concludes with the disciples leaving to preach the gospel, and it is unclear whether Mary departs with them. If the Mary of this text is Mary of Magdala, then she – although not referred to as an "apostle" in the NT – qualifies as an apostolic mother because she acts in a parallel fashion to the apostles, irrespective of her NT persona as benefactor (Lk. 8.2–3), demon-possessed woman (Lk. 8.2 parr.), witness to the empty tomb (Mk. 15.40 parr.), or the first person to testify to the resurrection (especially Jn. 20.1–10).[11]

9.2.2 Introduction: Women in the Undisputed Pauline Letters

Paul mentions women with some frequency in his letters.[12] In Phil. 4.1, he writes "I urge Euodia and I urge Syntyche to be of the same mind in

---

[10] J.M. Robinson, ed. *The Nag Hammadi Library in English*, 3rd ed. (San Francisco, CA: Harper & Row, 1988).

[11] E. de Boer, *Mary Magdalene: Beyond the Myth* (Harrisburg, PA: Trinity Press International, 1997); S. Haskins, *Mary Magdalene: Myth and Metaphor* (New York: Riverhead Trade, 1994); Mary Hinkle, "Mary Magdalene," in *Encyclopedia of Christianity Online*, dx.doi.org/10.1163/2211-2685_eco_M218, consulted on March 20, 2019; K.L. Jansen, *The Making of the Magdalene: Preaching and Popular Devotion in the Later Middle Ages* (Princeton, NJ: Princeton University Press, 2000); Jansen, "Mary Magdalena: Apostolorum Apostola," in *Women Preachers and Prophets through Two Millennia of Christianity*, ed. B.M. Kienzle and P.J. Walker (Berkeley, CA: University of California Press, 1998), 57–96; I. Maisch, *Mary Magdalene: The Image of a Woman through the Centuries* (Collegeville, MN: Liturgical Press, 1998); A. Marjanen, *The Woman Jesus Loved: Mary Magdalene in the Nag Hammadi Library and Related Documents* (Leiden: Brill, 1996); M. Meyer, "Making Mary Male: The Categories 'Male' and 'Female' in the Gospel of Thomas," *NTS* 31 (1985): 554–70; J. Schaberg, "How Mary Magdalene Became a Whore," *BibRev* 8 (1992): 30–7, 51–2. In tradition, Mary of Magdala ("Mary Magdalene") absorbs many other unnamed female characters in the Gospels into her persona such as the sinful woman who anoints Jesus' feet in Lk. 7.36–50.

[12] Although, according to 1 Cor. 14.34–5, Paul silences women in the churches, these two verses are not contained in all manuscripts. What is more, they occur in different locations: in Fuldensis, vv. 36–40 replace 34–40; Vaticanus, too, indicates a textual problem. Manuscript 88, copied from a Greek manuscript, does not contain vv. 34–5. In all likelihood, 1 Cor. 14.34–5 is a later intrusion.

the Lord." Likewise, in 1 Cor. 1.11, he explains: "For it has been reported to me by Chloe's people that there are quarrels among you, my brothers and sisters." All three are apostolic mothers although we know little more than their names.

9.2.2.1 Romans 16

In Romans 16, of the more than two dozen people greeted, seventeen are men and eight are women. No other Pauline letter has so many greetings. *Aspasasthe* occurs fifteen times in this section. Of those individuals described as contributing most to the ministry, seven are women and five are men. In this chapter, Paul uses fifteen different qualifying expressions for those greeted: sister (*adelphē*); deacon (*diakonos*, "envoy," i.e., Paul proxy,[13]); benefactor (*prostatis*); worker (*sunergos*, e.g., co-worker, also hard worker); first fruit (*aparchē*); beloved (*agapētos*); convert (*en Christō*); co-prisoner (*sunaichmalōt*);[14] approved (*dokimos*); relative (*sungenēs*, i.e., Paul's literal family member or Paul's figurative family member, either a fellow Jew or a fellow Jewish-Christian, possibly a co-missionary to the Gentiles); apostle (*apostolos*); chosen (*eklektos*); risked death (*ton eautōn trachēlon hupethēkan*, 16.4); saint (*hagios*); "in the Lord" (*en kuriō*; cf. above, "convert," *en Christō*); and "mother" (*mētēr*). Paul applies these qualifiers to the ten women listed as follows:

Phoebe	deacon, patron
Prisca	co-worker, risked life
Mary	hard worker
Junia	relative, co-prisoner, eminent apostle, convert
Tryphena	hard worker
Tryphosa	hard worker
Persis	beloved, hard worker, "in the Lord"
Julia	–
Rufus's mother	mother to Paul
Nereus's sister	–

These markers qualify the women as apostolic mothers. About most of the women, the above-mentioned quality is all that is known about

---

[13] Mitchell, Margaret M. "New Testament Envoys in the Context of Greco-Roman Diplomatic and Epistolary Conventions: The Example of Timothy and Titus," JBL 111 (1992): 641–62.

[14] *Sunaichmalōt mou*: "my" plus "with" (i.e., "fellow") indicates shared experience (cf. Phlm. 23). *Aichmalōt* frequently denotes women as war "booty." Concerning the question of which imprisonment and why: the only known imprisonment of Paul is the one in Rome. Paul cannot be writing Romans from Rome.

them. In a few cases, treated next, something more can be said. Each is taken up in the order of their appearance in Romans.[15]

9.2.2.2 Phoebe

The first person to be named in this chapter is Phoebe. Paul refers to her as a *diakonos* (administrative officer, assistant, envoy) of the church of the Corinthian port of Cenchreae. Some translate her title as "deaconess," possibly reading back from the third and fourth century when this role was restricted to women. Paul trusts Phoebe as his envoy – a role that includes acting as Paul's proxy, i.e., representing him in his absence. This was a position of exceptional status. Phoebe is also referred to as "benefactor" or "patron" (*prostatis*) – the only place in the New Testament where a woman is referred to with these distinctions. Paul introduces Phoebe with her credentials as his emissary to the church in Rome presumably because they are yet not acquainted with her.

9.2.2.3 Prisca

Paul refers to Prisca as a "fellow-worker" and wife of Aquila before whom she is listed. If she worked in tandem with her husband perhaps she had responsibility for outreach to women in a society that did not permit public social interaction between unmarried men and women. Alternatively, history preserves memory of a distinguished Roman matron named Prisca with the *nomen* Acilius who owned property in the Aventine district of Rome. Today St. Prisca's Church resides in its place. An excavation beneath it shows that it was built on two adjacent second-century villas. As *Akulan* is a Greek translation of Latin *Acilius*, Prisca Aquila may originally have been just one person playing the role of apostolic mother in Paul's ministry.

9.2.2.4 Mary

In Rom 16.6, Paul greets a woman named Mary. She is one of seven Jews named in this chapter. As the first Jew named as a "hard worker" (*polla ekopiasen*), she may have been a founding member of the church in Rome. Paul uses the verb *kopian* ("labor," "toil") as a technical term, denoting his own independent but cooperative missionary proclamation (cf. 1 Cor. 4.12; 15.10; 16.16; Gal. 4.11; Phil. 2.16; 1 Thess. 5.12).

---

[15] The order of their appearance in Romans 16 may or may not suggest a hierarchy of authority.

Without the same emphasis (*polla*), he applies the epithet to three other women in this passage: Persis, Tryphaena, and Tryphosa (Rom. 16.12). Because "hard worker" implies co-laboring in the spread of the gospel, Mary secures a position as apostolic mother.

9.2.2.5 Junia

In Rom. 16.7, Paul greets Junia, a female apostle, described alongside the apostle Andronicus. The feminine ending ("a") of Junia's name was considered an anomaly, such that it was often assumed without justification to be a man's name or in some cases changed to reflect a masculine form.[16] Junia is known as a relative (*sungeneis*), co-captive (*sunaichmalōtous*), and pre-Pauline convert (*oi kai pro emou gegonan en Christō*). Most significantly, she is also dubbed "outstanding" (or "signal") apostle (*oitines eisin episēmoi en tois apostolois*). Abiding questions include: If Junia was an apostle prior to Paul, did she meet the historical Jesus? Did Jesus commission her? Was she baptized by John? Paul's criterion for apostleship is witnessing the risen Christ. Did Junia witness the risen Christ? When and why did she go to Rome? What made Paul view her and Andronicus as *episēmoi* ("remarkable")?

---

[16] Without going into too much detail, the Greek word is in the accusative (used for direct objects) *Iounian* or "Junian": it can refer either to a man or a woman. Feminine is the most natural and (hence) compelling reading. Junia was a common Roman name. Junia as a male name has not been found in any evidence anywhere. The contracted form of Junianus is the only explanation of the name as masculine, but this name is unattested. Junia was the only ancient understanding of this passage, and Junia was the only modern interpretation with a very few exceptions. Luther propagated the masculine form, which he probably adopted from LeFevre. Bishop Lightfoot bears some responsibility for late nineteenth- and twentieth-century masculine readings. J.B. Lightfoot writes: "It seems probable that we should render the name *Iounian* by Junias (i.e. Junianus), not Junia" (*On a Fresh Revision of the English New Testament* [London: Macmillan, ¹1871, ³1891], 179). All translations (Latin, Syriac, Armenian, etc.) understood the name as feminine. Hence, Robert Jewett concludes that the masculine is "a figment of chauvinistic imagination" (*Romans*, Hermeneia [Minneapolis, MN: Fortress, 2007], 962). Eldon Epp recounts the history: "With the feminine presumably in the Greek text of Rom 16.7 for 365 years (with only one exception), what would prompt a committee of eminent scholars to render it as masculine in English? The answer would appear to reside with Lightfoot's context: the two persons in Rom. 16.7 were 'outstanding among the apostles,' so it must be a man, Junias, and this person's maleness could be predicated on the (specious) ground that 'Junias' was a shortened name for 'Junianus.' Hence, the shift that we observe from 'Junia' to 'Junias' in the RV of 1881 was hardly occasioned by noble, scholarly reasons (if it had been, Lightfoot, the quintessential scholar, might have been expected to have spelled them out)" (*Junia: The First Woman Apostle* [Minneapolis, MN: Fortress, 2005], 67).

We note that it is very rare for women to be held up as examples of leadership to men (*imitatio Pauli*).

9.2.2.6 *Tryphaena, Tryphosa, Persis*

Like Mary (see above), Paul addresses Tryphaena, Tryphosa, and Persis as "workers in the Lord" – a technical term qualifying all three as apostolic mothers. Unfortunately, we know nothing more about these women.

9.2.3 Non-Pauline Apostolic Mothers

9.2.3.1 *Philip's Daughters*

In Acts 21.8–9, we learn that Philip – one of the seven Greek-speaking Jewish men (including Stephen) who were appointed deacons to the Greek-speaking Jewish widows in the Jerusalem church – had four daughters: "The next day we left and came to Caesarea; and we went into the house of Philip the evangelist, one of the seven, and stayed with him. He had four unmarried daughters who had the gift of prophecy." Later tradition names these four women as Hermione, Irais, Chariline (Mariamne), and Eukhidia (Eutychis, Eutychiane or Eukhidia). Citing Papias, Eusebius (*Hist. eccl.* 3.31, 37; 5.17) writes that two daughters remained with Philip in his old age, after he had moved to Hierapolis. Eusebius also relates that one daughter, dying, miraculously rose from the dead. Eusebius regarded the women as examples of righteousness, referring to them as "great lights" (*megala stoicheia*) (*Hist. eccl.* 3.31). He regarded them as a benchmark of prophetic ministry in the church. Evidently, people traveled long distances to meet them. Tradition tells that only Irais and Chariline were buried in Hierapolis. Eusebius says that all four prophetesses and their father were buried together at Hierapolis. Other sources claim that the women were buried in Caesarea.

9.2.3.2 *Thecla*

Thecla was a purported follower of Paul. The earliest record of her life comes from the Acts of Paul and Thecla, a second-century text forming part of the Acts of Paul, although it also circulated separately. According to this text, she was a virgin from Iconium who heard and subsequently traveled, and taught Paul's teachings on chastity. As a result, she became estranged from Thamyris, her fiancé, and from her mother, who requested that the authorities punish them. A storm miraculously saves from her being burnt at the stake. When she travels to Pisidian

Antioch with Paul a member of the nobility (Alexander) attempts to rape her. Thecla fights him off. On trial for assaulting him, she is sentenced to be eaten by wild beasts. While in the arena, she hurls herself into a nearby lake as a baptism. She is rescued thanks to a series of miracles. In the fourth century, Gregory of Nyssa (*Hom. 14 in Cant.*) argues that she took up multiple forms of self-sacrifice. Owing to the wide circulation of the Acts of Paul and Thecla in the Eastern Church she is venerated as "apostle and protomartyr among women" and "equal to the apostles." As such she qualifies as an apostolic mother.

9.2.3.3 *Prisca and Maximilla*

Sometime in the middle of the second century (c. 135–175 CE), Prisca and Maximilla attempted to recover apostolic charisma as leaders in the Montanist movement. As Montanist prophetesses, followers claimed that Montanus and these two women traced their gift to a line of prophetic succession from prophets Quadratus and Ammia of Philadelphia to Agabus and the daughters of Philip.[17] Although much of what is known about them comes from anti-Montanist sources, Johannine literature seems to have been influential on this diverse movement (known as the New Prophecy). Montanists derived their prophetic inspiration from Jesus' promise of the Paraclete (Jn. 14.15–17, 26; 15.26); and, they identified a mountain in Phyrgia near Pepuza (Montanist headquarters) as the mountain from which the angel shows John the New Jerusalem in Rev. 21.2.[18] Prisca and Maximilla were evidently very popular leaders.[19] With Montanus, they expressed spiritual inspiration in ecstatic visions during which followers were compelled to fast and pray. Circa 177 CE, the churches of Asia Minor condemned the movement and its adherents.[20] Eventually, Montanist teachings came to be regarded as heretical by the orthodox church. Elsewhere followers were also excommunicated, but others remained (e.g., in Carthage).[21] Tertullian defended the movement, although he never joined their ranks.[22] By the sixth century, Justinian dispatched a

---

[17] William Tabernee, *Prophets and Gravestones: An Imaginative History of Montanists and Other Early Christians* (Peabody, MA: Hendrickson, 2009), 37, 40–1.

[18] Ibid., 20 n. 21.

[19] Ibid., 89.

[20] Ibid., 21–3.

[21] Ibid., 128.

[22] Ibid., 98 n. 1.

group to demolish the shrine at Pepuza. It was the ostensible location of
the tombs of Montanus, Priscilla, and Maximilla.[23]

9.2.3.4 Flora

Ptolemy's *Letter to Flora* is a so-called gnostic work preserved by
Epiphanius in his work *Against Heresies*, 33.3.1–33.7.10.[24] This short
work explains the relationship of the Jewish law to the *dēmiourgos*
("demiurge"). In the letter, Flora is called sister. Characterized as a
zealous student of Christian faith, she finds herself somewhere in the
middle of a complicated curriculum, with a fervent desire to learn more.
According to the letter, Flora asks the Valentinian teacher Ptolemy the
origin of the Jewish law. He replies that it is neither the work of God nor
the Devil. Rather it is the joint work of the *dēmiourgos* Moses and the
Jewish elders. The title of this work connotes the literary genre of
philosophical epistle.[25] Such tractates circulated publicly as formal
instruction. Nothing else is known of this woman, Flora. Some surmise
that Epiphanius concocted the letter as a straw-man argument against
positions he sought to debunk. Provided that Flora was a real person and
female student of Ptolemy's, she qualifies as an apostolic mother
through Ptolemy who, as a student of Valentinus, belongs in the line
of succession through Theudas back to Paul (Clement of Alexandria,
Strom. 7.17).[26]

9.2.3.5 Zenaida and Philonella

Although the sources of the tradition are unclear, Zenaida and
Philonella were female physicians who traced their lineage to Paul (as
cousins).[27] They studied medicine and began a medical clinic in the
mountains around Pelion near Demetriada in Thessaly. They act as
apostles in carrying out their medical vocation and, as such, qualify as
apostolic mothers.

---

[23] Ibid.

[24] Cf. Irenaeus, *Haer.* 1.8.5; 1.12. Bentley Layton, *The Gnostic Scriptures: Ancient
Wisdom for the New Age*, Anchor Bible Reference Library (New York: Doubleday,
1987), 306–7.

[25] Layton, *Gnostic Scriptures*, 307.

[26] Peter Lampe, *From Paul to Valentinus: Christians at Rome in the First Two
Centuries* (Minneapolis, MN: Fortress, 2003), 78.

[27] Omer Engelbert writes that a "a Greek text preserved at the Vatican" supports this
legend (*The Lives of the Saints* [New York: Barnes & Noble, 1994], 386). I was not
able to find other substantiating evidence.

9.3 CONCLUSION

These sixteen women represent the underacknowledged group of apostolic mothers of the church. The "chosen woman" in 2 Jn. 1 and the Samaritan woman at the well (Jn. 4.7) are excluded because in both cases she is unnamed. Women including Joanna, Susanna (Lk. 8.3), Mary the mother of James (if not Mary the mother of Jesus) (Mk. 16.1), Salome (Mk. 15.40, 16.1), Martha of Bethany (Lk. 10.38–42; Jn. 11.1, 5, 19–28, 30, 38–40; 12.2), Mary the sister of Martha (Jn. 11.1–2), Mary the wife of Clopas (Jn. 19.25), Julia (Rom. 16.15), Chloe (1 Cor. 1.11), Lois, Eunice (2 Tim. 1.5), Claudia (2 Tim. 4.21), Sapphira (Acts 5.1–11), Dorcas or Tabitha (Acts 9.36–42), Rhoda (Acts 12.13–15), Lydia (16.14–15), Damaris (Acts 17.34), Jezebel (Rev. 2.20–3) and others likely belonged to the group, but for now it is impossible to know. The significance of grouping women as "apostolic mothers" might be debated but the significance of their lives and work, most certainly, should not.

FURTHER READING

Cohick, Lynn H., and Amy Brown Hughes (eds.). *Christian Women in the Patristic World: Their Influence, Authority, and Legacy in the Second through Fifth Centuries.* Grand Rapids, MI: Baker Academic, 2017.

Denzey-Lewis, Nicola. *The Bone Gatherers: The Lost Worlds of Early Christian Women.* Boston, MA: Beacon, 2007.

Ehrman, Bart D. (ed. and trans.). The Apostolic Fathers. *LCL. 2 vols.* Cambridge, MA and London: Harvard University Press, 2003.

Epp, Eldon. *Junia: The First Woman Apostle.* Minneapolis, MN: Fortress, 2005.

Mitchell, Margaret M. "New Testament Envoys in the Context of Greco-Roman Diplomatic and Epistolary Conventions: The Example of Timothy and Titus," *JBL* 111 (1992): 641–62, repr. in *Paul and the Emergence of Christian Textuality.* WUNT 1/393, Tübingen: Mohr Siebeck, (2017), 89–110.

Moss, Candida. *Other Christs: Imitating Jesus in Ancient Christian Ideologies of Martyrdom.* New York: Oxford University Press, 2010.

Parkhouse, Sarah. "The Fetishization of Female Exempla: Mary, Thecla, Perpetua, and Felicitas," *NTS* 63 (2017): 567–87.

10 *1 and 2 Clement*

JANELLE PETERS

10.1 INTRODUCTION

Although the association behind *1* and *2 Clement* with Clement of Rome is ancient, the two texts have different genres and purposes. The former deals with church leadership generally and addresses particular individuals, while the latter focuses on almsgiving and church wealth distribution. Whereas martyrdom of Christians in the Roman arena appears in *1 Clement*, the traditional Games of Greek civic life appears in *2 Clement*. The two letters also diverge in their references to specific cities: *1 Clement* cites Corinth as its destination, but *2 Clement* does not repeatedly invoke the circumstances of a particular city. The biggest similarity between the two texts is that neither claims to be written by Clement of Rome, though for the sake of convenience the unknown authors of both are called "Clement."

1 Clement is a letter of deliberative rhetoric that purports to be from the "church of God residing in Rome." It is directed at the decision by the "church of God residing in Corinth" to depose its presbyters. Clement argues for the restoration of these leaders, using examples from Jewish Scriptures, apostles and martyrs, and pagans. As the letter mentions the envoys who carried it by name, it should not be classified as a general treatise. *Homonoia* (concord) is a dominant theme of the letter, as has been recognized since the work of W.C. van Unnik and Paul Mikat.[1] However, several other themes also permeate the letter. Clement goes from mentioning elements of civic life and heroes – as

---

[1] W.C. van Unnik, *Studies over de zogenaamde Eerste Brief van Clemens: Het Litteraire Genre* (Amsterdam: Noord Hollandische Witz., 1970); van Unnik, "Studies on the So-Called First Epistle of Clement: The Literary Genre," in *Encounters with Hellenism: Studies on the First Letter of Clement*, ed. C. Breytenbach, AGJU 53 (Leiden: Brill, 2004), 115–81; Paul Mikat, *Die Bedeutung der Begriffe Stasis und Aponoia für das Verständnis des 1. Clemensbriefes*, VAFLNW.G 155 (Köln: Westdeutscher Verlag, 1969).

does Hebrews – to proofs of the resurrection (e.g., the phoenix). Clement develops the role of scripture in ecclesial decision-making, repeatedly admonishing his audience that they know the scriptures well. Such details as the phoenix and scriptural knowledge do not seem necessitated by standard contemporary letter-writing conventions, and suggest that Clement is not simply writing a general treatise, but a document directed toward a particular audience whose reading practices he knows.[2]

Developing the offices of bishop and presbyter from earlier texts such as Philippians and 1 Peter, *1 Clement* features some fluidity in the titles and roles of church leadership. Chapter 44 claims that the apostles anticipated that "strife would arise over the office of bishop." The legal terminology of a codicil appears, showing that the apostles "added a codicil" in order to maintain an orderly succession of approved leaders. The men were variously appointed by the apostles or "other reputable" leaders. Clement insists that removing good bishops from office is a sin and calls deceased presbyters "blessed" for being fortunate enough to avoid such ignominy. He also appoints to the approval of the "whole church," indicating that a rigid hierarchical leadership structure had not yet developed. Clement advocates greater humility on the part of the great (48.6).

2 Clement, by contrast, delivers paraenesis about the redemptive power of almsgiving. Reminding its readers of eternal damnation and seeking virtue, the text advances charity as a superior means to salvation. Like 1 Corinthians, it mentions the Games and draws a contrast between the perishable and imperishable. However, as the author talks of sailing to the Games, the text envisions a scenario in which such civic competitive honors are far-removed and not actually part of one's own city.

10.2 *I CLEMENT*

1 Clement positions itself as a letter written from the church of Rome to the church of Corinth. For this reason, the innovative thesis by Rothschild to interpret the epistle as a fictive letter to clarify apostolic succession is not quite convincing – if the writer were seeking to adopt the literary characterization of the Corinthian church, why would

---

[2] Contra Clare K. Rothschild, *New Essays on the Apostolic Fathers* (Tübingen: Mohr Siebeck, 2017).

Paul's other churches in Rome not also have literary development?[3] Clement's focus is very much on one city's church writing to another city's church not to replace leadership in vague "apostolic tradition." The letter's unified style suggests an individual author writing in response to a single crisis at Corinth pertaining to ecclesial office, one that parallels what classicists have identified as a cultural change in the length of the terms of priesthood in imperial Greece from temporary to lifelong offices.

The letter claims to have been brought to Corinth by three envoys for the church of Rome, all of whom have Latinate names: Claudius Ephebus, Valerius Bito, and Fortunatus (65.1). These representatives are "faithful and temperate men who have lived blamelessly among us from youth to old age" (63.3). Rothschild detects a similarity to these names in Paul's letters that supports her thesis that the letter is a fiction, marshalling a revised version of the argument of Lightfoot that Clement refers to Paul's Fortunatus, Claudius, and Valeria (Claudius' wife).[4] Yet, Clement suggests that the Roman community is an established church with members who may have joined as children under their parents' supervision and thus with multiple generations of membership. The occasion for the letter is the Roman church's disapproval of the Corinthian church's deposition of its leaders. The Roman church gives examples of leaders from the Old Testament and from church history. According to Clement, the Corinthian church should put "a halt to the futile faction" (63.1), and those "who laid the foundation of the faction should be subject to the presbyters and accept the discipline that leads to repentance" (57.1). If *1 Clement* is choosing names from Paul, why would these names be the most significant? Invented names can be selected in a way that maximally makes an author's point. If Rothschild's argument is that 1 Corinthians provides the "substructure" of *1 Clement*, we must wonder why Fortunatus' companions Stephanas and Achaicus in 1 Corinthians are omitted and replaced by freed slave of Claudius and a freed slave of Valeria if Clement's intention is to recall the authority of 1 Corinthians. The letter itself chooses to name envoys, much like Paul does in Rom. 16.1–2, even though we have examples of early Christian letters that Clement knows that do not name their addressees, let alone their envoys (e.g., Hebrews). The purpose of naming the envoys is to establish that the letter is brought by

---

[3] Ibid., 67.

[4] Ibid., 43; J.B. Lightfoot, *Apostolic Fathers* (London: Macmillan, 1890), i. 29, i. 62, ii. 187.

people who have long participated in the churches of God, an appeal to antiquity (like the apostles who used their foreknowledge for a legal codicil) rather than conversion (which would allow for Clement's opponents to repent and return from their exile to hold positions of leadership). It is unclear why Claudius and Valeria would be implicated by the envoys instead of the apostles, given the letter's emphasis on the apostles and apostolic authority.

Time in *1 Clement* is somewhat relative. On the one hand, both churches are said to have long-standing traditions and members. They inherit their position from the "ancient" churches of the apostles, and there are multiple generations of leaders. However, on the other hand, the author of *1 Clement* switches from his example of Moses to the example of Peter with the phrase: "But to stop giving ancient examples, let us come to those who became athletic contenders in quite recent times; we should consider the noble examples of our own generation" (5.1). The author proceeds to mention the "good apostles" Peter and Paul (5.2) among these "recent" examples. While *1 Clement* has many of the topics of 1 Corinthians, including the body and love themes, it lacks the many themes of the earlier letter, such as proxy baptism, food sacrificed to idols, and slavery.

Concord is a major theme of the letter. This theme of *1 Clement* was seminally noted by Jaeger: "Concord (*homonoia*) has always been the slogan of peacemaking leaders and political educators, of poets, sophists, and statesmen in the classical age of the Greek polis."[5] Jaeger and then van Unnik used the concord theme to classify *1 Clement* as a letter of *symbouleutikon* (deliberative rhetoric).[6] *1 Clement* compares to a number of later first- and second-century authors, including Dio Chrysostom and Aelius Aristides. There remains general consensus that *1 Clement* centers on concord and uses deliberative rhetoric, exceeding the form of the occasional letter to verge on resembling a treatise on concord to the Corinthian church. Scholars widely agree that Clement's emphasis matches the imperial emphasis on concord in the estimated composition of the letter in the late first or early second century.[7]

---

[5] Werner Jaeger, *Early Christianity and Greek Paideia* (Cambridge, MA: Belknap Press, 1962).

[6] Van Unnik, *Studies over de zogenaamde Eerste Brief van Clemens*; van Unnik, "Studies on the So-Called First Epistle of Clement."

[7] Judith Perkins, *The Suffering Self: Pain and Narrative Representation in the Early Christian Era* (London: Routledge, 1995), 48; Sviatoslav Dmitriev, *City Government in Hellenistic and Roman Asia Minor* (Oxford: Oxford University Press, 2005), 171–2;

The author admonishes that following those who promote factions and disorder could result in disastrous harm to the community. The author argues that "real danger" is posed by the faction (14.2). Factionalism will increase, according to the author of *1 Clement*, if the author and audience persist in following a rebellious group. There is no mention of any discrepancy in the beliefs and practices of the divergent group other than the notation that the dissidents do not share the epistolary author's view that apostolic succession legitimates the current flow of leadership. Van Unnik and Mikat therefore proposed that the theme of "strife and faction" (14.2) is the impetus for the letter.[8] Van Unnik has been widely followed in calling *1 Clement* a *symbouletikon* on concord and peace, with scholars finding that the various themes of the letter can be paralleled in near contemporary political discourse from the likes of Dio Chrysostom, Plutarch, Cassius Dio, Tacitus, and Lucian of Samosata.

Like the author of Hebrews, Clement points to the Jewish Temple cult with its high priest (32; 40.5) at Jerusalem as an analogous and contemporary form of ecclesial order (41.1). Following Richard Horsley, Eyal Regev has noted that Clement goes further than Hebrews in making clear that the Jewish cult is independent of church order and still valid.[9] It thus seems that the "church of Rome" and "church of Corinth" have a form of mutual subjugation to apostolic succession based on historical revelation rather than the sheer assertion of power.

Kloppenborg disagrees with Bakke's proposal that the disagreement is between high and lower socioeconomic groups, which would be a scenario also suggested for Paul's Corinthian house-churches. Instead, Kloppenborg holds that the conflict is the result of a patron trying to usurp the authority of existing leaders. Kloppenborg reads the situation as one not specific to the Roman context but to the group dynamics of the wider Mediterranean, supporting his claim with evidence from the Ptolemaic period.[10] I have argued that the conflict be read more generally in terms of the Roman/Greek shift from democratic to lifelong

---

Cilliers Breytenbach, *Grace, Reconciliation, Concord: The Death of Christ in Graeco-Roman Metaphors* (Leiden: Brill, 2010), 298.

[8] Van Unnik, *Studies over de zogenaamde Eerste Brief van Clemens*; van Unnik, "Studies on the So-Called First Epistle of Clement"; Mikat, *Die Bedeutung der Begriffe Stasis und Aponoia*.

[9] Eyal Regev, "Relating to Judaism, Experiencing the Sacred," *The Temple in Early Christianity* (New Haven, CT: Yale University Press, 2019), 292–3.

[10] John Kloppenborg, "Pneumatic Democracy and the Conflict in 1 Clement," in *Christian Communities in the Second Century: Between Ideal and Reality*, ed. M. Grundeken and J. Verheyden, WUNT 342 (Tübingen: Mohr Siebeck, 2015), 61–81.

priesthood that happened during the late first- and early second-century Roman Empire in Greece.[11] While Ferguson could be correct in comparing the situation in *1 Clement* with the removal of an unworthy presbyter in Polycarp, there is very little mention of the moral rectitude or leadership talents of the presbyters involved.[12] Their main shortcoming is that they refuse to vacate their office for those more in keeping with the authority created by the apostles' codicil.

Many proposals have tried to identify the rebels at Corinth, and little consensus exists about them. Calling *1 Clement* "a clearly genuine letter," Horsley casts Clement from the Roman church as pitted against wealthy patrons of the Corinthian church using language of Roman class ideology such as "people," "rank," and "eminent."[13] Meanwhile, Welborn has portrayed the Corinthian community as one where "rash," "self-willed," and therefore younger members of the community challenge the authority of elders.[14] Because *1 Clement* briefly describes Peter and Paul as co-leading martyrs, other scholars have suggested that the author contended against a negative view toward Peter, which perhaps might provide a clue in deciphering Clement's preferred leaders. Tyson has considered that the author of Acts might have seen *1 Clement* since he amends Galatians to be more favorable to Peter, who shares heroic status with Paul in *1 Clement*. Nevertheless, Tyson also notes that Acts goes much further than *1 Clement* in needing to revamp Peter's image, including more information about Peter's leadership of the church.[15] Rothschild has argued that the focus on Paul in *1 Clement* combined with the text's inclusion of the golden calf incident (as proof of Mosaic leadership) and phoenix (as proof of the resurrection) demonstrate engagement with the Marcionite controversy, particularly given the early association of *1* and *2 Clement*.[16] However, neither of these proposals explains why the mention of Peter is scant, the Mosaic examples have contemporary parallels, and the phoenix can more easily be tied to the concern for

[11] Janelle Peters, "Rahab, Esther, and Judith as Models for Church Leadership in *1 Clement*," *JECH* 5 (2015): 94–110.

[12] Everett Ferguson, *The Early Church at Work and Worship*, vol. 1 (Eugene, OR: Cascade, 2013), 94.

[13] Richard Horsley, *Christian Origins: A People's History of Christianity*, vol. 1 (Minneapolis, MN: Fortress, 2006), 194.

[14] L.L. Welborn, *The Young Against the Old: Generational Conflict in 1 Clement* (London; Lanham, MA: Lexington Books/Fortress Academic, 2018), 27.

[15] Joseph B. Tyson, *Marcion and Luke-Acts: A Defining Struggle* (Columbia: University of South Carolina Press, 2006), 61.

[16] Rothschild, *New Essays*, 94–6, 109.

resurrection in 1 Corinthians and Roman symbols of politics and resurrection.

Likewise, there have been suggestions that *1 Clement* deals with the problem of female leadership. Women martyrs equal the apostles Peter and Paul, women are instructed to regulate their speech or (in later manuscripts) keep silent (21.7), and Judith and Esther serve as exemplars of renunciant leadership (55). Douglas points out that in order to champion women the text must fight against a broader patriarchal context that only understands women's valor as "manly."[17] The household codes of *1 Clement* are similar in not restricting women as much as promulgating elders – the mention of a household code functions in the same way of acknowledging patriarchal culture while resisting it. Louise Tsui-yuk Liu correctly points out that the use of the household example in *1 Clement* means that the letter "does not exclude the possibilities of female public roles or even leadership roles in a community past and present."[18]

10.2.1 Manuscripts

While Clement of Rome featured in the fourth-century *Homilies* and *Recognitions*, *1 Clement* languished in popularity and disappeared from Christian scholarship during the Middle Ages. There are two manuscripts that witness to the Greek text of the original letter. There are also two Coptic manuscripts, one Latin manuscript, and one Syriac manuscript.

The first Greek manuscript is Codex Alexandrinus (A), which lacks *1 Clement* 57.7–63.4. Codex Alexandrinus dates from the fifth century. It was rediscovered when Cyril Lucar, Patriarch of Constantinople, gave the manuscript to King Charles I of England, after King James I of England died before he could receive it. As Codex Alexandrinus contains both *1–2 Clement*, the *editio princeps* of *1 Clement* appeared in 1633 with *1* and *2 Clement* together. Codex Alexandrinus almost elevates *1–2 Clement* to the status of Scripture, given that these two texts accompany the Septuagint and the New Testament. They were placed after the Apocalypse and before the Psalms of Solomon, according to the table of contents prefixed to the manuscript.

---

[17] Sally Douglas, *Early Church Understandings of Jesus as the Female Divine: The Scandal of the Scandal of Particularity* (London: Bloomsbury, 2016), 123–5.

[18] Louise Tsui-yuk Liu, "Rahab as Perfect Servant in *1 Clement*: Negotiating Women's Role in Corinth," in *Biblical Women in Patristic Reception*, ed. Agnethe Siquans (Göttingen: Vandenhoeck & Ruprecht, 2018), 100.

The second Greek manuscript is Codex Hierosolymitanus (H). Philotheos Bryennios found the manuscript in the Library of the Most Holy Sepulchre in Constantinople in 1873. Codex Hierosolymitanus was written in 1056. Along with the Bible, it preserves the *Didache*, the *Epistle of Barnabas*, *1–2 Clement*, and the long recension of Ignatius' letters. The placement of *1 Clement* among these letters suggests that *1 Clement* was considered authoritative in the eleventh century.

Manuscripts of *1 Clement* also attest versions in other languages. There are two Coptic manuscripts that preserve portions of the text. The first dates to the fourth century. The second dates between the fifth and eighth centuries. A complete eleventh-century Latin manuscript (L) could represent a corruption of a second- or third-century translation to magnify the role of the Pope. Lastly, there is also a twelfth-century Syriac manuscript (S) of the New Testament. This manuscript positions *1* and *2 Clement* after the Catholic Epistles and Acts but before the Epistles of Paul. It divides *1* and *2 Clement* into lessons as it does for the Catholic Epistles and Acts.[19]

10.2.2 Date

1 Clement has been dated to the late first or early second century. *1 Clement* makes extensive use of Hebrews, which sets its *terminus a quo* at the late first century.[20] Moreover, Clement introduces the element of concord in his description of Lot's wife, saying that she was turned to stone because "she fell out of concord." Roman concern with marital concord as a parallel to imperial concord dates to the late first or early second century. The author calls Paul's church at Corinth "ancient" (47.6), which suggests that everyone in the original church no longer is alive but does not give a firm indication of the passage of time. As the deaths of Peter and Paul mentioned in the text (*1 Clem.* 5–6) date to the time of Nero, the text would have to date to later decades in order to accommodate the "more recent" martyrs dying including Danaids and Dircae. Such a late date is corroborated by the envoys who have belonged to the church from youth to old age (63.3). If the men were youths in the late 40s or early 50s CE, when Christianity reached Rome, the text would have to date to at least 90.[21] Since one

---

[19] Andrew Gregory, *1 Clement: An Introduction, The Writings of the Apostolic Fathers*, ed. Paul Foster (London: Bloomsbury, 2007), 22.

[20] Edgar J. Goodspeed, "First Clement Called Forth by Hebrews," *JBL* 30 (1911): 157–60.

[21] A notable exception to this argument is the 70 CE date assigned by Thomas J. Herron in his 1988 doctoral dissertation at the Pontifical Gregorian University on factors

presumes "ancient" is older than "old age," the range of *1 Clement*
would be roughly 90 to 120 CE.

External evidence suggests *1 Clement* was known by contemporary
Christian authors. Polycarp displays knowledge of *1 Clement*, though
he does not follow Clement in many aspects (e.g., only *1 Clement*
mentions Peter specifically).[22] Polycarp's *Philippians* ranges from
120 CE (Pol. *Phil.* 13, after Ignatius left for Rome) to 140 CE (Pol. *Phil.*
1–12, 14). Ignatius' *Romans* 3:1 might allude to *1 Clement*. Thus,
1 Clement was written no later than 120 to 140 CE.

10.2.3 Author

The stated author of *1 Clement* is not Clement of Rome. The letter
itself says that it is composed by the Roman church.[23] While the voice
of the letter is unified and suggestive of a single author, the letter takes a
collective view. As Head has recently underscored, it mentions envoys
who represent the sending church, who could have expanded on the
letter's message in the receiving church.[24] These envoys would seem to
militate against the recent suggestion of Clare Rothschild that the letter
is actually a fictive epistle meant only to be from the metaphorical
church in Rome to the metaphorical church in Corinth. Rothschild
explains the names thus: "Good forgeries anticipate attacks on their
authenticity."[25] However, such a move toward forgery would seem to
negate her other proposal that the text belongs to a genre of intentionally allegorical epistles that the audience would understand were metaphorical.[26] Paul Foster agrees with van Unnik that the author exceeds

ranging from the names of the envoys to the use of the present tense for the
Jerusalem Temple. See his *Clement and the Early Church of Rome: On the Dating
of Clement's First Epistle to the Corinthians* (Steubenville, OH: Emmaus
Road, 2008).

[22] Kenneth Berding, "Polycarp's Use of 1 Clement: An Assumption Reconsidered,"
JECS 19 (2011): 127–39.

[23] Pamela Eisenbaum connects the anonymity of Hebrews with the trend toward
letters that circulated with churches rather than individuals who circulated the
letter, e.g., 1 Clement, Martyrdom of Polycarp, and Letter of the Churches in
Vienne and Lyons. Pamela Eisenbaum, "Locating Hebrews within the Literary
Landscape of Christian Origins," in *Hebrews: Contemporary Methods – New
Insights*, ed. Gabriella Gelardini (Leiden: Brill, 2005), 220.

[24] Peter M. Head, "'Witnesses between You and Us': The Role of Letter-Carriers in 1
Clement," in *Studies on the Text of the New Testament and Early Christianity:
Essays in Honour of Michael W. Holmes on the Occasion of His 65th Birthday*, ed.
Daniel M. Gurtner, Juan Hernandez, and Paul Foster (Leiden: Brill, 2015), 477–93.

[25] See Rothschild, *New Essays*, 43, n. 38.

[26] Ibid., 65.

the amount of specificity customary for the genre of *sumbouletikon*.[27] A presumption is the right of the church of Rome to advise the church of Corinth on matters of church governance. *I Clement* is the first example of one church trying to exercise authority over another church, but there is no indication that its author has disciplinary power over the church of Corinth. Nor would the mention of Clement in the near-contemporary and Rome-based *Shepherd of Hermas* serve to indicate Clement had such power: "You are to write out two booklets and send one to Clement and one to Grapte. Clement then is to send it to the cities outside, for that is his function (*Vis.* 2.8)." The basic model of authorial authority in *I Clement* is consistent with a late first- or early second-century church in Rome.

10.2.4 Genre

I Clement has been labeled as a letter of *symbouletikon*, a composition of deliberative rhetoric. It draws a connection between the current church of Corinth and the Corinthian community to which Paul wrote I Corinthians. The most likely explanation for this is that the author considers both Peter and Paul authoritative, so to cite Paul's letter to the Corinthians is a logical device by which to develop authority and rapport with the audience. Though *I Clement* invokes the "ancient church" of I Corinthians, it also could refer to several other Pauline letters, leading some to speculate that the Pauline corpus had been established by this time.

However, the central Pauline letter in *I Clement* is I Corinthians. This may be seen particularly in chapter 47. The text instructs the church at Corinth: "Take up the epistle of that blessed apostle, Paul" (47:1). It equates the current church with the historical church at Corinth, making the contemporary church the spiritual heirs of the apostolic church there. The sin described in I Corinthians was "partisanship" that was trivial, because it represented loyalty toward "reputable apostles" (47:4). Now, the Corinthians have become "corrupted" (47:5).

I Clement directs its deliberative rhetoric toward a specific event, but it utilizes the contemporary practice of arguing from examples. As the use of examples was widespread in Roman-era historiography and

---

[27] See Andrew Gregory, *I Clement: An Introduction, The Writings of the Apostolic Fathers*, ed. Paul Foster (London: Bloomsbury, 2007), 27.

not in the Old Testament, the examples of *1 Clement* should be viewed
in the context of contemporary Jewish and Christian literature.
Clement shows a clear preference for Jewish and Christian as opposed
to Gentile traditions. The author's description of Gentile examples
contains no names and is quite general (55.1). Jewish and Christian
examples specify names and elaborate on events. Moreover, the author
prefers to label these examples with the term *hypodeigma* common in
Jewish and Christian texts instead of the *paradeigma* common in
literature from the wider contemporary culture.[28]

10.2.5 Concord, the City, and the Cosmos

Homonoia (concord) is a prominent term in *1 Clement*, a significant
difference from contemporary Jewish and Christian literature. The noun
occurs fourteen times in the letter and a verb form once. By contrast,
concord (in its noun and verb forms) is found eleven times in the LXX,
seven times in the letters of Ignatius, and twice in Hermas.[29] Clement
uses concepts from political rhetoric promoting concord and reconciliation such as the body topos. He also invokes concepts from Roman
ideology such as *homonoia* representing marital accord.

In addition to citing from the Pauline corpus (e.g., Rom. 1.29–32,
Rom. 6.1), *1 Clement* augments terms in Paul's 1 Corinthians. To Paul's
eris (1 Cor. 1:11, 3:3), Clement adds *stasis* (*1 Clem.* 3.2, 14.2, 54.2).[30]
Clement has the body metaphor known from contemporary political
discourse, its members (*1 Clem.* 37.5, 38.1). But Clement connects the
image of the body with that of the army in which each has his own rank
(*1 Clem.* 37.3). Clement cites the Pauline love language, but relates it
back to schism and concord rather than to personal hubris (*1 Clem.*
49.5).

Commensurate with the second-century interest with concord, concord is important in *1 Clement*.[31] Household order is mentioned in the
first chapter. The author says the church at Corinth taught its women

---

[28] Odd Magne Bakke, *Concord and Peace: A Rhetorical Analysis of the First Letter of
Clement with an Emphasis on the Language of Unity and Sedition* (Tübingen: Mohr
Siebeck, 2001), 59.

[29] Ibid., 73. The verb occurs at Lev. 20.5; Esth. 4.17; Dan. 2.43. The noun occurs at
Pss. 54.14, 82.5; Wis. 10.5, 18.9; Sir. 25.1; 4 *Macc.* 3.21, 13.23, 25.

[30] L.L. Welborn, "Take Up the Epistle of the Blessed Paul the Apostle: The Contrasting
Fates of Paul's Letters to Corinth in the Patristic Period," in *Reading Communities
Reading Scripture: Essays in Honor of Daniel Patte*, ed. Daniel Patte, Gary A.
Phillips, and Nicole Wilkinson Duran (London: Bloomsbury, 2002), 351.

[31] Peter Brown, *The Body and Society: Men, Women, and Sexual Renunciation in Early
Christianity* (New York: Columbia University Press, 1988), 16.

"to run their households respectfully, living under the rule of submission, practicing discretion in every way" (1.3). When *1 Clement* talks about the example of Lot's wife, her error of looking back becomes one of changing her mind and "falling out of harmony" (11.2).

The Genesis creation account features in multiple parts of *1 Clement*. A sustained discussion of the Genesis creation account is found in the well-known chapter 20 of *1 Clement*. W.C. van Unnik writes: "This chapter is considered to be one of the crown-witnesses for Stoic influence upon this letter. It is a clear proof that *1 Clement* has left the sphere of the Bible and that the *theologia naturalis* makes its *joyeuse entrée* in the church."[32] Here, the celestial bodies and the day–night cycle are described as being on a track (20.3). Humans, animals, and all living creatures are said to conform to preexisting divine laws (20.4). The seasons follow each other "in peace" (20:9). However, chapter 33 of *1 Clement* ascribes the Genesis creation of man and woman to divine intelligence. The author states that the Creator made man in the divine image, created male and female, and told creation to be fruitful and increase. Here, the fully numinous picture of God complements the scientific order in the universe that the author has already described. Neither cosmology seems intended to define the male and female attributes and attire, which is the case in 1 Corinthians.

10.2.6 Examples from the Old Testament

1 Clem. 9–12 adds and amplifies women from Jewish Scriptures in the heroes list of Hebrews 11. Heroes for Hebrews 11 feature only one named woman: Abel; Cain; Enoch; Noah; Abraham; Jacob; Sarah; Isaac; Esau; Joseph; Moses; Rahab; "Barak, Samson, Jephthah, of David and Samuel and the prophets"; and "women [who] received their dead."*1 Clement* adds women to this list by mentioning: Cain and Abel (4.1–6); Jacob and Esau (4.8); Joseph (4.9); Moses (4.10, 17.5); Aaron and Miriam (4.11); Dathan and Abiram (4.12); David and Saul (4.3); Peter, Paul, and female martyrs 5:1–6:2); Noah (7.6, 9.4); Jonah (7.7); Enoch (9.3); Abraham (10.1); Lot (11.1); Rahab (12.1, 3); Elijah, Elisha, Ezekiel, and the prophets (17.1); and Job (17.3). It also calls Rahab an example that prophecy could be found in a woman (12.3). Rahab mirrors the good traits of male exemplars Abraham and Lot.[33]

---

[32] W.C. van Unnik, "Is *1 Clement* 20 Purely Stoic?," in *Sparsa Collecta: The Collected Essays of W.C. Van Unnik* (Leiden: Brill, 1983), 53.

[33] Liu, "Rahab as Perfect Servant in *1 Clement*," 79.

Clement's use of the example of Dathan and Abiram appears to be a stock example of factionalism in contemporary Judaism. Philo, Paul, and Josephus all refer to the revolt of Korah in Numbers 16.[34] The widespread usage of the trope suggests that the crisis to which *1 Clement* is addressed might be more minor than major.

10.2.7 Sacrifice and Exile

In chapters 51 to 55, *1 Clement* argues for the sacrifice and exile of those causing the faction. To do this, he makes an appeal to "sacred Scriptures" (53.1). The text begins by noting that those who rebelled against Moses "descended into Hades, and Death will be their Shepherd," drawing on Num. 16.33 and Ps. 49.19 (51.4). Moses, on the other hand, is able to intercede for the rebels or to sacrifice himself along with them: "The servant speaks boldly to the Lord, and asks for the multitude to be forgiven – or pleads for himself to be blotted out with them" (53.5).

The author compares the scriptural example of Moses with faction leaders and then urges those faction leaders to do their "civic duty to God" (54.4). By this, Clement means that the ones who recognize themselves as the "cause of faction, strife, and schisms" be willing to withdraw themselves from the community (54.1). These individuals should then go wherever the congregation tells them, effectively giving the congregation the power to impose exile. Concomitant to this power of exile is the recognition of appointed presbyters (54.2). As *1 Clement* claims to be written from the congregation of Rome, this could also be a strengthening of interchurch authority.

With chapter 55, though, Clement seems to suggest that civic duty is inherently Jewish, suggesting an interest in positioning the congregation as Jewish and better adherents of Greek and Roman political values than other groups. The discussion moves to bringing in "examples from the Gentiles as well" (55.1). Here, Clement begins with the illustrations of kings and those who undertook exile to prevent their fellow citizens from devolving into schisms. But Clement cycles back to a conception of the congregation as Jewish by noting that "among ourselves" many have put themselves in prison or slavery. Both acts indicate the possibility to ransom others. Women were empowered to

---

[34] Margaret Mitchell, *Paul and the Rhetoric of Reconciliation: An Exegetical Investigation of the Language and Composition of 1 Corinthians* (Louisville, KY: Westminster John Knox Press, 1991), 139–40.

commit "manly" deeds, and these resemble Jewish heroines Judith and Esther.

10.2.8 Women

The inclusion of female figures in *I Clement* is significant, and Clement highlights the greater significance of women within the early churches than within contemporary culture. The deaths of women in the arena as "Danaids and Dircae" (6.2) is for *I Clement* the contemporary equivalent of the martyrdoms of the apostles Peter and Paul. In the list of examples from Jewish Scriptures, the author mentions both Lot's wife and Rahab, with the latter modeling the virtue of hospitality. Li has drawn attention to the elevated role of Rahab, who serves as proof that "not only faith was found in the woman, but prophecy as well."[35] Rahab is thus equivalent to the male prophets Elijah, Elisha, and Ezekiel. In chapter 55, *I Clement* cites precedents for choosing to live among the margins and the marginal from among "the Gentiles" and "ourselves." For the Gentiles, those going into exile or giving themselves over to death in the event of an oracle or plague are said to be "kings and rulers." For the churches, the examples are both men and women. While church members of both sexes became prisoners or slaves to save others, *I Clement* specifically draws attention to the accomplishment of women as performers of "numerous 'manly' deeds." The author then proceeds to adduce Judith and Esther.

10.2.9 Resurrection

I Clement's concern for resurrection occurs after a concern for the wait for the Lord with an analogy of the tree and temple in chapter 23. In chapter 24, the author points out that nature manifests several resurrections: the day follows the night, resurrecting light; the seed that appears dead from heat when sown into the parched ground is raised by the "magnificent foresight of the Master." These examples prove that resurrection happens in other contexts and should be considered reasonable by the readers of *I Clement*. Then, in chapter 25, the author calls the audience's attention to the "paradoxical sign" of the phoenix "in the regions near Arabia" (25.1). Using frankincense, myrrh, and other spices (25.2), the resurrecting bird constructs its own tomb. The phoenix is a natural sign that, along with the biblical example of Job,

---

[35] Shelly Li, "Imposing the Silence of Women: A Suggestion about the Date of the Interpolation in 1 Corinthians," in *Hermeneutics and the Authority of Scripture*, ed. Alan Cadwallader (Adelaide: ATF, 2011): 125–38.

demonstrates the reality of the resurrection (26) and the need for hope in God (27).[36] It reassures the church at Corinth that God has created the world in such a way to leave natural signs pointing to the divine order.[37] However, as it is situated precisely in Arabia and Heliopolis, the mythic bird also confirms a particularity to this divine order, much like *1 Clement*'s insistence that sacrifice happens only in Jerusalem (41).

10.2.10 Presbyters

1 Clement demonstrates both that the role of presbyters existed in a church with a Pauline tradition and that this role had not been firmly established and delineated. To prove warrant for leadership roles, *1 Clement* says in chapter 42 that Jesus commissioned apostles who then appointed bishops and deacons, roles that can be found in Jewish Scriptures. As an attempt to shore up support for these positions, the author says that the apostles "knew through our Lord Jesus Christ that strife would arise over the office of the bishop" (44.1). The legal term codicil reinforces the precedent set by the apostles to establish these roles. Moreover, the entire church has ratified leaders. By implication, then, the Corinthian church is opposing apostolic tradition, church law, and ecclesial plebiscite by removing its presbyters.

10.3 2 CLEMENT

Written as a text of paraenesis, *2 Clement* directs the attention of its audience to their own salvation in Jesus Christ, judge of the living and the dead. The text has a greater concern with hell than earlier writings, and it differs from *1 Clement* in describing belief in Christ as a calling from non-being. Such spiritualizing Christology led Vernon Bartlet in 1906 to describe *2 Clement* as more a product of the East and possibly Alexandrine, contrasting the text with the realism of *Hermas*.[38] Likewise, features like the section on the resolution of binaries at 12.2 (two/one, inside/outside, male/female) have led some commentators to interpret the text as directed against gnostic opponents, a thesis that

---

[36] Janelle Peters, "The Phoenix in *1 Clement*," *Studia Patristica* 93 (2017): 17–26.

[37] Janet E. Spittler, *Animals in the Apocryphal Acts of the Apostles: The Wild Kingdom of Early Christian Literature* (Tübingen: Mohr Siebeck, 2008), 29–30.

[38] Vernon Bartlet, "The Origin and Date of *2 Clement*," *Zeitschrift für die Neutestamentliche Wissenschaft und die Kunde der Älteren Kirche* 7 (1906): 123–35.

Kelhoffer has refuted.[39] Though 2 *Clement* lacks references to the later canonical Gospel of John, 12.2 contains a quotation of the Gospel of the Egyptians and shares the contemporary second-century (and geographically diffuse) interest in logia, with variations arising either from oral tradition or catechetical motives.[40] Recent commentators Garrison and Downs agree that the overall intent of these stylistics is to encourage almsgiving.[41] Kelhoffer notes that the envisaged situation applies patron–client relationships on a cosmic dimension, so that Christ would be the ultimate patron.[42]

It is probable that 2 *Clement* was a homily. According to a near contemporary, Justin Martyr, writing in Rome at almost the same time, "the memoirs of the apostles or the writings of the prophets are read – as much as there is time for" (*1 Apol.* 67.3).[43] The original homily could have been restricted to chapters 1–18, with the subsequent two chapters being added by a different author.[44] However, as Tuckett notes, "the differences in language and ideas in 19.1–20.4, even the usage of 'brothers and sisters' in place of the formerly consistent 'brothers,' are not significant enough to exclude the later chapters."[45]

10.3.1 Manuscripts

2 *Clement* has not yet been found in a manuscript without *1 Clement*. The manuscripts that we have of 2 *Clement* come from the scant manuscripts we have of *1 Clement*. The text of 2 *Clement* survived in three manuscripts: Codex Alexandrinus (1.1–12.5a, fifth century), Codex Hierosolymitanus (1056), and a Syriac manuscript (1169). The first edition that reintroduced the text to early modern scholarship

---

[39] James A. Kelhoffer, "*Second Clement* and Gnosticism: The *Status Quaestionis*," *Early Christianity* 8 (2017): 124–49; Kelhoffer, "Eschatology, Androgynous Thinking, Encratism, and the Question of Anti-Gnosticism in 2 Clement 12 (Part Two)," *VigChr* 72 (2018): 353–68.

[40] Annewies van den Hoek, "Divergent Gospel Traditions in Clement of Alexandria and Other Authors of the Second Century," *Apocrypha* 7 (1996): 43–62.

[41] Roman Garrison, *Redemptive Almsgiving in Early Christianity* (Sheffield: JSOT Press, 1993); David J. Downs, "'Love Covers a Multitude of Sins': Redemptive Almsgiving in 1 Peter 4:8 and Its Early Christian Reception," *JTS* 65 (2014): 489–514.

[42] James Kelhoffer, "Reciprocity as Salvation: Christ as Salvific Patron and the Corresponding 'Payback' Expected of Christ's Earthly Clients According to the Second Letter of Clement," *NTS* 59 (2013): 433–56.

[43] Christopher M. Tuckett, *2 Clement: Introduction, Text, and Commentary*, OAF (Oxford: Oxford University Press, 2012), 47–57.

[44] Foster, *The Writings of the Apostolic Fathers*, 35.

[45] Tuckett, *2 Clement*, 33.

coincided with the publication of the Codex Alexandrinus, which contains the Bible and the Clementine letters, in 1633.

10.3.2 Date

2 *Clement* probably dates to the first half of the second century. As 2 *Clement* appears to have Matthean and Lukan redactions of sayings of Jesus, the homily was probably written after 100 or 125 CE. There is a conceptual similarity between the late first- or early second-century *Shepherd of Hermas* and 2 *Clement* concerning redemptive almsgiving, leading Garrison to suggest that 2 *Clement* came from a Roman church with contact with the Roman church of *Hermas*.[46] Parvis dates the text to 150 CE for its lack of the fourfold gospel canon proposed by Irenaeus in 180.[47]

Nonetheless, 2 *Clement* displays access to a possibly pre-Q block of tradition found in Q 6.27–38, which could be a pre-Q block given that these verses are also found in *1 Clement*, Polycarp, and the *Didache*.[48] This would suggest that it would be wise to keep the date closer to other texts from the Apostolic Fathers and from a period in which a pre-Q block of tradition would not have been overwhelmed by the authority of the gospels in the process of being canonized.

10.3.3 Author

According to Eusebius (*Hist. eccl.* 3.28.4), Clement is not the author of 2 *Clement*, because older authors do not acknowledge him as such. While scant mention existed for 2 *Clement*, Eusebius found *1 Clement* well-attested (*Hist. eccl.* 4.23.11; 5.6.3).[49] Concannon has revived Lightfoot's observation that only 2 *Clement* consistently uses the first person singular in order to argue against Harnack's later thesis that Soter could be the author of 2 *Clement*.[50]

There are a few self-references by the author toward the end of the treatise. At 18.2, the author claims to be "eager to pursue

---

[46] Garrison, *Redemptive Almsgiving*, 142.

[47] Paul Parvis, "2 Clement and the Meaning of the Christian Homily," *ExpT* 117 (2006): 265–70.

[48] Stephen E. Young, *Jesus Tradition in the Apostolic Fathers: Their Explicit Appeals to the Words of Jesus in Light of Orality Studies* (Tübingen: Mohr Siebeck, 2011), 269.

[49] Bart D. Ehrman, *Forgery and Counterforgery: The Use of Literary Deceit in Early Christian Polemics* (Oxford: Oxford University Press, 2012), 75.

[50] Lightfoot, *Apostolic Fathers*, 196–7. Cavan W. Concannon, *Assembling Early Christianity: Trade, Networks, and the Letters of Dionysios of Corinth* (Cambridge: Cambridge University Press, 2017), 194.

righteousness." In chapter 19, there is a reflexive meditation on the act of reading: "I am reading you a request to pay attention to what has been written, so that you may save yourselves and the one who is your reader" (19.1).

This double reference has led some to position that 1–18 and 19–20 are written by two different authors. The most significant difference between the two authors would be the authors' addresses to "brothers" (1.1; 4.3; 5.1; 5.5; 7.1; 8.4; 9.11; 10.1; 11.5; 13.1; 14.1, 3; 16.1) and "brothers and sisters" (19.1; 20.2). Tuckett has noted that the change to "brothers and sisters" does not automatically imply two authors, agreeing with earlier scholarship that saw the text as a unity.[51]

10.3.4 Genre

While the text is known as a letter to ancient authors such as Eusebius, Jerome, and Rufinus, it lacks epistolary features such as personal greetings, identification of recipients, personal experiences of the author, and the ancient theme of absence and presence.[52] As a document, it is a performative one, since passages such as 15.2, 17.3, and 19.1 suggest that the document was read aloud to a community of Christians. However, to label the text a sermon would be to make it one of the first such documents, the other being Melito's Paschal Homily.[53] It also differs from the sermons on "the memoirs of the apostles or the writings of the prophets" described by Justin in *1 Apol.* 67. The author perhaps categorizes his text in the negative at 15.1, by saying that he has not given a small *symboulia*, piece of advice, about self-control.[54] Meanwhile, 19.1 claims that the work is an *enteuxis*, a petition or supplication. Baasland and Pratscher are thus probably correct to call the text a "homily" as opposed to a more general sermon.[55]

---

[51] Tuckett, *2 Clement*, 27.

[52] Ibid., 18.

[53] C. Stegemann, "Herkunft und Entstehung des sogenannten zweiten Klemensbriefes," PhD dissertation, Department of Church History, Rheinischen Friedrich-Wilhelms-Universität, 1974.

[54] Tuckett, *2 Clement*, 22–3.

[55] Ernst Baasland, "Der *2.Klemensbrief* und die frühchristliche Rhetorik: Die erste christliche Predigt` im Licht der neueren Forschung," in *ANRW* 2.27.1, ed. Wolfgang Haase and Hildegard Temporini (Berlin: de Gruyter, 1993), 78–157, at 100; Wilhelm Pratscher, *Der Zweite Clemensbrief, Kommentar zu den apostolischen Vätern* (Göttingen: Vandenhoeck & Ruprecht, 2007), 125.

10.3.5 Manuscripts

The extant copies of 2 *Clement* are all in manuscripts that contain
1 Clement. We do not possess a copy of the text that has not already
been associated with *1 Clement*. Of the manuscripts of *1 Clement*, only
three have 2 *Clement*. These are Codex Alexandrinus (fifth century),
Codex Hierosolymitanus (1056), and the Syriac manuscript of the New
Testament dated 1169. The two Coptic manuscripts of *1 Clement* lack a
surviving portion of 2 *Clement*.

10.3.6 Themes

There are several themes in 2 *Clement*. The author exhorts his audience
to fasting, almsgiving, prayer, repentance, health, and the day of judgment. Correcting interpretations that the emphasis in 2 *Clement* falls
on almsgiving, Parvis points out that the variegated themes focus on
moral improvement and conversion. Parvis discerns a set of exhortative
pairs: blindness and sight, sickness and healing, moral drunkenness and
sobriety: "Praying more frequently, let us attempt to make progress in
the commandments of the Lord, that we might all, being of one mind, be
brought together in life" (17.3); "Let us pursue virtue all the more, and
let us leave behind vice, as the forerunner of our sins" (10.1).[56] Like
Hermas, this moral exhortation might be a case of love-patriarchalism
intended to create unity. Such a focus on moral improvement and unity
would be congruent with the nature of 2 *Clement* as a homily.

10.3.6.1 Eternal Judgment

Judgment holds a central place for the argumentation of 2 *Clement*,
beginning with the incipit: "Brothers, we must think about Jesus Christ
as we think about God, as about the judge of the living and the dead"
(2 *Clem.* 1.1). The goal is to prevent individual believers from destruction (17.1). There is a clear contrast between those who have acted
correctly and renounced "pleasures of the soul" with those who have
"deviated from the path" (17.7).

While the rhetoric that 2 *Clement* uses appears to be dire, it seems
that there is an intent toward conversion for the whole community as
well as those who might be more susceptible to deviating from the
correct moral constitution. The author uses the first person plural
pronoun for those who are "foolish" (19.2).

---

[56] Parvis, *The Writings of the Apostolic Fathers*, 38.

Perhaps greater than this evaluation of the individual comportment of believers is the judgment against the Roman Empire. The author of *2 Clement* says that the rulership of this world will be shocked when they see that the current world order no longer has power. Control over the world will have shifted to Jesus (17.5). The Roman Games are invoked by calling the arena a "spectacle" (17.5).

10.3.6.2 *Almsgiving*

Like the *Shepherd of Hermas*, *2 Clement* evinces a concern for almsgiving that redeems sins of believers and reconciles the church.[57] The language of the text frames salvation as a "reward" (3.3; 6.5, 6; 15.1). Being "charitable" is recommended as a virtue and reiterated as not being "attached to money" (4.3). *2 Clement* invokes the Jesus logion that no one can serve two masters, reminding that one cannot serve both God and wealth (6.1). Developing the theology of Tob. 12.8–9 and 1 Pet. 4:8, the homily argues that charitable donations outrank both fasting and prayer as forms of repentance (16.4).[58]

The size of the donation conceivably does not matter as the author notes that the unjust "become rich." In exhorting its audience to have faith, *2 Clement* 20 specifically references both men and women as "brothers and sisters." Like the egalitarian sentiment of the crown that Paul expresses in 1 Corinthians 9, which envisions those in the community as being capable of beating Paul for the imperishable crown, *2 Clement* includes both men and women in the trope of the agony of faith and its accompanying laurels. This suggests that women are not included merely for their recurring role as financial supporters of the early church, but that *2 Clement* is including them in the discipline of the church.

10.3.6.3 *Athletics*

In chapter 20, athletics are mentioned in connection with money. The author uses one of the athletic metaphors known from Paul's 1 Corinthians: training for and competing in the contest in the present world in order to gain an imperishable crown. *2 Clement* only invokes the more elite stephanitic games, not those consisting of a monetary prize. Without the wait for the reward, believers would "be engaged in commerce rather than devotion to God" (20.4). De Wet has interpreted

---

[57] Garrison, *Redemptive Almsgiving*, 107–8.
[58] Downs, "Love Covers a Multitude of Sins."

this as a use of the patriarchal athletic apparatus of the Roman Empire to regulate the church body and appeal to outsiders.[59] However, since women had less enfranchisement in official athletic events, such a metaphor would have had the effect of putting more of an onus for discipline on male patronage and perhaps held more of an appeal to non-members who had esteem for traditional Greek games instead of the Roman spectacles (probably those from the Greek East and possibly those who were male).

10.3.6.4 Presbyters

Unlike 1 Clement, the issue of presbyters is not a recurring theme in 2 Clement. In chapter 17, there is a mention of presbyters as authoritative, but the faction deposing the presbyters is not present. Instead, there are merely church members who do not believe the presbyters that they should repent (17.3, 17.5). Rather, these members are at risk of not remembering the commandments and being "dragged away by worldly desires" (17.5).

10.4 CONCLUSION

As was noted in antiquity, the authors of 1 and 2 Clement differ. Both texts are cohesive documents unto themselves, though they share some conceptual overlap with each other and with the Roman political discursive tradition of writing on concord. 1 Clement specifically addresses a single situation in Corinth involving non-appointed presbyters. The text seeks to advance the position of the churches within Roman and Stoic values such as concord and political unity. 2 Clement is a more general exhortation on moral conversion, focusing on common themes in early Christian literature (e.g., almsgiving, unity). It does not refer to a single event in the congregation of Corinth, and it does not frame its message as one of Roman churches to those inheriting the Pauline legacy at Corinth.

The picture of the early church that emerges from these two texts is simultaneously one of unity of communities and diversity of theological opinions. Churches in different cities correspond and collaborate with each other, and individual church communities evince interest in maintaining harmony within their communities by means of social and

---

[59] Chris L. de Wet, "'No small counsel about self-control': Enkrateia and the Virtuous Body as Missional Performance in 2 Clement," HTS Teologiese Studies/ Theological Studies 69 (2013), Art. #1340, 10 pages.

financial generosity. There is a notion, in *1 Clement*, that the current church presbyter-bishop leadership inherits its authority from the apostles, with Clement referring to the legalistic term "codicil." However, the nexus of ecclesial authority remains within each individual community. No one bishop, such as a Clement of Rome, helms one church or several churches. *1 Clement* must persuade rather than demand that the Corinthian church reinstate its presbyters by appealing to examples from Roman, Greek, and Jewish traditions and the moral rectitude of the letter's carriers. In a lengthy letter, Clement's primary instruction is to restore presbyters, departing from the Pauline custom of imparting multipronged instruction on everything from sexual relationships to idol food. Likewise, the prospect of eternal judgment is used to convince the audience of *2 Clement* to engage in almsgiving rather than an established tithing schedule or a clear ministry prescription such as the food service for the widows in Acts 6. The authors of *1* and *2 Clement* appear as moral authorities, but they have a lesser role in both the day-to-day activities and general running of their church audiences than did Paul and the other apostles.

FURTHER READING

Donfried, Karl Paul. *The Setting of Second Clement in Early Christianity.* NovTSup 38. Leiden: Brill, 1974.

Fuellenbach, John. *Ecclesiastical Office and the Primacy of Rome: An Evaluation of Recent Theological Discussion of First Clement.* Washington, DC: Catholic University of America Press, 1980.

Gregory, Andrew. *1 Clement: An Introduction, The Writings of the Apostolic Fathers*, ed. Paul Foster. London: Bloomsbury, 2007.

Lindemann, Andreas. "The First Epistle of Clement," in *The Apostolic Fathers: An Introduction*, ed. Wilhelm Pratscher. Waco, TX: Baylor University Press, 2010, 47–69.

Peters, Janelle "Rahab, Esther, and Judith as Models for Church Leadership in *1 Clement*," *JECH* 5 (2015): 94–110.

Stanton, G.R. "2 Clement VII and the Origin of the Document," *Classica et Mediaevalia* 28 (1967): 314–20.

Stewart Sykes, Alistair. *From Prophesy to Preaching. A Search for the Origins of Christian Homily.* VgChrSup 59. Leiden: Brill, 2001.

Tuckett, Christopher M. *2 Clement: Introduction, Text, and Commentary.* OAF. Oxford: Oxford University Press, 2012.

11 The Letters of Ignatius

JONATHON LOOKADOO

> Word is that this one (Ignatius) was sent away from Syria to the city of
> Rome to become the food of beasts on account of the witness to Christ.
> Indeed, he was taken through Asia under a most careful watch of guards
> and strengthened the communities of each city in which he stayed with
> his discourses and exhortations.
>
> Eus. *Hist. eccl.* 3.36.3–4[1]

11.1 INTRODUCTION

Writing in the fourth century, Eusebius puts forward what may be
regarded as the traditional story of Ignatius of Antioch. Little is said of
his birth or early life. Eusebius' account begins in earnest with the
apparent arrest of Ignatius in Syria or, more specifically, in Antioch.
Ignatius is then forced to travel with a cohort guarding him overland
through Asia. While in Smyrna and Troas, he wrote seven letters: five
to nearby communities of believers in western Asia (*Ephesians;
Magnesians; Trallians; Philadelphians; Smyrnaeans*), one to believers
in Rome (*Romans*), and one to a fellow ecclesial leader named Polycarp
(*Polycarp*). In his *Letter to Polycarp*, Ignatius says that he would like to
write more but is unable to do so because he is being forced to sail on to
Neapolis (Ign. *Pol.* 8.1). This is the last that is heard from Ignatius
himself. To follow the story to the end we must consult documents
that postdate Ignatius' letters. These end with Ignatius' death by the
beasts that he had earlier hoped would become his tomb (Ign. *Rom.* 4.2).

This is not to say that the traditional narrative answers every
question about the weeks and months prior to Ignatius' death or even
that this narrative is the only story to tell about him. While Eusebius

---

[1] Greek text from G. Bardy (ed.), *Eusèbe de Césarée: Histoire Ecclésiastique, Livres
I–IV*, 2nd ed., SC 31 (Paris: Cerf, 1986), 146–8. Unless otherwise noted, all translations
are my own.

elsewhere locates Ignatius' death to the 221st Olympiad and the tenth year of Trajan's reign (107 CE), the Byzantine historian John Malalas appears to date Ignatius' death near the end of Trajan's reign, perhaps between 115 and 117 CE (*Chron.* 11.276). Likewise, two early accounts developed regarding Ignatius' trial. In one version, Ignatius is summoned by Trajan while Trajan is in Antioch. In another story, Ignatius' trial occurs in Rome before Trajan and the Senate.[2] Although these ambiguities and alternatives arose early in the transmission of Ignatian materials, they are not the only difficulties that have been observed regarding Ignatius. Recent scholarship has found ambiguity when attempting to identify Ignatius' opponents, uncertainty when trying to define whether and how Ignatius used authoritative texts, and doubts when endeavouring to determine when Ignatius wrote and whether his letters are genuine. It is to this last matter that the chapter turns next.

11.2 DATE AND AUTHENTICITY

Questions about when Ignatius wrote and whether the letters are authentic reach back at least to the aftermath of the Protestant Reformation.[3] The issues of the letters' date and authenticity have been freshly questioned since the 1990s. Building on the work of Robert Joly,[4] Reinhard Hübner and Thomas Lechner argue that Polycarp's *Letter to the Philippians* shows evidence of interpolation at Pol. *Phil.* 13.2.[5] According to this line of thought, the later addition appears to contradict what Polycarp says in Pol. *Phil.* 9.1. The interpolation at Pol. *Phil.* 13.2 along with the reference to "copies" (*mimēmata*) at Pol. *Phil.* 1.1 are regarded as the work of a forger who is also responsible for penning

---

[2] These versions are often distinguished as the *Antiochene Acts* and the *Roman Acts.* See J.B. Lightfoot, *The Apostolic Fathers: Part II, S. Ignatius, S. Polycarp*, 2nd ed., 3 vols. (London: Macmillan, 1889), 2.363–540, 573–88.

[3] H. de Quehen, "Politics and Scholarship in the Ignatian Controversy," *Seventeenth Century* 13 (1998): 69–84; P. Hartog, "A Multifaceted Jewel: English Episcopacy, Ignatian Authenticity, and the Rise of Critical Patristic Scholarship," in *Defending the Faith: John Jewel and the Elizabethan Church*, ed. A. Ransom, A. Gazal, and S. Bastow (University Park: Pennsylvania State University Press, 2018), 263–83.

[4] Robert Joly, *Le dossier d'Ignace d'Antioche* (Brussels: Éditions de l'Université de Bruxelles, 1979).

[5] R. Hübner, "Thesen zur Echtheit und Datierung der sieben Briefe des Ignatius von Antiochien," *ZAC* 1 (1997): 48–50; T. Lechner, *Ignatius adversus Valentinianos? Chronologische und theologiegeschichtliche Studien zu den Briefen des Ignatius von Antiochien*, VCSup 47 (Leiden: Brill, 1999), 6–65.

the Ignatian letters. Doubt about the reliability of Eusebius' testimony has added to uncertainty about the reliability of Ignatius' letters. If such arguments are accepted, they would dislodge the Ignatian letters from a date in the early second century. Irenaeus' citation of Ign. *Rom.* 4.1 at the end of the second century determines the latest possible date that can be posited for the letters (*Haer.* 5.28.4), but one must still attempt to locate the Ignatian letters more precisely in the second century. Hübner appeals to similarities between Ignatius' language about Jesus in Ign. *Eph.* 7.2; *Pol.* 3.2 and reports about Noetus in Hippolytus, *Haer.* 9.10.9–10; 10.27.1–2. Both Ignatius and Noetus utilize paired adjectives that appeal to paradoxes in Christ (e.g., born–unborn; visible–invisible).[6] Lechner finds close resemblances between the star-hymn in Ign. *Eph.* 19.2–3 and reports about Theodotus in Clement of Alexandria, *Exc.* 74. He argues that Ignatius' letter provides a proto-orthodox response to Theodotus' Valentinian christological narrative.[7] The cumulative results of such arguments suggest a date for the Ignatian letters around 160–175 CE. If one follows Hübner and Lechner the letters must be regarded as inauthentic and forged in Ignatius' name by a later second-century writer.

The challenge put forward by Hübner and Lechner has shown no signs of weakening but neither has it resulted in consensus. Indeed, it appears that the number of ways in which scholars can now reflect on Ignatius' date and authenticity have only proliferated. Three primary tendencies can be adduced.[8]

To begin with, the arguments of Hübner and Lechner have continued to receive support and to be developed by others who explore Ignatius alongside second-century texts. Two ways of arguing for this position should be mentioned. First, the letters may be placed directly in dialogue with other texts. For example, Ignatius' comments on Jesus' bodily resurrection (Ign. *Smyrn.* 3.1–3) could be understood as an anti-marcionite interpretation of a tradition similar to Lk. 24.37–9.[9] Second,

---

[6] Hübner, "Thesen," 53–9; Hübner, "Die antignostische Glaubensregel des Noët von Smyrna (Hippolyt, Refutatio IX,10,9–12 und X,27,1–2) bei Ignatius, Irenaeus und Tertullian," *MTZ* 40 (1989): 279–311.

[7] Lechner, *Ignatius*, 246–300.

[8] J. Lookadoo, "The Date and Authenticity of the Ignatian Letters: An Outline of Recent Discussions', *Currents in Biblical Research* 19 (2020): 88–114.

[9] M. Vinzent, "'Ich bin kein körperloses Geistwesen': Zum Verhältnis von κήρυγμα Πέτρου, 'Doctrina Petri', διδασκαλία Πέτρου und IgnSm 3," in *Der Paradox Eine: Antignostischer Monarchianismus im zweiten Jahrhundert*, R. Hübner, VigChrSup 50 (Leiden: Brill, 1999), 241–86.

one might also consider the purpose for writing a pseudepigraphic corpus in the third quarter of the second century. Instead of assuming the letters should be interpreted in the context of Asia Minor, they may support the development of the bishop's role in Rome.[10] Whether the intended audience is located in Rome or Asia, proponents of this position hold in common a late date for the letters of Ignatius (c. 160–180 CE) and the belief that the letters were falsely attributed to Ignatius.

A second position maintains that the letters are authentically Ignatian and should be dated to the first third of the second century. Although Hübner's challenge may be regarded as valuable since the question of the letters' authenticity, on the one hand, must be separated from the issue of the letters' date, on the other, arguments for a specifically late date have not persuaded all.[11] Just as Ignatius' letters can be read alongside texts from the latter half of the second century, so also they can be read in conjunction with first-century texts from the Jesus movement. Ignatius' epistolary style and emphasis on harmony, unity, and peace may fit within the Second Sophistic rhetorical environment of the early second century.[12] Moreover, if Ignatius did not write these letters, it is difficult to see how he would be a sufficiently authoritative persona in whose name to forge a letter collection. Although not everyone would follow Eusebius in dating Ignatius to the time of Trajan, this position interprets Ignatius' letters as documents in the early decades of the second century.

A third perspective argues for an authentically Ignatian corpus of letters that should be dated in the middle of the second century. This view would date Ignatius' compositions later than Trajan or the early years of Hadrian's reign but prior to Polycarp's death.[13] It acknowledges that Ignatius' letters contain elements – such as an emphatically high

---

[10] W. Schmithals, "Zu Ignatius von Antiochien," *ZAC* 13 (2009): 181–203; F. Prostmeier, "*Cui bono*," in *Die Briefe des Ignatios von Antiochia: Motive, Strategien, und Kontexte*, ed. T.J. Bauer and P.v. Möllendorff, Millennium Studies 72 (Berlin: De Gruyter, 2018), 169–99.

[11] A. Lindemann, "Antwort auf die Thesen zur Echtheit und Datierung der sieben Briefe des Ignatius von Antiochien," *ZAC* 1 (1997): 185–94; M.J. Edwards, "Ignatius and the Second Century: An Answer to R. Hübner," *ZAC* 2 (1998): 214–26.

[12] Allen Brent, *Ignatius of Antioch and the Second Sophistic: A Study of an Early Christian Transformation of Pagan Culture*, Studien und Texte zu Antike Christentum 36 (Tübingen: Mohr Siebeck, 2006).

[13] P. Foster, "The Epistles of Ignatius of Antioch," in *The Apostolic Fathers*, ed. P. Foster (London: T&T Clark, 2007), 84–9; T.D. Barnes, "The Date of Ignatius," *ExpT* 120 (2008): 119–30.

view of the bishop – that are difficult to locate early in the second century but also refuses to link Ignatius' letters to texts from the late second century. The third position resists making a false dichotomy between letters that are early and authentic or late and forged.[14] It also implicitly demonstrates the influence of the challenge by Hübner and Lechner by expanding the number of positions and possible dates that one may assign to Ignatius' epistles.

Two findings come out of this discussion of recent scholarship on the date and authenticity of Ignatius' letters. Most significantly, the issues of date and authenticity are no longer narrowly connected in scholarship. One may argue for a genuinely Ignatian corpus but date the letters later than the Trajanic date given by Eusebius. While dates at the earliest end of the range are closely linked to an authentic Ignatian corpus and dates at the latest end of the spectrum presume pseudepigraphic letters, there are positions in the middle where Ignatius' letters could be regarded as either authentic or forged. By separating these two issues, the band of possible dates for Ignatius' letters ranges from roughly 105 to 180 CE.

A second matter that comes out of these reflections concerns the sorts of evidence that may be used to argue about the date and authenticity of Ignatius' letters. Three pieces of evidence have been central to recent discussions. These include the reliability of Eusebius' dating of Ignatius' martyrdom, the difficulty of interpreting Pol. *Phil.* 1.1; 9.1; 13.2, and the placement of Ignatius' letters vis-à-vis second-century theological discussions as well as the Second Sophistic movement.[15] With regard to the last piece of evidence, the question is how precisely Ignatius' letters can be dated in the second century on the basis of comparison with other second-century authors, coins, and inscriptions. One may wonder what other pieces of evidence are useful to consider when determining the date and authenticity of the letters. Are Ignatius' comments about the Lord's Day (*kyriakē*; Ign. *Magn.* 9.1) best interpreted in accordance with Marcion?[16] Or is the evidence too ambiguous

---

[14] A. Stewart, *The Original Bishops: Office and Order in the First Christian Communities* (Grand Rapids, MI: Baker Academic, 2014), 239.

[15] For a concise statement of evidence, see H. Löhr, "The Epistles of Ignatius of Antioch," in *The Apostolic Fathers: An Introduction*, ed. W. Pratscher (Waco, TX: Baylor University Press, 2010), 84–5.

[16] M. Vinzent, *Christ's Resurrection in Early Christianity and the Making of the New Testament* (Farnham: Ashgate, 2011), 213.

to place Ignatius' letters so precisely?[17] Ignatius refers to personified aeons (*aiōnes*; Ign. *Eph.* 19.2), which are best known from their connection to so-called gnostic writings.[18] Yet personified aeons are also found in texts that predate or are roughly contemporaneous with Ignatius' letters (1 En. 1.9; Epictetus, *Diatr.* 2.5.13; Euripides, *Heracl.* 900).[19]

Further clarification is needed to advance current debates regarding the date and authenticity of Ignatius' letters. For now, one may note two things. First, scholarship on Ignatius' letters has continued to study other elements of Ignatius' letters productively and can do so even when there is disagreement about their date and authenticity.[20] Second, although the Eusebian evidence for Ignatius' date is far from certain, a date for Ignatius' martyrdom during Trajan's reign remains a plausible way of understanding the letters. The remainder of this chapter assumes an authentically Ignatian set of letters.[21]

11.3 AUDIENCE AND OPPONENTS

While the questions of date and authenticity have received an enormous amount of recent attention, they are not the only matters of interest when reading Ignatius' letters. If the letters are accepted as genuinely Ignatian, these texts may also shed light on the early Christian communities to which they are addressed. As an early Christian leader from Antioch addresses groups and individuals in western Asia and Rome, the letters offer a glimpse into three major regions of the Roman Empire (Syria, Asia, Rome/Italy) as well as shedding light on issues that believers faced in particular cities. The letters also refer to named individuals. Ignatius mentions the leaders of Ephesus (Onesimus; Ign.

---

[17] U. Heil, "Ignatios von Antiochia und der Herrentag," in *Die Briefe des Ignatios von Antiochien: Motive, Strategien, und Kontexte*, eds. T.J. Bauer and P.v. Möllendorff, Millennium Studies 72 (Berlin: De Gruyter, 2018), 201–27.

[18] Lechner, *Ignatius*, 267–70.

[19] J. Lookadoo, "A Note on the Use of Αἰών in the Letters of Ignatius of Antioch," *ETL* 94 (2018): 693–703.

[20] For a recent example, see the essays in T.J. Bauer and P.v. Möllendorff (eds.), *Die Briefe des Ignatios von Antiochien: Motive, Strategien, und Kontexte*, Millennium Studies 72 (Berlin: De Gruyter, 2018).

[21] For further argumentation in support of this position, see C. Trevett, *A Study of Ignatius of Antioch in Syria and Asia*, Studies in the Bible and Early Christianity 29 (Lewiston, ME: Edwin Mellen, 1992), 3–9; P. Trebilco, *The Early Christians in Ephesus from Paul to Ignatius*, WUNT 166 (Tübingen: Mohr Siebeck, 2004), 629–32; J. Lookadoo, *The High Priest and the Temple: Metaphorical Depictions of Jesus in the Letters of Ignatius of Antioch*, WUNT 2.473 (Tübingen: Mohr Siebeck, 2018), 15–22.

Eph. 1.3; 6.2), Magnesia on the Maeander (Damas; Ign. *Magn.* 2), Tralles (Polybius; Ign. *Trall.* 1.1), and Smyrna (Polycarp; Ign. *Eph.* 21.1; *Magn.* 15; *Pol.* inscr.). Ignatius also refers to the leader of the believers in Philadelphia but does not name the bishop (Ign. *Phld.* 1.1). He names several other believers, particularly elders and deacons (Ign. *Eph.* 2.1; *Magn.* 2.1; *Rom.* 10.1; *Smyrn.* 13.2; *Pol.* 8.2). Burrhus, Philo, and Rhaius Agathopus receive special mention. They seem to have accompanied Ignatius for portions of his journey while serving as messengers (Ign. *Eph.* 2.1; *Phld.* 11.1–2; *Smyrn.* 10.1; 12.1).[22] The women whom Ignatius names at the end of the Smyrnaean communication are also of note (Ign. *Smyrn.* 13.2; *Pol.* 8.2–3), since Tavia, Alce, and the widow of Epitropus appear to play leading roles in Smyrnaean households and the community of believers gathered in that city. Although Ignatius does not offer much detail about the believers that he names, the fact that they are named strongly suggests that Ignatius knew and was part of a network of believers that wove its way through many of the cities in the Mediterranean world.

While addressing individuals and communities in western Asia and in Rome, the letters also contain evidence that all was not well in and around these communities. Two criteria emerge within the letters that Ignatius views as central characteristics of early Christian communities.[23] To begin with, he demonstrates consistent concern about who Jesus is and what his addressees believe about Christ. Ignatius offers short summaries of Jesus' life (Ign. *Trall.* 9.1–2; *Smyrn.* 1.1–3.3) and poetic statements that make use of both parallelism and narratival allusions (Ign. *Eph.* 7.2; *Pol.* 3.2).[24] Ignatius understands the prophets with respect to Christ (Ign. *Phld.* 8.2–9.2).[25] Believers are lauded for ignoring teachers who impart different ways of understanding Jesus

---

[22] D. Batovici, "Contrasting Ecclesial Functions in the Second Century: 'Diakonia', 'Diakonoi', 'Episkopoi' and 'Presbyteroi' in the *Shepherd of Hermas* and Ignatius of Antioch's *Letters*," *Augustinianum* 51 (2011): 309–10.

[23] T.A. Robinson, *Ignatius of Antioch and the Parting of the Ways: Early Jewish–Christian Relations* (Peabody, MA: Hendrickson, 2009), 125.

[24] On the role of the incarnational narrative in Ignatius' letters, see M.J. Svigel, *The Center and the Source: Second Century Incarnational Christology and Early Catholic Christianity*, Gorgias Studies in Early Christianity and Patristics 66 (Piscataway, NJ: Gorgias, 2016), 47–174.

[25] F. Bergamelli, "Gesù Cristo e gli archivi (*Filadelfiesi* 8,2): Cristo centro delle scritture secondo Ignazio di Antiochia," in *Exegesi e catechesi nei padre (secc. IV–VII)*, ed. S. Felici (Rome: LAS, 1993), 35–47; G. Vall, *Learning Christ: Ignatius of Antioch and the Mystery of Redemption* (Washington, DC: Catholic University of America Press, 2013), 27–33.

(Ign. *Eph.* 9.1), while Jesus provides the basis upon which believers should set their hope and establish their ethics (Ign. *Magn.* 11; *Smyrn.* 6.1–7.2). Yet Ignatius offers an additional criterion to aid his audiences in forming healthy communities. Believers must demonstrate unity with one another under proper authorities. In addition to naming bishops in direct support of people whom Ignatius views as rightful overseers in the community, he extends the harmony for which he calls to include all believers while linking bishops, presbyters, and deacons to a heavenly hierarchy that includes God the Father, Jesus Christ, and the apostles (e.g., Ign. *Eph.* 3.2; *Magn.* 2.1–3.2; *Trall.* 2.1–3.1; *Smyrn.* 8.1; *Pol.* inscr.).[26]

If the way in which believers describe Jesus and unify around ecclesial officials provide central standards by which Ignatius identifies a faithful community, he also raises problems that had arisen within the communities. Two oft-mentioned matters in Ignatian scholarship include how Ignatius' opponents viewed Jesus and Judaism. Indeed, a longstanding debate among Ignatian scholars concerns whether Ignatius' repeated comments on these issues should be understood with reference to a single collection of Jewish-Docetists or to two groups, one set of Jewish believers and another set of believers with docetic Christologies.[27] Although Ignatius never fully outlines his opponents' views or why he disagrees with them, he juxtaposes the word Judaism (*Ioudaismos*) opposite the beliefs that he expects his readers to take (Ign. *Magn.* 8.1; 10.3; *Phld.* 6.1). While it is unclear precisely how best to term Ignatius' christological opponents, he repeatedly speaks of Jesus' blood, flesh, suffering, death, and physicality after his resurrection so that one suspects at least some readers had encountered teachings about Jesus that downplayed Jesus' bodily nature, death, or both (e.g., Ign. *Eph.* 1.1; 7.2; 18.2–19.1; *Magn.* 11; *Trall.* 9.1–11.2; *Rom.* 6.3; *Phld.* 9.2; *Smyrn.* 1.1–3.3; *Pol.* 3.2). Ignatius' consistent concern for unity and obedience to the bishop may provide evidence for a third set of opponents in the letters, namely, those who oppose either specific ecclesial officials or

---

[26] A. Brent, "The Ignatian Epistles and the Threefold Ecclesiastical Order," *JRH* 17 (1992): 18–32.

[27] For an example of the one-opponent hypothesis, see J.W. Marshall, "The Objects of Ignatius' Wrath and Jewish Angelic Mediators," *JEH* 56 (2005): 1–23. For two opponents, see M. Myllykoski, "Wild Beasts and Rabid Dogs: The Riddle of the Heretics in the Letters of Ignatius of Antioch," in *The Formation of the Early Church*, ed. J. Ådna, WUNT 183 (Tübingen: Mohr Siebeck, 2005), 341–77.

the role of the bishop entirely.[28] Although it is likely the case that
Ignatius' comments about bishops stem from his own experience,[29] it
is difficult to ascertain whether these comments reveal the remains of
an organized set of opponents.

11.4 ISSUES IN IGNATIUS' LETTERS

The issues covered so far are standard introductory issues for early
Christian texts and are important for studying Ignatius' letters. As
important as the questions of date, authenticity, audience, and opponents are, however, they are not the only matters to consider when
reading Ignatius. It will be helpful, therefore, to explore a few characteristic concerns within the letters. The Ignatian focus on Jesus, the people
of God, and how his addressees should act may serve as useful
starting points.

11.4.1 Jesus

Ignatius describes Jesus in both the highest and the lowest of terms.
Because disputes about Jesus were likely a source of conflict among at
least some people in or around Ignatius' audiences, the previous section
alluded to some of what Ignatius says about Jesus when discussing
opponents. Ignatius' recurrent references to Jesus as God and his consistent emphasis on Jesus' flesh and suffering allow him to depict Jesus
as a mediatorial figure who is present in the communities to which
Ignatius writes.

The first mention of Jesus by name that readers encounter in
modern editions of Ignatius' letters comes in Ign. *Eph.* inscr. While
greeting the Ephesians, Ignatius remarks on "the will of the Father
and of Jesus Christ our God." Although the precise number of times
that Ignatius describes Jesus as God (*Theos*) is difficult to ascertain
owing to text critical uncertainties,[30] Ignatius' portrayal of Christ in

---

[28] C. Trevett, "Prophecy and Anti-Episcopal Activity: A Third Error Combatted by
Ignatius?," *JEH* 34 (1983): 1–18.

[29] K. Piepenbrink, "Zur Perzeption des kirchlichen Amtes durch einen
'Märtyrerbischof': Die Perspektive des Ignatios und ihre historische
Kontextualisierung," in *Die Briefe des Ignatios von Antiochien: Motive,
Strategien, und Kontexte,* ed. T.J. Bauer and P.v. Möllendorff, Millennium Studies
72 (Berlin: De Gruyter, 2018), 131–52, at 137–45.

[30] P.R. Gilliam, *Ignatius of Antioch and the Arian Controversy,* VCSup 140 (Leiden:
Brill, 2017), 8–48. For Ignatius' attribution of Jesus as *Theos* elsewhere in the letters,
see Ign. *Eph.* 1.1; 7.2; 18.2; 19.3; *Trall.* 7.1; *Rom.* inscr. (twice); 3.3; 6.3; *Smyrn.* 1.1;
10.1; *Pol.* 8.3.

divine terms extends beyond the use of a single noun. As he insists to the Magnesians, Jesus is unified with the Father (Ign. *Magn.* 1.2; 8.2; 13.2). This union between the Father and Son extends "before the ages" (Ign. *Magn.* 6.1) and remains true in the present (Ign. *Magn.* 7.2). Following Ignatius' logic, Jesus can be described as timeless, invisible, and untouchable (Ign. *Pol.* 3.2). Ignatius' letters thus portray Jesus in elevated terms by presenting him as God and as one who is uniquely united to the Father.

Such high ways of speaking about Jesus do not prohibit Ignatius from speaking of Jesus' humanity in emphatic terms. One of the most striking expressions occurs at the end of the letter to the Ephesians, where Ignatius lists monumental disruptions to the normal economy of the world that occurred when God appeared "humanly" (*anthropōpinōs*; Ign. *Eph.* 19.3). Earlier in the letter, Ignatius vividly speaks of "God's blood" (Ign. *Eph.* 1.1), while he also mentions the birth (Ign. *Eph.* 18.2–19.1; *Magn.* 11) and death (Ign. *Eph.* 7.2; *Smyrn.* 1.2; *Pol.* 1.2) of Jesus regularly in the letters. Allusions to Jesus' suffering also recur in Ignatius' rhetoric (Ign. *Rom.* 6.3; *Phld.* inscr.). Talk of agony ultimately gives way to resurrection and the hope of life found therein (Ign. *Magn.* 9.1; *Trall.* 9.2). Throughout the letters, Ignatius emphasizes Jesus' flesh (*sarx*). He illustrates the fleshly reality of Jesus' corporeal existence before and after the resurrection with reference to the food and drink that he consumed (Ign. *Trall.* 9.1; *Smyrn.* 3.1–3).

One means by which Ignatius brings these portrayals of Jesus together is by referring to the unity of flesh and spirit that Jesus embodies (Ign. *Eph.* 7.2; *Smyrn.* 3.3; 12.2). Jesus belongs to David's line and is also Son of God (Ign. *Eph.* 20.2; *Smyrn.* 1.1).[31] Such paradoxical claims allow him to serve as mediator between the Father and human beings. For Ignatius, Jesus is both a high priest who makes known the secrets of God to human beings and a door that offers the people access to the Father (Ign. *Phld.* 9.1). Jesus' cross brings the Ephesians into God's building (Ign. *Eph.* 9.1), while his union with the Father positions him perfectly to teach and speak in revelatory ways on the Father's behalf (Ign. *Eph.* 15.1; *Magn.* 8.2; *Rom.* 8.2). Because of Jesus' union with the Father, harmony of flesh and spirit, and willingness to suffer, he is able to serve as humanity's physician (Ign. *Eph.* 7.2). While discussions of

---

[31] P. Hartog, "The Impact of the Christological Controversies: Comparing the Ignatian Kerygma and Romans 1," in *Docetism in the Early Church: The Quest for an Elusive Phenomenon*, ed. J. Verheyden, R. Bieringer, J. Schröter, and I. Jäger, WUNT 402 (Tübingen: Mohr Siebeck, 2018), 178–82.

Jesus in Ignatius' letters are by no means as refined as debates in the fourth and fifth century will become, his letters may be suitably understood as a stepping stone on one of the criss-crossed paths that eventually led to Nicaea and Chalcedon.[32]

11.4.2 The People of God

As Ignatius keeps a taut line drawn between the flesh and spirit in Jesus, so also he maintains tensions in the letters when depicting his audiences. On the one hand, he styles believers in terms that point to their participation in a superterrestrial reality. Whether through prayer or by means of the ecclesial leaders whom Ignatius meets, he can write as if he has met the people where they are, even though the congregations are represented by a small number of their leaders (Ign. *Eph.* 1.3; *Rom.* 1.1). The leaders of God's people participate in celestial ministrations as they embody the Father, Jesus, and the apostles while serving the people (Ign. *Magn.* 2.1–3.2; *Trall.* 2.1–3.1; *Smyrn.* 8.1). The Ephesians are described as God's temple(s), something that Ignatius attributes to them in the present (Ign. *Eph.* 9.1–2; 15.3). Yet Ignatius portrays them being drawn into an even larger building that represents all of God's people (Ign. *Eph.* 9.1). On the other hand, things were not completely right in the communities to which Ignatius wrote his letters. He offers advice to the Ephesians regarding how to act in view of outsiders who antagonize the community (Ign. *Eph.* 10.2–3). While he describes the bishop at Philadelphia as "in harmony with the commandments" (Ign. *Phld.* 1.2), he repeatedly directs the Philadelphians to obey the bishop, suggesting that all may not be as it seems (Ign. *Phld.* 3.2–3; 4; 7.1–8.1). The opponents that have been discussed earlier in the chapter appear to be either mixed in among Ignatius' addressees or circling around the outskirts of their communities (Ign. *Eph.* 9.1; *Magn.* 8.1–10.3; *Smyrn.* 4.1). Ignatius pulls on his depiction of the ideal community while simultaneously warning them against problems that lurk nearby.

Unity plays a multifaceted role in Ignatius' understanding of God's people.[33] It does not absolve the communities of the tensions in which they live but properly calibrates the tension. The most striking way in which Ignatius discusses unity has to do with the harmony between believers, their bishop, and other leaders (Ign. *Trall.* 3.1; *Phld.* 7.1; *Pol.*

---

[32] T.G. Weinandy, "The Apostolic Christology of Ignatius of Antioch: The Road to Chalcedon," in *Trajectories through the New Testament and the Apostolic Fathers*, ed. A.F. Gregory and C.M. Tuckett (Oxford: Oxford University Press, 2005), 71–84.

[33] Vall, *Learning Christ*, 91–6.

6.1). Ignatius goes so far as to admonish his audience to do nothing "without the bishop" (Ign. *Trall.* 2.2; *Smyrn.* 8.2). Nor is Ignatius concerned only about solidarity with the bishop. He wishes for all members to live in harmony with one another (Ign. *Magn.* 6.2; *Trall.* 13.2; *Pol.* 6.1–2). The unity expressed in these communities mimics what Ignatius expects to be true between believers and God (Ign. *Trall.* 7.1; *Phld.* inscr.) as well as the union found between Jesus and the Father (Ign. *Magn.* 7.1–2; *Phld.* 7.2).[34] Concord among God's people includes anthropological unity as they seek to bring together fleshly and spiritual things in themselves (Ign. *Eph.* 8.2). Ignatius' challenging statements about the people of God – who are both participants in heavenly realities and people who struggle to live within complicated communities – are best understood within the unifying project that his letters portray as beginning from the work of Jesus Christ and extending through the people whom he has set apart.

11.4.3 The Life of the People of God

Ignatius did not write merely to tell an audience about its identity or to convince them to be united under a particular group of leaders. While these rhetorical aims comprise portions of some letters, Ignatius offers additional instruction about what the life of the people of God should be like. Life is precisely what Ignatius tells the Ephesians that the cross brings to believers (Ign. *Eph.* 18.1). The beginning and end of life can be summarized in two words: faith and love (Ign. *Eph.* 14.1; *Smyrn.* 6.1).[35] Ignatius' language may suggest that he views faith as something that is most vital in the initial stages of believers' lives, while love sustains one through the end. However, it is better to see these terms as the means by which Ignatius expresses the fundamental content of a believer's entire life.[36]

Ignatius also conceives of life in terms of imitation and uses dynamic terms in order to effect a sense of movement in his audiences. He understands his own life as an act of imitating Christ's suffering and

---

[34] D.J. Downs, "The Pauline Concept of Union with Christ in Ignatius of Antioch," in *The Apostolic Fathers and Paul*, ed. T.D. Still and D.E. Wilhite (London: Bloomsbury T&T Clark, 2017), 143–61.

[35] S. Zañaratu, "Les concepts de vie et de mort chez Ignace d'Antioche," *VC* 33 (1979): 329-30.

[36] O. Tarvainen, *Faith and Love in Ignatius of Antioch*, trans. Jonathon Lookadoo (Eugene, OR: Pickwick, 2016), 2; trans. of *Glaube und Liebe bei Ignatius von Antiochien*, Schriften der Luther-Agricola-Gesellschaft 14 (Helsinki: Luther-Agricola-Gesellschaft, 1967), 17.

tells the Philadelphians to imitate Jesus in the same way that Jesus followed his Father (Ign. *Rom.* 6.3; *Phld.* 7.2).[37] Believers are called to learn suitable ways to live, since they would cease to exist if Christ mimicked their actions (Ign. *Magn.* 10.1). The love that husbands should exhibit toward their wives is portrayed in terms of Christ's love for the church (Ign. *Pol.* 5.1). Ignatius complements these depictions of a believer's life as an imitation of Christ with active terminology that encourages believers to act rightly. Believers are instructed to "run together" in accordance with God's mind or to the God's temple (Ign. *Eph.* 3.2; *Magn.* 7.2). They must gather together regularly (Ign. *Magn.* 4; *Phld.* 7.1). Ignatius even calls believers to suffer together like soldiers prepared for battle (Ign. *Pol.* 6.1–2).

Dynamic expressions thus reveal the type of life that should be evident in God's people. Yet again the life that Ignatius' letters envision can be described in terms of unity. While there are two quite different ways in which one may live – one of life and one of death (Ign. *Magn.* 5.1) – faith and love are a key way in which Ignatius provides ethical cohesion to his instructions. Ignatius employs a merism that allows his audience to conceive of the entire life in terms of faith and love (Ign. *Eph.* 14.1). When understood in connection to the cross, faith and love pave the way to union with God (Ign. *Eph.* 9.1). Everything in life becomes good if Ignatius' audiences believe in love (ἐν ἀγάπῃ πιστεύητε; Ign. *Phld.* 9.2). To employ a more vivid Ignatian image from Ign. *Pol.* 6.2, faith and love form part of the armour by which believers are prepared to encounter those things that oppose them and thereby run together toward the life that is found by imitating Christ.

11.5 ISSUES IN IGNATIAN SCHOLARSHIP

Ignatius emphasizes Jesus in each of his letters in both the highest and lowest terms. He identifies the people of God as participants in celestial realities but also refers to problems circling in and around his audience. His letters describe the life that this people should live in terms of faith, love, and imitation. All of these are tied together by Ignatius' thoroughgoing focus on unity. While scholarship on Ignatius' letters has devoted attention to each of these issues, this does not exhaust the topics that have sparked interest. It may be useful to select two examples of issues

---

[37] H.H.D. Williams, "'Imitate Me': Interpreting Imitation in 1 Corinthians in Relation to Ignatius of Antioch," *Perichoresis* 11 (2013): 80–3.

in Ignatian scholarship: sources and traditions in Ignatius' letters and the best reading strategy with which to interpret the letters.

11.5.1 Sources, Traditions, and Scripture in Ignatius' Letters

A question that has perpetually intrigued readers concerns where Ignatius' letters might be located in relation to other cultural, rhetorical, and literary sources in the second-century Roman Empire. While similarities between the epistles and other Second Sophistic rhetors have been utilized in conjunction with arguments for dating Ignatius, comparison of the letters to Second Sophistic rhetoric remains important for interpreting the letters in themselves and for placing them in relation to ancient rhetoric.[38] Ignatius' disparaging comments about Judaism have made his letters important for those exploring the complex process of how Jews and Christians differentiated themselves from one another.[39] While some have viewed the limited number of citations of Jewish scripture as contributing to the sense that Ignatius is attempting to distinguish his own "Christian" position from a "Jewish" one, the time may have come to reevaluate Ignatius' use of scripture as well as the function of scriptural texts in the letters.[40] Ignatius' language also bears similarities to passages found in the Wisdom of Solomon and 4 Maccabees. However, it is difficult to determine precisely whether Ignatius had literary knowledge of these texts or if he drew upon vocabulary from similar traditions.

Students of Ignatius' letters have enquired most vigorously about possible literary and tradition-historical relationships between Ignatius' letters and the texts now contained in the New Testament.[41] The most active work has explored similarities and possible connectons between Ignatius' letters and those of Paul.[42] Ignatius' imitation ethic, his

---

[38] W. Wischmeyer, "Die Briefe des Ignatios von Antiochia und die zweite Sophistik," in *Ein neues Geschlecht? Entwicklung des frühchristlichen Selbstbewusstseins*, ed. M. Lang, NTOA 105 (Göttingen: Vandenhoeck & Ruprecht, 2014), 170–8.

[39] D. Boyarin, *Judaism: The Genealogy of a Modern Notion* (New Brunswick, NJ: Rutgers University Press, 2018), 112–18.

[40] J. Lookadoo, "Ignatius of Antioch and Scripture," *ZAC* 23 (2019): 201–27. For a fuller perspective of Jewish scripture in the Apostolic Fathers, see J.C. Paget, "The Old Testament in the Apostolic Fathers," in *Studies on the Text of the New Testament and Early Christianity: Essays in Honor of Michael W. Holmes on the Occasion of His 65th Birthday*, ed. D.M. Gurtner, J. Hernández, and P. Foster, NTTSD 50 (Leiden: Brill, 2015), 453–76.

[41] For more on this topic, see Chapter 5 by P. Foster in the current volume.

[42] E.g., E. Norelli, "La tradition paulinienne dans les lettres d'Ignace," in *Receptions of Paul in Early Christianity: The Person of Paul and His Writings through the Eyes of*

comments about wisdom and the cross as stumbling block in Ign. *Eph.*
17.2–18.1, and his encouragement to put away old leaven in favor of the
new leaven (Ign. *Magn.* 10.2) collectively present strong evidence that
Ignatius knew 1 Corinthians. Ignatius' knowledge of Ephesians as well
as 1 and 2 Timothy is likely, while cases may be made that Ignatius was
aware of other letters now contained in the Pauline corpus. One may
also study rhetorical motifs and theological themes in the two sets of
letters. For example, although both men may differ in their understanding of the purpose of suffering, Ignatius' remarks on suffering resemble
thoughts found in Paul's writings. Indeed, the choice to write letters at
all may exhibit an Ignatian debt to the Apostle.

Yet the study of Ignatius' letters alongside other texts extends
beyond questions about Ignatius and Paul's letters to include knowledge
of early Christian Jesus-traditions. Ignatius' origins in Antioch and the
possible Syrian origins of the Gospel of Matthew have led some to
examine Ignatius and Matthean traditions. In addition to Ignatius'
remark that Jesus was baptized in order to fulfill all righteousness (Ign.
Smyrn. 1.1; see Mt. 3:15), his discussions of the Father's plantings have
also been juxtaposed with the words of the Matthean Jesus (Ign. *Trall.*
11.1; *Phld.* 3.1; see Mt. 15.13). In addition, it is possible that Ignatius
knew the Gospel of John, had heard of Johannine traditions, or at least
thought in Johannine ways. Ignatius' characterization of Jesus in Ign.
Magn. 7.1–8.2 and description of the Spirit's knowledge of where it has
come from and where it is going (Ign. *Phld.* 7.1) sound similar to phrases
found in John's Gospel. While it is difficult to prove Ignatian literary
dependence on John or any other early Christian text owing to the fact
that Ignatius does not formally cite other gospels or letters, Ignatius'
letters exhibit similar vocabulary and motifs to those found in some
documents that are now contained in the New Testament.

11.5.2 How to Read Ignatius' Letters

An additional matter of interest to those who study Ignatius' letters
concerns a methodological decision about how to read these letters. If
Ignatius' letters are read as individual compositions written to particular groups of believers in Asia Minor and Rome, then the study of the
letters might work on analogy to Pauline studies in recent decades,
which have largely examined Paul's letters individually before enquir-
ing about what the letters say about the author's overall viewpoint.

His Early Interpreters, ed. J. Schröter, S. Butticaz, and A. Dettwiler, BZNW 234
(Berlin: De Gruyter, 2018), 519–52.

Mikael Isacson has put forward a strong thesis arguing that the letters should be read as differentiated works to varied audiences.[43] Pablo Cavallero has likewise offered a reading of Ignatius' *Letter to the Romans* that treats the text as a self-contained whole without reference to any other letters.[44] This way of interpreting Ignatius' letters allows readers to examine how elements in individual letters work together to communicate Ignatius' thought to local groups of readers.

Alternatively, if the letters are best understood as part of a collection, a corpus-based hermeneutic would allow Ignatius' letters to mutually interpret one another. If Ignatius wrote the letters in quick succession, it may be that there is little reason to suspect that he changed his mind or said things in a dramatically different way. Moreover, if Ignatius' letters were forged with a single purpose and audience in mind, the letters may be best read as the single work of a pseudepigrapher. Studying the Ignatian collection as a whole also opens new vistas from which to view the letters. Scholars may ask questions about what order the letters should be read in, thereby cautioning readers against too easily accepting the Eusebian listing as normative.[45] It is also possible to enquire about the center of the collection. As the fourth of seven letters, *Romans* takes central position in most recent printed editions of Ignatius' texts. Since the focus on martyrdom and the failure to mention ecclesial officials differ from other letters, it may be that *Romans* marks the middle of the corpus.[46] Yet Ignatius writes four letters from Smyrna (*Eph.*; *Magn.*; *Trall.*; *Rom.*) and addresses letters to the community and an individual in Smyrna (*Smyrn.*; *Pol.*). Since Smyrna is geographically central between Ignatius' start in Antioch and his goal of Rome, it may provide the axis around which the rest of the letters and locations rotate.[47]

As these reading strategies continue to be considered, one's decision about authorship and authenticity will likely factor into how one thinks

---

[43] M. Isacson, *To Each Their Own Letter*, ConBNT 42 (Stockholm: Almqvist & Wiksell, 2004), 20–30.

[44] P.A. Cavallero, "La retórica en la *Epístola a los romanos* de san Ignacio de Antioquía," *Helmantica* 48 (1997): 269–322.

[45] See the exemplary discussion in M. Theobald, *Israel-Vergessenheit in den Pastoralbriefen: Ein neuer Vorschlag zu ihrer historisch-theologischen Verortung im 2. Jahrhundert n. Chr. Unter besonderer Berücksichtigung der Ignatius-Briefe*, SBS 229 (Stuttgart: Katholisches Bibelwerk, 2016), 259–75.

[46] Prostmeier, "*Cui Bono*," 181–9; Theobald, *Israel-Vergessenheit*, 270–5.

[47] P.v. Möllendorff, "Sonne über Smyrna: Überlegungen zur Konstruktion von Kirche und Raum in den Briefen des Ignatios von Antiochia," in *Die Briefe des Ignatios von Antiochien: Motive, Strategien, und Kontexte*, ed. T.J. Bauer and P.v. Möllendorff, Millennium Studies 72 (Berlin: De Gruyter, 2018), 153–67.

that Ignatius' letters should be interpreted. If the letters are authentic and were sent to particular groups of believers, it may be best to interpret them as discrete compositions. If the letters were authored collectively by a pseudepigrapher, individual peculiarities in the letters may give way to a holistic, corpus-based hermeneutic. However, the decision on authenticity need not determine which reading strategy one should utilize. Authentic letters may still be read as part of a collection, while an individual reading of pseudepigraphic letters may shed light on why a later author wrote multiple letters in Ignatius' name.

11.6 CONCLUSION

This chapter has introduced important issues to consider when studying Ignatius' letters as they were composed in the second century. To use more precise terminology, the essay has focused on the middle recension of the letters, particularly the Greek text of Ignatius' letters as it has been printed in modern editions of the texts. Yet it is worth noting that Ignatius' letters are available in other lengths and languages than what has been taken up in this chapter. A short recension of Ignatius' letters is available in Syriac containing only three letters in a shorter form than the letters are elsewhere attested. The middle recension consists of the seven letters that have been discussed in this essay. In addition to the Greek text of the letters, they are also extant in Latin, Coptic, Armenian, and Arabic, along with Syriac fragments. The last of the major recensions is known as the long recension and has been found in Greek and Latin. In addition to containing more letters (13 total; 12 letters by Ignatius, 1 letter to Ignatius), the long recension includes interpolated versions of the letters in the middle recension. Nor is this the end of the writings that have been attributed to Ignatius or written about Ignatius. Four medieval Latin letters contain correspondence between Ignatius, the Apostle John, and the Virgin Mary, while other narratives record Ignatius' trial and martyrdom. The variety of Ignatian letters and of the narratives about him may be surprising given the sparsity of information that comes from prior to the third century, but this same variety hints at the multiplicity of ways in which one may study Ignatius' letters.[48]

---

[48] The easiest way to access the various recensions remains Lightfoot's *Apostolic Fathers*. For an up-to-date translation of the middle and long recensions as well as some other texts related to Ignatius, see Stewart, *Ignatius of Antioch*.

When Eusebius wrote about Ignatius early in the fourth century, he dated the letters to the time of Trajan and emphasized both his focus on martyrdom and his exhortations to believers. Recent scholarship has questioned the certainty with which Eusebius' Trajanic date ought to be accepted and has found a wealth of additional language, imagery, and theology to consider within the letters. Yet Eusebius, recent scholars, and the many readers of Ignatius' letters in between have found them to be variously a source of intrigue, a supply of historical data, and even a spring of piety. At the very least, the letters continue to be important sources for students of early Christianity and a vital point of interest within the collection known as the Apostolic Fathers.

FURTHER READING

Corwin, V. *St. Ignatius and Christianity in Antioch*. Yale Publications in Religion 1. New Haven, CT: Yale University Press, 1960.

Foster, P. "The Epistles of Ignatius of Antioch," in *The Apostolic Fathers*, ed. P. Foster. London: T&T Clark, 2007, 81–107.

Löhr, H. "The Epistles of Ignatius of Antioch," in *The Apostolic Fathers: An Introduction*, ed. W. Pratscher. Waco. TX: Baylor University Press, 2010, 91–115.

Schoedel, W.R. *Ignatius of Antioch*. Hermeneia. Minneapolis, MN: Fortress, 1985.

Stewart, A. *Ignatius of Antioch: The Letters*. Popular Patristics Series 49. Yonkers, NY: St. Vladimir's Seminary Press, 2013.

Trevett, C. *A Study of Ignatius of Antioch in Syria and Asia*. Studies in the Bible and Early Christianity 29. Lewiston, ME: Edwin Mellen, 1992.

Vall, G. *Learning Christ: Ignatius of Antioch and the Mystery of Redemption*. Washington, DC: Catholic University of America Press, 2013.

12 Polycarp's *Epistle to the Philippians* and the *Martyrdom of Polycarp*

PAUL A. HARTOG

12.1 INTRODUCTION

Polycarp was an important Christian leader of the first half of the second century. Although he wrote many letters, only one has survived – his *Epistle to the Philippians* (Pol. *Phil.*). A narrative of his death is also extant, the *Martyrdom of Polycarp* (*Mart. Pol.*). Collections of the Apostolic Fathers have consistently included both works. Hill and Beatrice have argued that Polycarp stands behind various traditions from "the elder" cited by Irenaeus.[1] A canon list ascribes a *Didaskalia* to Polycarp.[2]

Irenaeus passed on memorable anecdotes about Polycarp. He depicted Polycarp as an "apostolic elder" who confronted opponents and converted a number of their followers (*Adv. Haer.* 3.3.4). In a "Letter to Victor," Irenaeus also mentions Polycarp visiting Anicetus in Rome. They discussed differing fasting and Eucharistic traditions, and Anicetus even allowed Polycarp to celebrate the Eucharist (Eusebius, *Hist. eccl.* 5.24.11–18).

Irenaeus described a Polycarpian association with "John" in *Adv. Haer.* 3.3.4 (= Eusebius, *Hist. eccl.* 4.14.1–8), *Adv. Haer.* 5.33.4 (= Eusebius, *Hist. eccl.* 3.39.1), "Letter to Victor" (= Eusebius, *Hist. eccl.* 5.24.11–17), and "Letter to Florinus" (= Eusebius, *Hist. eccl.* 5.20.4–8). Irenaeus claimed that both he and Florinus had heard Polycarp teach, and that he could still recall Polycarp's discussions of his interactions with "John," who had "seen the Lord" and had described Jesus' miracles

---

[1] P.F. Beatrice, "Der Presbyter des Irenäus, Polykarp von Smyrna und der Brief an Diognet," in *Pléroma: Salus Carnis*, ed. E. Romero-Pose (Santiago de Compostela: Universidad de Santiago de Compostela, 1990), 179–202. C.E. Hill, *From the Lost Teaching of Polycarp: Identifying Irenaeus' Apostolic Presbyter and the Author of "Ad Diognetum,"* WUNT 186 (Tübingen: Mohr Siebeck, 2006).

[2] J.B. Lightfoot, *The Apostolic Fathers*, 2nd ed. (London: Macmillan, 1889), vol. II.1, 447, 351 n.1.

and teachings. These traditions appear within broader lore about John's influence on Asia Minor, including the Quartodeciman debates. One senses development and adaptation of traditions over time.[3]

Alternative "images" of Polycarp appear in the *Vita Polycarpi*, the "Harris" fragments, the *Bios kai Martyrion*, and several patristic homilies.[4] According to Dehandschutter, the *Vita Polycarpi* "mirrors a radically *different* tradition about Polycarp" than the Irenaean material.[5] The work never mentions John and emphasizes an alternative Pauline connection, apparently reflecting an anti-Quartodeciman perspective. Conversely, the Harris fragments closely connect Polycarp's life work with John, and Polycarp's execution becomes a sort of surrogate martyrdom for John, who did not suffer execution.[6] Through such materials, one can trace reception trajectories and alternative "images" of Polycarp.

12.2 THE *EPISTLE TO THE PHILIPPIANS*

Irenaeus praised Pol. *Phil.* as a "very powerful" epistle (*Adv. Haer.* 3.3.4). While Irenaeus' "Letter to Florinus" mentions other letters of Polycarp (Eusebius, *Hist. eccl.* 5.20.8), they do not survive. Eusebius quoted from both chapters 9 and 13 of Pol. *Phil.* (*Hist. eccl.* 3.36.13–15), and Jerome affirmed that the epistle was still read publicly in Asia (*Vir. ill.* 17).

12.2.1 Text and Manuscript Tradition

The text of Pol. *Phil.* is found in nine Greek manuscripts, but every manuscript abruptly transfers from Pol. *Phil.* 9.2. to *Barn.* 5.[7] The Greek manuscripts thereby manifest derivation from a common exemplar.

---

[3] P. Hartog, *Polycarp's Epistle to the Philippians and the Martyrdom of Polycarp*, OAF (Oxford: Oxford University Press, 2013), 15–16.

[4] See B. Dehandschutter, *Polycarpiana: Studies on Martyrdom and Persecution in Early Christianity*, ed. J. Leemans, BETL 205 (Leuven: Leuven University Press, 2007), 259–77.

[5] See also P. Maravel, *Vie d'Abercius – Vie de Polycarpe: Deux biographies légendaires d'évêques du IIe siècle*, Roue à livres 82 (Paris: Les Belles Lettres, 2017).

[6] F.W. Weidmann, *Polycarp and John: The Harris Fragments and their Challenge to the Literary Traditions* (Notre Dame, IN: University of Notre Dame Press, 1999), 94–6; J.M. Kozlowski, "Polycarpus Ioannis aemulator?: Compensative Character of Polycarp's Death in *Martyrium Polycarpi*," *Vetera Christianorum* 52 (2015): 165–76.

[7] F.R. Prostmeier, "Zur handschriftlichen Überlieferung des Polykarp- und des Barnabasbriefes. Zwei nicht beachtete Deszendenten des Cod. Vat. gr. 859," *VC* 48 (1994): 48–64; Dehandschutter, *Polycarpiana*, 29–34.

Eusebius provides the full Greek text of chapter 9 and most of chapter 13. For the remainder, we are essentially dependent upon the Latin version. Portions of the epistle (including parts of chapter 12) appear within scattered Syriac fragments, and an Armenian version also remains extant.

12.2.2 Authenticity, Integrity, and Unity

Pol. *Phil.* serves as the earliest testimony to the Ignatian letters, and historically it has been intertwined with Ignatian questions. Ignatius is explicitly mentioned in two chapters (chaps. 9 and 13), and his passing through Philippi seems implied in a third (chap. 1). Chapter 1 commends the Philippians for receiving and escorting "the imitators of true love, those bound with saint-worthy fetters."[8] Chapter 9 relates that the Philippians personally witnessed the endurance of "the blessed Ignatius and Zosimus and Rufus." Chapter 13 mentions Ignatius' request to forward his correspondence to Syria, and it commends the attached letters of Ignatius. Polycarp appends a request for any "certain" news concerning Ignatius and his companions (13.2).

Scholars opposed to the authenticity of the Ignatian correspondence have dealt with this Polycarpian witness in different ways. Some have maintained that Pol. *Phil.* is a wholesale forgery, but the arguments have not overturned the general assumption of the work's genuineness. Another tactic has been to contend that the references to Ignatius were interpolated into Polycarp's epistle. A stream of scholars have highlighted the apparent contradiction between the statement that Ignatius and his companions were "in the place appointed them with the Lord" (9.2) and the request for further information about Ignatius and "those who are with him" (13.2).

Four considerations may mitigate this tension. First, the pertinent phrase in 13.2 only survives in the Latin, and the original Greek was probably *Ignatios kai tōn met' autou* ("Ignatius and those with him" or "Ignatius and his companions"), based upon comparable renditions elsewhere in the epistle. Second, the phrase "in the place appointed them" echoes *1 Clem.* 5.3–4, which focuses upon Paul and Peter, and Pol. *Phil.* 9.1 references "Paul and the rest of the apostles." Third, Ignatius himself anticipated, and even desired, his martyrdom (Ign. *Rom.* 5.2). Fourth, from his location in Smyrna, Polycarp may have taken the expected execution in Rome for granted, while still desiring

---

[8] English translations of Polycarpian materials throughout come from Hartog, *Polycarp's Epistle.*

a report with "more certain" (*certius*) details. Polycarp was probably assuming the execution of Ignatius and his companions based upon the passing of time, but he had not yet heard any definite details and thus requested fuller news.

Harrison, using the apparent tension between 9 and 13, argued that our extant Pol. *Phil.* comprises two authentic letters merged together.[9] An earlier one (chapters 13–14) was written shortly after Ignatius left Philippi, and it served as a cover letter to an Ignatian collection. A second letter (chapters 1–12) was written in the 130s, and was directed at Marcion's teachings. According to Irenaeus, Polycarp publicly opposed Marcion, whom he castigated as "the firstborn of Satan" (*Adv. Haer.* 3.3.4). Pol. *Phil.* uses the same designation of the opponents in chapter 7, who are also "antichrists" and "of the devil." Nevertheless, the specific teachings opposed in Pol. *Phil.* do not easily match known Marcionite doctrine.

Later scholars modified Harrison's thesis, by arguing that the second letter was written within a few years of Ignatius' trip, and/or by maintaining that chapter 14 was part of the second letter.[10] Holmes has posited that the cover letter included 1.1 as well as chapters 13 and 14, but he himself does not ultimately land on this alternative.[11] As Tugwell maintains, "the arguments against the integrity of the single letter are not decisive."[12]

12.2.3 Date

According to Eusebius, Ignatius was martyred during the rule of Emperor Trajan (*Hist. eccl.* 3.36), who reigned from 98 to 117. In recent scholarship, the tendency has been to move beyond a Trajanic placement into the Hadrianic era (117–138).[13] Although early Christian sources both directly and indirectly place Ignatius' martyrdom in Trajan's era, the internal evidence of the *Epistle to the Philippians* is

---

[9] P.N. Harrison, *Polycarp's Two Epistles to the Philippians* (Cambridge: Cambridge University Press, 1936).

[10] C.N. Jefford, *Reading the Apostolic Fathers*, 2nd ed. (Grand Rapids, MI: Baker, 2012), 75.

[11] M.W. Holmes, "Polycarp of Smyrna, Epistle to the Philippians," in *The Writings of the Apostolic Fathers*, ed. P. Foster (London: T&T Clark, 2007), 122–3.

[12] S. Tugwell, *The Apostolic Fathers*, Outstanding Christian Thinkers (London: Continuum, 2002), 131.

[13] M.W. Holmes, *The Apostolic Fathers: Greek Texts and English Translations*, 3rd ed. (Grand Rapids, MI: Baker, 2007), 170.

ambiguous. The balance of the evidence may perhaps point toward a placement around 120 or the years prior.[14]

12.2.4 Genre and Style

Pol. *Phil.* follows the common epistolary form, including a letter opening, a letter body, and a letter closing. Maier maintains that Pol. *Phil.* represents "a literary genre of epistolary advice or exhortation."[15] Holmes has categorized the work as "a complex hortatory letter."[16] Polycarp reflects a conservative allegiance to received teaching, combined with pastoral sensitivity.

The letter opening provides the sender ("Polycarp and the elders with him") and recipients ("the church of God sojourning in Philippi"). A greeting of mercy and peace ensues, followed by a statement of rejoicing. Polycarp rejoiced that the Philippians received and escorted Christian prisoners (1.1), and he also rejoiced at the fruit-bearing "firm root" of the Philippians' faith (1.2). The letter transitions into the body with the *dio* ("therefore") statement in 2.1. The theme of "righteousness" is introduced in 3.1.

The letter closing includes a final benediction (12.2), an exhortation to prayer (12.3), an acknowledgment of the Philippian request to forward correspondence to Syria (13.1), an introduction to the appended Ignatian correspondence (13.2), a request for more definite news concerning Ignatius and his companions (13.2), commendations of Crescens and his sister (14), and a closing farewell (14).

12.2.5 Occasion

Pol. *Phil.* originated in the transport of Ignatius through Smyrna and Philippi, on his way to martyrdom in Rome. The Philippian congregation contacted Polycarp, requesting that he forward their letter to the church in Antioch (13.1), requesting copies of Ignatius' letters (13.2), and requesting guidance concerning "righteousness" (3.1). Polycarp had also learned of the moral failure of Valens, who had succumbed to avarice (11.1–4). Moreover, he was concerned about the threat of false doctrine (7.1–2).

---

[14] B. Dehandschutter, "The Epistle of Polycarp," in *The Apostolic Fathers: An Introduction*, ed. W. Pratscher (Waco, TX: Baylor University Press, 2010), 122; Hartog, *Polycarp's Epistle*, 40–5.

[15] H.O. Maier, "Purity and Danger in Polycarp's Epistle to the Philippians: The Sin of Valens in Social Perspective," *JECS* 1 (1993): 229.

[16] Holmes, *Apostolic Fathers*, 273.

The Polycarpian opponents denied that Jesus Christ came "in flesh," and Polycarp accuses them of distorting the Lord's sayings for the sake of their own desires (7.1). They also denied a future resurrection and judgment (7.1). The false teaching seems to resemble the so-called docetic views opposed in the Ignatian correspondence (Ign. *Magn.* 10–11; Ign. *Trall.* 9–10; Ign. *Smyrn.* 2). According to Bauer, "A more precise description of the docetism noted by Polycarp is not possible."[17] Moreover, recent scholarship has greatly nuanced our understanding of "docetic" perspectives in early Christianity.[18] Scholars disagree whether Polycarp's warnings represented a real threat in Philippi or reflected opposition in Polycarp's own Asia Minor.

12.2.6 Purpose and Themes

Polycarp wrote concerning "righteousness" at the Philippians' request (3.1). He points them to Paul's letters, which build up faith (3.2). He centers the fulfillment of "the command of righteousness" in faith, hope, and especially love (3.3). The letter body includes congregational duty codes (4.2–6.2), warnings against opponents (6.3–7.2), admonitions to endurance (8–9), further paraenesis (8.1–10.3), and a discussion of Valens and his wife (11.1–12.1).

The theme of "righteousness" (*dikaiosunē*) recurs throughout the letter body (2.3; 3.1; 4.1; 5.2; 8.1; 9.1–2). Another recurrent theme is avarice (2.2; 4.1; 4.3; 5.2; 6.1; 11.1–2). According to Polycarp, "avarice is the beginning of all difficulties" (4.1). He also underscores the importance of forgiveness (2.3; 6.2), which may be tied to his recommendation of mercy toward Valens, the former elder who fell into avarice, along with his wife (11.1–4).

"Endurance" is also connected with obeying "the word of righteousness" (9.1). Jesus himself "endured all things, in order that we might live in him" (8.1). Believers are to imitate his example of endurance, being willing to suffer for his name's sake (8.2). Martyrs enjoy reward because they did not love the present world (9.2).

Scholars have debated whether the focus of "righteousness" targets Valens' fall into avarice (11.1) or the threat of aberrant teaching (7.1–2). Holmes contends that the "central interpretive question" of Pol. *Phil.* is

---

[17] J.B. Bauer, *Die Polykarpbriefe*, KAV 5 (Göttingen: Vandenhoeck & Ruprecht, 1995), 502.

[18] See J. Verheyden, R. Bieringer, J. Schröter, and I. Jäger (eds.), *Docetism in the Early Church: The Quest for an Elusive Phenomenon*, WUNT 402 (Tübingen: Mohr Siebeck, 2018).

"the relationship (or lack thereof)" between "the two main issues of avarice and heresy."[19] Meinhold argued that Valens had accepted a bribe from Marcion, but there is nothing distinctively Marcionite about the false teaching opposed in Pol. *Phil.*[20] Jefford believes that Valens' lapse threatened the community's stability and theological self-understanding.[21] Holmes adds that Polycarp was committed to protecting the community's integrity, "both its beliefs and its behaviors."[22] A more direct connection seems implied by 7.1. The opponents allegedly distorted the Lord's teachings to fit their own desires. More specifically, they denied both a future resurrection and judgment, thereby undermining moral exhortation (2.2–3.1).[23]

12.2.7 Intertextuality and Sources

Pol. *Phil.* frequently quotes or alludes to documents now in the New Testament. Some of the stronger candidates for influence include Romans, 1 Corinthians, Galatians, Ephesians, Philippians, 1 Timothy, 2 Timothy, 1 Peter, and 1 John, as well as Jesus materials reflected in the Synoptics. Eusebius already noted Polycarp's employment of 1 Peter (*Hist. eccl.* 4.14.9), but his use of 1 Timothy and 1 John is also striking.[24] Polycarp borrowed from *1 Clement* as well.[25] Given his epistolary purposes, Polycarp drew heavily from paraenetic materials.

Confident conclusions are hampered by several considerations. Orality and literacy were webbed phenomena within the culture. Ancient authors often borrowed from sources in a fluid manner. Moreover, Polycarp seems to have been working from memory. Regarding Jesus materials, one must consider the possible influence of oral traditions as well as Gospel texts. Furthermore, Synoptic overlap complicates attempts to trace backward to a specific Gospel text. Young

---

[19] M.W. Holmes, "Polycarp of Smyrna," in *Dictionary of the Later New Testament & Its Developments*, ed. R.P. Martin and P.H. Davids (Downers Grove, IL: InterVarsity, 1997), 935.

[20] P. Meinhold, "Polykarpos," *Pauly-Wissowa Realencyclopädie der classischen Altertumswisssenschaft* 21 (1952): 1686–7.

[21] Jefford, *Reading*, 78.

[22] Holmes, *Apostolic Fathers*, 274.

[23] P. Hartog, "The Relationship between Paraenesis and Polemic in Polycarp, Philippians," *StPatr* 65 (2013): 27–37.

[24] J. Lookadoo, "Polycarp, Paul, and the Letters to Timothy," *NovT* 59 (2017), 366–83; P. Hartog, "The Opponents in Polycarp, Philippians, and 1 John," in *Trajectories through the New Testament and the Apostolic Fathers*, ed. A.G. Gregory and C.T. Tuckett (Oxford: Oxford University Press, 2005), 375–91.

[25] K. Berding, "Polycarp's Use of 1 Clement: An Assumption Reconsidered," *JECS* 19 (2011): 127–39.

has argued that recourse to "oral tradition" *can* explain all instances of Synoptic-like materials in Pol. *Phil.*, and it is *best* to do so.[26] Young underscores the lack of verbal exactitude in the Synoptic-like quotations. Yet a similar level of inexactitude characterizes various quotations from other works, probably owing to the considerations above (the fluid nature of citation and the task of working from memory).[27] Polycarp likely would not have "looked up" his sources. Most of his references are "tacit allusions" rather than "explicit quotations."[28]

Pol. *Phil.* introduces four excerpts with a formulaic "knowing that" (1.3; 4.1; 5.1; 6.1). The first three cases parallel Eph. 2.8–9, 1 Tim. 6.7, and Gal. 6.7, while the final instance ("we are all debtors of sin") does not exactly parallel any extant literature. Polycarp cites the "Scriptures" in 12.1 while introducing material found in Ephesians 4, which in turn quotes the Psalms.[29] At times Polycarp clusters quotations, including materials from *1 Clement* (in 4.2–3), materials from 1 John (in 7.1–2), and materials from 1 Peter (in 8.1–2). Berding has examined Polycarp's "unmistakable" and "marked" tendency "to cluster Pauline citations and allusions after each of the three references to the apostle" (3.2; 9.1; 11.2–3).[30]

Polycarp drew a continuity between the prophets, the Lord, and the apostles (6.3). He recurrently refers to the sayings, teachings, and commandments of the Lord (2.3; 6.3; 7.1; 7.2). The prophets foretold the coming of Christ, and the apostles served as appointed representatives who preached the good news (6.3; cf. 9.1). Paul is referenced in 3.2, 9.1, and 11.2–3, and he is the only apostle mentioned by name. Polycarp was writing to the Philippians, a Pauline congregation, and apparently intended to imitate Paul in character and advice.[31]

12.2.8 Theology and Paraenesis

The letter opening highlights "God Almighty and Jesus Christ our Saviour." The benediction in the letter closing also refers to "the God and Father of our Lord Jesus Christ and the eternal high priest himself, the Son of God Jesus Christ" (12.2). The benediction later refers to "our

---

[26] S.E. Young, *Jesus Tradition in the Apostolic Fathers* (Tübingen: Mohr Siebeck, 2011), 284.

[27] K. Berding, *Polycarp and Paul*, VCSUP 62 (Leiden: Brill, 2002), 191–206.

[28] Oxford Society of Historical Theology (eds.), *The New Testament in the Apostolic Fathers* (Oxford: Clarendon, 1905), 84.

[29] See P. Hartog, "Polycarp, Ephesians, and 'Scripture,'" *WTJ* 70 (2008): 255–75.

[30] Berding, *Polycarp and Paul*, 349, 360.

[31] Ibid., 126–41.

Lord Jesus Christ" and "his Father who raised him from the dead" (12.2).
The letter emphasizes both the death and resurrection of Jesus
Christ (1.2; 2.1–2; 8.1; 9.2) but does not reflect interest in the details of
his life. Pol. *Phil.* mentions Jesus' exaltation, eschatological coming, and
future judgment (2.1; 6.2). Polycarp specifically underscores Jesus'
sinlessness (8.1).

The Holy Spirit is conspicuous by his absence. Although the Spirit
is the *arrabōn* ("guarantee" or "pledge") in the Pauline epistles, Jesus
Christ is the *arrabōn* in Pol. *Phil.* (8.1). The use of *pneuma* in 5.3 may be
the sole reference to the Holy Spirit (cf. Gal. 5.17), although it may be a
reference to the human spirit (cf. 1 Pet. 2.11).

Echoing Ephesians 2, Polycarp insisted that his readers had been
saved "by the will of God through Jesus Christ," by grace and not
by works (1.3). Polycarp highlighted the threefold virtue list of
faith, hope, and love (3.3). His epistle repeatedly mentions *pistis* (1.2;
3.2; 4.2; 9.2; 10.1; 12.2; 13.2) and *pisteuō* (5.2; 8.2). His eschatology is
simple and focuses upon the realities of resurrection and judgment
(2.1–2; 5.2; 6.2; 7.1; 11.2). The false teachers of 7.1 deny both resurrection
and judgment.

The contents of the letter are more paraenetic than doctrinal.
Readers are to "follow the example of the Lord" (10.1). Irreproachable
conduct provides no occasion for blaspheming the Lord (10.2–3). The
epistle includes exhortations for wives (4.2), widows (4.3), deacons (5.2),
younger men (5.3), and elders (6.1). Polycarp emphasizes and emulates
the role of prayer in the Christian life (6.2; 7.2; 12.2) and encourages
prayer for political authorities (12.3). He discusses the avaricious
conduct of Valens, a former elder, and his wife (11.1), appealing for
their restoration to fellowship. The epistle calls for a spirit of forgiveness (2.3; 6.2).

12.3 THE *MARTYRDOM OF POLYCARP*

According to the twentieth chapter of *Mart. Pol*, the summary report
came "through our brother Marcion" (20.1), having been written by
Evarestus (20.2). These two claims have stimulated questions. Was
Marcion the letter carrier, authoritative source, or author?[32] Was

---

[32] B. Dehandschutter, *Martyrium Polycarpi: Een literair-kritische studie*, BETL 52
(Leuven: Leuven University Press, 1979), 187–9; M.W. Holmes, "Recovering a
'Lost' Author: Marcion of Smyrna," *HBT* 31 (2009): 111–22.

Evarestus an amanuensis, author, or redactor?[33] The colophones further claim that Pionius copied the materials from Socrates, who copied them from Gaius, who transcribed them from manuscripts in Irenaeus' possession (22.2–3). One wonders if redaction could have accompanied Gaius's copying. Some scholars have doubted the reliability of many or all of these colophonic claims concerning the transmission of the work.[34] In any case, the nature of the work seems to reflect the influence of "social or collective memory." First-person plural language pervades the narrative, and the text seeks to form group identity.

12.3.1 Text and Manuscript Tradition

Mart. Pol. is preserved in over a handful of Greek manuscripts. Much of the work is included in the fourth book of Eusebius' *Historia ecclesiastica*. Latin, Syriac, Coptic, and Armenian versions are also extant. Khomych has investigated the Old Slavonic version, concluding that it "may possibly provide an independent witness to the text."[35]

Six of the Greek manuscripts form the "menologia' text tradition, while Codex *Mosquensis* provides a distinct witness, including extra materials. Among these extra traditions in the "Moscow Epilogue" is Polycarp's encounter with Marcion, in which Polycarp exclaimed, "I do recognize you – I recognize the firstborn of Satan." The "Moscow Epilogue" further develops Irenaeus' connection with Polycarp, and it adds the lore of Irenaeus hearing a trumpet-like voice announcing that "Polycarp has been martyred."

12.3.2 Overview

Polycarp was one of twelve individuals martyred (19.1). The martyrs were preliminarily whipped, until their torn skin revealed the underlying soft tissues (2.2), and some were stretched on sharp seashells (2.4). Germanicus faithfully faced wild animals, even pulling one upon himself to hasten his death (3.1). By contrast, Quintus (a recent immigrant from Phrygia) offered pagan sacrifice under duress (4).

---

[33] C.N. Jefford, *The Apostolic Fathers and the New Testament* (Peabody, MA: Hendrickson, 2006), 24.

[34] C.R. Moss, "On the Dating of Polycarp: Rethinking the Place of the Martyrdom of Polycarp in the History of Christianity," *Early Christianity* 1 (2010): 568–70; cf. J.A. Hoover, "False Lives, False Martyrs: 'Pseudo-Pionius' and the Redating of the *Martyrdom of Polycarp*," *VC* 67 (2013): 471–98.

[35] T. Khomych, "A Forgotten Witness: Recovering the Early Church Slavonic Version of the Martyrdom of Polycarp," in *Persecution and Martyrdom in Late Antiquity*, ed. J. Leemans, BETL 241 (Leuven: Peeters, 2010), 127–8.

The angry crowd cried out, "Away with the atheists! Search for Polycarp!" (3.2). But Polycarp escaped to a country house outside the city (5.1) and then to a second rural home (6.1). A tortured slave, however, revealed Polycarp's whereabouts (6.1). The authorities arrested Polycarp and hauled him to the stadium, first upon a donkey and then within a carriage (8.1–2). The irenarch and his father attempted to persuade Polycarp to recant while in transit, but he remained firm. His leg was injured while being forced from the carriage (8.3).

At the stadium, the proconsul also pressured for a recantation. Instead, Polycarp waved at the pagan crowd and exclaimed, "Away with the atheists!" He declared, "For eighty-six years I have been serving him, and he has done me no wrong. Indeed how can I blaspheme my king who saved me?" Polycarp solemnly declared, "I am a Christian" (10.1). The proconsul further threatened with wild beasts and fire, but Polycarp retorted, "Bring on what you wish" (11.2). The proconsul's herald announced, "Polycarp has confessed himself to be a Christian three times!" (12.1).

Because the animal contests had ended, the crowd shouted for Polycarp to be burned (12.3). Polycarp voiced an extended prayer from the stake (14.1–3). The fire encircled but did not burn him, so an executioner plunged a dagger into him (16.1). Polycarp's corpse was burned (18.1), but fellow Christians gathered his remains and laid them in a fitting location (18.2).

12.3.3 Portrayal of Polycarp's Character

The narrative emphasizes the age of Polycarp, "an elderly man" and "a godly old man" (7.2; 7.3). Those arresting him marveled at his "age and composure" (7.2). The proconsul advised Polycarp to consider his age (9.2). Polycarp had been highly honored even before his martyrdom, "on account of his good conduct" (13.2). He was credited with "blameless conduct from the beginning" (17.1). He was both a "distinguished teacher" and an "eminent martyr" to be imitated (1.2; 19.1). Polycarp was "remembered by all," including the pagans (19.1).

Polycarp is described as "an apostolic and prophetic teacher in our times and bishop of the catholic church in Smyrna" (16.2). The storyline highlights his prophetic ability: "For every saying that he uttered from his mouth was accomplished and will also be accomplished" (16.2). Specifically, while in a trance, he saw a burning pillow and prophetically proclaimed, "It is necessary for me to be burned alive" (5.2; cf. 12.3).

Polycarp also displays a model prayer life. While he was hiding outside the city, he spent his time "doing nothing night and day other than praying for all and for the churches throughout the world, as was his habit" (5.1). When the authorities came to arrest him, he asked for "an hour to pray undisturbed' (7.2), and went on to pray for a full two hours (7.3). In prayer, he remembered "all of those who had ever even met him" and "the universal church throughout the inhabited world" (8.1).

12.3.4 Compositional Integrity and Date of Composition

In the mid-twentieth century, Campenhausen and Conzelmann developed intricate redaction theories. Zwierlein has recently privileged the Old Armenian version as a reflection of the Ur-form, yet maintains that it also includes some interpolated materials and excises some original materials.[36] Redaction theories have served as thought-provoking hypotheses, but it has proven difficult to nail down exact redactional processes and specific interpolated passages. Using the Eusebian retelling as a standard by which to measure interpolations appears problematic, as it seems likely that Eusebius excised and changed materials that did not fit his own purposes.[37]

Moss has argued that the extant version was likely composed in the first half of the third century.[38] She highlights "the rhetorical use of first-person reports, the legal incongruities, the Biblical parallelism, the use of the term 'Catholic Church,' the behavior of Quintus, the *apologia* for the absence of relics, the *inventio*-styled epilogues, the concern about the status of the martyrs, and the lack of early witnesses to the account."[39] According to Moss, "the account is a forgery and the author is a fraud," but the essential motivation of composition was not necessarily polemical.[40]

Yet the account's emphasis is not upon the use of remains as relics, but upon burial in a "suitable" location.[41] Second-century texts oppose voluntary martyrdom (Justin, *2 Apol.* 2), reflect enthusiasm in the face of martyrdom (Marcus Aurelius, *Meditations* 11.3), mention the gathering of remains (*Mart. Lyons* 1.59–63), and describe the well-known burial places of revered figures (Papias in Eusebius, *Hist. eccl.*

---

[36] O. Zwierlein, *Die Urfassungen der Martyria Polycarpi et Pionii und das Corpus Polycarpianum*, 2 vols., UALG 116.1/2 (Berlin: de Gruyter, 2014).

[37] S. Parvis, "The *Martyrdom of Polycarp,*" in *The Writings of the Apostolic Fathers*, ed. P. Foster (London: T&T Clark, 2007), 134.

[38] Moss, "On the Dating," 539–74.

[39] Ibid., 547, 568–70.

[40] Ibid., 557–8.

[41] Holmes, "Dating the *Martyrdom,*" 194.

3.31; 5.24; *Martyrdom of Justin* 5).[42] Holmes has added argumentation that plausibly places *Mart. Pol.*'s use of "catholic" within the second century (cf. Ign. *Smyrn.* 8.2).[43] Den Boeft and Bremmer have examined further parallels between small details in *Mart. Pol.* and second-century practices.[44] The characterizations within *Mart. Pol.* have been compared to facets of second-century sophistic literature and leaders.[45] On the other hand, Johnson has situated Polycarp's prayer within a third-century liturgical context.[46]

Lucian's *Peregrinus* (a late second-century work) mocks enthusiasm for death, the gathering of remains, and the possible dedication of a "shrine" at the pyre (26, 28, 39). Kozlowski contends that *Mart. Pol.* was probably written after Irenaeus' *Adversus haereses* and was likely influenced by *Peregrinus*, thus preferring a placement in the late second century.[47] Hartog has argued for Lucian dependence in the opposite direction, and is open to a composition of *Mart. Pol.* within the 160s or early 170s.[48] Another consideration is the possible relationship between *Mart. Pol.* and *Mart. Lyons.* Dehandschutter confidently claimed that *Mart. Pol.* "uncontroversially" influenced *Mart. Lyons*, though Moss argues otherwise.[49] In any case, similar facets in *Mart.*

---

[42] Cf. E.L. Gibson, "The Jews and Christians in the *Martyrdom of Polycarp*: Entangled or Parted Ways?," in *The Ways that Never Parted: Jews and Christians in Late Antiquity and Early Middle Ages*, ed. A.H. Becker and A.Y. Reed (Tübingen: Mohr Siebeck, 2003), 156.

[43] Holmes, "Dating the *Martyrdom*," 186–8.

[44] J. den Boeft and J. Bremmer, "Notiunculae martyrologicae IV," *VC* 45 (1991): 107–11; J. den Boeft and J. Bremmer, "Notiunculae martyrologicae V," *VC* 49 (1995): 146–51.

[45] M. denDulk and A.M. Langford, "Polycarp and Polemo: Christianity at the Center of the Second Sophistic," in *The History of Religions Today*, ed. T.R. Blanton IV, R.M. Calhoun, and C.K. Rothschild, WUNT 340 (Tübingen: Mohr Siebeck, 2014), 211–40. See also C.K. Rothschild, "Evaluating Masculinity: The Quintus Incident in Light of the Second Sophistic," in *New Essays on the Apostolic Fathers*, WUNT 375 (Tübingen: Mohr Siebeck, 2017), 159–73.

[46] M.E. Johnson, "Sharing 'the Cup of Christ': The Cessation of Martyrdom and Anaphoral Development," in *Studies in the Liturgies of the Christian East*, ed. S. Hawkes-Teeples, B. Groen, and S. Alexopoulos, Eastern Christian Studies 18 (Leuven: Peeters, 2013), 109–26.

[47] J.M. Kozlowski, "*Tanto Perfusus est sanguine, ut* ... Dependence of *Passio Perpetuae* 21,1–3 upon *Martyrium Polycarpi* 14,2 and 16,1," *Eirene* 52 (2016): 392.

[48] P. Hartog, "Lucian of Samosata's *Death of Peregrinus* and Second-Century Christian Martyrdom," *StPatr* 74 (2016): 57–69.

[49] Dehandschutter, *Polycarpiana*, 60; T.D. Barnes, *Early Christian Hagiography and Roman History*, Tria Corda 5 (Tübingen: Mohr Siebeck, 2010), 61–2; cf. C.R. Moss, "Polycarphilia: The Martyrdom of Polycarp and the Origins and Spread of Martyrdom," in *The Rise and Expansion of Christianity in the First Three*

Lyons may reflect the contextual plausibility of *Mart. Pol.* (or at least its core) being composed in the second century.

Holmes continues to argue for a date of composition within a year of Polycarp's execution, reflecting the future verb *praksei* in 18.3: "the Lord *will permit* us to celebrate the birthday of martyrdom."[50] Many assume that such an annual celebration had never yet happened, and so the narrative was written within a year of the execution. Lightfoot acknowledged, "But this inference is far from certain."[51] The future tense of *praksei* alone does not necessarily say anything about past practice, whether the community had already been celebrating Polycarp's "birthday." The deference to divine will ("the Lord *will permit* us to celebrate") fits the narrative's larger theme of divine sovereignty. Temporal distancing between the execution and the composition of the narrative allows more space for the role of "social memory" in forming the work. Finally, one should consider the possibility that a redactor or copyist (cf. *Mart. Pol.* 22–3) adapted earlier materials.

12.3.5 Historicity

Several scholars have discussed the location in the stadium and the unusual legal proceedings there. There is no formal charge by accusers, no trial before the *bēma* or magistrate's tribunal, and no *krisis* or formal sentence. Parvis acknowledges "the strangeness of the legal proceedings," but turns the evidence into an argument for basic reliability.[52] An author creating the narrative *in toto* would have followed normal legal procedures more closely.[53] Holmes further contends that Roman *stadia* were commonly used for Roman spectacles.[54]

Mart. Pol. undoubtedly manifests "reflection" and "interpretation."[55] The narrative is not a report of the *bruta facta* but a theologized work of hagiographical edification intended to form communal character. As Lieu explains, "the text is in the end all to which we have

---

Centuries of the Common Era, ed. C.K. Rothschild and J. Schöter, WUNT 301 (Tübingen: Mohr Siebeck, 2013), 415–16.

[50] Holmes, "Dating the *Martyrdom*," 183 n.9.

[51] Lightfoot, *Apostolic Fathers*, II.1, 609.

[52] Parvis, "*Martyrdom*," 143.

[53] Ibid., 142–5.

[54] Holmes, "Dating the *Martyrdom*," 184.

[55] M.W. Holmes, "The *Martyrdom of Polycarp* and the New Testament Passion Narratives," in *Trajectories through the New Testament and the Apostolic Fathers*, ed. A.G. Gregory and C.T. Tuckett (Oxford: Oxford University Press, 2005), 423.

direct access, but it itself created a reality or 'universe of meaning' for its readers."[56] If the core composition is moved into the years following the actual martyrdom, then Polycarp's image may have been posthumously adapted to address post-mortem issues.

Chapter 14 includes a prayer Polycarp purportedly uttered while tied to the stake. Interpreters agree that the highly stylized prayer does not convey Polycarp's *ipsissima verba* at the point of execution. The prayer, however, carries import for the history of both theology and liturgy. The prayer twice refers to Jesus as *pais*, which commonly reflects "primitive"-sounding early Christian tradition.[57] Yet the language of "the cup of Christ" and "a rich and acceptable sacrifice" resembles liturgical prayers. The prayer mentions God the Father, his blessed and beloved Son Jesus Christ, and the Holy Spirit. Nevertheless, the doxological material is not as succinct as polished Trinitarian declarations would later become.[58]

The Jews play an adversarial role, focused at three distinct junctures (12.2; 13.1; 17.2–18.1). According to the narrative, the Jews (along with the pagans) cried out against Polycarp: "This one is the teacher of impiety, the father of the Christians, the destroyer of our gods, the one teaching many neither to sacrifice nor to worship!" (12.2). Such a sentiment ("destroyer of our gods") seems strange upon the lips of Jews. The narrative depicts the Jews as helping to gather wood and kindling for the fire, "as is their custom" (13.1). The Jews also insist that Polycarp's corpse be guarded, lest the Christians abandon Jesus as the Messiah and worship Polycarp instead (17.2). The centurion noted this Jewish opposition, and burned the body, "as is their custom" (18.1).

The existence of Jewish–Christian tensions at Smyrna is inherently plausible (cf. Rev. 2:9–10). But facets of the portrayal stretch historical credibility – Jews shouting about "our gods," collecting kindling on the "great Sabbath," and worried that Christians might substitute Polycarp for Jesus as the Messiah. The phrase "as is their custom" further underscores the problematic stereotyping. Moreover, the narrator conflates Jewish and other opposition, thus constructing a united "other"

[56] J.M. Lieu, *Image and Reality: The Jews in the World of the Christians in the Second Century* (Edinburgh: T&T Clark, 1996).

[57] G. Buschmann, *Das Martyrium des Polykarp*, KAV 6 (Göttingen: Vandenhoeck & Ruprecht, 1998), 265.

[58] P. Hartog, "The Nascent 'Trinitarian' Worship of *Martyrdom of Polycarp* 14 and Ephesians 1," in *The Holy Trinity in the Life of the Church*, ed. K. Anatolios (Grand Rapids, MI: Baker, 2014), 39–53.

contrasted with Christian self-identity. This social construction owes as much to "theological schema" as to historical accuracy.[59]

12.3.6 Date of Execution

Eusebius' *Hist. eccl.* 4.14–15 relates Polycarp's martyrdom immediately after discussing Marcus Aurelius' regnal succession, which occurred in 161 CE. Eusebius' *Chronicle* places Polycarp's martyrdom in 167/168. Yet *Mart. Pol.* 21 claims that Polycarp was executed on the second of Xanthicus, "a great Sabbath," seven days before "the calends of March," while Philip of Tralles was Asiarch and Statius Quadratus was proconsul. Most scholars assume that chapter 21 contains some helpful material for consideration, even if a secondary addition. By comparing *Mart. Pol.* 21 with chronological evidence in Aelius Aristides, numerous scholars have opted for 155/156 CE. Barnes has reexamined the evidence and concluded that 156/157 CE or later seems more probable, although some of the evidence within chapter 21 seems contradictory.[60]

Mart. Pol. 7.1 claims that Polycarp was arrested on "the day of preparation" (Friday), and Polycarp seems to be executed on the next day (Saturday), designated as "the great Sabbath" (cf. Jn. 19:31). Within the *Mart. Pionius*, the "great Sabbath" signifies a day on which both Jews and Gentiles got off work (2.1; 3.6). The seventh before "the calends of March" fell on a Saturday in 155 and did so again in 156 (a leap year). Overall, a placement between 155 and 161 seems most plausible.

12.3.7 Genre and Style

The *Mart. Pol.* is framed in epistolary form, with both a letter opening and a final greeting. The letter opening names the sender ("the church of God sojourning at Smyrna") and the recipient ("the church of God sojourning in Philomelium, and to all those of the holy and universal church sojourning in every place"). The Philomelians were requested to forward the letter to believers further out (20.1).

The *Mart. Pol.* is a narrative with "a clear didactic and kerygmatic purpose in view."[61] A supernatural air enlivens the account. It claims

---

[59] J.M. Lieu, "Accusations of Jewish Persecution in Early Christian Sources, with Particular Reference to Justin Martyr and the *Martyrdom of Polycarp*," in *Tolerance and Intolerance in Early Judaism and Christianity*, ed. G.N. Stanton and G.G. Stroumsa (Cambridge: Cambridge University Press, 1998), 283.

[60] T.D. Barnes, "A Note on Polycarp," *JTS* 18 (1967): 433–7. Cf. Parvis, "*Martyrdom*," 130.

[61] Lieu, *Image*, 58.

that the fires were "cool" to the martyrs (2.3). As Polycarp entered the stadium, a *vox caelestis* proclaimed, "Be strong, Polycarp, and act like a man!" (9.1). The fire purportedly made a vault around Polycarp, yet the aroma of baking bread and the smell of incense or spices flowed forth (15.2). A dove flew out when the executioner plunged a dagger into Polycarp, and an abundance of blood poured forth and quenched the fire (16.1).

The narrative claims that only believers heard the voice from heaven (9.1). In the case of the vaulted fire around Polycarp, only those "to whom it was granted to see" witnessed the miracle (15.1). But in the case of the dove and abundance of blood, "the whole crowd marveled at such a great distinction between the unbelievers and the elect" (16.1). Attempts to explicate such claims through naturalistic explanations are interesting on a rational level but ring hollow within the narrative world, in which the supernatural claims help form Christian self-iden-tity.[62] As Ehrman recognizes, such claims "are designed to show God's stamp of approval on a martyrdom of this kind."[63]

12.3.8 Intertextuality

Very few biblical texts appear. Chapter 1 seems to draw from Philippians 2.4: "not only looking out for that which concerns ourselves but also that which concerns our neighbours." Chapter 2 includes a passage resembling 1 Corinthians 2.9, although somewhat similar material appears in the Hebrew Scriptures.[64]

The *Mart. Pol.* sketches parallels with the passion of Jesus, draws from Pauline reflections of self-donation, and echoes the martyrdom of Stephen and the martyr reflections of Revelation. Most of the resem-blances are too weak to establish direct literary dependence. Lieu con-cluded that 4 Maccabees offers several parallels, but reasoned that textual dependence cannot be verified.[65] Some scholars have noted similarities between Polycarp and Socrates traditions.[66]

---

[62] Parvis, "Martyrdom," 137–8.

[63] B. Ehrman, *Lost Christianities: The Battles for Scripture and the Faiths We Never Knew* (Oxford: Oxford University Press, 2003), 138.

[64] P. Hartog, "1 Corinthians 2:9 in the Apostolic Fathers," in *Intertextuality in the Second Century*, ed. D.J. Bingham and C.N. Jefford, BAC 11 (Leiden: Brill, 2016), 98–125.

[65] Lieu, *Image*, 80.

[66] L.S. Cobb, "Polycarp's Cup: *Imitatio* in the *Martyrdom of Polycarp*," *JRH* 38 (2014): 224–40.

Polycarp was "a partner of Christ" (*Mart. Pol.* 6.2). Like Jesus, Polycarp was betrayed by a close companion, receiving "the punishment of Judas himself" (6.2). The irenarch bore the name of "Herod," the same name as a ruler in Jesus' passion (6.2). Similar to Jesus, Polycarp entreated, "The will of God be done" (7.1). Officials came to arrest both Jesus and Polycarp as if seizing a robber or bandit (7.1). Polycarp, like Jesus, is served a last meal, although Polycarp hosted those who had come to arrest him (7.2). Both entered into town on a donkey (8.1), both were pierced by an executioner (16.1). Unlike Jesus, Polycarp was not nailed but was rather bound to his stake, insisting that he did not require nails to be secured (13.3).[67]

12.3.9 Theology

In Polycarp's prayer at the stake, God is described as "the God of angels and of powers and of all the creation and of the entire race of the righteous who live before you" (14.1) and as "the undeceiving and true God" (14.2).

Christ is portrayed as being with the martyrs in their suffering, even conversing with them (2.2). Polycarp confessed Jesus as his saving King (9.3). Jesus "suffered for the salvation of the whole world of the saved, the blameless on behalf of sinners" (17.2). While martyrs are to be loved, only the Son of God is to be worshiped (17.3). He is the "King and Teacher" (17.3). Jesus is described as "the savior of our souls and pilot of our bodies and shepherd of the universal church throughout the world" (19.2). God brings believers into "his eternal kingdom" through "his Son, the only begotten Jesus Christ" (20.2). While the colophones acknowledge the reign of earthly rulers, they praise the eternal dominion of Jesus Christ (21).

The Holy Spirit is only mentioned in Polycarp's prayer from the stake (14.1; 14.3) and in the colophonic materials (22.4). The prayer praises and glorifies the Holy Spirit along with the Son and Father (14.3). The colophones likewise glorify the Holy Spirit along with the Father and the Lord Jesus Christ (22.3).

The martyrs focused upon the "good things reserved for those who endure," insisting that they would escape the eternal fire of punishment, although suffering the fire of execution (2.3; 11.2). Polycarp received "the crown of immortality" (17.1; 19.2) by defeating "the

---

[67] C.R. Moss, "Nailing Down and Tying Up: Lessons in Intertextual Impossibility from the *Martyrdom of Polycarp*," *VC* 67 (2013): 117–36.

unrighteous ruler," a reference to Satan (19.2; cf. Rev. 2.10).[68] Behind
the human persecution stands "the Devil" (3.1). He is "the jealous and
envious and evil one" as well as "the adversary of the race of the
righteous" (17.1).

On four occasions, *Mart. Pol.* refers to the "universal" or "catholic"
(*katholikē*) church (inscr., 8.1; 16.2; 19.2). Believers are sojourners
(inscr.) and comprise "the God-loving and God-fearing race" (3.2), also
designated as "the race of the righteous" (14.1; 17.1). *Mart. Pol.* notes "a
great distinction between the unbelievers and the elect" (16.1). The Lord
sovereignly orchestrates the experience of martyrdom, and "makes his
choice from his own servants" (20.1).[69]

Governmental authorities are to be respected as divinely established powers, as long as it "does us no harm" (10.2). The colophonic
materials contrast the rule of temporal authorities with the eternal
reign of Christ (21; 22.3).

12.3.10 View of Martyrdom

The ancient world reflected upon the "noble death."[70] *Mart. Pol.* underscores the nobility of the protagonist, combined with the themes of
bravery and composure (2.1–2; 3.1; 5.1; 7.2; 9.1; 12.1). The extant work
particularly emphasizes a "martyrdom in accordance with the Gospel."
Such martyrdoms happen "according to the will of God" (2.1), and are to
be framed by divine sovereignty, ascribing to God "the authority over all
things" (2.1).[71] More specifically, "we do not praise those who hand
themselves over, because the gospel does not so teach" (4). The opening
chapters also describe such a martyrdom as other-centered (1.2) and
characterized by nobility and perseverance (2.2).

Mart. Pol. serves as "an ideological exploration of the *image of
evangelical martyrdom.*"[72] Even as Polycarp imitated the passion of

---

[68] P. Hartog, "The Devil's in the Details: The Apocalyptic 'Adversary' in the
    Martyrdom of Polycarp and the *Martyrs of Lyons*," in *Studies on the Text of the
    New Testament and Early Christianity*, ed. D.M. Gurtner, J. Hernández Jr., and P.
    Foster, NTTSD 50 (Leiden: Brill, 2015), 432–52.

[69] P. Hartog, "The Christology of the *Martyrdom of Polycarp*: Martyrdom as Both
    Imitation of Christ and Election by Christ," *Perichoresis* 12 (2014): 137–52.

[70] A.J. Droge and J.D. Tabor, *A Noble Death: Suicide and Martyrdom among
    Christians and Jews in Antiquity* (San Francisco, CA: HarperOne, 1992).

[71] See Holmes, "*Martyrdom.*"

[72] P.-W. Lai, "Dialogue and Ideology in the *Martyrdom of Polycarp*: A Bakhtinian
    Analysis," *StPatr* 52 (2012): 37–45.

Christ, so the readers are exhorted to imitate Polycarp's endurance, "because it transpired according to the gospel of Christ" (19.1). The readers were to "walk by the word of Jesus Christ according to the gospel" by following in the "footsteps" of Polycarp (22.1). Although a "martyrdom according to the Gospel" may be illustrated by passion parallels between Jesus and Polycarp, its essence does not lie in such details. Events like riding into town on a donkey and being pierced in the side are beyond one's control, and thus cannot constitute the substance of a martyrdom to be imitated.

Mart. Pol. warns against rash voluntary martyrdom. Quintus turned himself into authorities and even convinced others to do so, but he subsequently apostasized (4). Quintus is described as a "Phrygian," and Buschmann links his "hasty enthusiasm" to Montanist perspectives. Yet not all "Phrygians" were Montanists (Eusebius, *Mart. Lyons* 5.1.49). Christians of various commitments manifested zealous enthusiasm for martyrdom, as demonstrated by the Ignatian correspondence (Ign. *Rom.* 2.2; 4.1–2; 7.1; cf. *Apocryphon of James; Letter of Peter to Philip*). Moreover, early Christian martyr texts reflect a spectrum of activity vs. passivity. Within *Mart. Pol.*, Germanicus "pulled the beast upon himself" (3.1). Agathonike "threw herself on the stake" (*Mart. Carp.* A.4). The early Christian response to willful martyrdom was "nothing simple or systematic," as "significant variations and inconsistencies" existed.[73] Nevertheless, *Mart. Pol.* emphasizes the calm resignation of Polycarp, who remains focused upon the welfare of others. For this reason, he willingly took refuge outside town (5.1; 6.1), but also calmly greeted the authorities when they arrived (7.2).

The narrative relates the perceived sanctity of Polycarp's body both before and after martyrdom (13.2; 17.1; 18.2). The Christian community steadfastly cared for Polycarp's remains, which were eventually interred in a "fitting" place (17–18; cf. *Mart. Lyons* 1.57–63). The celebration of his "birthday" and accompanying commemorations were designed to honor previous martyrs and to prepare for future ones as well (18.3; cf. Tertullian, *Cor.* 3; *Scorp.* 15). Nevertheless, although martyrs were loved as "disciples and imitators of the Lord," only the Son of God was to be worshipped (17.3).

---

[73] F.W. Weidmann, "'Rushing Judgment'? Willfulness and Martyrdom in Early Christianity," *USQR* 53 (1999): 61–9.

12.4 CONCLUSION

Polycarp has been called the most important Christian leader of the first half of the second century.[74] His influence was felt far beyond his Smyrnaean congregation, as evidenced by his interactions with the Philippian church and with Anicetus of Rome. He assisted Ignatius of Antioch and impacted Irenaeus of Lyons. Polycarp's extant *Epistle to the Philippians* remains an important work in its own right, through its portrayal of early Christian morals and congregational life. The stated theme of the largely paraenetic letter is "righteousness" (Pol. *Phil.* 3.1), though the thirteenth chapter also mentions sending along the Ignatian correspondence, as requested. Although not exceptionally innovative or creative, Polycarp's epistle weaves together received traditions in order to address false teaching, the avarice of Valens, and forgiving mercy. In particular, the letter reflects the reception of various works now appearing in the New Testament.[75] The *Martyrdom of Polycarp* portrays "a martyrdom in accordance with the Gospel." As a work of hagiographical edification, the *Martyrdom* aims to form social identity and communal character. Christians, as "the race of the righteous," are contrasted with both Jews and pagans. The narrative depicts Polycarp as an apostolic teacher, prophetic figure, person of prayer, and eminent martyr. The account underscores his imitation-worthy submission to God's will, concern for others, patient endurance, and nobility. The work continues to inspire and to attract scholarly interest and critical investigation. Ongoing debates remain regarding the *Martyrdom*'s compositional integrity, dating, and historical reliability.

FURTHER READING

Berding, Kenneth. *Polycarp and Paul: An Analysis of their Literary and Theological Relationship in Light of Polycarp's Use of Biblical and Extra-Biblical Literature*. Supplements to Vigiliae Christianae 62. Leiden: Brill, 2002.

Buschmann, Gerd. "The Martyrdom of Polycarp," in *The Apostolic Fathers*, ed. Wilhelm Pratscher. Waco, TX: Baylor University Press, 2010, 135–57.

Dehandschutter, Boudewijn. "The Epistle of Polycarp," in *The Apostolic Fathers*, ed. Wilhelm Pratscher. Waco, TX: Baylor University Press, 2010, 117–33.

---

[74] Hill, *From the Lost Teaching of Polycarp*, 1.

[75] Paul Hartog, *Polycarp and the New Testament*, WUNT 134 (Tübingen: Mohr Siebeck, 2002).

Polycarpiana: Studies on Martyrdom and Persecution in Early Christianity. Leuven: Leuven University Press, 2007.

Hartog, Paul. *Polycarp and the New Testament: The Occasion, Rhetoric, Theme, and Unity of the Epistle to the Philippians and Its Allusions to New Testament Literature.* WUNT 2.134. Tübingen: Mohr Siebeck, 2002.

Polycarp's Epistle to the Philippians and the Martyrdom of Polycarp: Introduction, Text, and Commentary. Oxford: Oxford University Press, 2013.

Holmes, Michael. "Polycarp of Smyrna, *Epistle to the Philippians*," in *The Writings of the Apostolic Fathers*, ed. Paul Foster. London: T&T Clark, 2007, 108–25.

Parvis, Sara. "The *Martyrdom of Polycarp*," in *The Writings of the Apostolic Fathers*, ed. Paul Foster. London: T&T Clark, 2007, 126–46.

13 *Didache*

CLAYTON N. JEFFORD

13.1 INTRODUCTION

Several patristic authors witness to a tradition of ancient instruction
frequently identified as "Teaching of Apostles" (*didache apostolōn*).[1]
While the precise nature of that corpus stayed hidden to scholars for
centuries, clearly its contents were considered important in various
regions of the early Christian Mediterranean world. This renown is
demonstrated, for example, by the fourth-century Alexandrian bishop
Athanasius, who observed in his annual letter declaring the time for
Easter observance in 367 CE that "Teaching of the Apostles" (*didache
tōn apostolōn*) was accepted in his diocese, though he omitted it from
any "canon" of works thought worthy for liturgy.[2] What could be
identified about the features of the tradition remained vague from
patristic sources generally, however, clarified only in part during the
ninth century when Patriarch Nicephorus of Constantinople described
the length of the text in his *Stichometry* as 200 "lines" (*stichoi*). Beyond
this, little was known of the tradition prior to 1873, at which time
Metropolitan Philotheos Bryennios of Nicomedia came upon a version
of the text within *Codex Hierosolymitanus 54* (= H), stored at the
Jerusalem Monastery of the Holy Sepulcher in Constantinople (modern
Istanbul).[3] That codex, dated by inscription to June 11, 1056, contains a
tractate bearing two distinct titles: a brief heading "Teaching of the
Twelve Apostles" (*didache tōn dōdeka apostolōn*) and a longer one at
the beginning of the opening line, "Teaching of the Lord through the

---

[1] See, e.g., Eusebius, *Hist. eccl.* 3.25.4. For a summary of ancient references and usages,
see K. Niederwimmer, *The Didache*, trans. L.M. Maloney, Hermeneia (Minneapolis,
MN: Fortress, 1998), 4–18.

[2] Athanasius, *Ep. fest.* 39.

[3] Early scholars referred to this text as "J" for "Jerusalem Manuscript." A digitized
version is available online at the Library of Congress under the title "Pangios Taphos
54"; see www.loc.gov/item/00279389694-jo/.

Twelve Apostles to the Nations" (*didache kuriou dia tōn dōdeka apostolōn tois ethnesin*). While neither header was necessarily original to the tradition – the shorter title having possibly served as an incipit based on the longer form – such markers indicate this manuscript represents some form of the ancient Christian tradition of teaching now known by early church historians as the *"Didache"* (*didache*).[4]

Following the Bryennios text of H, scholars commonly divide the work into four distinct sections primarily indicative of the tradition's orientation. These appear generally as follows:

1. The "two ways" (1.1–6.3)
2. Teachings on liturgical matters (7.1–10.7)
3. Teachings on community matters (11.1–15.4)
4. Concluding short apocalypse (16.1–8)

Such rough delineations identify the general movement of the work, but apart from this structural framework, several subcategories more fully define the wider parameters of the *Didache's* organization and complicate scholarly understanding of the tradition. For example, materials in 1.3b–2.1 are typically seen as a secondary addition (either by the author or some later editor) and are often identified by the title *"sectio evangelica."* At the same time, the concluding portion of the "two ways" in 6.1–3 is not uniformly supported by all available literary evidence,[5] and may reflect extensive evolution within the formation of the tradition. So too, various topics introduced by the phrase "and concerning" (*peri de*) extend from the conclusion of the "two ways" section into the later division on community concerns (6.3–11.11), suggesting this range of themes should be viewed as inherently connected via their structure. But whether they are original to the tradition remains unknown. Apart from such exceptions, one may safely consider the text to follow the four basic categories listed above.

What results from such division is the need to explain some purpose for the origination of the tradition according to its divisions. Scholarly views differ widely, but generally the following is typical of majority opinions:

1. The text acquired a basic written form either by the late first or early second centuries.

---

[4] For discussion of the title, consult N. Pardee, *The Genre and Development of the Didache*, WUNT 2/339 (Tübingen: Mohr Siebeck, 2012), 105–25.

[5] As for example with the Latin *Doctrina apostolorum* and parallel from *Barn.* 21.1–9.

2. The tradition was linked to Matthean tradition by providing materials for the Gospel itself, by sharing materials known both to the author and to the evangelist, or by being constructed with knowledge of the Gospel.

3. The work was not likely designed for a single community but was intended for related groups working together loosely.

4. The primary purpose of the tradition was to assimilate non-Jewish converts into an ancient Christian "way" of messianic faith, which either originally included or came to embrace rituals of baptism and Eucharist.

5. A secondary goal of the text was to address complications related to leadership and itinerant apostles and prophets.

Exactly who and where such interests may have produced the tradition remains debated, but typically researchers attribute its manufacture to an unknown individual usually labeled "the Didachist," with perhaps one or more editors having made emendations over time. As to provenance, the regions of Egypt and Syria (particularly that of Antioch) are most often offered, though Galilee is also a reasonable possibility. Present trends of thought tend to favor Syria.

13.2 STRUCTURE OF THE TEXT

Beyond the fourfold division of the text identified above, scholars normally recognize smaller units of instruction scattered throughout the work that help to categorize the individual concerns of the writing. Following the structure given by H, the first section, or the "two ways" (1.1–6.3), may be divided into the following substructures:

1. 1.1–6.3   The "two ways"
    a. 1.1–3a   Teachings on "love of God," "love of neighbor," and Golden Rule
    b. 1.3b–2.1   The so-called *sectio evangelica*
    c. 2.2–4.14   Way of life
        i. 2.2ff.   Instruction focused on the Decalogue
        ii. 3.1ff.   Instruction focused on wisdom tradition
        iii. 4.9–11   Brief "household code"
    d. 5.1–2   Way of death
    e. 6.1–3   Conclusion

Most scholars consider this segment to preserve some of the oldest materials within the work. Drawn from a predominantly Jewish framework of orientation, there is near uniform agreement that these teachings originally served as some form of catechetical instruction for new converts to "the way," primarily to familiarize non-Jews with a Judaic view of incipient Christian values.

The opening teachings (1.1–3a) provide an overture to the remainder of the section, featuring clear parallels to scripture focused on the "two ways" theme known from antiquity.[6] Between this opening and the formal "way of life" material lies the so-called *sectio evangelica* (1.3b–2.1), which offers sayings that largely reflect teachings of Jesus from the famous "sermon" of Matthew (here 5.26, 39–47) and Luke (here 6.27–35). This is the one portion of the text that favors Lukan wording and structure over Matthean forms. As observed above, its presence is often thought to be from a secondary hand, and its form is often missing in whole or in part among manuscript witnesses. Next arises the "teaching of life" proper (2.2–4.14), here presented in two formulas: the first begins at 2.2 and is oriented around the Decalogue of Exod. 20.13–15 and Deut. 5.17–19; the second starts at 3.1 and integrates the phrase "my child," a common motif drawn from Jewish wisdom literature. Both constructions feature basic Judaic ethical teaching acceptable for even non-messianic audiences, including a rhetorical technique that provides a fence of lesser prohibitions to avoid violation of the Decalogue's original proscriptions. The conclusion of these directives culminates with a short "household code" (4.9–11), seen elsewhere in different forms throughout early Christian writings. Thereafter appears a brief rendering of the "way of death" (5.1–2), whose components look like a distilled counter description to the earlier "way of life." The entirety of the section concludes with basic warnings to remain faithful to all afore-mentioned directives (6.1–3), though manuscript traditions are not in agreement concerning the wording of this material, especially 6.3, which reflects tenets of ancient "Noachide laws" seen elsewhere in Acts 15.29.

2. 7.1–10.7   Teachings on liturgical matters
   a. (6.3)   Concerning food
   b. 7.1–4   Concerning baptism
   c. 8.1   Concerning fasting
   d. 8.2–3   Concerning prayer
   e. 9.1–10.7   Concerning eucharistic prayer
   f. (11.3–11)   Concerning apostles and prophets

---

[6] Cf. Deut. 30.15/Prov. 12.28/Sir. 15.17/Mt. 7.13–14; Deut. 6.5/Mt. 22.37/Mk. 12.30/ Lk. 10.27a; Lev. 19.18/Mt. 22.39/Mk. 12.31/Lk. 10.27b; Tob. 4.15/Mt. 7.12/Lk. 6.31.

While most scholars begin this section with 7.1, the introduction of each topic with the words "and concerning" (*peri de*) compels some supposition that 6.3 be included. As observed above, it is unclear from existing manuscripts whether this subject was original to the construction of the tradition, but inclusion is logical here, even if it derives from a secondary hand.

In some sense the opening five elements of the sequence belong together in their relation to basic liturgical concerns, though the additional instruction on apostles and prophets (11.3–11) diverges from this pattern and extends the section beyond the usual structural partition between chapters 10 and 11. The opening comment to accept all foods, with avoidance of what is offered to idols only (6.3), relates more to Jewish food obligations, reflecting concerns of the apostolic decree (Acts 15.29) and specific teachings of Jesus on "bearing the yoke" (Mt. 11:28–30). Yet the closing comment about food offered to idols ("it serves dead gods") indicates the liturgical nature related to rituals of eating, as well as the need to know of each believer's commitment to follow the one true God in such practices. The second teaching on baptism (7.1–4) offers instruction on ritual initiation associated with Jewish conventions (baptism in cold, running water), yet provides exception for use of standing water, perhaps warm, as well as the practice of pouring water on the head ("affusion") rather than immersion when necessary. In each instance, use of the Trinitarian formula and pre-baptismal fasting is essential. The nature of worthy fasting follows in 8.1, warning the reader not to fast "with the hypocrites" (*meta tōn hypokritōn*). Identification of "the hypocrites" remains unspecified, but allusion to fasting on Mondays and Thursdays advises they represent some form of rival Jewish practice. So too, 8.2–3 also warns against praying "with the hypocrites," offering instead the model of the so-called Lord's Prayer (see Mt. 6.9–13) under the rubric of "as the Lord instructed in his gospel." Believers should offer this prayer three times a day. The tag phrase "the hypocrites" joins the concerns of 8.1 and 8.2–3 within the tradition, much as they appear in Mt. 6.1–18 (there with additional instruction on almsgiving).

The prayer of 8.2–3 links with two ensuing prayers in 9.1–10.7 to form a triad of materials allied with early Christian supplication. Whether this structure originates with the tradition is unclear, since the Matthean form of the Lord's Prayer in 8.2–3 does not appear elsewhere in Christian literature prior to the early third century. Nevertheless, the prayers of chapters 9 and 10 relate to blessings over food and drink associated either with an ancient agape feast ritual or in reflection of the roots of later Eucharistic practice. In either case, most scholars believe these petitions to be among the oldest ritual prayers within Eucharistic tradition. Curiously, though, they show no sign of being linked with any passion theology, unlike the Eucharistic invocations in the gospels. In the first prayer (actually two interlinked prayers), thanks for the cup (9.2) is given "for the holy vine of David" (*hyper tēs hagias ampelou Dauid*) made known through Jesus, while thanks "concerning the broken bread" (*peri tou klasmatos*; 9.3–4) specifies "for the life and knowledge" (*hyper tēs zōēs kai gnōseōs*) revealed through Jesus. The scattering and gathering of these fragments of bread are seen to reflect the faith community itself, at one time divided but now reunited. After these supplications, the hearer is warned to let only those who are worthy participate in the ritual activities (a likely reference to those baptized in chapter 7), recalling in support the Lord's prohibition "do not give what is holy to dogs" (*mē dote to hagion tois kusi*), which is known elsewhere only from Mt. 7.6. The Matthean context of this warning is not itself liturgical, however, which suggests the proscription may possibly derive from a later hand. The second prayer, found in chapter 10, is more extensive that those of chapter 9, giving thanks "for your holy name" (*hyper tou hagiou onomatos*; 10.2) made to dwell within believers, which provides "for the knowledge, faith, and immortality" (*hyper tēs gnōseōs kai pisteōs kai athanasias*) made known through Jesus. The Father is then thanked for food and drink, spiritual food and drink and eternal life, and divine strength (10.3–4). This is followed by a plea for the gathering of the church into God's kingdom (10.5), together with a benediction of

> Hosanna to the God of David!
> If anyone is holy, let them come;
> If anyone is not, let them repent!
> The Lord come (*Maranatha*)! Amen.

In conclusion, the hearer is told to let prophets "give thanks" (*eucharistein*) as they may choose. Again, as with 9.5, scholars debate whether this instruction is original to the tradition.[7]

Technically, 11.3–11 on apostles and prophets belongs in the following section, but is mentioned here (as with 6.3) because of its

---

[7] So too, *Apostolic Constitutions* and a Coptic fragment offer a prayer over the "ointment/fragrance" here, though H does not preserve this blessing.

introduction by the phrase "and concerning." The topic of instructions about roles and rights of apostles and prophets does not fall otherwise within the discussion of liturgical matters.

3.   11.1–15.4   Teachings on ecclesiastical matters
    a.   11.1–11   Teachers, apostles, and prophets
    b.   12.1–5   Those who come in the name of the Lord
    c.   13.1–7   Those who come as prophets
    d.   14.1–4   Gathering for worship
    e.   15.1–2   Appointing bishops and deacons
    f.   15.3–4   Acting in community

The materials preserved here speak directly to activities of community management, primarily with respect to several duties of leadership. Otherwise, two sections (14.1–4; 15.3–4) relate to gathering for community worship and interpersonal interaction.

Chapter 11 begins with counsel about the nature of those who teach (11.1–2), as well as how true teachers are to be received. The topic of teachers and those who offer instruction arises several times throughout the text (see 4.9; 6.1; 11.10–11; 13.2; 15.2), becoming a mainstay of the entirety of the work. Yet with 11.3 the focus of discussion turns toward itinerant apostles and prophets (or apostolic prophets?) and whether such persons should be acknowledged within the community. While the motif of teaching remains of concern (so 11.10–11), the primary question becomes how one may adequately evaluate such individuals, since to do so introduces a perilous process of testing the very spirit of prophecy – a procedure not to be undertaken lightly. Not all manuscripts include 11.3–12, though, which suggests the section either was not original to the tradition or was met with varying degrees of acceptance. The nature of prophets is continued in 13.1–7, where the text discusses prophets within the community and how they must be treated as "your high priests" (*hoi arxiereis hymōn*), receiving the first fruits of the community's labors. The concern for prophecy in 11.3–12 and 13.1–7 is divided by a brief comment on which additional outsiders may unite with the community under other circumstances (12.1–5), offered primarily via the caveat that such persons must support themselves through their crafts. This structural divide suggests prophets in chapter 11 are *not* to be considered the same as those in chapter 13, the former being itinerant (and apostolic?) in nature and the latter perhaps being an established part of the community's leadership. The question of governance is continued in 15.1–2, where one is told to "appoint/elect overseers/bishops and ministers/deacons" (*cheirotonēsate episkopous kai diakonous*) as community leaders, to be honored "with the prophets and teachers" (*meta tōn prophētōn kai didaskalōn*). The identification of only two offices of leadership (bishops and deacons) is sometimes seen as problematic in discussions of the rise of ecclesiastical offices (though see Phil. 1.1), where a threefold division of bishop–presbyter–deacon dominates the literature.[8]

Beyond matters of community structure, materials at 14.1–3 and 15.3–4 are focused on community interaction related to worship. Chapter 14 counsels worshippers to give thanks with pure conscience, having resolved quarrels among themselves in advance. The materials of 15.3–4 continue with this theme, insisting on peaceful correction among believers in recognition that those who refuse instruction be shunned until they repent. In each instance scripture is invoked as a source of authority: 14.3 appeals to Mal. 1.11, 14, while 15.4 refers to prayers and charity reflecting what is known "from the gospel of our Lord" (*en tō euangeliō tou kyriou hēmōn*), a possible reference to Mt. 6.1–18.

4.   16.1–8   Concluding short apocalypse

The tradition is completed with a short section related to elements of the future. These materials are decidedly apocalyptic in tone and include warnings for the hearer to be ready. Also here are specific descriptions of the final signs prior to when "the Lord will come and all his saints with him" (*hēxiei ho kyrios kai pantes hoi hagioi met' autou*; 16.7), a clear reference to Zech. 14.5. The sense of these lines is somewhat unexpected, since the tradition does not otherwise focus on the end times. Undoubtedly the purpose of this closing is to emphasize the eschatological importance of the hearer's correct response to instructions given in previous chapters.

Much of what appears here shows clear dependence on materials found in Mt. 24.10–25.13.[9] But numerous additional parallels to the Apostle Paul's instruction in 1 Thess. 4.13–18 (signs of the coming Parousia) suggest the tradition either predates both passages or takes stock of each in its own way. Various other allusions from Hebrew scripture populate the section as well, seen for instance with Dan. 7.13, Joel 2.2, and Zech. 13.8–9, thus to suggest a heavy reliance on biblical tradition as the background of these teachings.

---

[8] See A.C. Stewart, *The Original Bishops* (Grand Rapids, MI: Baker, 2014).
[9] Cf. Mk. 13.13–37; Lk. 12.35–40.

What is not clear from the tradition is whether 16.8 served as the original conclusion of the tradition. The editor of H, for instance, offered a series of stylistic marks in the codex here in a manner atypical of his conclusion for other writings within the work. No other manuscript parallels are accessible for comparison, which has led some scholars to offer reconstructions of a textual conclusion that includes brief additional materials no longer available.[10]

13.3 MANUSCRIPT WITNESSES

The rediscovery of H gave opportunity for scholars to identify the presence of a parallel form of the tradition preserved in Book 7 of the late fourth-century *Apostolic Constitutions* (= ApCon). While not exact in their agreement about the text, the two works are sufficiently analogous to suggest basic assumptions concerning the common tradition behind each manuscript.[11] As illustrated above, the fourfold division of the tradition suggested by H is preserved as well in ApCon. For this editor, the teaching clearly carried great authority, serving as the backbone onto which additional materials such as scripture were then attached. In addition to the witnesses of H and ApCon, one may perhaps include a third witness from Georgian tradition identified in the 1930s by Georg Peradse that basically reflects materials otherwise found in H. This last evidence remains unclear with regard to date and setting, however, not having been secondarily verified by any independent scholar.[12]

Beyond these three witnesses – none of which reflects a context prior to the late fourth century – only fragmentary parallels to the tradition are evident. Most of these comprise similar "two ways" teachings, seen for instance in the texts of *Barnabas* 18–21, the Latin *Doctrina apostolorum*, the *Didascalia apostolorum*, the *Apostolic Church Order* and its *Epitome*, a brief fragment in POxy. 1782, the *Syntagma doctrinae*, and *Fides Nicaena*. Of these, the *Didascalia*, *Syntagma*, and *Fides* also preserve parallels to 8.1 and 13.3, though

---

[10] Cf. R.E. Aldridge, "The Lost Ending of the *Didache*," *VigChr* 53 (1999): 1–15.

[11] Though this is not assumed by all scholars, thus the hesitancy of B. Steimer, *Vertex traditionis* (Berlin: de Gruyter, 1992), 12.

[12] So G. Peradse, "Die 'Lehre der zwölf Apostel' in der georgischen Überlieferung," *ZNW* 31 (1932): 111–16, and Peradse, "Zum Text der georgischen Didache," *ZNW* 31 (1932): 206. This evidence is highly debated. Holmes thinks it "a modern translation rather than an independent witness"; so M.W. Holmes, *The Apostolic Fathers*, 3rd ed. (Grand Rapids, MI: Baker, 2007), 340.

without the contexts found in H. In addition, the Coptic pages of Coptic Brit. Mus. Or. 9271 preserve a version of the prayers in 10.3b–12.2a, while Ethiopic tradition includes various additional fragments.[13] Beyond these, limited parallels to the work appear in diverse later treatises, though distance from the original form of the tradition makes their testimony only of limited value.

Since most published editions and commentaries on the *Didache* rely primarily on the eleventh-century witness found in H, a series of questions necessarily arises. One might ask, for instance, to what extent scholars should be comfortable following the primary testimony of a medieval manuscript for reconstructions of any original form of the tradition. To be sure, ApCon offers general support for H as conservator of the ancient teaching, but the various infelicities between the two treatises serve as a reminder that no easily established original text is evident from a ready comparison of the works. Likewise, as is clearly evident from the form of the tradition preserved in ApCon, one should question the degree to which later, post-Constantinian values may have entered into the rendering of H. This is suggested by use of the Trinitarian formula in two slightly different forms in chapter 7 (wording missing in ancient baptismal rituals generally), an almost exact replication of Matthew's so-called Lord's Prayer in chapter 8 (not otherwise attested prior to Tertullian at the beginning of the third century), the teaching not to give holy things to dogs in 10.5 (a reflection of the fourth-century mantra "holy things for the holy"?), and concern for the offices of bishop and deacon in 15.1–2. Such language and concerns, while not indicative of a late origin for the tradition necessarily, certainly reflect the interests and practices of the fourth/fifth-century church. Finally, since the majority of manuscript evidence from early sources does not include much beyond chapters 1–5, one must question whether patristic allusions to the "teaching" (noted in the Introduction above) are not themselves actually made in reference to some limited version of the tradition now reflected in writings such as the *Apostolic Church Order* or *Doctrina apostolorum*. If true, one might envisage why patristic authors such as Athanasius saw the tradition as suitable for instruction only and not for liturgy.

[13] See most recently, A. Bausi, "La nuova versione etiopica della Traditio apostolica: edizione e traduzione preliminare," in *Christianity in Egypt: Literary Production and Intellectual Trends*, ed. P. Buzi and A. Camplani (Rome: Institutum Patristicum Augustinianum, 2011), 19–69.

13.4 LITERARY PRESERVATION OF ORAL TRADITION

Recent scholars have come to focus on the likely oral nature of the sources behind the *Didache*, from which one might deduce that materials preserved there reflect a living community and on the likelihood no single provenance or date of origin for the tradition will ever be identified.[14] In result, one must be concerned for the broad usage of the tradition's evolving formation within various first- and second-century Christian literatures outside the canon. In the case of the *Didache*, this has likely resulted in the collection of diverse sources and traditions assembled, shaped, and reshaped by unknown editors, sometimes indicated by changing terminology and views within the tradition. The implications are patent in the case of the *Didache* to the extent that establishing a firm date for the composition of the text holds little meaning if one imagines sources behind the work were largely in transition (not static) and may have circulated in various provisional forms for decades (if not centuries) before being recorded in literary records. One need only look at instances of "two ways" teaching from late Jewish and patristic literature as suitable examples, though the range of readings among New Testament manuscripts during the early centuries of textual transmission suggests this process to be typical of epistolographical and codicological practices that extended well into the Middle Ages.

This leads one to wonder if what remains from literary witnesses is a valid reflection of what was first recorded historically as the text of the *Didache*. For example, ancient sources are not in agreement concerning either the content or extent of the work, often preferring only the preservation of the "two ways" (typically with omission of certain passages), indicating lack of uniformity (or featuring creativity) for the ending of that same section in chapter 6, sometimes including (though mostly omitting) the famous "*myron* (Greek)/*stenoufi* (Coptic) prayer" of 10.7b, and at odds over how to conclude the apocalyptic materials of chapter 16 (which end abruptly in H). Should one simply claim the editors made diverse, stylistic choices in their work (which they clearly did) or, as an alternative, that they had only limited sources of the tradition at their disposal? Most likely the form of the *Didache* known

---

[14] See I.H. Henderson, "*Didache* and Orality in Synoptic Composition," *JBL* 111 (1992): 283–306, and Henderson, "Style-Switching in the *Didache*: Fingerprint or Argument?," in *The Didache in Context*, ed. C.N. Jefford, NovTSup 77 (Leiden: Brill, 1995), 177–209.

to later editors varied widely because the text itself was not yet firmly established, reflecting to some extent lack of uniformity within the tradition and/or weak oversight in establishing its authority within specific communities. In other words, if the tradition did not mirror a universally recognized standard for a limited community (or range of communities), then there was little to prevent its constant alteration (undoubtedly through adaptation for use in oral mode) by those who employed its materials.[15] In many respects one observes that a living tradition of instruction (not necessarily a literary text) required revision according to its employment. Whether this is the basis on which the *Didache* arose versus the more popular, scholarly perspective that an explicit literary text was composed over a precise period of time remains unresolved.

13.5 INTERRELATED OR EVOLVED?

Subsequent to the question of oral (versus literary) backgrounds, the issue remains whether the *Didache* was penned as a single literary unity or evolved from modest beginnings into something like the complex form now preserved in H. At the beginning of scholarly research in the late nineteenth century, there was a general assumption that the tradition was a unified production from a particular "time and place." These two elements varied among scholars, ranging from penchants for the mid-first to mid-second centuries and from Egypt to Asia Minor. Nonetheless, at least a majority of researchers chose some such milieu.

With the publications of Jean-Paul Audet in the 1950s[16] there was a gradual shift toward another view that the *Didache* reflects the contribution of more than one hand, or at least the involvement of a single hand over more than one period of time. In the 1960s[17] Robert Kraft identified this genre of literature as "evolved," and this perspective soon gained traction among students of the text. Kurt Niederwimmer held differently, however, seeing the *Didache* as the work of a single hand that unified a variety of sources,[18] and more recently Aaron Milavec has argued for a return to the idea that the *Didache* represents a single (if

---

[15] This is supported by Gamble, who reviews various ways in which early Christian texts were employed; see H.Y. Gamble, *Books and Readers in the Early Church* (New Haven, CT; London: Yale University Press, 1995), 203–41.

[16] J.-P. Audet, *La Didache: instructions des apôtres*, ÉB (Paris: Gabalda, 1958).

[17] R.A. Kraft, *Barnabas and the Didache*, AF 3 (New York: Nelson & Sons, 1965).

[18] K. Niederwimmer, *Die Didache*, KAV 1 (Göttingen: Vandenhoeck & Ruprecht, 1989) (ET = *The Didache* [Minneapolis, MN: Fortress, 1998]), and Niederwimmer, "Der

broadly scattered) community and unified period of time (mid-first century).[19] In this sense the work may reflect a set of conditions in early Christian community life that was over time eradicated through the rise of "orthodoxy" and its hegemony. In result, the "teaching" should be seen as interconnected from its beginning and attributable to a single, unified perception, the reflection of a specific moment in ancient Christian development.

Yet certain elements of the tradition seem to defy many such assumptions of unity. One may ask, for example, whether it is fair to draw such conclusions given the paucity of literary support and in light of the late date of the manuscripts. So too, divergent aspects of the text are not so easily explained by such broad sweeping assumptions. For example, concerns arise about whether use of the Trinitarian formula was common in the late first century, whether the *Didache* employs the term "gospel" (*euangelion;* so 8.2; 11.3; 15.3–4 [twice]) for a particular tradition of oral teachings identified with the figure of Jesus or instead as reference to a specific text,[20] the unique employment of the Lord's Prayer from Matthew as exemplary of universal Christian prayer (mentioned above),[21] and enigmatic references to "worldly mystery of the assembly" (*eis mystērion kosmikon ekklēsias;* 11.11) and "Christ merchant" (*christemporos;* 12.5) that appear here as unique usages within ancient literature. Such curious elements within H are not readily clarified from a holistic, interrelated portrait of a uniquely primitive experience. In many respects they are better assumed to reflect a process of accrual, having been added while the community that produced the text changed or as those who contributed to the tradition at various moments in history confronted new and novel situations that required emendation within the textual growth.

This issue remains unresolved, though it is significant to *Didache* studies, since a desire to see the text as representative of a singular setting in early Christian circles intrigues scholars. Yet such a limiting view evades many fundamental problems within H and requires resourceful clarification to explain the vagaries of that manuscript

---

Didachist und seine Quellen," in *The* Didache *in Context*, ed. C.N. Jefford, NovTSup 77 (Leiden: Brill, 1995), 15–36.

[19] A. Milavec, *The Didache* (New York; Mahwah, NJ: Newman, 2003).

[20] See H. Koester, *Ancient Christian Gospels* (London; Philadelphia, PA: Trinity, 1990); J.A. Kelhoffer, "'How Soon a Book' Revisited: EUANGELION as a Reference to 'Gospel' Materials in the First Half of the Second Century," *ZNW* 95 (2004): 1–34.

[21] S.E. Young, *Jesus Tradition in the Apostolic Fathers*, WUNT 2/311 (Tübingen: Mohr Siebeck, 2011), 218–25.

witness. Scholars thus remain divided between those who accept and those who reject any of scholarship's proposed, unified origins.

13.6 IMPLICATIONS OF STRUCTURE

The question of literary integrity leads quite naturally to the problem of textual divisions within H. Recently Nancy Pardee has brought the issue into clear focus, isolating shifts between specific teachings, subsets, and general categories of thought.[22] To ignore this topic is to miss an essential aspect of the work, that is, the purpose of the author reflected in the construction of the text. Some features may be offered by way of illustration.

One may ask, for example, whether some early author initiated a single textual tradition with extensive complexity as suggested by the witness of H. To argue that "two ways" materials were recorded for the purpose of catechesis is reasonable. But should one accept the premise that the remainder of the text, including various liturgical rituals and regulations of the community (chapters 7–15), are likewise intended for the newly initiated? Alternatively, one may surmise the work was composed for specific leaders responsible for rituals and regulations, thereby requiring that "two ways" instruction for catechumens should be included for use by such instructors. This latter option seems more likely on the surface, yet certain problems remain, as seen from the following explicit controversial passages.

13.6.1 The "*sectio evangelica*" Section (1.3b–2.1)

Since these materials appear in their most complete form in H as opposed to all other parallel manuscripts, one might argue this section was *not* original in its entirety (contrary to H) but reflects editorial emendation. This challenge to literary composition presents a complicated issue as illustrated by available evidence. Several witnesses contain none of these materials, including *Barnabas, Doctrina, Syntagma*, and *Fides*. Otherwise, *Didascalia* includes only 1.3b ("bless those who curse you") and 1.5b ("for the Lord wishes to give to all from his gifts"), though this appears elsewhere in chapter 4. Other manuscripts include other portions of the section, seen for example in POxy. 1982 (1.4 only), ApCon (1.3b–5a only), and the Georgian version (1.3b–4; 2.1).[23] Such a

---

[22] Pardee, *Genre and Development*.

[23] In addition to these manuscripts, one might consider the *Didache*'s opening words "teaching of the lord" (*didache kyriou*) to resemble the notion of "teachings of

variety of readings recommends that something must have been here in the original form of the tradition, but oddly only H seems to have preserved the entire section. Yet, to argue that H alone reflects the original is thus to dismiss all other partial literary parallels, which is awkward.

13.6.2 Chapter 6 as Transitional

On the one hand, chapter 6 serves as the conclusion of the "two ways" materials while serving as the beginning of the liturgical instruction. This is a logical literary link between sections, but to assume this was the original intention of the tradition bears explanation. Many parallels to H do not contain instruction beyond the "two ways" and, when they do, the form of chapter 6 differs widely. Variance appears in *Barnabas*, *Doctrina*, and *Apostolic Church Order*, and (with some slight change of wording) in ApCon and the Georgian version. That the manuscripts show no uniformity indicates again something stood in the original tradition, though that form remains unclear. As indicated above concerning the materials that follow in chapters 7–11, the tradition's series of "now concerning" phrases overlaps at 6.3 and extends into the ecclesiastical section at 11.3. This formula currently unites all these materials into a coherent unit in H. But should one say that the author saw chapter 6 as the structural conclusion of the "two ways" while simultaneously framing the end of the chapter as an organizational start for the following teachings? The complexity of this situation has received extensive review.[24]

13.6.3 Appointing Bishops and Deacons (15.1–2)

One final example involves the problem of how a text may be read from opposing perspectives. The instruction about assigning bishops and deacons for the community comes unexpectedly within the text, introducing a topic not otherwise anticipated between instructions on worship (14.1–3) and suitable community interaction (15.3–4). In truth,

---

Christ" (*didagmata tou Christou*) reflected in Justin, *1 Apol.* 14.4, which may provide early historical evidence for at least the core of *Did.* 1.3b–5 within second-century teaching traditions; see A. van den Hoek, "Divergent Gospel Traditions in Clement of Alexandria and Other Authors of the Second Century," *Apocrypha* 7 (1996): 59 n. 15.

[24] See, e.g., Niederwimmer, *The Didache*, 120–4; J.A. Draper, "Torah and Troublesome Apostles in the Didache Community," *NovT* 33 (1991): 347–72; H. van de Sandt and D. Flusser, *The Didache* (Assen: Van Gorcum; Minneapolis, MN: Fortress, 2002), 238–70; Milavec, *The Didache*, 771–82; Pardee, *Genre and Development*, 134–40.

these two sections link together naturally without the instructions of 15.1–2. Those who argue for the original presence of this material typically identify the introductory "therefore" (oun) as indication that issues of worship and community relations necessitated some remark by the author on selection of valid liturgical and ecclesiastical authorities. In opposition, those who view the material as secondary see no special purpose to the term and subsequently view the instruction as out of place and awkward in the larger framework of the text. As such, it reflects a secondary editor concerned for later issues.

This leads to the question of whether the tradition is structurally complex because it represents a series of revisions. The view of a progressive, evolved tradition insists that divisions within the text are necessarily complex because of the events during which the text evolved. This may be in part because the original author made subsequent revisions, or this may be because later editors emended the initial tradition. The degree to which editorial interference occurred is notable given the brevity of the work, but basic elements may be outlined in the structure identified above. Over the course of sixteen brief chapters the text of H covers an amazing variety of topics, much like later handbooks of ecclesiastical instruction. Unlike later handbooks, however, there is no uniformity of style or clear structural framework. To complicate the matter further, one sees alternating patterns of "you singular" and "you plural" language without obvious rationale, relatively low christology[25] intermingled with high Trinitarian phraseology, decidedly Jewish rituals (prayers) and related language intermingled without concern for strict Jewish practices, references to gospel teachings and authority alongside apparently pre-gospel traditions, etc. In other words, while there is much to argue for the antiquity of the tradition, there is also much to recommend that some limited liturgical standards and wording typical of post-Constantinian Christian practice found their way into the text as it now stands in H. Should one not then assume multiple hands are present based on the complexity of the text's structure, thus to make the tradition an example of "evolved literature"? This is likely the case, though scholarship remains in dispute on this idea.

---

[25] See J.A. Overman, "Problems with Pluralism in Second Temple Judaism: Matthew, James, and the Didache in Their Jewish-Roman Milieu," in *Matthew, James, and Didache*, ed. H. van de Sandt and J.K. Zangenberg (Atlanta, GA: SBL, 2008), 259–70 (esp. 265). Not all authors see the christology as "low," however; see M.J. Smith, "The Lord Jesus and His Coming in the Didache," in *The Didache*, ed. J.A. Draper and C.N. Jefford (Atlanta, GA: Society of Biblical Literature, 2015), 363–407.

13.7 PURPOSE AND FUNCTION

A majority of scholars accept the tradition is intended for catechesis, likely directed at inclusion of non-Jewish devotees into a Jewish-oriented community of messianic faith. The initial alignment around the "two ways" and Decalogue suggest this assumption, especially since such essentials continued in a similar role for later generations. The materials are clearly instructional; their orientation is directed toward ethical living.

Yet the remaining chapters on baptism, prayer, acceptance of outsiders, and directions on community organization are hardly relevant to the situation of a catechumen. True, later editors (e.g. with ApCon) included all this material as part of basic training programs – but not for catechumens. Instead, these materials were used to instruct priests and other leaders of the community. To this end one might imagine the tradition came to be employed as a touchstone for the training of leaders themselves, who then were responsible for the integration of catechumens into the broader group. This much seems evident. But one must question whether later use of the *Didache* reflects the way in which it was originally designed to function.

This begs the question of whether there was previously another purpose for the text. Here one may divide possible usages into two categories: the author's wish to preserve materials already in use within the community and/or the author's desire to offer original answers to questions that arose as the community's situation evolved.

As to "preservation," evidently numerous materials preserve and employ ancient sources as a mainstay of instruction. Thus, the "two ways" of chapters 1–5 reflect early practices known from Jewish and Hellenistic literature, including the writings of Qumran. Yet other materials are preserved here as well. The prayers of chapters 9–10 are clearly archaic in form and, reflecting parallel usages elsewhere,[26] likely echo liturgical practices of the oldest faith community rather than evidence of novel wording designed for use in new contexts. In many respects these may be among the oldest portions of the text. So too, the baptismal practices and Lord's Prayer in chapters 7–8 also suggest ancient forms preserved for immediate use.

---

[26] See J. Schwiebert, *Knowledge and the Coming Kingdom* (London; New York: T&T Clark, 2008); J.J. Clabeaux, "The Ritual Meal in Didache 9–10: Progress in Understanding," in *The Didache*, ed. J.A. Draper and C.N. Jefford (Atlanta, GA: Society of Biblical Literature, 2015), 209–30.

As to "innovation," certain allowances arise throughout that are meant to emend earlier customary traditions. These include 1.5, where one is told to give to all who ask (since God wishes gifts to be given to all), while immediately thereafter in 1.6 (following Sir. 12.1) one is instructed to withhold charity until the one who receives is known, despite yet again being instructed later to welcome anyone who comes in the name of the Lord (12.1) and to give freely as instructed by the gospel (15.4); 6.2, where one is told that if unable to bear the whole yoke of the Lord, one should do as one can; 7.2–3, where for baptism one is permitted to use warm and/or still water and to pour such on the head three times if cold and/or running water is unavailable; 10.7, where prophets are allowed to give thanks as they wish despite explicit instructions for the ritual of thanksgiving in previous materials; and, 13.4, where one is told that first fruits of a crop may be given to the poor if the usual recipients (community prophets) are not present. Regardless of whether such words derive from the author or a later editor, they clearly reflect an emendation of the tradition's teaching. Further, instructions on how the community should treat itinerant apostles and prophets (11.3–13.7) suggest an historical moment in the community's development in which the tolerant lifestyle of the audience faces new circumstances – the role of outside authorities. With the writing of these instructions it is clear that the authority of a local voice seeks to frame rules of engagement in such matters. Clearly and without question, innovation exists at least in this single, precise moment.

Related to the issue of "preservation versus innovation" is whether the instruction is to be viewed as authentic, "actionable" teachings or, instead, as "idealized" understanding of the life of faith.[27] The issue of "idealized vision" reflects the situation of ancient messianic communities of the first and second centuries, who often were displaced from their homelands by war, famine, legislative abuse, etc. and realized an intrinsic loss within the new circumstances of a different society with a need to preserve some memory of homeland traditions. As such, instruction of the next generation of a community needed the reminder of such values. In the mid- to late first and early second centuries, the period in which most scholars now place the tradition, this same situation deserves deliberation.[28] One must also ask whether the tradition

---

[27] By way of contemporary illustration, see J. D'Alisera, *An Imagined Geography* (Philadelphia, PA: Penn University Press, 2004).

[28] This is described in some detail by H. Wendt, "From the Herodians to Hadrian: The Shifting Status of Judean Religion in Post-Flavian Rome," *Forum* 6 (2017): 145–70.

was first composed in a setting soon lost to memory. Modern attempts to place the text in a single set of circumstances may be to force a specific context on the development of the work without justification. This may be true if the earliest traditions came from circumstances later abandoned. For example, the original community may have left some ancestral home owing to unfavorable circumstances such as the Jewish wars of 66–73 CE. Thus, attempts to locate the provenance of the tradition based on elements in the text (e.g. use of "broken bread scattered on the hills" [9.4] as representative of Syria or comments about "the Lord's own day" [14.1] as typical of writers from Asia Minor) may seek to establish the text in a secondary framework rather than its original setting. Nevertheless, variables such as these may never be identified with certainty.

13.8 CONCLUSIONS

In the final analysis, the *Didache* reflects an ancient tradition of teaching comprised of "two ways" training, liturgical rituals, and ecclesiastical instruction. Its origins remain unknown, though scholars usually place its roots in Syria – specifically Antioch – with Egypt a possible if less likely provenance. Some researchers set the tradition within our most ancient Christian literature from the middle first century, while others attribute it to an early second-century setting after the composition of the gospels. In either case, clearly it preserves some of the church's oldest instructional materials. The author (or editor) of the corpus – the so-called Didachist – remains a figure of conjecture, if such ever actually existed. Later editors clearly played some role. While patristic authors refer to the tradition in limited ways, it likely circulated in fluctuating forms until its adoption by the fourth-century ApCon. Our best known witness (H) derives from the early eleventh century and suggests use of the tradition may have begun as catechetical training with a decidedly Jewish tone, though ensuing usage likely varied based on context and need.

FURTHER READING

Draper, J.A., and C.N. Jefford, eds. *The Didache: A Missing Piece of the Puzzle in Early Christianity*. ECL 14. Atlanta, GA: Society of Biblical Literature, 2015.

Garrow, A.J.P. *The Gospel of Matthew's Dependence on the* Didache. London; New York: T&T Clark, 2004.

Milavec, A. *The Didache: Faith, Hope, and Life of the Earliest Christian Communities, 50–70 C.E.* New York; Mahwah, NJ: Newman, 2003.

Niederwimmer, K. *The Didache: A Commentary.* Hermeneia. Translated by L.M. Maloney. Minneapolis, MN: Fortress, 1998.

Pardee, N. *The Genre and Development of the Didache.* WUNT 2/339. Tübingen: Mohr Siebeck, 2012.

van de Sandt, H., and D. Flusser. *The Didache: Its Jewish Sources and Its Place in Early Judaism and Christianity.* CRINT 3/5. Assen: Van Gorcum; Minneapolis, MN: Fortress, 2002.

14 The *Epistle of Barnabas*

REIDAR HVALVIK

The so-called *Epistle of Barnabas* is one of the first writings after the New Testament to deal with two burning issues in early Christianity: How ought the "Old Testament" to be interpreted – over against Jewish interpretations, and how should the Christians define themselves in relation to non-Christian Jews and their beliefs and practices? The author's rather unique answers are both intriguing and provoking.

14.1 *BARNABAS* IN THE EARLY CHURCH

The first person to refer to *Barnabas*[1] is Clement of Alexandria (c. 150–215). In order to find support for an argument, he writes: "I need merely call as witness the apostolic figure of Barnabas (one of the Seventy and a co-worker of Paul)" (*Strom.* 2.116.3).[2] In another place he refers to "the apostle Barnabas" (*Strom.* 2.35.5) and quotes him several times, often referring to his name (*Strom.* 2.67.3; 2.84.3; 5.63.2). Origen (c. 185–254) quotes the letter, once referring to it as "the general epistle of Barnabas" (*Cels.* 1.63), and on another occasion he writes about "Barnabas in his Epistle" (*Princ.* 3.2.4). Didymus the Blind (c. 313–398) writes in his commentary of Zechariah: "Barnabas, likewise, who along with Paul was himself appointed apostle for the uncircumcised, sent a letter to those with faith in the Gospel, and directed it to his sons and daughters, as it were"[3] (*Comm. Zech.* 10; see also *Comm. Ps.* 300.11–13).

---

[1] In the following "*Barnabas*" (italicized) refers to the writing; "Barnabas" refers to the unknown author.

[2] Quoted from Clement of Alexandria, *Stromateis Books 1–3*, trans. John Ferguson, Fathers of the Church 85 (Washington, DC: The Catholic University of America Press, 1991), 233. The reference is to *Barn.* 16.7–9.

[3] Quoted from Didymus the Blind, *Commentary on Zechariah*, trans. Robert C. Hill, Fathers of the Church 111 (Washington, DC: The Catholic University of America Press, 2006), 241.

These references show that *Barnabas* was used and in high esteem in the East, a fact made visible by the inclusion of the epistle in the fourth-century *Codex Sinaiticus*. There it is placed after Revelation and before *The Shepherd of Hermas*.

There is no firm evidence that *Barnabas* circulated in the West in late antiquity. Admittedly Tertullian speaks about such a letter (*De. pud.* 20.2), but he obviously has Hebrews in mind. Jerome (c. 347–419) mentions Barnabas and his letter (*Vir. Ill.* 6), identifying him as an apostle and Paul's co-worker, and in one place referring to the epistle's wording (*Comm. Ezech.* 43.18–22). Jerome almost certainly knew the letter through his many connections in the East, particularly Didymus (see *Vir. Ill.* 109).

14.2 AUTHORSHIP

The abovementioned witnesses from the early church make a clear connection between the author of *Barnabas* and the Cyprian Levite Joseph, also known as Barnabas and a co-worker of Paul (Acts 4.36; 13.1–15.39; Gal. 2.1–13; 1 Cor. 9.6). The reason for this connection is unknown and without a basis in the text of the epistle. Since the author does not name himself it is accurate to say that the author is anonymous, rather than pseudonymous (consequently it is inappropriate to refer to him as Pseudo-Barnabas, as sometimes is done).

The attribution to the Levite Barnabas seems, however, quite unlikely. This Barnabas, who according to Gal. 2.13 was eager to follow Jewish dietary laws, could hardly be the author of the radical allegorizing of these laws in *Barn.* 10. Moreover, he could not have included himself in saying "Before we believed in God, our heart's dwelling place was ... full of idolatry and was the home of demons" (16.7).[4] For the same reason, it is quite improbable that the author was a converted rabbi, as has been suggested.[5] From the letter itself, the author seems to be a gentile Christian, regarding himself as a teacher (1.8; 4.9). It is true that the writing has a Jewish(-Christian) character, but this is most certainly related to the sources utilized by the author.

---

[4] Translations from *Barnabas* are generally taken from Michael W. Holmes, *The Apostolic Fathers: Greek Texts and English Translations*, 3rd ed. (Grand Rapids, MI: Baker Academic, 2007). In some cases quotations are from Bart Ehrman, *The Apostolic Fathers*, LCL, 2 vols. (Cambridge, MA: Harvard University Press, 2003); this will be noted.

[5] So Leslie W. Barnard, "Judaism in Egypt A.D. 70–135," in Barnard, *Studies in the Apostolic Fathers and their Background* (Oxford: Blackwell, 1966), 41–55, at 47.

14.3 PROVENANCE

The location of *Barnabas* is not known, and various places of origin
have been proposed. A majority of scholars argue for Alexandria, while
others have proposed Syria-Palestine or Western Asia Minor. The argument for Asia Minor is based on the fact that Ignatius in his letter to the
Philadelphians (8.2) refers to people who said "If I do not find (it) in the
archives, I do not believe (it to be) in the gospel."[6] The "archives"
clearly refers to the Old Testament, and Ignatius' opponents seem to
be people claiming that Scripture is the only norm for Christian teaching. According to Klaus Wengst, this rare theological point of view
matches Barnabas and substantiates a historical and geographical relationship between them.[7] The information about Ignatius' opponents is,
however, so scanty that it is impossible to draw secure conclusions and
Wengst's proposal has got little, if any, support.

Syria-Palestine has been proposed as a place of origin owing to the
similarities between *Barnabas* and theological traditions found in
writings from this region. Pierre Prigent, among others, has drawn
attention to Qumran, rabbinical traditions, the ideas expressed by
Stephen in Acts 6–7, Justin, and the *Odes of Solomon*.[8] Among the
rabbinical traditions are details about the two goats on the Day of
Atonement in *Barn.* 7 (see below). Noteworthy are also the many parallels between *Barnabas* and Justin (coming from Syrian Palestine); they
probably used some parallel sources.[9] Likewise, there are some striking
parallels between phrases and ideas found both in *Barnabas* and the
Odes of Solomon. It can be argued with high probability that the language of the *Odes* influences *Barnabas* (see esp. *Barn.* 5.5–7 and *Odes
Sol.* 31.10–13).[10] Also to be mentioned is *Didache*,[11] which seems to
utilize the same Two Ways traditions as *Barnabas*.

---

[6] Translation from William R. Schoedel, *Ignatius of Antioch: A Commentary on the
Letters of Ignatius of Antioch*, Hermeneia (Philadelphia, PA: Fortress, 1985), 207.

[7] Klaus Wengst, *Tradition und Theologie des Barnabasbriefes*, Arbeiten zur
Kirchengeschichte 42 (Berlin: de Gruyter, 1971), 113–18.

[8] Pierre Prigent and Robert A. Kraft, *Épître de Barnabé*, SC 172 (Paris: Les Éditions du
Cerf, 1971), 22–4.

[9] See Oskar Skarsaune, *The Proof from Prophecy: A Study in Justin Martyr's Proof-
Text Tradition: Text-Type, Provenance, Theological Profile*, NovTSup 56 (Leiden:
Brill, 1987), 110–13.

[10] See Michael Lattke, *Odes of Solomon: A Commentary*, Hermeneia (Minneapolis,
MN: Fortress, 2009), 437. Admittedly, the place of origin for the *Odes of Solomon* is
debated, but Syria (or Palestine) is the most plausible candidate.

[11] Provided that *Didache* originated in Syria-Palestine, which is most likely.

Alexandria (or more generally: Egypt) is the provenance proposed by the majority of scholars.[12] The arguments for this position are as follows: First, the earliest witness to *Barnabas* is Clement of Alexandria; later both Origen and Didymus the Blind show knowledge of the epistle (see above). Secondly, Barnabas shows a great liking for allegorical interpretation, generally associated with Alexandria and exemplified by Philo and the *Letter of Aristeas*. Thirdly, Barnabas writes that "all the priests of the idols are circumcised" as well as the people of Egypt (9.6). According to some scholars, this demonstrates Barnabas' location in Alexandria because he knew that the priests in Egypt were circumcised though he incorrectly claimed the same for all pagan priests.

In modern scholarship, there is, however, increasing recognition of the vulnerability of these arguments. First, the fact that *Barnabas* was popular in Alexandria does not prove that it originated there. This fact can be clearly illustrated by the popularity of the *Shepherd of Hermas* in Alexandria – even if it was written in Rome/Italy. This writing was considered inspired by Clement of Alexandria (*Strom.* 1.29.181), and he, Origen, and Didymus the Blind (*Comm. Zech.* 5; 9 and 13) refer to this writing. This means that early attestation is no secure basis for determining the place of origin. Besides, Wengst has pointed out that *Barnabas'* unique theological position did not gain support in early Christianity.[13] It is thus likely that it was disputed in its original milieu. Consequently, it is more probable that it circulated in places with no knowledge of such a local debate and possibly with limited understanding of the author's distinctive position. When *Barnabas* is referred to by Alexandrian authors, it is only about harmless questions. The main reason for its popularity was probably the assumed connection to an apostolic author. Since it was regarded as a "catholic epistle" by authorities like Clement and Origen, it is no surprise that it was included in *Codex Sinaiticus*.

Secondly, *Barnabas'* use of allegory is neither decisive since this form of exegesis was utilized by authors in various locations, e.g., Melito, Justin, Irenaeus, and Tertullian. Admittedly there are some thematic and exegetical points of contact between Barnabas and Philo. However, as David Runia emphasizes, "the actual interpretations that

---

[12] See James Carleton Paget, *The Epistle of Barnabas: Outlook and Background*, WUNT 2.64 (Tübingen: Mohr Siebeck, 1994), 30–42.

[13] Wengst, *Tradition*, 113.

the author supports are in most respects at a great remove from Philo's thought."[14] There are, however, some noteworthy similarities between *Barnabas* and the *Letter of Aristeas*, which may be taken as evidence of an Alexandrian origin for *Barnabas*.[15]

In the discussion of *Barnabas'* provenance, we also have to take into account the author's use of sources. This fact makes the case even more complicated and invites a broad investigation about the availability of the assumed sources. When it comes to the actual provenance of *Barnabas*, we have to admit that there is actually no decisive argument that can settle the matter. The factors mentioned above are mainly indications of *affinity* between *Barnabas* and theological traditions typical for various areas. The affinities are indeed strongest with Syria-Palestine and Alexandria (Egypt), probably in that order. It is very likely that *Barnabas* was written in a geographical area with a distinct Jewish presence and where Christians came into contact with Jews. This fits well with both Syria-Palestine and Alexandria.

14.4 DATE

Like the question of provenance, the date of *Barnabas* is much debated. The explicit reference to the destruction of the temple (16.2–3) means that the epistle must post-date 70 CE, and Clement of Alexandria's use of the text provides a fixed terminus *ante quem* (c. 200 CE). The absence of any mention of the Bar Kokhba revolt (132–135 CE) with the following ban of circumcision and prohibition against entering Jerusalem, so useful in anti-Jewish polemic (cf. Justin, *Dial.* 16 and Tertullian, *Adv. Jud.* 3.4; 13.4), makes it most likely that *Barnabas* should be dated before 132 CE.

Two texts in *Barnabas* are brought into the discussion of dating: 4.3–6a and 16.3–4. There are good reasons to believe that the first text (which mainly consists of quotations from Scripture) is taken from tradition and originally applied to an earlier period of time.[16] It is therefore probably best not to base the date of *Barnabas* on this text.[17]

[14] David T. Runia, *Philo in Early Christian Literature: A Survey* (Assen: Van Gorcum, 1993), 93.

[15] See *Let. Aris.* 150/*Barn.* 10.11 and *Let. Aris.* 165/*Barn.* 10.8.

[16] Wengst, *Tradition*, 21–2, 105–6.

[17] For two different detailed treatments, see Carleton Paget, *The Epistle of Barnabas*, 9–17 and Reidar Hvalvik, *The Struggle for Scripture and Covenant: The Purpose of the Epistle of Barnabas and Jewish-Christian Competition in the Second Century*, WUNT 2.82 (Tübingen: Mohr Siebeck, 1996), 25–32.

This leaves us with 16.3–4: "Moreover, he says again, 'See, those who have destroyed this temple will themselves build it.' This is happening (*ginetai*). For because of their war, it was destroyed by their enemies. And now (*nyn*) the servants of the enemies will themselves rebuild (*anoikodomēsousin*) it" (trans. Ehrman).

Verse 3 obviously refers to the temple in Jerusalem, and the enemies who destroyed it are clearly the Romans. The problem is that we do not know of any rebuilding of the Jewish temple, and certainly not with the assistance of the Romans. Besides, there is a temporal tension between *ginetai* (and *nyn*), indicating the present nature of the building, and *anoikodomēsousin*, indicating that it is still in the future. What then, does the text refer to? There are two entirely different answers to this question. First, some scholars look for a historical situation where a future rebuilding of the temple was hoped for, though not yet a reality. The most common proposal is that it refers to the reign of Nerva who reformed the *fiscus Iudaicus*, the tax imposed on the Jews in the Roman Empire after the first Jewish War. Precisely what the reform implied is debated, but it is essential that Nerva issued coins with the legend FISCI IVDAICI CALVMNIA SVBLATA ("the removal of the wrongful accusation of the *fiscus Iudaicus*")[18] on the one side and a palm tree, a Roman emblem of Judea and Judaism, on the other. This indicates that Nerva entertained a friendly attitude toward the Jews, and it has been suggested that this also gave rise to a hope of the rebuilding of the temple.[19] On this basis, *Barnabas* may be dated to 96–98 CE.

The second line of interpretation takes *Barn.* 16.4 as a reference to Hadrian's building of the temple of Jupiter on the site of the Second Temple in his new Aelia Capitolina – based primarily on the information given by Dio Cassius (*Hist.* 69.12).[20] While the former interpretation stressed the future form of "rebuild," this interpretation stresses the present form of the verb *ginetai*: "This is happening (now)." This must mean that something is, in fact, going on, at least the preparation

---

[18] For the interpretation of the legend, see Nathan T. Elkins, *The Image of Political Power in the Reign of Nerva, AD 96–98* (New York: Oxford University Press, 2017), esp. 84–8.

[19] See Peter Richardson and Martin B. Shukster, "Barnabas, Nerva, and the Yavnean Rabbis," *JTS* n.s. 34 (1983): 31–55, at 41–4; Carleton Paget, *The Epistle of Barnabas*, 22–7.

[20] See Wengst, *Tradition*, 111–13 and Ferdinand R. Prostmeier, *Der Barnabasbrief*, Kommentar zu den Apostolischen Vätern 8 (Göttingen: Vandenhoeck & Ruprecht, 1999), 111–19.

for the actual building. Besides, this interpretation takes seriously that the Romans are in charge of the building. On this basis, one can argue that *Barnabas* was written around 130–132 CE.

Against the second interpretation, it has been objected that the word "rebuild" requires that Barnabas is referring to the Jewish temple. It is correct that Barnabas in 16.1 is speaking about the temple in Jerusalem, but in his mind, this was not the house of God – and thus not unlike a pagan temple. If we take this into consideration, it becomes less strange that Barnabas can speak about a "rebuilding" of the temple, since the Jupiter-temple could be seen as a replacement of the Jewish temple. Besides (as an argument against the first interpretation), a rebuilding of the Jewish temple does not fit the tenor of *Barn.* 16, where the author stresses that the "wretched people went astray and set their hope on the building, as though it were God's house … You now know that their hope was in vain" (16.1–2). In this context, it would be strange to find a reference to a rebuilding – or the hope for a rebuilding – of the Jewish temple. In the author's mind, what he is referring to is the fulfillment of the prophecy of the destruction of the temple in Jerusalem – for Scripture had revealed "that the city and the temple and the people of Israel were destined to be handed over" (16.5).[21]

There are some uncertainties about the exact historical course of the establishment of Aelia Capitolina (and the placement of the Jupiter-temple), but it is most likely that it was planned and founded when Hadrian visited the region in 129–130.[22] Even if Barnabas only had heard rumors of a new city named after Jupiter Capitolina, he would probably expect that a temple would be erected at the same site as the destroyed Jewish temple.

It must be admitted that all arguments for the dating of *Barnabas* are based on some speculation and inadequate sources. The time of Nerva (96–98) cannot be ruled out, though a time during the reign of Hadrian (c. 130–132) seems to fit the text better.

---

[21] See Adolf Harnack, *Die Chronologie der altchristlichen Litteratur bis Eusebius*, vol. 1 (Leipzig: Hinrichs'sche Buchhandlung, 1897), 423–7; more recently Hvalvik, *Struggle*, 20–2 and James N. Rhodes, *The Epistle of Barnabas and the Deuteronomic Tradition: Polemics, Paraenesis, and the Legacy of the Golden-Calf Incident*, WUNT 2.188 (Tübingen: Mohr Siebeck, 2004), 78–87, esp. 83–4.

[22] See Mary T. Boatwright, *Hadrian and the Cities of the Roman Empire* (Princeton, NJ: Princeton University Press, 2000), 196–203 and Menahem Mor, *The Second Jewish Revolt: The Bar Kokhba War, 132–136 CE* (Leiden: Brill, 2016), esp. 121–9.

14.5 MANUSCRIPTS, EDITIONS, AND TRANSLATIONS

The full text of *Barnabas* survives only in two Greek manuscripts, both rediscovered and published in the nineteenth century: *Codex Sinaiticus* ([S] from the fourth century) and *Codex Hierosolymitanus* 54 ([H] from 1056). A Latin translation of 1.1–17.2 (L), possibly made as early as the third century, is preserved in one single manuscript; the further textual witnesses are fragmentary.[23]

The most complete critical edition of the Greek text is that of Prigent and Kraft (*Épître de Barnabé* in Sources chrétiennes); Wengst's edition[24] is useful because it reveals many different text-critical choices. Convenient editions with the Greek text and facing English translation are those of Ehrman (2003) and Holmes (2007).[25]

14.6 GENRE

Both in the early references to *Barnabas* and in the manuscript tradition, the writing is referred to as an "epistle." In recent research, *Barnabas* is, however, almost unanimously said to be a treatise or tract.[26] Admittedly there are some epistolary features, but they are explained as a literary device. It has also been suggested that *Barnabas* is a written homily,[27] but very few scholars would be so definitive.[28]

As a matter of fact, there are many traits in *Barnabas* that seem to be reminiscent of a preaching or teaching situation. Most apparent are the references to hearing (7.3; 13.2); to be noted are also the many imperatives calling the addressees to attention, e.g., "understand" (*noiete* – 4.14; 7.1; 8.2), "pay attention" (*prosechete* – 7.4, 6, 7, 9; 15.4; 16.8), "learn" (*mathete* – 5.5; 6.9; 9.7, 8; 14.4; 16.2, 7, 8), and "see" (*ide* – 6.14; 7.10; 8.1; 12.10, 11). Mention must also be made of the direct address, which occurs in two forms: "brothers (and sisters)" (*adelphoi* – 2.10; 3.6; 4.14; 5.5; 6.10, 15) or "children" (*tekna* – 7.1; 9.3, 7; 15.4). These traits are best explained if we assume that the author makes use

---

[23] For details, see Prostmeier, *Barnabasbrief*, 11–34.

[24] Klaus Wengst, *Didache (Apostellehre), Barnabasbrief, Zweiter Klemensbrief, Schrift an Diognet*, Schriften des Urchristentums (Munich: Kösel, 1984), 101–202.

[25] See note 4 above.

[26] So, e.g., Prostmeier, *Barnabasbrief*, 86–9.

[27] Leslie W. Barnard, "The Epistle of Barnabas – A Paschal Homily?," *VigChr* 15 (1961): 8–22.

[28] See, however, Ellen Bradshaw Aitken, *Jesus' Death in Early Christian Memory: The Poetics of the Passion*, NTOA 53 (Göttingen: Vandenhoeck & Ruprecht, 2004), 90–2.

of material earlier employed in oral teaching/preaching, though it is hardly adequate to call the writing as a whole a homily.

When it comes to the epistolary features, they are numerous, not only the opening greeting (1.1) and concluding farewell (21.9). More important is the reference to sending (1.5), the author's emphasis on writing for his addressees (4.9; 6.5; 17.2; 21.9), and the direct "I–you" address (4.6; 17.1). It seems reasonable to argue that this is more than a literary device;[29] the writing may, in fact, have been sent (or intended to be sent). For that reason, *Barnabas* could be labeled as a literary letter or "epistolary treatise."[30]

14.7 STRUCTURE

In 1.5 Barnabas says that he writes to the addressees in order that they may have "perfect knowledge (*gnōsis*)" to accompany their faith, and in 18.1 he states: "let us turn to another area of knowledge and teaching (*gnōsin kai didachen*)." These are the primary markers of sections in the text, which results in the following rough structure:

1:        Greeting and introduction
2–16:   First main section: Knowledge from the Scriptures
17:       Transition
18–20:   Second main section: Knowledge from the Two Ways teaching
21:       Closing

There are also several (more or less) evident thematic changes in the text; they are indicated by the headings in the following overview.

14.8 THE CONTENT OF *BARNABAS*: AN OVERVIEW

14.8.1 Introduction

In chapter 1 the author presents himself as one known to his addressees; he has earlier spoken to them (1.3–4), but since then he has apparently learnt many things and is eager to share something of what he himself has "received" – in order that they may have perfect knowledge (1.5). He does not claim to be a teacher (1.8a), though he indeed is aware of his role as a mediator of vital knowledge. This is related to the fact that God "through the prophets . . . has made known to us what has happened and

---

[29] See Hvalvik, *Struggle*, 66–81 and Carleton Paget, *Epistle of Barnabas*, 42–5.
[30] See Lutz Doring, *Ancient Jewish Letters and the Beginnings of Christian Epistolography*, WUNT 1.298 (Tübingen: Mohr Siebeck, 2012), 213.

what now is; and he has given us the first fruits of the taste of what is yet to be" (1.7a). Here we meet for the first time the author's emphasis on God's revelation through the prophets or through Scripture, i.e., "the Old Testament." We also note a certain focus on what is going on at the time (cf. the reference to "the present circumstances" in 1.8b).

The present situation is apparently also reflected in 2.1, where Barnabas is saying that "the days are evil." Therefore it is necessary to be on guard and to seek out "the righteous requirements of the Lord (*ta dikaiōmata kyriou*)." This term (*ta dikaiōmata* [*kyriou*]) occurs several times in the epistle, notably in the concluding section: "It is good, therefore, to learn all the Lord's righteous requirements that are written here and to walk in them" (21.1), and in connection with the word "commandments" (4.11; 10.2; 16.9). This indicates that for Barnabas the Scriptures primarily contain requirements and commandments, in which one should walk; in fact, they describe the "way of light."

14.8.2 Sacrifices and Fasts That Please God

The following section (2.4–3.6) quotes a series of Old Testament texts to demonstrate that the Jewish observances of sacrifices and fasts are futile. The first quotation (from Isa 1.11–13) is introduced thus: "For he has made it clear to us through all the prophets that he needs neither sacrifices nor whole burnt offerings nor general offerings," and it is followed by the statement that God "has abolished these things, in order that the new law of our Lord Jesus Christ ... might have its offering, one not made by humans." The kind of sacrifice that pleases God is love for truth and a broken heart (cf. 2.8, 10).

In this section, we recognize that the author says that some quotations from Scripture are spoken to "us" (2.4, 10; 3.3) while others are directed to "them" (2.7; 3.1), i.e., Israel/the Jewish people (cf. 5.2).[31] Words of rebuke are spoken to Israel, a people that, according to the author, has gone astray. "We" – the Jesus believers – are not without understanding and should perceive that our Father is speaking to us because "he wants us to seek how we may approach him, rather than go astray as they (*ekeinois*)[32] did" (2.9). To go astray seems to be an

---

[31] "They" are never referred to as "Jews" in *Barnabas* though it is interesting to note that the early Latin translation generally renders "Israel" as *populous Iudaeorum* (e.g., in 4.14; 5.2; 16.5) and twice as *Iudaeis* (6.7; 12.2).

[32] It is noteworthy that this pronoun (*ekeinos*) is introduced in 2.9 without any further explanation. Since one of the functions of this pronoun is to refer to "well-known or notorious personalities" (BDAG s.v.), it seems justified to think that both Barnabas and his addressees were well acquainted with Jews.

imminent risk and will be a reality if the addressees adhere to the Jewish understanding of the law. The correct understanding of Scriptures is thus vital and possible because God has "revealed everything to us in advance, in order that we might not shipwreck ourselves as proselytes to their law" (3.6).

14.8.3 The Present Time and Salvation

The urgent tenor of the text (note the reference to "the evil one" who may cause that "we" are hurled "away from our life" in 2.10b) is followed up in the next section (4.1–14): "We must therefore investigate the present circumstances very carefully and seek out the things that are able to save us" (4.1a; cf. 4.9b). The author warns against lawlessness and fellowship with sinners, stressing that the stumbling block is at hand (referring to an unknown apocalyptic text and Daniel 7). He then asks his addresses to be on guard and "not become like some people by piling up your sins, saying that the covenant is both theirs and ours. For it is ours"[33] (4.6f; trans. Ehrman). This is a key verse in the epistle, indicating a peculiar one-covenant theology, stressing that only the people who believe in Jesus have a covenant, not Israel/the Jews. This is based on the fact that the Israelites turned to idols (the golden calf) and that Moses smashed the tables of the covenant (4.7–8). Barnabas continues to exhort his readers to resist "the black one" and hate the works of "the evil way"; on the contrary, they should become "a perfect temple of God" (4.9b–11). Moreover, seeing how Israel was abandoned "let us be on guard lest we should be found to be, as it is written, 'many called, but few chosen'" (4.14b).[34]

---

[33] This text is based on the Latin translation, followed by, e.g., Ehrman (Loeb) and Wengst (Schriften des Urchristentums). Holmes's edition is based on an emendation proposed by J.N. Rhodes ("Barnabas 4.6b: The Exegetical Implications of a Textual Problem," *VigChr* 58 [2004]: 365–92) arguing against following the Latin text because it goes against basic rules of textual criticism, i.e., to follow the shorter and more difficult text (i.e., the reading of S), on which Rhodes bases his emendation. Despite its merits, Rhodes's conjecture is unconvincing, among other things because one cannot claim that this is the most difficult text; besides the text as quoted above (based on L) makes good sense, especially in light of Barnabas' treatment of the same issue in 13.1. For an apt refutation of Rhodes's proposal, see J. Carleton Paget, "Barnabas and the Outsiders: Jews and Their World in the Epistle of Barnabas," in *Early Christian Communities between Ideal and Reality*, ed. M. Grundeken and J. Verheyden, WUNT 1.342 (Tübingen: Mohr Siebeck, 2015), 177–202, at 182–3, n. 25.

[34] This could be a quotation from Mt. 22.14; for a balanced treatment of the question, see J. Carleton Paget, "The *Epistle of Barnabas* and the Writings that Later Formed the New Testament," in *The Reception of the New Testament in the Apostolic*

14.8.4 The Son of God and His Suffering

In chapters 5–8 the focus is on the Son of God and his suffering, with an emphasis on Scripture as prophecy. Chapter 5 contains several statements about Christ's incarnation and ministry: he was manifested in the flesh "that he might destroy death and demonstrate the reality of the resurrection of the dead" (5.6), and he came to prepare "the new people for himself" (5.7). He preached and performed miracles to Israel – because he loved them, and when he chose his apostles, he demonstrated that "he did not come to call the righteous, but sinners" (5.8–9). To these positive statements reflecting the gospel tradition, Barnabas adds that the Son of God came in the flesh "that he might complete the full measure of the sins of those who persecuted his prophets to death" (5.11). Here, too, there may be some links to the synoptic tradition (cf. Lk. 11.47–51), but Barnabas argues on the basis of prophetic words (e.g., Zech. 13.7) showing that Christ's wounds came from "them," the Jews (5.12–14). In 6.1–7 there are further Old Testament testimonies stressing the responsibility of the Jews for Christ's suffering.

Barnabas 6.8–19 is a relatively independent and original midrash-like exposition of Exod. 33.1, 3 about entering the good land, "flowing with milk and honey," which is interpreted as setting one's hope upon Jesus (6.9). The land is identified with the flesh of Jesus (Jesus becoming man) based on the connection between the Hebrew words *'adam* (man) and *'adamah* (earth/land). Milk and honey is nourishment for new-born children; consequently one can only enter into the promised land (= Christ) through a new birth – which is the result of the new creation by the forgiveness of sins (6.11, 14), clearly referring to baptism. Interesting also is the interpretation (related to Ezek. 36.26) about stony hearts replaced by hearts of flesh: this refers to Christ who became flesh and dwells in us (as a temple) (6.14–15). Based on this argumentation the sayings about the creation of man (Gen. 1.26, 28 – quoted in 6.11, 13c) are said to be referring to believers in Jesus who will be rulers of the earth – and heirs of the covenant (6.12a, 18, 19b).

The author starts chapter 7 by (again) emphasizing that God has "revealed everything to us beforehand," saying that the Son of God suffered to give "us" life and showing that he must suffer at "their

Fathers, ed. A. Gregory and C. Tuckett (Oxford: Oxford University Press, 2005), 229–49, at 232–3.

hands" (7.1–2, 5). In the following section (7.6–8.7) Barnabas concentrates on the interpretation of Scripture by focusing on types of Christ.
Already in 7.3 Isaac, who was offered upon the altar, is mentioned as a
type (typos) of Christ; in 7.6–11 the two goats on the Day of Atonement
(Lev. 16) are – in different ways – presented as types of Jesus (7.7, 10c).
The text contains some noteworthy extra-biblical details, e.g., that the
two goats should be "alike, fine, and equal" (Barn. 7.6 and 10) – a
regulation only found in Mishna (m.Yoma 6.1); similarly the "piece of
scarlet wool" around the head of the scapegoat (Barn. 7.8) is probably
based on Mishna (m.Yoma 4.2).

In chapter 8 the author explains the ritual of the Red Heifer
(Num. 19 – with extra-biblical Jewish traditions): the heifer/calf is
Jesus, the sinful men who offer it are those who brought him to the
slaughter, and so forth (8.2). In Barnabas' version of the ritual, three
children shall sprinkle the people one by one; they represent the
apostles (8.5). The meaning of these things is clear to "us" but
quite obscure to "them," "because they did not listen to the voice of
the Lord" (8.7). In other words: to the Christians, the real meaning of the
Scriptures is evident, to the Jews it is not.

14.8.5 The Right Understanding of Scripture: Circumcision and Food

In the next section (9.1–10.12), the right understanding of Scripture is
also in focus. It starts with a discussion of circumcision, though in a
spiritual way – of the heart and ears. With reference to various texts
(e.g., Jer. 4.4), Barnabas reveals that the Lord "circumcised our ears in
order that when we hear the word, we might believe" (9.4). Thus he
presents an alternative understanding of circumcision, evident in 9.4. In
this verse the author is claiming (1) that "the circumcision in which
they [the Jews] have trusted has been abolished," (2) that God has
"declared that circumcision was not a matter of the flesh" (but rather
of the heart/ear), (3) that "they" (the Jews) "disobeyed" (by practising
circumcision of the flesh), and (4) that they did so because an evil angel
deluded them.

As part of his argumentation, Barnabas refers to Abraham "who first
instituted circumcision" (9.7), and notes that he circumcised his
318 men (cf. Gen. 14.14; 17.23). What does this mean? According to
Barnabas it is a foreshadowing of Jesus and the cross – based on the
numerical value of the letters in the Greek alphabet: 318 = TIH, where
T (300) represents the cross and IE (ten and eight) represents Jesus

(IE being the first two letters in his name, a common abbreviation for IESOUS).[35]

Chapter 10 deals with the interpretation of Mosaic dietary laws. Already from the beginning, Barnabas argues that "it is not God's commandment that they should not eat; rather Moses spoke spiritually" (10.2b; cf. 10.9). This means that the laws are not related to food but to moral behavior. The Jews do not understand this, but "we, however, having rightly understood the commandments" since God has "circumcised our ears and hearts" (10.12).

14.8.6 The Water and the Cross Foreshadowed

The next section (11.1–12.11) is about how the Lord has foreshadowed the water and the cross. The first topic is water (baptism), possibly because of a potential connection between circumcision and baptism (cf. Col. 2.11–12). Again the contrast between the two peoples is evident: "Now concerning the water, it is written with reference to Israel that they would never accept the baptism that brings forgiveness of sins, but would create a substitute for themselves" – referring to Jer. 2.12–13 as a proof-text. Then further texts are quoted, probably taken from a collection of testimonies related to baptism, and a statement about "us" descending into the water of baptism (11.11).

In chapter 12 the author deals with types (*typoi*) of Jesus and the cross (12.2, 5, 6, 10). The underlying point seems to be that the Scriptures can only be understood when they are interpreted Christologically: "all things are in him and for him" (12:7c). The most important types are Moses stretching out his hands in the war with Amalek (Exod. 17.8–16) and the bronze serpent (Num. 21.4–8), both symbols of the cross.

14.8.7 Heirs and Covenant

In the following section (13.1–14.9) Barnabas discusses "whether this people or the former people is the heir, and whether the covenant is for us or for them" (13.1; cf. 4.6–8). First, he cites from Gen. 25.21–23 concerning Rebecca's two sons, representing two peoples; its meaning seems to be taken for granted ("You ought to understand" – 13.3). Obviously "this people" (the Christians) are represented by Jacob, the younger one who should be the greater of the two sons.

---

[35] On this text, see R. Hvalvik, "Barnabas 9:7–9 and the Author's Supposed Use of Gematria," *NTS* 33 (1987): 276–82.

The next argument is based on the story about Joseph's two sons, Ephraim and Manasseh (13.4–6). Barnabas gives a tendentious rendering of the story from Gen. 48, with the result that only the younger son, Ephraim, is blessed by Jacob. The interpretation seems to be taken more or less for granted: Ephraim represents "this people," which should "be first and heir of the covenant" (13.6). As the last argument, Barnabas quotes Gen. 17.5 about Abraham being "the father of the nations who believe in God without being circumcised" (13.7). Once more the author seems to think that the meaning is clear: the heirs are the uncircumcised Gentiles – not the Jews. It is important to note that Barnabas at this point claims that "our knowledge is now perfect" (trans. Ehrman; cf. Barnabas' expressed purpose in 1.5).

In 13.1 two related topics were announced: inheritance and covenant. In 14.1 Barnabas directs attention to the latter topic: "let us see if he has actually given the covenant that he swore to the fathers he would give to the people" [= the Jews]. His answer is yes and no: "He has indeed given it; but they were not worthy to receive it because of their sins." As proof for this, he provides a paraphrase of texts from Exodus and Deuteronomy concerning the giving of the Law at Sinai. Barnabas' point is simple: Moses received the tablets from the Lord, but the tablets were soon broken – owing to the idolatry of the people. In other words: the covenant was given, but never received by the people. Nothing is said about the new tablets that were given later on.

Barnabas never asks *if* the Christians received the covenant; he immediately turns to the question "how did we receive it?" The answer is clear: the Lord himself gave it to "us" – "by suffering for us" (14.4b–c). The proof-text is Isa. 42.6–7, understood as a text about the Father commanding Christ: "I have given you as a covenant to the people, a light to the nations" (14.7).

14.8.8 The Sabbath

Chapter 15 introduces a new topic, the Sabbath – though it may be linked to the previous chapter by the word "Sinai" (15.1; cf. 14.2). Barnabas starts with a free rendering of the commandment given at Sinai but is eager to give the word "Sabbath" a new definition. On the basis of Gen. 2.2–3, he interprets the phrase "he finished in six days" in light of Ps. 89.4 and concludes: "Therefore, children, in six days – that is, in six thousand years – everything will be brought to an end" (15.4). This shows that Barnabas thinks within the frame of a world week made up of six millennia followed by an eschatological Sabbath. In line with this definition, Barnabas claims that "the presents Sabbaths" are not acceptable to God (15.8). This means that the Jewish observance of the Sabbath is based on a total misunderstanding of God's commandment.

14.8.9 The Temple

The author's polemical tone continues in chapter 16: "Finally, I will also speak to you about the temple, and how those wretched people went astray and set their hope on the building, as though it were God's house" (16.1). The topic is most likely treated because of the centrality of the temple – even after its destruction, but also owing to events in Barnabas' own time (cf. 16.4; see Section 14.4 above on date). With reference to Isa. 40.12 and 66.1, Barnabas claims that God has abolished the temple (16.2). While the Jewish temple was not God's house, he nevertheless argues that "a temple of God" exists. Since "we" are a new creation owing to the forgiveness of sins, God dwells in us (16.8); this is thus a spiritual temple (16.10b).

14.8.10 The Two Ways

Chapter 17 marks the end of the main part of the epistle, but the beginning of chapter 18 makes clear that the author has something more to say; he is moving to another knowledge (*gnōsis*) and teaching, the teaching of "the two ways" (18.1–20.2). Here the author (like the author of *Didache*) seems to be dependent on an earlier, probably Jewish source. Even though the teaching is introduced as something new, the two-ways imagery, with its contrast between light/righteousness and darkness/death, is well prepared in the preceding chapters (see 1.4; 4.10; 5.4; 10.10; 11.6; 12.4; 14.5–6). While Barnabas and his readers represent the "way of righteousness" (1.4; cf. 5.4), the Jews are a people in opposition to God's righteous way (12.4). For that reason the "way of darkness" becomes something more than a description of paganism; in *Barnabas* it also becomes a description of Judaism.

14.8.11 Conclusion

Throughout the letter, Barnabas has shown what God requires and what he rejects. In the conclusion it is thus appropriate to urge his addressees to walk in, i.e., to live according to, "the Lord's righteous requirements" (21.1). This is urgent since "the Lord, and his reward is near" (21.3). Barnabas continues to exhort his readers to fulfill every commandment and writes that he has been eager to write as well as he could in order to cheer them up (21.8–9).

14.9 OCCASION AND PURPOSE

Why was *Barnabas* written? This question is very much dependent on how one understands the references to the Jews (labeled "they," "Israel," "the former people" etc.). The author's focus on and the polemic against Jews and Jewish law observance is an undeniable fact, but what kind of historical realities (if any) does it reflect? Some scholars claim that Barnabas' interest in Jews and Judaism is completely academic or theoretic,[36] not rooted in social realities. This point of view was also prevalent a century ago, at a time when ancient Judaism was referred to as "late Judaism" (German: *Spätjudentum*), imagined almost like a dying religion. Likewise "the parting of the ways" was understood as an indisputable reality already before the close of the first century. More recent research has made it clear that Judaism continued as a vigorous force after 70 CE, and that contact between Jews and Christians continued for a very long time ("the ways that never parted"). Against this background, it seems more likely that Barnabas related to a social reality. This also works better with the text itself; it is not characterized by a distant academic attitude but – at least in some parts – by a most serious concern. This is particularly true for the sayings found in 2.9 (about God who "wants us to seek how we may approach him, rather than *go astray as they did*") and 3.6 ("in order that we might not *shipwreck ourselves* as proselytes to their law").

According to some scholars there was a specific event or situation that led to the writing of *Barnabas*, e.g., the concerns that an imminent rebuilding of the temple in Jerusalem might lead to a Jewish resurgence.[37] Since there is no clear evidence for such a rebuilding, it may be better to imagine a kind of ongoing rivalry between Jews and Christians, and that some Christians were being tempted to consider Judaism as a more valid religion and that Jews really were people of the covenant.[38] Such a scenario requires some contact or nearness between the Jewish and Christian communities, and the author's treatment, e.g., of fasting is an indication that this was, in fact, the case: Without being an essential issue in the Mosaic Law, fasting became increasingly so in

---

[36] So, e.g., Wengst, *Tradition*, 102.
[37] E.g., Martin B. Shukster and Peter Richardson, "Temple and *Bet Ha-midrash* in the Epistle of Barnabas," in *Anti-Judaism in Early Christianity, Vol. 2: Separation and Polemic*, ed. Stephen G. Wilson (Waterloo: Wilfrid Laurier University Press, 1986), 17–31 and Carleton Paget, *Epistle of Barnabas*, 66–8.
[38] Hvalvik, *Struggle*.

post-70 Judaism. In other words, Barnabas seems to know Judaism in his own time, not only as a theoretical construction from the Scriptures.

Recently James Rhodes[39] has offered an alternative reading of *Barnabas*, downplaying the Jewish polemic and stressing the strong ethical tenor of the text. In his view, the author's purpose is primarily to exhort his audience to covenant fidelity and eschatological perseverance. Barnabas' primary concern with Israel lies in the fact that their past failings may serve as an example to warn Christians against a sense of complacency.

Rhodes has rightly drawn attention to Barnabas' ethical emphasis (cf. 4.11–12), but it is not adequate to say that the polemic against Jews generally is used as a moral lesson for his addressees. Barnabas is definitely concerned with God's commandments, and he speaks well of Moses as a lawgiver (10.11), but Barnabas' ethical teaching is also integrated with his polemic against the Jews' understanding of Scripture: "But how could those people grasp or understand these things? But we, however, having rightly understood the commandments, explain them as the Lord intended" (10.12).

Further, Rhodes argues that the golden calf incident is a rhetorical hyperbole and a paradigmatic event exposing Israel's disobedience rather than the termination of the covenant. Thus the incident functions as a warning for Christians. This is, however, not what the text actually says. In chapter 14 (which repeats and complements chapter 4), it is said that the Israelites did not receive the covenant because of their sins (14.1); this could obviously be used as a warning, but this is not the case. Instead, Barnabas simply affirms that the Christians have received the covenant – without any reservations.[40]

14.10 MAJOR TRENDS IN RECENT RESEARCH

Until Hans Windisch's commentary in 1920[41] *Barnabas* was commonly treated as an epistle written by an author with a distinct theology and for a distinct purpose. Windisch, however, argued that the author – or rather: the editor – made use of different sources with different theologies and that the result was a poorly connected patchwork. This

---

[39] Rhodes, *The Epistle of Barnabas*.

[40] For a forceful refutation of Rhodes's thesis, see Carleton Paget, "Barnabas and the Outsiders," 189–92.

[41] Hans Windisch, *Der Barnabasbrief*, Handbuch zum Neuen Testament, Ergänzungsband: Die Apostolischen Väter III (Tübingen: Mohr Siebeck, 1920).

approach was followed by the major studies by Pierre Prigent and Robert Kraft in the 1960s: the focus was to a large extent on the sources.[42] According to Kraft, an author like Barnabas did not digest his sources, "he has not integrated them by means of a perspective which may be called, in a special way, his own. Rather, his tradition speaks through him."[43]

A similar point of view is found in Klaus Wengst's book from 1971: by distinguishing between tradition and the author's own contribution Wengst searched for the theology of *Barnabas*.[44] He concluded that *Barnabas* was a product of school tradition, but, in contrast to earlier research, he stressed the unity of the letter: there was no discrepancy between the traditions and the editorial comments.

In dialogue with – and in opposition to – the earlier source-critical research James Carleton Paget (1994) argued that Barnabas compiled and reworked earlier traditions to serve his own purposes.[45] He further argued that the most striking features of the epistle are its anti-Judaism and its approach to Scripture. The anti-Jewish tenor of the writing reflects that Judaism was an influential factor in the author's environment, and Carleton Paget suggests that such a situation may have existed in Alexandria before the Trajanic revolt. Barnabas argues against people within his own community whom he feared might be attracted to the Jewish way of life.

Without arguing for a specific historical situation, Hvalvik (1996) similarly focused on Barnabas' anti-Jewish element and the interpretation of Scripture; the former reflects a situation where Judaism was felt as an attractive competitor and thus a threat to the Christian community.[46] This way of understanding the anti-Jewish element in *Barnabas* has more recently been challenged by Rhodes (see above on occasion and purpose).

---

[42] Pierre Prigent, *Les Testimonia dans le christianisme primitif: L'Epître de Barnabé 1–16 et ses sources* (Paris: Gabalda, 1961) and Robert A. Kraft, "The Epistle of Barnabas, its Quotations and their Sources" (PhD dissertation, Harvard University, 1961).

[43] Robert A. Kraft, *Barnabas and the Didache*, The Apostolic Fathers: A New Translation and Commentary 3 (New York: Thomas Nelson & Sons, 1965), 2.

[44] Wengst, *Tradition*.

[45] Carleton Paget, *Epistle of Barnabas*. To a certain extent, this was also the view of Francesco Scorza Barcellona, *Epistola di Barnaba*, Corona Patrum I (Torino: Società Editrice Internazionale, 1975), 13.

[46] Hvalvik, *Struggle*.

During the last century research on *Barnabas* has changed radically, from focusing on sources to a focus on the epistle itself. Moreover, from being a literary foil, the "Jews" in the text have been perceived as reflecting real people and social realities. This does not mean that *Barnabas* is written against Jews (*adversus Judaeos*), but their presence in the addressees' neighborhood gave rise to questions that the author tried to answer.

14.11 THE *EPISTLE OF BARNABAS* IN THE HISTORY OF EARLY CHRISTIANITY

It is not easy to define *Barnabas* within the history of early Christianity – simply because the author in many ways is a loner: "This document is a special case. ... It is not representative of early Christianity."[47] Indeed, the epistle shares several traditions with New Testament writings (in particular the Synoptic gospels and Paul's letters), but it is not possible to detect an undeniable dependence on any of them.[48] Nevertheless, Barnabas struggled with the same burning issues as did other early Christian writers, particularly the role of the Mosaic Law.

Paul tried to settle the case in salvation-historical terms: the Law was added because of transgressions (Gal. 3.19). For the author of Hebrews, the key is the idea of an old and a new covenant (Heb. 8.6–13; cf. 2 Cor. 3.6, 14). Marcion "solved" the problem by claiming that the Old Testament was valid for Jews, but not for Christians, since it was the product of an inferior god, creator of the world and giver of the Law. Unlike these authors, *Barnabas* takes an unhistorical approach, claiming that there is one covenant only – given to the Christians alone. In reality *Barnabas* divides the Mosaic Law into two parts, arguing that all ritual/cultic regulations should be interpreted allegorically, referring merely to moral questions. Thus the Law is reduced to moral

---

[47] Hans Conzelmann, *Gentiles, Jews, Christians: Polemics and Apologetics in the Greco-Roman Era*, trans. M. Eugene Boring (Minneapolis, MN: Fortress, 1992), 261; cf. Philipp Vielhauer, *Geschichte der urchristlichen Literatur: Einleitung in das Neue Testament, die Apokryphen und die Apostolischen Väter* (Berlin: De Gruyter, 1975), 612: "Der Barn[abasbrief] ist wohl das seltsamste Dokument der urchristlichen Literatur, ein zeit- und theologiegeschichtlich schwer einzuordnender Einzelgänger."

[48] See Carleton Paget's essay referred to in note 34; note also Harnack, *Chronologie*, 415–18.

commandments – but, according to Barnabas, that is what the Lord intended (10.12).

Even if Barnabas' logic is clear enough, his terminology sometimes reveals reliance on a traditional salvation-historical model, e.g., the terms "abolish" (2.6; 9.4), "new law" (2.6), "new people" (5.7; 7.5) and "former/first people" (13.1). Such tensions disclose the difficulties by *Barnabas'* unhistorical model. Not surprisingly it was not pursued by later authors.

More generally there is nothing to suggest that Barnabas actually influenced any early Christian writer. Admittedly he was quoted by some Alexandrian authors, but it should be noted that none of the references applies to critical topics in *Barnabas*. Typically, "none of its occasionally massive anti-Jewish statements were cited in the early church."[49]

The inclusion of the epistle in *Codex Sinaiticus* certainly indicates that it was highly regarded in some circles, but probably not on account of its peculiar theological position. It is more likely that *Barnabas* was used and referred to because of its assumed connection to a person from the apostolic age and because it contains a lot of proto-orthodox sayings, particularly concerning Christ and his salvific work. For instance, Barnabas is alone among the Apostolic Fathers in interpreting Christ's passion in expressly sacrificial terms, stating that he offered his body "as a sacrifice for our sins" (7.3).[50] He also emphasizes that Christ died "so that we might be cleansed by the forgiveness of sins, that is, by his sprinkled blood" (5.1) and that baptism brings forgiveness of sins (11.1, 11; cf. 6.11; 16.8). Barnabas is very much aware of the problem of human sinfulness: sin is not merely a problem for Israel (cf. 5.11; 12.2; 14.1, 5) but also for the "new people" (7.5; cf. 4.13; 19.10, 12). Interestingly, only Barnabas among the Apostolic Fathers connects the fall with Genesis 3 (12.5) – which later became the orthodox position.

In general Christology has a central place in the epistle, and the author prefers to refer to Jesus as the "Son of God" (5.9, 11; 7.2, 9; 12.9, 10; cf. 6.12; 12.8; 15.5) and "Lord" (2.6; 5.1, 5; 7.2; 12.10–11; 14.5); only twice as "Christ"/"Messiah" (2.6; 12.10). He argues against calling Jesus "son of man" and "son of David," stressing his position as "son of God"

---

[49] Ferdinand R. Prostmeier, "The Epistle of Barnabas," in *The Apostolic Fathers: An Introduction*, ed. Wilhelm Pratscher (Waco, TX: Baylor University Press, 2010), 27–45, at 39.

[50] J.N.D. Kelly, *Early Christian Doctrines*, 4th ed. (London: A&C Clark, 1968), 165; for the following, see ibid., 163, 194.

and "Lord" (12:10–11). He presupposes his presence in creation (6.12), refers to his resurrection and ascension (on the same day; 15.9) and states that he is destined to judge the living and the dead (7.2; cf. 5.7) – thus conveying common theological positions.

FURTHER READING

Carleton Paget, James. *The Epistle of Barnabas: Outlook and Background.* WUNT 2.64. Tübingen: Mohr Siebeck, 1994.
  "Barnabas and the Outsiders: Jews and Their World in the Epistle of Barnabas," in *Early Christian Communities between Ideal and Reality*, ed. M. Grundeken and J. Verheyden. WUNT 1.342. Tübingen: Mohr Siebeck, 2015, 177–202.
Ehrman, Bart. *The Apostolic Fathers.* LCL 2 vols. Cambridge, MA: Harvard University Press, 2003.
Holmes, Michael W. *The Apostolic Fathers: Greek Texts and English Translations*, 3rd ed. Grand Rapids, MI: Baker Academic, 2007.
Hvalvik, Reidar. *The Struggle for Scripture and Covenant: The Purpose of the Epistle of Barnabas and Jewish–Christian Competition in the Second Century.* WUNT 2.82. Tübingen: Mohr Siebeck, 1996.
Prigent, Pierre, and Robert A. Kraft. *Épître de Barnabé.* SC 172. Paris: Les Éditions du Cerf, 1971.
Prostmeier, Ferdinand R. *Der Barnabasbrief.* Kommentar zu den Apostolischen Vätern 8. Göttingen: Vandenhoeck & Ruprecht, 1999.
Rhodes, James N. *The Epistle of Barnabas and the Deuteronomic Tradition: Polemics, Paraenesis, and the Legacy of the Golden-Calf Incident.* WUNT 2.188. Tübingen: Mohr Siebeck, 2004.

15 The *Shepherd of Hermas* as Early Christian Apocalypse

DAN BATOVICI

15.1 INTRODUCTION

The *Shepherd of Hermas*[1] packs a striking number of conundrums, textual, compositional, theological, and reception historical. To begin with, despite the fact that there are more papyri of this book than any of the other Apostolic Fathers, as well as than most New Testament books taken separately, we still do not have the complete text in Greek. As a result, in current critical editions the last chapters are supplied from the Latin (and Ethiopic) translations. It is also the longest AF book, replete of allegorical material, occasionally inconsistent and largely repetitive, which leads modern readers every now and again to describe it as naive, dilettante, and incompetent, or plainly boring.[2] Moreover, the manner in which the book is written in large narrative sections with seemingly poor connection from one to another has occasioned several theories of multiple authorship.

The theology and even the literary genre of the *Shepherd of Hermas* proved complicated to pin down. The book presents Hermas going through a number of visions and subsequently receiving lengthy eluci-dations of these visions from the Shepherd – the angel of penitence – as heavenly mediator, suggesting thus that we are dealing with an apoca-lyptic work. Yet there are so many differences between the *Shepherd* and other early Christian and Jewish apocalypses that scholars have to explain what type of apocalypse this is in order to make it fit current definitions of the genre. From a theological point of view, a striking

---

[1] In the following, "the *Shepherd*" and "the *Shepherd of Hermas*" designate the book, and "Hermas" and "the Shepherd" the two main characters of the book.
[2] Examples are gathered in Edith McEwan Humphrey, *The Ladies and the Cities: Transformation and Apocalyptic in Joseph and Aseneth, 4 Ezra, the Apocalypse and The Shepherd of Hermas*, JSPSS 17 (Sheffield: Sheffield Academic Press, 1995), 119, and B. Diane Lipsett, *Desiring Conversion: Hermas, Thecla, Aseneth* (New York: Oxford University Press, 2011), 19.

peculiarity of the *Shepherd* is that neither Jesus nor Christ are ever mentioned in the book, yet its intricate "highest-angel" Christology has also caused puzzlement and led to even more complex scholarly solutions.

Yet for all its "faults" the book has enjoyed a remarkable reception. Important early patristic authors considered it scriptural in some ways (Irenaeus of Lyons), or an inspired writing (Clement of Alexandria and Origen), and used it freely along with biblical texts in their arguments (Didymus of Alexandria). Canonical lists of Late Antiquity include the *Shepherd* as a secondary (Eusebius of Caesarea) yet nevertheless recommended book (the Muratorian Fragment, Athanasius of Alexandria). Codex Sinaiticus of the fourth century includes it as well, together with the *Epistle of Barnabas*, after the Greek Old and New Testament. Its extant papyri show that the book was copied all throughout early and late antique Christianity, virtually up until this writing medium fell out of use. Last but not least, there are – complete, partial, or misattributed – translations in several languages of Antiquity. In modern times, these problems (and several other) and highlights have attracted a lot of scholarly attention and continue to do so.

15.2 PLOT, COMPOSITION, SOURCES, GENRE

15.2.1 Plot

The *Shepherd* is divided in its manuscripts into three main parts: five *Visions*, twelve *Mandates*, and ten *Similitudes*.[3] *Vision* 1 introduces Hermas: he sees the skies opening and a woman from his past who makes him aware of his impure thoughts. A second woman, personifying the Church, then provides some explanation to a confused Hermas.

---

[3] The main commentaries on the *Shepherd* are M. Dibelius, *Der Hirt des Hermas*, Die Apostolischen Väter. IV/HNT (Tübingen: Mohr Siebeck, 1923); G.F. Snyder, *The Shepherd of Hermas*, The Apostolic Fathers: A New Translation and Commentary 6 (Camden, NJ: T. Nelson, 1968); N. Brox, *Der Hirt des Hermas*, KAV 7 (Göttingen: Vandenhoeck und Ruprecht, 1991); C. Osiek, *The Shepherd of Hermas: A Commentary*, Hermeneia (Minneapolis, MN: Fortress Press, 1999). Critical editions, with annotated translations and extensive introductions, are available in R. Joly, *Hermas. Le Pasteur*, SC 53 (Paris: Cerf, 1958, ²1968); J.J. Ayán Calvo, *Hermas. El Pastor*, Fuentes Patrísticas 6 (Madrid: Editorial Ciudad Nueva, 1995); U.H.J. Körtner and M. Leutzsch, *Papiasfragmente. Hirt des Hermas* (Darmstadt: Wissensch. Buchgesell. 1998). The latter remains unsurpassed for textual purposes. More recent editions, with simplified apparatus and English translations, include B.D. Ehrman, *The Apostolic Fathers*, LCL 25, vol. 2 (Cambridge, MA: Harvard University Press, 2003) and M.W. Holmes, *The Apostolic Fathers: Greek Texts and English Translations*, 3rd ed. (Grand Rapids, MI: Baker Academic, 2007).

In *Vision* 2, Hermas sees again the woman personifying the Church, who offers him a book to copy for the benefit of his and other communities; later on, a young man will explain to him that the woman – whom he thought to be the Sibyl! – is in fact the Church.

Vision 3 is by far the longest: the woman Church shows to Hermas the construction of the eschatological church in the shape of a tower. A detailed description of the construction follows, and the *Vision* is completed by extensive explanations on the scope of the building and the significance of the different stones used in, or excluded from, the ongoing construction. In *Vision* 4 Hermas encounters the beast, explained as an allegory of an indeterminate future threat. Surviving the beast, Hermas sees again the personified Church, who explains to him what he just saw and how to stay safe.

Vision 5 introduces the Shepherd, the angel of penitence, who presents himself as having been sent to stay with Hermas for the rest of his days and, with the purpose of dictating the *Mandates* and *Similitudes* for Hermas to write down. He also takes over, from the Church impersonation of the previous Visions, the role of heavenly mediator for the rest of the book.

The twelve *Mandates* follow, containing a wide array of ethical and largely spiritual concerns, developed from one another, ranging from faith and fear of God to self-restraint and lists of vices and virtues. The ten *Similitudes* then develop in an allegorical manner several topics, some manifesting social concerns regarding the less fortunate, the poor, and the widows. *Similitude* 9 stands apart in that it picks up and extensively builds upon the material in *Vision* 3, that of the eschatological tower.[4] *Similitude* 10 concludes the book with an exhortation for following closely the teachings of the book, and with the promise of future revelations.

15.2.2 Composition

The three main parts of the *Shepherd of Hermas* differ from one another in literary outlook and content to the extent that there are scholars who contest not only Hermas' ability to write, but altogether the notion that the book has only one author.

For instance, the fact that the Church impersonation is replaced by the Shepherd as heavenly mediator in *Vision* 5, that Hermas is never

---

[4] Carolyn Osiek, "The Genre and Function of the *Shepherd of Hermas*," in *Early Christian Apocalypticism: Genre and Social Setting*, ed. Adela Yarbro Collins, Semeia 36 (Decatur, GA: Society of Biblical Literature, 1986), 114: "the literary devices of revelatory agent and symbolic visions are sustained throughout."

explicitly named after *Vision 4*,[5] and that *Vision* 5 reads less like a vision (compared to the preceding ones) and more like an introduction to the rest of the book, suggests that an important caesura takes place between the two *Visions*. Based on these and many other similar clues that point to a lack of unity, Stanislas Giet, for instance, famously proposed in 1963 that we should distinguish three authors behind the book we read today, corresponding to three successive layers of composition: (a) the first four *Visions*, then (b) *Similitude* 9 drawing on the previous *Visions*, followed by (c) the rest of the book, from *Vision* 5 to the *Similitude* 8, with the *Similitude* 10 as conclusion.[6]

Much like other similar theories, one of which argues for as many as six authors,[7] Giet's proposal did not gain support and seems to have been conclusively refuted.[8] The debate seems to have subsided for now, and the current scholarly consensus leans toward the notion that the *Shepherd* is the labor of one author, who worked in successive stages of redaction.[9] Most of the recent scholarship on this book takes as point of departure the text as reconstructed in critical editions.

---

[5] As a result, the Georgian translation, which does not contain the first four Visions, misattributes the work to "Saint Ephrem."

[6] Stanislas Giet, *Hermas et les Pasteurs: Les trois auteurs du Pasteur d'Hermas* (Paris: Presses Universitaires de France, 1963).

[7] Particularly W. Coleborne, in "A Linguistic Approach to the Problem of Structure and Composition of the Shepherd of Hermas," *Colloquium* 3 (1969), 133–42, and Coleborne, "The Shepherd of Hermas: A Case for Multiple Authorship and Some Implications," in *Studia Patristica X*, ed. Frank Leslie Cross, TU 107 (Berlin: Akademie-Verlag, 1970), 65–70. Other stances are surveyed by Osiek, *The Shepherd of Hermas*, 9.

[8] Robert Joly argued for one author in "Hermas et le Pasteur," *Vigiliae Christianae* 21 (1967), 201–18, and Joly, "Le milieu complexe du Pasteur d'Hermas," in *ANRW* 2.27.1 (Berlin: De Gruyter, 1993), 524–51. Also Philippe Henne, *L'unité du Pasteur d'Hermas: Tradition et rédaction* (Paris: J. Gabalda, 1992), and Henne, "La pénitence et la rédaction du 'Pasteur' d'Hermas," *Revue Biblique* 98 (1991): 358–97.

[9] E.g., David Hellholm, *Das Visionenbuch des Hermas als Apokalypse: formgeschichtliche und texttheoretishce Studien zu einer literarischen Gattung*, Coiectanea Biblica, New Testament series 13 (Lund: Gleerup, 1980), 12; Brox, *Der Hirt des Hermas*, 32–3; Humphrey, *The Ladies and the Cities*, 126–9; Osiek, *The Shepherd*, 13–15; Bogdan G. Bucur, *Angelomorphic Pneumatology: Clement of Alexandria and Other Early Christian Witnesses*, SVC 95 (Leiden/Boston, MA: Brill, 2009), 114–15 n. 7; Lipsett, *Desiring Conversion*, 23; Grundeken, *Community Building*, 11–16. See, e.g., the manner in which the strategies employed in the successive layers of writing are described in Jörg Rüpke, "Der Hirte des Hermas: Autorenprofil und Textstrategien eines Visionärs des zweiten Jahrhunderts n. Chr.," in *Autoren in religiösen literarischen Texten der späthellenistischen und der frühkaiserzeitlichen Welt*, ed. Eve-Marie Becker und Jörg Rüpke, CRPGRW 2 (Tübingen: Mohr Siebeck, 2018), 181–97.

15.2.3 Sources

Before moving on to the similarly complicated issue of genre, it is important to note in brief that the sources of the *Shepherd* are less obvious than for other texts. The only book it explicitly quotes is the pseudepigraphon *Elad and Modad* in *Vision* 2.3.4 [7]. The very notion that the author of the book would have known the writings that later formed the New Testament was called into question: as Chapter 5 by Paul Foster in this volume exemplifies, in a strict sense it is likely – but not certain – that 1 Corinthians, Ephesians and the Epistle of James are used in the *Shepherd*. A recent contribution has readdressed in a broader approach the relationship between the "Pauline legacy" and the *Shepherd*, arguing that the author of the latter can be construed as a Pauline interpreter who writes his book in dialog with Pauline themes.[10]

15.2.4 Genre

The literary genre of the *Shepherd of Hermas* also presents us with a puzzle. Based on the *Visions* alone, the Shepherd would sit well with the apocalypses, but this is not so clear for the rest of the book: even though the revelatory framework is kept throughout – mainly by the dialogue between Hermas and the angel of penitence as heavenly mediator – the *Mandates* seem to be written in the genre of Jewish–Hellenistic homily, and the *Similitudes* in an allegorical vein. For the apparent lack of eschatological material and of the teachings related to the future, common in other apocalypses, the *Shepherd* is sometimes not taken into account as an apocalypse.[11]

Indeed, in order to make it fit in current definitions of the apocalyptic genre, scholars tend to add further qualifications, for instance describing the book as "apocalyptic procedure in action, but with a clear-cut focus on the present and serving catechetical purposes."[12]

---

[10] Jonathan E. Soyars, *The* Shepherd *of Hermas and the Pauline Legacy*, NovTSup 176 (Leiden/Boston, MA: Brill, 2019).

[11] For instance, on account of its minimal apocalyptic theological content or apocalyptical eschatology, J.C. Wilson concludes: "It is as if the author is trying his best to write an apocalypse but fails"; in J. Christian Wilson, *Five Problems in the Interpretation of the Shepherd of Hermas: Authorship, Genre, Canonicity, Apocalyptic, and the Absence of the Name "Jesus Christ,"* MBPS 34 (Lewiston, ME: Mellen Biblical Press, 1995), 41.

[12] J. Verheyden, "The Shepherd of Hermas," *ExpT* 117 (2006): 398. A survey of literature that tends to use "qualifying adjectives" for the Shepherd being an apocalypse is available in Osiek, *The Shepherd*, 10.

The seminal definition put forward by John J. Collins[13] is also applied to the *Shepherd* in a qualified manner, since the book does not display the spatial component of the transcendent reality of the supernatural world, as none of Hermas' visions is otherworldly.[14] Carolyn Osiek, for instance, employs David Hellholm's amendment to the definition – namely that the apocalypse is "intended for a group in crisis with a purpose of exhortation and/or consolation by means of divine authority"[15] – to argue that the key to the morphological differences between the *Shepherd of Hermas* and other less debatable apocalyptic texts lies with its function, proposing that this book too addresses a crisis of some kind.[16]

In any event, the *Shepherd* is an apocalypse inasmuch as it is taken on its own terms, and a commendable aim is to make sense of its peculiar type of apocalypse rather than listing elements from other apocalypses that this book lacks. The challenge remains to explain the apocalyptically diluted material in the *Mandates* and *Similitudes*, where, at a first glance, only the apocalyptic general frame is preserved.[17] David Hellholm

---

[13] John J. Collins, "Introduction: Towards the Morphology of a Genre," in *Apocalypse: The Morphology of a Genre*, ed. J.J. Collins, Semeia 14 (Atlanta, GA: Society of Biblical Literature, 1979), 1–59, at 9: "'Apocalypse' is a genre of revelatory literature with a narrative framework, in which a revelation is mediated by an otherworldly being to a human recipient, disclosing a transcendent reality which is both temporal, insofar as it envisages eschatological salvation, and spatial insofar as it involves another, supernatural world."

[14] Given the polythetic approach taken in applying this definition, in the same volume Adela Yarbro Collins includes this book in the genre apocalypse, since it does display apocalyptic eschatology and "revelation mediated by otherworldly beings"; A. Yarbro Collins, "The Early Christian Apocalypses," in *Morphology*, 61–121, at 74. So does Humphrey, *The Ladies and the Cities*, 124.

[15] D. Hellholm, "The Problem of Apocalyptic Genre and the Apocalypse of John," in *Early Christian Apocalypticism: Genre and Social Setting*, ed. A. Yarbro Collins, Semeia 36; Decatur, GA: Society of Biblical Literature, 1986), 13–64, at 27.

[16] C. Osiek, "The Genre and Function of the Shepherd of Hermas," in *Early Christian Apocalypticism: Genre and Social Setting*, ed. A. Yarbro Collins, Semeia 36 (Decatur, GA: Society of Biblical Literature, 1986), 113. *Hermas* would be then a case in which "the social reality prompts a response of ethical exhortation within a framework of apocalyptic myth; at the same time, apocalyptic myth gives meaning and shape to a prophetic and paraenetic interpretation of the social reality," on the same page.

[17] In D. Batovici, "Apocalyptic and *Metanoia* in the Shepherd of Hermas," *Apocrypha* 26 (2015): 151–70, for instance, I argued that the Shepherd's teaching about *metanoia* (repentance) contains an interiorized apocalyptic *sui generis* in as much as (a) the various stages of Hermas' (the character) spiritual transformation in dialogue with the otherworldly mediator match the layered definition of *metanoia* offered by the Shepherd in 30.2 and (b) *metanoia* in this book can be conceived of as a dialog of sorts between the Lord and the believer. This, in turn, would show an embedded manner

argues that the entire book is an apocalypse not only because the revelatory dialogue form – between Hermas and the angel of penitence – is kept throughout but, for instance, also because *Similitude* 9 contains a vision proper, concluded in *Similitude* 10.1.1 [111] by the coming of "that angel who had turned me over to the Shepherd," which is the "Son of God" and the "glorious angel" (*endoxos angelos*) of *Similitude* 9.1.1–3 [78]. Furthermore, the book includes an encompassing hierarchy of revelation: the Son of God as the one who gives the commission, the woman Church and the Shepherd as main mediators, various secondary mediators (e.g., the young man of *Vision* 3.10.7 [18] and the twelve virgins of *Similitude* 9.2 [79] and 9.10–11 [87–8]), as well as transmitters (e.g., Grapte and Clement in *Vision* 2.4.3 [8], and Hermas through the whole book) and addressees for what has been revealed: the communities in Rome and beyond (*Vision* 2.4.3 [8] and *Similitude* 10.4.1 [114]).[18]

15.3 THEMES AND THEOLOGICAL PECULIARITIES

In its own peculiar brand of apocalypse, the *Shepherd of Hermas* is a work deeply concerned with the present weaknesses of the community, with catechetical as well as social implications: on the one hand the author addresses baptism, self-control, endurance in view of salvation, and the possibility of post-baptismal repentance, on the other the relationship between the rich and the poor in the community.

15.3.1 Church, Baptism, Repentance

Several individual themes have been proposed by scholars as the main focus of the book. Some scholars have found this to be the Church (as suggested by the extended description of the allegorical tower in *Vision* 3 and *Similitude* 9), others baptism (on the basis of the peculiar teaching on post-baptismal repentance of the book), others yet repentance (as the "tool" through which the shortcomings of the believer can be evaded), or the pervading theme of sin. These are indeed important, intertwined

in which apocalyptic features are present in the Mandates and Similitudes, beyond the general frame provided by the seer–otherworldly mediator dialog. In any event, "Hermas is not merely the messenger of *metanoia*, but the *exemplum*"; Lipsett, *Desiring Conversion*, 20.

[18] D. Hellholm, "Der Hirt des Hermas," in *Die Apostolischen Väter: Eine Einleitung*, ed. W. Pratscher (Göttingen: Vandenhoeck & Ruprecht, 2009), 244–6. The English translation is available in W. Pratscher (ed.), *The Apostolic Fathers: An Introduction* (Waco, TX: Baylor University Press, 2010).

themes that develop upon one another, and there is perhaps little gain in establishing somewhat artificially a hierarchy between them.

The Church is certainly a key focus throughout the *Shepherd*: the woman personifying the Church is the initial heavenly mediator and revelatory agent in the first four *Visions*, and the two most developed revelatory narratives – the allegory of the tower-in-construction in *Vision* 3 and *Similitude* 9 – are of the eschatological Church. Hermas is informed, in *Vision* 2.4.1 [8], that the woman in his first vision (whom he initially mistook for the Sybil) is in fact the Church, who is elderly in appearance because "she was created before all things" and that "for her sake was the world created." The church is polymorphic in the *Shepherd*: first, she is a lady (*kyria*) in *Vision* 1 and her "image ... incorporates aspects of the biblical Wisdom traditions."[19] She is then an elder woman (*presbytera*) in *Vision* 2, explained in *Vision* 3.11.2 [19] as a result of "weakness and doublemindedness" of the believers, whereas later on she gradually rejuvenates, appearing eventually as a young woman (*parthenos*) due to their improvement, in *Vision* 3.13 [21]. In the construction of the eschatological tower, the believers are received, placed, or rejected according to their accomplishments or misgivings. The image of the Church as the eschatological tower in construction reflects therefore a tension or contrast in the *Shepherd* between the contingent and ideal Church, the former being potentially affected in many ways, and the *Shepherd* offers extensive lists with possible sins in *Vision* 3, in *Similitude* 9, and elsewhere.

As long as the eschatological tower is in construction, there is still place for improvement, and in the *Shepherd* the pedagogical tool of choice for that is repentance (*metanoia*), which has long been proposed as the main theme of the book. Much of the scholarship on repentance here focuses on the Shepherd's somewhat ambiguous teaching about the possibility of repeating repentance after baptism. This is indeed peculiar in the sense that it seems to oppose and react to a rigorist context by allowing repentance after baptism, while being at the same time itself rigorist, as it allows for one repentance alone of the baptized sinner.[20] In this sense, even though the author knows the rite of baptism for the newcomer by immersion into water, taken to mean the forgiveness of previous sins (*Mandate* 4.3.1 [31]), his focus is on the consolidation in view of salvation rather than the

---

[19] Verheyden, "The Shepherd of Hermas," 399.
[20] Grundeken, *Community Building*, 133–4.

expansion of the community, and therefore on the conversion of the
insider instead.[21]

Since this teaching indicates an effort in the early church to deal with
instances of serious sin after baptism, the question did arise as to whether
we can see here the beginning of a movement toward a sacrament of
penance, yet this understanding did not win the day: "Although some
scholars, interested in a history of dogma, have read *The Shepherd* looking
for the beginnings of an institutional discipline of penance, *metanoia* here
seems not so much a ritual or ecclesial mandate as a broad change of heart
and social practice to which the protagonist, his household, and all the
saints are called."[22] As such, the 150 occurrences of *metanoia* and its
cognates in the *Shepherd* place the believer in a dialog of sorts with God:
penitence can be construed as a divine gift, which believers are still to
accomplish.[23] "Having" and "doing" *metanoia* are not the same thing in
the *Shepherd of Hermas*, only the latter being within the grasp of the
believer, and that has to happen before the completion of the eschatological tower. There is still hope of *metanoia*, as in *Similitude* 8.7.2 [73],
but it should be fulfilled as soon as possible, 8.8.3 [74].

In *Mandate* 4.2.2 [30], the Shepherd describes what repentance is for
the believer, and equates it with understanding (*synesin*): being in
charge of repentance, it is him who gives understanding (*synesin*) to
those who repent, which in turn makes the sinners understand that they
have done evil before the Lord and, as they recognize this evil, they
repent, cease to do evil, only do good plentifully, and "humble their soul
and torment it, for they have sinned." As such, understanding (*synesin*)
is the benefaction for the act of repentance, which is incidentally also
what Hermas continually asks from the Shepherd, with regard to the
visions he sees and the parables he hears throughout.[24] Therefore,
metanoia in the *Shepherd of Hermas*, even when it is understood to
mean conversion, is geared toward those who are already in, consoli-
dating rather than expanding the community.

15.3.2 The Son of God

The peculiar Christology of the *Shepherd* has long puzzled modern
readers. Neither "Jesus" nor "Christ" are ever mentioned in the book,

---

[21] Ibid., 128–33.
[22] Lipsett, *Desiring Conversion*, 20.
[23] Grundeken, *Community Building*, 138: "It is true that μετάνοια is a God-given
opportunity. ... There is, however, an element of personal responsibility as well."
[24] On this see Batovici, "Apocalyptic and *Metanoia*," 166–8.

nor is the passion nor the resurrection. The *Shepherd* speaks of the Son of God, but not as the Messiah or the fulfillment of Scriptures. He is the foundation of the world in *Similitude* 9.2.1 [79] and of the Church (and through him believers are saved and in his name are they baptized) in *Similitude* 9.12.1–8 [89], and elsewhere. There are in fact only a few traces of the canonical Jesus. In *Similitude* 5.6.2–6 [59] the Shepherd explains that the Son of God cleansed the sins of the people through his hard efforts, and vv. 5 and 6 speak of him dwelling in the flesh (*sarx*) "on this earth," and perhaps *Similitude* 9.12.3 [89] where the Son of God is represented allegorically as "a new door" because "he was revealed in the final days." These instances come closest in this book to imply Jesus' activity.[25]

This situation has led some scholars to wonder at the fact that the *Shepherd* has never been condemned for its odd Christological teaching at any point of its generally positive reception. The author of the book seems to know and speak of God, Son, and Holy Spirit, but the exact relationship between them remains in many ways obscure, and the various interpretations proposed for this tend to be as complicated as the text itself.

In a fairly recent contribution, Bogdan Bucur analyzes the way in which the *pneuma* language is used in the *Shepherd* to describe an angelic being as well as the Son of God, and proposes that in view of the broader tradition of designating angelic beings by the term "spirit," the Son of God is technically a supreme "holy spirit" to which all other "holy spirits" are subordinated. To Bucur, the fact that in this book the believer can be indwelled – interchangeably and without contradiction – by "the angel," "the spirit," or "the Lord" is explained in the context of "the *Shepherd*'s view of the heavenly world: Father, Son and holy spirits/angels."[26] Bucur understands the Holy Spirit in the *Shepherd* by setting it in a larger early Christian context – found also in Clement of Alexandria and Revelation – which reworks the notion of "the seven supreme angels into an angelomorphic representation of the Holy Spirit."[27] As such, the book is shown to share an older tradition that combines an angelormorphic pneumatology with a spirit Christology within a binitarian framework, within which the *Shepherd* is concerned mainly with God and the supreme "holy spirit," the Son of God.

---

[25] Ibid., 40–1.
[26] Bucur, *Angelomorphic Pneumatology*, 127.
[27] Ibid., 128.

This interpretation has the advantage that it accounts for why the *Shepherd* was so popular in early Christianity, explaining the oddities of its Christology by setting it in a broader interpretative context, in the company of Revelation, Justin Martyr, and Clement of Alexandria.

15.4 TITLE, AUTHOR, PROVENANCE, DATE, COMMUNITY

15.4.1 Title

The title as we use it today, "The Shepherd of Hermas" is a modern construct, much like the "Apostolic Fathers" as a collection. In Codex Sinaiticus (fourth century) it is simply *Poimēn*, "(The) Shepherd," which is also implied in the *titulus* found in codex Athous Grigoriou 96 (fourteenth century) – "the beginning with God of the book named the Shepherd," *archē syn theō bibliou legomenēs poimēn*. "The Shepherd" is also for the most part the designation in patristic literature. In the Latin manuscripts of the oldest translation, the *argumentum* includes the title *Liber Pastoris nuntii paenitentiae*, "the book of the Shepherd, the angel of penitence." The Ethiopic stands apart, bearing the title "(the book) of Hermas the prophet," or simply "of Hermas."

15.4.2 Author

The author of the book, however, remains elusive. External evidence is scarce. In his *Commentary on Romans* 10.31, Origen identifies him with the Hermas greeted among others by Paul in Rom. 16.14, but there is little reason to retain this information. Another tradition, preserved in the Muratorian Fragment and in other sources, claims that the book was written in Rome by Hermas while his brother, Pius, was the bishop of Rome. The book itself describes him as a freedman, husband and father, sinner, not very successful in his business, exemplifying both upward and downward social mobility.[28] While Hermas does not seem to claim to be a leader in his community, "he speaks with divinely inspired authority"[29] nonetheless. Since most things we know about him come from the manner in which he describes himself in the

---

[28] Alexander Weiss, "Hermas' 'Biography': Social Upward and Downward Mobility of an Independent Freedman," *Ancient Society* 39 (2009): 185–202.

[29] Verheyden, "The Shepherd of Hermas," 401.

narrative, a productive venue of research is to study the strategies employed in his self-portrayal. For instance, Hermas – the author – has the heavenly mediator tell him, in a book offered for copying in a vision, that his wife should hold her tongue, "in which she does evil" (*Vision* 2.2.3 [6]).[30]

In recent scholarship it was suggested that Hermas was a craftsman or perhaps an entrepreneur involved in viticulture or the wine trade.[31] Interestingly, based on the peculiarities of vocabulary and imagery of *Vision* 3, Jörg Rüpke suggests that Hermas might have been a salt farmer.[32] He also shows how the construction of the author goes hand in hand with not only the legitimacy but also of the plausibility of the received visions as far as the implied audience is concerned, with Hermas' self-description being a key element in his strategy of legitimizing the content of his message, as received through revelation.[33]

15.4.3 Provenance and Date

There is little reason to reject the idea that the *Shepherd* was written in (or otherwise related to) Rome: apart from the note in the Muratorian Fragment, the city and the river Tiber are mentioned in the opening scene, and Via Campana at the beginning of *Vision* 4. The date, however, is a far less clear matter, reflecting problems common to dating early Christian literature. As mentioned, the Muratorian fragment associates it with the episcopate of Pius, which Eusebius (*Eccl. hist.* 4.11) places around 140–154 CE.[34] Although the testimony of the Fragment is problematic in more than one way, this interval is normally taken as the time at which the book was completed.

A certain Clement is mentioned in *Vision* 2.4.3 [8] as the nominated copyist of the revelation entrusted to Hermas, but the identification of

---

[30] For a reading of the shift in gender symbolism – specifically eliminating maternal figures and feminine imagery – in the process of the writing the various successive recensions of the *Shepherd*, see Lora Walsh, "Lost in Revision: Gender Symbolism in *Vision* 3 and *Similitude* 9 of the *Shepherd of Hermas*," HTR 112 (2019): 467–90.

[31] For references, see Osiek, *The Shepherd of Hermas*, 21.

[32] Jörg Rüpke, "Apokalyptische Salzberge: Zum sozialen Ort und zur literarischen Strategie des 'Hirten des Hermas,'" *Archiv für Religionsgeschichte* 1 (1999): 148–60, esp. 155–60.

[33] See, e.g., Jörg Rüpke, "Der Hirte des Hermas: Plausibilisierungs- und Legitimierungsstrategien im Übergang von Antike und Christentum," ZAC 8 (2005): 276–98.

[34] The fact that Origen, in his *Commentary on Romans* 10.31, identifies the author of the book with the Hermas greeted among others by Paul in Rom. 16.14 (latter mentioned also by Eusebius and Jerome) is normally mentioned in discussions on dating, but it is usually discarded.

this character with Clement of Rome, though appealing, is unsecure and should be treated with caution.[35] Overall, scholars tend to consider that the writing of the book took place over a longer period of time, encompassing the first half of the second century.[36] Andrew Gregory, however, draws attention to the fact that "there seems no reason why the *terminus a quo* needs be any later than some time after the Neronian persecution," and consequently argues that "the Shepherd should be dated to the period c. 70 to c. 150."[37] Whatever one takes to be the consensus on this matter, one needs to keep in mind that narrowing down this interval is more of an educated guess than a fact established in any satisfactory way.

15.4.4 Community

Despite social historical approaches having been attempted on the *Shepherd* with very interesting results, there is still very little we know of the community of Hermas, as much of this information is filtered through the rhetorical strategy of the book.[38] With regard to early church offices, all expected terms are mentioned – *diakonia, presbyteroi, episkopoi* – but their function remains fuzzy to the point that it is doubtful that the *Shepherd* can be used as evidence for either the presence of the office of deacons in second-century Rome[39] or the lack of mono-episcopal communities,[40] as is sometimes suggested. Presbyters, however, are present and they are presiding: in *Vision* 2.4.2–3 [8], Hermas is to read the revealed book in his town, "together with the presbyters who lead the church." In the context of an argument

---

[35] See, e.g., Joly, *Hermas: Le pasteur*, 14 and 97–8; Snyder, *The Shepherd of Hermas*, 39; Brox, *Der Hirt des Hermas*, 136–7; Osiek, *The Shepherd of Hermas*, 59; Ehrman, *Apostolic Fathers* 2, 169; Holmes, *The Apostolic Fathers*, 35; Grundeken, *Community Building*, 4–5. For an exception, see J.B. Lightfoot, *The Apostolic Fathers, Part I: S. Clement of Rome*, vol. I (London: Macmillan, 1890), 348. More recent authors, even when they are entertaining this possibility, tend to remain cautious, e.g., P. Lampe, *From Paul to Valentinus: Christians at Rome in the First Two Centuries* (Minneapolis, MN: Fortress Press, 2003), 206, n. 1.

[36] E.g., Osiek, *The Shepherd of Hermas*, 20.

[37] Andrew Gregory, "Disturbing Trajectories: *1 Clement*, the *Shepherd of Hermas* and the Development of Early Roman Christianity," in *Rome in the Bible and the Early Church*, ed. Peter Oakes (Carlisle: Paternoster Press, 2002), 149. See also Grundeken, *Community Building*, 9.

[38] Grundeken, *Community Building*, 1.

[39] Mark Grundeken, "Diakone in Rom? Das Zeugnis des Hirten des Hermas," *VigChr* 72 (2018): 93–101.

[40] Dan Batovici, "Contrasting Ecclesial Functions in the Second Century: Diakonia, Diakonoi, Episkopoi and Presbyteroi in the *Shepherd of Hermas* and Ignatius of Antioch's *Letters*," *Augustinianum* 51 (2011): 307.

according to which the style of leadership in Rome was one in which "individual churches had individual leaders" and when these gathered they "were collectively known as presbyters" in their capacity as members of the gathering, while likely being *episkopoi* for their own congregations, Alistair C. Stewart shows that Hermas is a household leader, and therefore reads *Vision* 2.4.2–3 [8] as evidence for the congregation of the leaders at city level, beyond their communities; Stewart also argues that in their communities the *episkopoi* (and the *diakonoi*) had mainly economic duties, regarding hospitality and supporting those in need and the widows, in *Similitude* 9.26.2 [103] and 9.27 [104].[41]

The *Shepherd* envisages otherwise a somewhat exclusive community of the elect, where there are potentially many problems but also where – ideally – the members are looking to better or redeem themselves.[42] We have mentioned already that the author has the heavenly mediator tell him that his wife should hold her tongue in *Vision* 2.2.3 [6], and despite the presence of at least one female figure in the community – Grapte in *Vision* 2.4.3 [8] – "overall Hermas envisions 'traditional' male-centred gender roles."[43] Charity as the pious duty to help the less fortunate is an important side theme in the book, albeit as something that benefits the giver rather than borne out of compassion.[44] Furthermore, the *Shepherd* seems to reflect the eucharistic meal as the community (real) meal, followed by an after-dinner symposium.[45]

Overall, the *Shepherd* seems to presuppose a non-elite Roman context, with some, even though "limited literary education," in which a freedman can enjoy considerable upward and downward economical and social mobility.[46] In a crowded urban milieu, Hermas can be imagined as a local entrepreneur appealing to his audience with a call to repentance through apocalyptic descriptions in a Christian neighborhood where he is in competition with other

---

[41] Alistair C. Stewart, *The Original Bishops: Office and Order in the First Christian Communities* (Grand Rapids, MI: Baker Academic, 2014), 117–18.

[42] Grundeken, *Community Building*, 69–84, argues that the *Shepherd* displays sectarian tendencies, since the community of the elect is also presented in a certain tension with the "outside" world.

[43] Ibid., 113.

[44] Ibid., 114–27.

[45] Ibid., 142–70.

[46] Osiek, *The Shepherd of Hermas*, 21.

religious players, as the false prophets described as fortune-tellers in
Mandate 11 [43].[47]

15.5 RECEPTION

15.5.1 The Manuscript Transmission

The transmission of the *Shepherd* is no less intricate a matter than
those discussed so far, which in turn raises interesting reception-
historical problems. On the one hand, it has the highest number of
witnesses of all Apostolic Fathers: if there is a papyrus of each the
Didache, *Barnabas*, and Ignatius, there are twenty-three Greek papyri
of the *Shepherd*. This count is considerably higher than that of most
New Testament books taken separately – with the exception of John
and Mathew – even though the significance of such a comparison
remains unclear.

On the other hand, as mentioned in the introduction (Section 15.1),
we do not have the complete Greek text of the *Shepherd*: the papyri are
for the most part highly fragmentary, Codex Sinaiticus preserves only
about a third of its text, and the only more complete witness – codex
Athous Grigoriou 96 of the fourteenth century – lacks its ending. In fact,
since Codex Sinaiticus became known to the Western academic world
in the middle of the nineteenth century, and both the papyrus finds and
the publication of the text in Athous Grigoriou 96 are in the late
nineteenth century, for the longest time the *Shepherd* was known in
the West only through its Latin translations. The Latin branch of reception seems to have been particularly thriving, as there are over thirty
manuscripts from the ninth to the sixteenth century, which were
followed – after the change of the medium from parchment to printing –
by twelve editions from the seventeenth century up to today.[48]

The remaining antique translations are interesting in various ways.
The Ethiopic, for instance, is important because it preserves the whole
text and is rather old and translated directly from Greek. It is also
interesting because in this form the *Shepherd* seems to have been held

---

[47] Harry O. Maier, "Romans Watching Romans: Christ Religion in Close Urban
Quarters and Neighbourhood Transformations," *Religion in the Roman Empire* 6
(2020) 104–121..

[48] The latest is Christian Tornau and Paolo Cecconi (eds.), *The Shepherd of Hermas in
Latin: Critical Edition of the Oldest Translation Vulgata*, TU 173 (Berlin/Boston,
MA: De Gruyter, 2014).

in high esteem in the Ethiopian church.[49] The Coptic translation, much like a large part of the literature preserved in this language, is fragmentary and incomplete, but it preserves enough material to suggest that this was probably meant as a translation of the whole work, rather than perhaps an excerpted sample.[50] On the contrary, the Middle-Persian translation is in fact a "Manichean adaptation" of an excerpt from the Ninth Similitude of the *Shepherd*.[51]

Peculiar still in this regard is the Georgian translation, found so far in only one manuscript, likely translated from Arabic, for which no witness has emerged so far.[52] The text starts with *Vision* 5 and is preserved under the name of "Saint Ephrem" not only in the title, but also in introductory formulae for the lines that would otherwise belong to the character Hermas, for example, "and saint Ephrem said," that have no equivalent in the Greek. The confusion is made possible by the fact that in the Greek text the Hermas character, who speaks in the first person throughout, is not mentioned by name after *Vision* 4, which in turn suggests that the Georgian or Arabic translators did not have the first four *Visions* at hand when they translated the text.

Interestingly, in the studies on the *Shepherd* there has been a longstanding assumption that its text might have initially circulated split into two books, only later concatenated in the whole we know today: *Visions* 1–4 on the one hand and the rest of the work, prefaced by *Vision* 5 on the other. This is based on an influential reconstruction of the P.Mich. II 2.129 by Campbell Bonner,[53] whose proposal has ramifications also in the studies on the Latin and Coptic transmission of the *Shepherd*, where it tends to be taken as an established fact. However, this can be shown to be a reconstruction that is far more exact than the evidence allows for: while it is likely that parts of the *Shepherd* have

---

[49] Ted Erho, "The Shepherd of Hermas in Ethiopia," in *L'Africa, l'Oriente Mediterraneo e l'Europa: Tradizione e Culture a Confronto*, ed. P. Nicelli, Africana Ambrosiana 1 (Milano: Biblioteca Ambrosiana, 2015), 97–117.

[50] Dan Batovici, "Some Observations on the Coptic Reception of the *Shepherd of Hermas*," *Comparative Oriental Manuscript Studies Bulletin* 3.2 (2017): 81–96.

[51] W. Sundermann, "Hermas, The Shepherd of," in *Encyclopaedia Iranica*, Vol. XII, Fasc. 3 (2004), 232–4, at 232. The latest edition is available in B. Burtea, "Interpretatio manichaica am Beispiel des mittelpersischen Turfan-Fragments M 97," *Annals of the Sergiu Al-George Institute* 4–5 (1995–6 [2002]): 47–67.

[52] Bernard Outtier, "La version géorgienne du Pasteur d'Hermas," *Revue des études géorgiennes et caucasiennes* 6–7 (1990–1): 211–15. The critical edition is still in preparation by the same author.

[53] Campbell Bonner, *A Papyrus Codex of the Shepherd of Hermas (Similitudes 2–9) with a Fragment of the Mandates*, Humanistic Series XXII (Ann Arbor: University of Michigan Press, 1934).

circulated excerpted for various purposes – as is the case with many other texts – there is no positive evidence for a purposeful circulation of these two clear-cut parts of the book.[54] In fact, among the ancient translations, it is only the Georgian that knows the *Shepherd* starting with *Vision* 5 alone, but probably this has little to say about the Egyptian circulation of the *Shepherd* before the times of Clement of Alexandria, who already quotes from all parts of the book.

Finally, a brief mention is due to the solitary and generally ignored witness to the *Shepherd* found in the Armenian Catena of the Epistle of James, where an excerpt from *Mandate* 9 is adduced to explain James 1.8; this is translated from the Greek catena of James although the introductory formula that in Greek means "From the Shepherd, in the 9th Mandate,"[55] does not preserve his name in Armenian.

15.5.2 Patristic References and Canonical Lists

Complementary to the manuscripts found in these traditions, the *Shepherd* was mentioned in various ways by several patristic authors and canonical lists. The book is quoted or referenced by name as an authoritative writing in Irenaeus of Lyons and Clement of Alexandria. The former seems to regard it as a scriptural text, but it is not clear whether as a first- or second-tier book.[56] Clement of Alexandria uses, when mentioning Hermas' visions, his technical vocabulary of prophecy, which shows that for him the *Shepherd* is an account of genuine revelation.[57] Origen too held the book in high esteem and explicitly deemed it inspired, but it does not appear among his list of New Testament books.[58]

It is sometimes considered that the *Shepherd* was important in the earliest Christianity only and that it faded as soon as the New

---

[54] Dan Batovici, "Two Notes on the Papyri of the *Shepherd of Hermas* and Its Egyptian Transmission," *Archiv für Papyrusforschung* 62 (2016): 384–95.

[55] Charles Renoux (ed.), *La chaîne arménienne sur les Épîtres catholiques: I. La chaîne sur l'Épître de Jacques*, Patrologia Orientalis 43.1, No. 193 (Turnhout: Brepols, 1985), 76.

[56] See, e.g., D. Jeffrey Bingham, "Senses of Scripture in the Second Century: Irenaeus, Scripture, and Noncanonical Christian Texts," *JR* 97 (2017): 26–55, who argues that it is secondary.

[57] Dan Batovici, "Hermas in Clement of Alexandria," in *Papers Presented at the Sixteenth International Conference on Patristic Studies held in Oxford 2011, Volume 14*, ed. M. Vinzent, Studia Patristica 65 (Leuven: Peeters, 2013), 41–51.

[58] Edmon L. Gallagher, "Origen on the Shepherd of Hermas," *Early Christianity* 10 (2019): 201–15, concludes that for Origen the *Shepherd* "was scripture but not canon," at 215.

Testament canon started forming, but it is worth keeping in mind that even by the end of the fourth century a prominent author such as Didymus of Alexandria is using quotations from this book intertwined with quotations from biblical books, in theological arguments.[59] In all these cases it is generally clear that the *Shepherd* is an important, scriptural book, but it is unclear whether it is also a canonical one or, in other words, whether it is a first-tier rather than a second-tier book.

The same ambiguity surrounds the significance of the fact that the *Shepherd* was copied in Codex Sinaiticus in the middle of the fourth century together with the Greek Old and New Testament: on the one hand they are included in an artefact that resembles a "complete Bible," but on the other it is grouped at the end with the *Epistle of Barnabas*. In any event, the question of whether Codex Sinaiticus – and Codex Alexandrinus of the fifth century, which includes *1* and *2 Clement* similarly at the end – is a Bible as we think of it today, closed between two covers, or another type of scriptural collection (for instance, one that can include second-tier along with first-tier books) remains unclear.[60]

The *Shepherd* is also mentioned in a number of book lists, and here we find ourselves on firmer ground. These are normally considered "canonical lists," but if they are, they are so in different ways as they serve different purposes and seem to respond to different sets of concerns. These lists tend nonetheless to be in agreement in that the *Shepherd* is a second-tier book: the so-called Muratorian Fragment, Eusebius of Caesarea (*Eccl. hist.* 3.25.), and Athanasius of Alexandria (*Festal letter* 39), as well as Rufinus of Aquileia (*Exposition of the Creed* 37–8), are all explicitly denying it a place on the first tier of books. However, at the same time, they all keep it in a secondary tier of books, which are in most cases recommended or even prescribed reading.

Before concluding, it is worth mentioning that there are two witnesses that seem to reject the *Shepherd* entirely, a patristic author and a list: Tertullian (*On Modesty* 10.12 and 20.2) rejects it as "that apocryphal Shepherd of adulterers," and *Decretum Gelasianum* 4.5 of the sixth century, which lists it not on the second tier of writings, but among the "apocryphal books which are not to be received."

---

[59] On this basis, Bart D. Erhman, "The New Testament Canon of Didymus the Blind," *VigChr* 37 (1983): 1–21, argues that the *Shepherd* and other early Christian books were probably canonical to this important patristic author.

[60] For an argument that they are included as secondary, see Dan Batovici, "The Apostolic Fathers in Codex Sinaiticus and Alexandrinus," *Biblica* 97 (2016): 581–605.

On balance, the *Shepherd*'s reception as an authoritative writing in Early Christianity shows that it was, in various contexts, *at least* a secondary recommended reading. Several lists are explicit about this; for the remaining sources there is no ground to establish that it was a first-tier writing. In other words, we are lacking witnesses for which this book was not only scriptural but also canonical.

15.6 IN LIEU OF CONCLUSION

What to make, then, of the *Shepherd of Hermas*? The document remains enigmatic and it continues to stand apart among the other Apostolic Fathers. Most of the issues raised in scholarship about this text remain overall unresolved as the book resists attempts to mirror-reading its context, occasion, and purpose, obscured in its repetitive rhetoric and allegoric material. The *Shepherd* seems overall first and foremost concerned with improving and strengthening – rather than expanding – the community of believers, and in the service of that aim it conjures its own brand of apocalyptic, complex lists of shortcomings and pitfalls met with exhortations and precepts, with personal and social concerns, and a call to endurance and repentance in view of salvation, with a sense of urgency.

FURTHER READING

Brox, Norbert. *Der Hirt des Hermas*. Kommentar zu den Apostolischen Vätern 7. Göttingen: Vandenhoeck & Ruprecht, 1991.

Bucur, Bogdan G. "Angelomorphic Pneumatology in the *Shepherd of Hermas*," in *Angelomorphic Pneumatology: Clement of Alexandria and Other Early Christian Witnesses*. Supplements to Vigiliae Christianae 95. Leiden: Brill, 2009, 113–38.

Grundeken, Mark. *Community Building in the Shepherd of Hermas: A Critical Study of Some Key Aspects*. Supplements to Vigiliae Christianae 131. Leiden: Brill, 2015.

Hellholm, David. "The Shepherd of Hermas," in *The Apostolic Fathers: An Introduction*, edited by Wilhelm Pratscher. Waco, TX: Baylor University Press, 2010, 215–42.

Lipsett, B. Diane. *Desiring Conversion: Hermas, Thecla, Aseneth*. New York: Oxford University Press, 2011.

Maier, Harry. "Shepherd of Hermas," in *Oxford Research Bibliographies*. Oxford: Oxford University Press, 2016. www.oxfordbibliographies.com

Osiek, Carolyn. *The Shepherd of Hermas: A Commentary*. Hermeneia. Minneapolis, MN: Fortress Press, 1999.

Snyder, Graydon F. *The Shepherd of Hermas*. The Apostolic Fathers 6. London: Thomas Nelson & Sons, 1968.

Verheyden, Joseph. "The Shepherd of Hermas." *ExpT* 117 (2006): 397–401.

16 The *Epistle to Diognetus* and the *Fragment of Quadratus*

MICHAEL F. BIRD AND KIRSTEN H. MACKERRAS

16.1 INTRODUCTION

The document known to us as the *Epistle to Diognetus*[1] is a perplexing text. Its origins are obscure since the author is anonymous, the identity of the recipient remains unknown, the text has several lacunae, the integrity of the final two chapters is questionable, and nothing in the document indicates a specific date or provenance. What is more, *Diogn.* is entirely unknown to Christian authors of the patristic and medieval periods since no-one mentions or cites the document as far as we know.

Whatever its origin, the document was quickly forgotten and lost until its discovery in Constantinople in 1436 in a fishmonger's shop. The text of *Diogn.* was preserved in a single manuscript, codex Argentoratensis Graecus ix, dated to the thirteenth/fourteenth centuries, located at the end of a series of works by Justin Martyr. The document was eventually taken to France and was first published in 1592 by Henri Estienne. The manuscript was housed in the library of Strasbourg, but was destroyed by a fire during the Franco-Prussian war of 1870, and is now extant only in transcriptions made by several scholars.[2]

---

[1] For recent translations, see K. Wengst, *Didache (Apostellehre), Barnabasbrief, Zweiter Clemensbrief, Schrift an Diognet*, SUC 2 (Darmstadt: Wissenschaftliche Buchgesellschaft, 1984), 312–41; Bart D. Ehrman, *The Apostolic Fathers*, LCL 24, 2 vols. (Cambridge, MA: Harvard University Press, 2003), 2.121–60; Michael W. Holmes, *The Apostolic Fathers: Greek Texts and English Translations*, 3rd ed. (Grand Rapids, MI: Baker, 2007), 686–720; Rick Brannan, *The Apostolic Fathers: A New Translation* (Bellingham, WA: Lexham, 2017), 277–89. Translation in this chapter are from Holmes unless otherwise indicated.

[2] L.B. Radford, *The Epistle to Diognetus* (London: SPCK, 1908), 7–10; Henri Irénée Marrou, *A Diognète: Introduction, edition critique, traduction et commentaire*, SC 33.2, 2nd ed. (Paris: Cerf, 1997), 5–10, 33–7; Holmes, *Apostolic Fathers*, 689–90; Ehrman, *Apostolic Fathers*, 127–8; Clayton N. Jefford, *The Epistle to Diognetus (with the Fragment of Quadratus): Introduction, Text, and Commentary*, OAF (Oxford: Oxford University Press, 2013), 7–8.

Further, the document is misnamed: it is not an epistle, but more properly an apologetic treatise with an epistolary opening and a homiletical appendix. In addition, *Diogn.* does not really belong to the "apostolic fathers"; given its genre and contents it should be situated among the second-century apologists.[3] The Italian patristic scholar Andrea Gallandi (1709–1779) included *Diogn.* in his 1765 edition of the apostolic fathers thinking *Diogn.* to have been written by Paul's colleague Apollos.[4] Gallandi's authorial conjecture never found support in subsequent scholarship, but the inclusion of *Diogn.* among the apostolic fathers stuck even if *Diogn.* was thereafter included as "custom rather than right."[5]

Diogn. is – enigmatic origins and wrongful classifications aside – a literary masterpiece of Christian apologetics and rhetorical prowess. J.B. Lightfoot considered it "the noblest of early Christian writings,"[6] and Avery Dulles called it "the pearl of early Christian apologetics"[7] – apt endorsement for a document that offers a moving exposition of the vocation of Christians as the soul of the world, a robust affirmation of Christian theism and the Son's incarnation, a poignant account of the atonement, a powerful presentation of God's mercy for the unrighteous, and a concerted exhortation toward the imitation of God. The document, says Jefford, "present a fascinating view into how early Christian authors were able to harness biblical features for their rhetorical agendas and, in this particular case, to create a text whose style offers a simple beauty that is easily appreciated."[8] Thus, *Diogn.* is something of a sublime crescendo in early Christian literature.

Concerning the fragment of Quadratus, Eusebius preserves a single sentence of Quadratus' *Apology* in his own *Church History* (*Hist. eccl.* 4.3.1–2). Quadratus was remembered as the first Christian apologist, who addressed the Emperor Hadrian, and attempted to demonstrate the reasonableness of Christian faith. In terms of genre, Quadratus belongs

---

[3] Kirsopp Lake, *The Apostolic Fathers*, LCL 25, 2 vols. (Cambridge, MA: Harvard University Press, 1913), 2.348; Robert M. Grant, *Greek Apologists of the Second Century* (Philadelphia, PA: Westminster, 1988), 178–9; Frances Young, "Greek Apologists of the Second Century," in *Apologetics in the Roman Empire: Pagans, Jews, and Christians*, ed. M. Edwards, M. Goodman, and S. Price (Oxford: Oxford University Press, 1999), 87–8.

[4] Holmes, *Apostolic Fathers*, 5.

[5] Lake, *Apostolic Fathers*, 2.348.

[6] J.B. Lightfoot, *Saint Paul's Epistles to the Colossians and to Philemon*, 3rd ed. (London: Macmillan and Co., 1879), 156.

[7] Avery Dulles, *A History of Apologetics* (Eugene, OR: Wipf & Stock, 1999), 35.

[8] Jefford, *Diognetus*, 12–13.

to the apologists, but chronologically among the apostolic fathers. Like Papias and Polycarp, Quadratus had personal links to first-century Christian leaders. The fragment Eusebius preserves attests to the memory of Jesus as a healer, with supplicants of healing constituting a living witness to Jesus' miracles.

16.2 AUTHORSHIP, DATE, AND RECIPIENT OF *AD DIOGNETUM*

The author of *Diogn.* does not self-identify, and there is next to no internal evidence to assist in a positive identification,[9] thus proposals for the authorship have been wide-ranging.[10] The fact that codex Argentoratensis Graecus located *Diogn.* at the end of a collection of writings by Justin Martyr and titled *Diogn.* as "of him [Justin] to Diognetus" meant that Justin was an early candidate for the author.[11] However, it was quickly recognized by researchers that the text is stylistically very different from Justin, hence for a long time the manuscript was known as Ps[eudo]-Justin.[12] Other proposals have included Aristides, Tatian, Melito of Sardis, Theophilus of Antioch, Pantanaeus of Alexandria, and Hippolytus of Rome. Probably the two best educated guesses are Quadratus[13] and bishop Polycarp of Smyrna.[14] Sadly, the arguments for any particular author are either circumstantial or conjectural.[15] In the end, all we know for certain is that the author is educated and erudite, a teacher of Christianity in an ostensibly hostile context. Beyond that, one might agree with the judgment of bishop Polycarp in

---

[9] The author of the homilies – not original to *Diogn.* 1–10 – calls himself, "a disciple of apostles" and a "teacher of Gentiles" in 11.1.

[10] Radford, *Diognetus*, 21–31; Marrou, *Diognète*, 242–3; Henry G. Meecham, *The Epistle to Diognetus* (Manchester: Manchester University Press, 1949), 16–17; Horacio E. Lona, *An Diognet: Übersetzt und erklärt*, KfA 8 (Freiburg: Herder, 2001), 64–5; Jefford, *Diognetus*, 15–29.

[11] See Marrou, *Diognète*, 12–13, 24–5.

[12] Radford, *Diognetus*, 22; Meecham, *Diognetus*, 61–2.

[13] I.A. Dorner, *History of the Development of the Doctrine of the Person of Christ*, trans. W.L. Alexander (Edinburgh: Clark, 1861), 374–7; P. Andriessen, "The Authorship of the *Epistula ad Diognetum*," *VC* 1 (1947): 129–36.

[14] Pier Franco Beatrice, "Der Presbyter des Irenäus, Polykarp von Smyrna und der Brief an Diognet," in *Pléroma Salus Carnis. Homenaje a Antonio Orbe, S.J.*, ed. Eugenio Romero-Pose (Santiago de Compostella, 1990), 179–202; Charles E. Hill, *From the Lost Teaching of Polycarp: Identifying Irenaeus' Apostolic Presbyter and the Author of* Ad Diognetum, WUNT 186 (Tübingen: Mohr/Siebeck, 2006), 128–65.

[15] The prospect of a medieval or renaissance forgery was entertained by James Donaldson (1866) and critiqued by Johannes Dräseke (1881); see Radford, *Diognetus*, 10–11.

Kenneth Berding's pedagogical fiction, where Polycarp says of the author, "I don't know who he was, but he clearly was a true brother in the Lord."[16]

Given the resonance of *Diogn.* 1–10 with Christian apologetic works of the second century (esp. Aristides, Justin Martyr, Theophilus of Antioch, and Clement of Alexandria), the similarity of *Diogn.* 11–12 with second-century homiletical/catechetical writings (esp. *2 Clement*, Melito of Sardis, Hippolytus of Rome), plus the allusions to persecution (5.17; 7.7; 10.8), a date in the mid- to late second century is generally preferred by most commentators.[17]

The name of the designated addressee, *Diognetus* (*Diognētos*), was common enough in antiquity and is found among various writings, inscriptions, and papyri.[18] Scholars have speculated as to which Diognetus might have been intended. (1) A certain Diognetus was tutor to the emperor Marcus Aurelius, whom Aurelius admired for his freedom from superstition and sound educational advice (*Med.* 1.6).[19] (2) The procurator Tiberius Claudius Diogenes of Alexandria is known from papyri dated between 197 and 203 CE, and he is even called "the most excellent Diognetus" in one papyrus that is similar to the opening address in *Diogn.* 1.1[20] (3) An inscription in Smyrna dated 150–210 CE mentions a grandfather and grandson both called Diognetus.[21] Of course, the reality remains that we cannot determine who the recipient is.[22] Moreover, *Diognetus* might even be an entirely fictitious entity, a cipher for Roman enquirers of Christianity – a plausible suggestion given that "Diognetus" means literally "heir/child of Dios/Zeus" and could conceivably symbolize a pagan reader.[23] What we can say, from a narrative perspective, is that the implied reader is an educated pagan interested in learning about Christianity (1.2, "I gladly welcome this interest of yours"). Beyond that, apologetic literature was often composed for internal consumption among sectarian groups, so Christian readers might be ancillary to any pagan recipients.

---

[16] Kenneth Berding, *The Apostolic Fathers: A Narrative Introduction* (Eugene, OR: Wipf & Stock, 2017), 88.

[17] Jefford (*Diognetus*, 28) states: "Following the bulk of contemporary scholarship, the text is most likely to be attributed to some moment during the 2nd century, with a preference for the latter decades of that period."

[18] BDAG, 250; Meecham, *Diognetus*, 93; Lona, *Diognet*, 72; Jefford, *Diognetus*, 26.

[19] Radford, *Diognetus*, 44.

[20] Marrou, *Diognète*, 254–6, 267–8; Grant, *Greek Apologists*, 179.

[21] Hill, *Lost Teaching of Polycarp*, 160–5.

[22] See surveys in Marrou, *Diognète*, 254–9; Jefford, *Diognetus*, 15–29.

[23] Lona, *Diognet*, 73–4; Jefford, *Diognetus*, 25.

16.3 GENRE, PURPOSE, INTEGRITY, AND STRUCTURE

Concerning genre, *Diogn.* is an apologetic treatise prefaced as an epistle, while the final two chapters exhibit clear homiletical and catechetical features. On the whole, *Diogn.* 1–10 is best characterized as an apologetic–protreptic treatise that issues an invitation to Roman elites to embrace the Christian faith by refuting idol-worship, critiquing Judaism, praising Christian belief and conduct, and engaging in a manner of moral discourse that would be potentially attractive to those with Stoic and/or Platonic sympathies.[24] Thereafter, *Diogn.* 11–12 constitute homilies that use traditional materials to instruct a catechumen in the incarnation and exhorts them toward a knowledge that abounds in fruitfulness. As for overall purpose, Paul Foster comments: "These arguments are an attempt to convince those outside the community that Christianity is a rigorous and attractive faith, worthy to be pursued by all who cherish reason and despise superstition … [*Diogn.* is] a vivid snapshot of an early attempt to rationally present the integrity of Christianity to a society that was both pluralistic and hostile."[25]

The textual integrity of *Diogn.* is something of a conundrum. There are gaps in the text between 7.6 and 7.7 and at 10.8; at both points the original copyist noted the lacunae with a comment in the margins. This implies that the exemplar behind codex Argentoratensis Graecus was to some degree defective. In addition, the final two chapters, *Diogn.* 11–12, stand apart from *Diogn.* 1–10 as a homiletical composition, which assumes a Christian rather than pagan audience; it abounds in OT allusions, which are sparse in *Diogn.* 1–10; its purpose is catechetical rather than forensic argumentation, and so *Diogn.* 11–12 is fairly judged to be a later addition.[26] A minority of scholars regard these chapters as original to the work[27] or perhaps a separate work by the same

---

[24] On the protreptic–apologetic nature of *Diogn.*, see C.S. Wansink, "*Epistula ad Diognetum*: A School Exercise in the Use of Protreptic," *Church Divinity* (1986): 97–109; David Aune, *The Westminster Dictionary of New Testament and Early Christian Literature and Rhetoric* (Louisville, KY: Westminster John Knox, 2003), 136–9; Lona, *Diognet*, 27–34; Jefford, *Diognetus*, 52–4.

[25] Paul Foster, "The Epistle to Diognetus," in *The Writings of the Apostolic Fathers*, ed. P. Foster (London: T&T Clark, 2007), 156.

[26] See discussion of their unity and integrity in Radford, *Diognetus*, 31–8; R.H. Connolly, "Ad Diognetum xi–xii," *JTS* 36 (1936): 2–15; Meecham, *Diognetus*, 64–8; Lona, *Diognet*, 47–8; Jefford, *Diognetus*, 43–51.

[27] Andriessen, "Authorship," 135–6; Marrou, *Diognète*, 219–27; Hill, *Lost Teaching of Polycarp*, 106–27, 167; esp. Marco Rizzi, *La questione dell'unità dell' "Ad Diognetum*," SPM 16 (Milan: Università Cattolica del Sacro Cuore, 1989).

author.[28] *Diogn.* 11–12 was perhaps added to represent the type of catechesis that a pagan convert to Christianity like "Diognetus" would require to grow in the faith.

Concerning structure, the prologue of *Diogn.* 1.1 announces three questions that are addressed in the document: (1) What god do the Christians trust and worship? (2) What is the nature and reason for their love for each other? and (3) Why has this new group of people and their strange way of life emerged? Thereafter, *Diogn.* 2–6 provides an examination of the religion of the Greeks and the superstitions of the Jews with a view to reproving them and dissuading their continued observance (*Diogn.* 2–4),[29] and then the Christians are praised in an encomium for their virtue, veracity, victory, and vivifying effect upon the world (*Diogn.* 5–6). *Diogn.* 7 is something of a bridging section, which links the Christians to God's providence and plans, and announces that the sending of God's word is to save by persuasion, with Christians portrayed as the "proofs of his presence" (*Diogn.* 7.9). Beyond that, *Diogn.* 8–9 constitutes an exposition of God's purposes, revelation, and the sending of God's beloved child to save the powerless and the unrighteous. Then, in *Diogn.* 10, it is asserted that faith leads to knowledge, which leads to love, and love is an imitation of God's goodness. The homilies in *Diogn.* 11–12, resourcing traditional materials, include an exposition of the incarnation of the Logos and an exposition of the two trees planted in the garden according to Gen 2.9. Put in a tabulated form, the structure of *Diogn.* looks like this:

1.1–2	Prologue and Three Questions
2.1–10	The Folly of Pagan Idolatry
3.1–4.6	The Superstitions of the Jews
5.1–6.10	Encomium to the Christian *Genos*
7.1–8.11	The Christian God and his Son
9.1–6	The Christian God's Power to Salvation
10.1–8	The Imitation of God
11.1–8	A Homily on the "Epiphany of the Word"[30]
12.1–9	A Homily on Knowledge and Life

[28] L.W. Barnard, "The Enigma of the Epistle to Diognetus," in *Studies in the Apostolic Fathers and Their Background* (Oxford: Blackwell, 1966), 165–71; T.J. Lang, *Mystery and Making of a Christian Historical Consciousness: From Paul to the Second Century*, BZNW 219 (Berlin: Walter de Gruyter, 2017), 149.

[29] Aune, "Diognetus," 139.

[30] Grant, *Greek Apologists*, 178.

16.4 MAIN INFLUENCES AND PLACE IN
EARLY CHRISTIANITY

Diogn. draws on a rich assortment of philosophical, scriptural, apologetic, and theological texts and traditions.

First, as Meecham observed, the author's mind "moves in Platonic groves."[31] The sign of platonic influence is particularly evident in *Diogn.* 6. with a strong affirmation of soul–body dualism highly reminiscent of Plato's *Phaedo* (62b, 65a–d) and *Phaedrus* (245c–250c).[32] Likewise, the exhortation to be an imitator of God, well-attested in Christian tradition (Eph 5.1; Ignatius, *Eph.* 1.1; 10.3; 6.3; Polycarp, *Phil* 8.2; Justin, *Apol* 1.10), meshes neatly with Plato's own vision of virtue as an imitation of divinity (*Phaedrus* 176b; *Theatetus* 252c–253b, *Timaeus* 38a–b).[33] It is not altogether impossible that some platonic influences are mediated via Philo who, like the author, believes in God's invisibility (*Diogn.* 7.2; Philo, *Opif.* 29; *Spec.* 1.20; *Gai.* 318; cf. Col. 1.15); God's people are those who "see" God (*Diogn.* 10.2; Philo, *Ling.* 56; *Post.* 92; *Imm.* 3; *Somn.* 1.171), and God's people are sojourners (*Diogn.* 5.5, 17; 6.8; Philo, *Conf.* 77–82; *Agr.* 74; *Ebr.* 100; *Mos.* 1.35–6).[34] The worldview behind *Diogn.* is a platonic duality of the material and the spiritual realms, and Christians are expected to live faithfully in the former while relying on the latter.

Second, allusions to the Old Testament are invoked are several junctures.[35] To begin with, the critique of idolatry in *Diogn.* 2.1–10 clearly stands in the tradition of Isaiah 44 and Wisdom of Solomon 13–14. Otherwise Genesis looms in relation to humanity being created in "his own image" (*Diogn.* 10.2 = Gen. 1.26–7); the Isaianic servant is manifestly evoked (*Diogn.* 9.2 = Isa. 53.4, 11); there is a likely allusion to Malachi's day of the Lord's coming in judgment (*Diogn.* 7.6 = Mal. 3.2); and mention of the immortal soul in a mortal tent is indicative of Wisdom of Solomon (*Diogn.* 6.8 = Wisd. 9.15). Unlike Justin Martyr there is no proof from prophecy, and unlike Aristeas there is no spiritual reinterpretation of the Old Testament. Instead, the Old Testament provides the resource for a critique of pagan idolatry, the scaffolding

---

[31] Meecham, *Diognetus*, 34.
[32] Ibid., 117; Jefford, *Diognetus*, 64, 224–5.
[33] Martin Heintz, "*Mimētē Theou* in the *Epistle to Diognetus*," *JECS* 12 (2004): 107–19; Jefford, *Diognetus*, 65.
[34] David T. Runia, *Philo in Early Christian Literature: A Survey* (Minneapolis, MN: Fortress, 1993), 130; cf. Meecham, *Diognetus*, 3, 10.
[35] See Jefford, *Diognetus*, 87–91.

for a creational monotheism, the background story for God's redemptive plan, and the semantic register for explaining the Son's work of salvation.

Third, while the text has manifold echoes of the Synoptic Gospels, they do not form any rhetorical pivot in the argument, and they appear spasmodically and only faintly. Nonetheless Synoptic traditions are perhaps present in relation to the fitness of doing good on the Sabbath (*Diogn*. 4.3 = Mt. 12.12, Mk. 3.4, Lk. 6.9); the need to love one's enemies (*Diogn*. 6.6 = Mt. 5.44, Lk. 6.27); in the affirmation of God's goodness (*Diogn*. 8.8 = Mt. 19.17, Mk. 10.18, Lk. 18.19); God making it possible for people to enter the kingdom of God (*Diogn*. 9.1 = Mt. 19.26, Mk. 10.27; the need to not be anxious for food or clothing (*Diogn*. 9.6 = Mt. 6.25, 28, 31); and in mention of the "kingdom of heaven" (*Diogn*. 10.2 = e.g., Mt. 4.17).

Fourth, if we have to identify the largest single influence on *Diogn*. then it would have to be the Apostle Paul.[36] Ernst Dassman comments that, "The utilization of Pauline theology reaches an astonishing intensity in the epistle to Diognetus,"[37] and "not merely in the abundance of Pauline terminology, which the author cites or paraphrases into his own account, but rather in the exposition of central concerns found in Pauline theology."[38] Although the only explicit citation of Paul is in the homiletic section (*Diogn*. 12.5 = 1 Cor. 8.1), the whole of *Diogn*. is permeated with Pauline allusions and echoes. The Paulinisms are the

---

[36] Rudolf Brändle, *Die Ethik der "Schrift an Diognet": Eine Wiederaufnahme paulinischer und johanneischer Theologie am Ende des zweiten Jahrhunderts*, ATANT 64 (Zurich: Theologischer Verlage, 1975), 206–16; Andreas Lindemann, "Paulinische Theologie im Brief an Diognet," in *Kerygma und Logos: Beiträge zu den geistesgeschichtlichen Beziehungen zwischen Antike und Christentum*, ed. A.M. Ritter (Göttingen: Vandenhoeck & Ruprecht, 1979), 337–50; Ernst Dassman, *Der Stachel im Fleisch: Paulus in der frühchristlichen Literatur bis Irenäus* (Münster: Aschendorff, 1979), 254–9; Rolf Noormann, "Himmelsbürger auf Erden: Anmerkungen zum Weltverhältnis und zum 'Paulinismus' des Auctor ad Diognetum," in *Die Weltlichkeit des Glaubens in der Alten Kirche*, ed. B. Aland, C. Schäublin, D. Wyrwa, and U. Wickert, BZNW 85 (Berlin: Walter de Gruyter, 1997), 199–229; Michael F. Bird, "The Reception of Paul in the *Epistle to Diognetus*," in *Paul in the Second Century*, ed. M.F. Bird and J.R. Dodson, LNTS 412 (London: T&T Clark, 2011), 70–90; Matthew Thomas, *Paul's "Works of the Law" in the Perspective of Second Century Reception*, WUNT 2.468 (Tübingen: Mohr/Siebeck, 2018), 119–21.

[37] Dassman, *Der Stachel im Fleisch*, 254 ("Zu einer erstauntliche Intensität gelangt die Verwertung paulinischer Theologie dann bereits im Diognetbrief").

[38] Ibid., 255 ("nicht allein die Fülle paulinischer Wendungen, die der Verfasser zitierend oder paraphrasierend in die eigene Darstellung einfließen läßt, sondern ein Eingehen auf zentrale Anliegen der paulinischen Theologie").

most apparent when it comes to a critique of circumcision (*Diogn.* 4.1, 4 = Phil. 3.2-5; Rom 2.17, 25–9); the depiction of Christians as possessing a heavenly citizenship (*Diogn.* 5.9 = Phil. 3.20); the catalogue of hardships (*Diogn.* 5.8–17 = 1 Cor. 4.10–13; 2 Cor. 4.7–12; 6.8–10); Christian custodianship of a divine mystery (*Diogn.* 10.7 = 1 Cor. 2.1, 7; Col. 2.2); the inscrutability of God (*Diogn.* 8.5 = 1 Cor. 2.9–10); the contrast between Spirit and flesh (*Diogn.* 5.8, 6.5–6 = Romans 7–8; Galatians 4–5); and the announcement of God saving the lawless and unrighteous by sending the Son of God who by his righteousness could justify them (*Diogn.* 9.1–5 = Rom 3.24–6, 4.4–5, 5.6–8, 6.23, 8.3, 32, Gal. 4.4, Tit. 2.14, 3.4). The author explains the Christian view of God, human plight, and salvation largely in Pauline categories.[39]

Fifth, the author constantly supplements Pauline elements with Johannine tropes.[40] The author describes how the world hates Christians, as the Johannine Jesus predicted (*Diogn.* 5.17, 6.5 = Jn. 15.18–19, 25, 1 Jn. 3.13); Christians are in the world but don't belong in the world (*Diogn.* 6.3 = Jn. 15.19); God sent Jesus to show his love to the world, not to condemn the world (*Diogn.* 7.4–6 = Jn. 3.17); the inscrutability of God has a Johannine ring (*Diogn.* 8.5 = Jn. 1.18); then there is a Johannine bulge with the description that "God loved humanity" and "sent them his only-begotten son" as evidence that God "so loved you first" (*Diogn.* 10.2-3 = Jn. 3.16; 1 Jn. 4.19). The author has married the Johannine view of the Logos, divine love, and the cosmos with the Pauline narrative of the corruption of the flesh, the condemnation of humanity, and justification through faith in Christ.

Sixth, the homilies intensify the merging of Pauline and Johannine motifs, interweaving them with Old Testament allusions, and capping off with burgeoning ecclesial interpretative traditions.

The author, like the post-apostolic "elders," Polycarp, and Quadratus, is identified as a "disciple of the apostles" who ministers and hands down traditions to "disciples of truth" (*Diogn.* 11.1 = *traditions of the elders*, 2; Papias *frag.* 2; Jerome, *Vir. Ill.* 19; Irenaeus, *Adv. Haer.* 3.3.4; 4.32.1). Furthermore, he appears as Paul *redivvus* when describing himself as a "teacher of the Gentiles" (*Diogn.* 11.1 = 1 Tim. 2.7), learned in the "mysteries of the Father" (*Diogn.* 11.2 = 1 Cor. 2.7; 4.1; Eph 1.9; 3.3–9; 6.19; Col. 1.26-7), and heralds a message

---

[39] Bird, "Reception of Paul," 87–8.
[40] See Brändle, *Die Ethik der "Schrift an Diognet*," 217–21; Charles E. Hill, *Johannine Corpus in the Early Church* (Oxford: Oxford University Press, 2006), 361–6; Jefford, *Diognetus*, 73–7.

that like Paul is both "preached" and "believed" (*Diogn.* 11.3 = 1 Tim. 3.16). Then, like a piece of the Johannine prologue falling out of the sky, is a short narration about the pre-existent "Word" appearing in the world with all its grace (*Diogn.* 11.3–5 = Jn. 1.1–14; 1 Jn. 1–3 1.1). Interweaved with it is an Irenaean-like statement of the *regula fidei* ("rule of faith") that marks the various epochs of redemptive-history: "The fear of the Law is sung and the grace of the Prophets is known and the faith of the Gospels is established and the tradition of the apostles is guarded and the grace of the church exults" (*Diogn.* 11.6, trans. R. Brannan).[41]

Most of *Diogn.* 12 can be considered an allegorical exposition of the "tree of knowledge" and "tree of life" in Genesis 2–3, where the author underscores the symbiotic nature of "knowledge" and "life." In the one explicit citation from Paul, the author then warns that "knowledge puffs up, but love builds up" (*Diogn.* 12.5 = 1 Cor. 8.1). Thereafter, the contrast of Eve's corruptibility and the Virgin's fidelity reflects second-century interpretive schemes found in Justin (*Dial.* 100), Irenaeus (*Adv. Haer.* 3.22.4), and Tertullian (*de Carn. Christi* 17). Another Irenaean-like summary of the *regula fidei* closes off the homilies where the Old Testament "Passover of the Lord" (*Diogn.* 12.9) stands as a metonym for God's saving acts for and through his people.

As to where *Diogn.* precisely fits into early Christianity, several observations can be offered.

First, there are natural connections between *Diogn.* and Alexandrian Christianity.[42] The use of philosophy and rhetoric antici-pates writers like Clement of Alexandria, especially his *Protrepticus*. The Logos christology fits firmly between the Alexandrian first-century Jewish philosopher Philo and the third-century Christian theologian Origen. The dispensing of Judaism has analogies with the *Epistle of Barnabas* (c. 130 CE).

Second, *Diogn.* has much in common with the second-century apologists, notably Aristides, Justin Martyr, Theophilus of Antioch, Tatian, and Clement of Alexandria. On the species of apologetics that *Diogn.* employs, it is best considered as a type of "To the Greeks" argument mixing public exhortation with anti-pagan polemics.[43]

---

[41] Mention of the "gospels" (*euangelia*) in the plural could be one of the earliest references to the written gospels as a collection of multiple books.

[42] Lona, *Diognet*, 67–9; Holmes, *Apostolic Fathers*, 687.

[43] Markus N.A. Bockmuehl, *Jewish Law in Gentile Churches: Halakah and the Beginning of Christian Public Ethics* (Grand Rapids, MI: Baker, 2003), 196.

Third, the critique of Judaism in *Diogn.* 3–4 reflects the growing tradition of anti-Jewish rhetoric found in the letters of Ignatius, the *Epistle of Barnabas*, Melito of Sardis, and Justin Martyr. Strangely, in *Diogn.* there is no critique of Jewish unbelief in Jesus as Messiah, or any contest over who are the true heirs of Israel's religious heritage. The author trades mostly in stereotypical pagan denunciation of Jews (e.g., Tacitus, *Hist.* 5.5; Cicero, *Pro Flacco* 28.67). Judaism offers no preparation for Christianity, since Christianity is a "mystery" without antecedent (4.6; 5.3; 7.1). The author affirms God's election of the Jews and that they are beloved by God (4.4). He commends the Jews for not worshipping idols and for affirming one God as creator and master. Yet he regards the Jerusalem cultus with its sacrifices as essentially the same as pagan sacrificial worship (3.2–3).[44] Jewish sacrificial worship is defunct because of divine self-sufficiency: God simply does not need it (3.4–5). There is also a rejection of Jewish "superstition" epitomized by Sabbath observance, the allegedly arbitrary festivals, refusing to eat things that God has made for human consumption, prohibition of doing good on the Sabbath, taking pride in circumcision – "the mutilation of the flesh" – as a sign of election, and considering Christians as "foreigners." Such things are considered not a mark of piety, but of foolishness and folly (4.1–5; 5.17). This rehearses the Pauline rejection of Jewish "boundary markers" as a sign of election.[45] The difference is that the author has taken the Roman cavil of Christianity as a *superstitio* (Tacitus, *Ann.* 15.44; Suetonius, *Ner.* 16.2; Plin. *Ep.* 10.96) and deflected it back on to the Jews. In sum, the author rejects Jewish sacrifices, superstitions, and separation, because he strives to differentiate Christianity from Judaism. This argumentative maneuver would be expedient if one were commending Christianity to pagan intellectuals after the Jewish uprisings in Cyprus and Cyrenaica (115–117 CE) and the Bar Kochba revolt (132–135 CE) in a place like mid-to-late second-century Alexandria.[46]

---

[44] This rehearses Jewish and Christian critiques of the Jerusalem cultus, such as "I desire mercy, not sacrifice" (Hos. 6.6; cf. Mt. 9.13; 12.7), "the Most High does not live in houses made by human hands" (Acts 7.48), and an apocryphal saying attributed to Jesus by the Ebionites, "I have come to destroy the sacrifices. And if you do not stop making sacrifice, God's wrath will not stop afflicting you" (*Gos. Eb.* § 7 [trans. B. Ehrman]).

[45] See Bockmuehel, *Jewish Law*, 217 n. 134; Thomas, *Paul's "Works of the Law,"* 122–4.

[46] Tobias Nicklas, "*Epistula ad Diognetum* (Diognetus): The Christian 'New Genos' and its Construction of the Others," in *Sensitivity towards Outsiders: Exploring the Dynamic Relationship between Mission and Ethics in the New Testament and Early*

Fourth, an intriguing question is how *Diogn.* can be related to the "heretic" Marcion and the various Gnostic movements of the mid-second century. Christian J.B. Bunsen proposed that *Diogn.* was written by Marcion to Marcus Aurelius' tutor Fronto in 135 CE, just prior to Marcion's break with the Roman church. He alleges that, "There is nothing in the Epistle to Diognetus which might not have been written by Marcion; but there is much in it which, as far as history goes, nobody could have written except young Marcion, or his unknown foster-brother in soul."[47] While the acute Hellenism, intense Paulinism, and critique of Judaism are certainly conducive toward a Marcionite trajectory, ultimately *Diogn.* cannot be correlated with Marcion's theological project or with broadly Gnostic sympathies. *Diogn.* has no demiurgal creationism. In fact, the author expresses utter derision for intermediary figures such as a "subordinate," "angel," "ruler," and "elements," who are inferior to the Logos (7.2–3; 8.2); from which we may infer a disinclination toward the aeons and archons of Gnostic cosmologies. Similarly, there is no separation of the God of creation from the God of redemption (*Diogn.* 7.2–5; 8.7–11; 10.2). Throughout *Diogn.* the God of the Jews (3.2) is the Christian God of love, who sent his beloved child, a lover of humanity no less (8.7–8, 11, 9.2, 10.2–3), a totally unacceptable proposition to any Marcionite. Plus, there is a positive if minimal use of the Old Testament and the creedal-like statements in the homilies with law, prophets, and "gospels" are as un-Marcionite as one can be (11.6; 12.9). Against Bunsen we'd aver that almost anyone except Marcion could have written *Diogn.*[48]

When it comes to the place that *Diogn.* occupies in early Christianity, taking our cue from Jefford, we'd maintain that *Diognetus* largely reflects what early Christianity had already become by the end of the second century, namely, a Gentile religious movement whose Jewish Christian roots had been cultivated in an environment of Greek philosophy and scriptural exegesis. This yielded a loose network of house churches whose most pressing concerns were continued evangelization, advocacy of a particular ethical lifestyle for its members,

---

Christianity, ed. J. Kok, T. Nicklas, D. T. Roth, and C. M. Hays, WUNT 2.364 (Tübingen: Mohr/Siebeck, 2014), 501–2.

[47] Christian J.B. Bunsen, *Christianity and Mankind, Their Beginnings and Prospects*, 7 vols. (London: Longman, Brown, Green, and Longmans, 1854), 1.170–2; cf. Charles Merritt Nielsen, "The Epistle to Diognetus: Its Date and Relationship to Marcion," *ATR* 52 (1970): 77–91.

[48] Radford, *Diognetus*, 22–5; Meecham, *Diognetus*, 16; Brändle, *Ethik der "Scrift an Diognet*," 62–3; Bird, "Reception of Paul," 88–90.

self-definition by self-differentiation from Judaism and paganism, and making tacit apologetic toward imperial authorities to secure the right to exist in the Greco-Roman polis.[49]

16.5 THEOLOGY

(1) *God*. The author explicitly answers the question as to "what God" Christians trust in and worship (*Diogn.* 1.1). There is a clear embrace of Jewish aniconic monotheism with a rejection of the worship of idols and the elements (2.1–10; 8.2), a careful distinction between God and creation (3.2–5; 7.2, 7; 10.2, 7), affirmation of God's oneness, uniqueness, aseity omnipotence, invisibility, perfections, immortality, and majesty (3.2, 5; 7.2; 8.8; 9.2; 10.5), belief in divine providence, foreordination, election, and calling (4.4–5; 6.10; 7.2, 5; 9.1). God's abode is in the heavens (10.7) and God's deeds are principally creation (3.2, 4; 4.2, 4; 7.2; 8.7; 10.2; 12.3), revelation (8.6, 11; 9.6), and salvation (8.9; 9.6; 12.9).

In terms of character, God is not a tyrant ruling by terror; to the contrary, he is gentle and meek (7.3–5; 10.5), also tender-hearted, patient, kind, good, and merciful (8.7–8; 9.2), a lover of humanity (10.2–4). In an elegant list of descriptors God is considered "nourisher, Father, teacher, counselor, healer, mind, light, honor, glory, strength, life" (*Diogn.* 9.6, trans. R. Brannan). The contribution of the homilies to the document's theology is God as "Father" and sender of the "Word" who desires humanity to cultivate true knowledge (11.2; 12.8). The primary characteristics of God in *Diogn.* are benevolence, patience, and love. While *Diogn.* mentions the "Father" and "Son" there is no mention of the Holy Spirit. The document is distinctly binitarian not trinitarian.

(2) *Christology*. The document has no mention of "Jesus" or "Christ" and focuses instead largely on God's "Son" (*huios*) and "child" (*pais*). While *pais* is never used for Jesus in the New Testament, it is perhaps incorporated from Isa. 52.12 (LXX), and a similar switch between *huios* and *pais* occurs in the Didache (*Did.* 7.1, 3 [*huios*] and 9.2–3, 10.2–3 [*pais*]). The filial aspect is stressed with reference to the "beloved child" (*Diogn.* 8.11), "Son of God" (9.4), and the

---

[49] Jefford, *Diognetus*, 98.

"only-begotten Son" (10.2 [trans. J. Lightfoot]). Other titles include "King" (7.4), "Judge" (7.6), "Lord" (7.7), and "Saviour" (9.6).

The son/child sent to earth is certainly a divine agent, but this is not a subordinationist christology.[50] For a start, the son/child is explicitly differentiated from any subordinate and intermediary powers (7.2). In addition, the "omnipotent Creator" sent the "Designer and Creator of the universe" to be a benevolent ruler over humans, which entails that the son/child stands on the creator side of the creator–creature divide. Moreover, the son/child is described as being sent by a king who has a son "who is a king," by God "as God," and "as a human to humans." This is as a clear statement of the son/child as "truly human and truly divine" and being "consubstantial with the Father's divine nature and consubstantial with our human nature" as one can imagine prior to Nicaea and Chalcedon (7.2, 4).

The homilies replicate many of these themes with its account of the pre-existent "Son" as the "Word" and "Eternal One," who reveals God, who instructs and infuses grace among the saints (11.2–5, 7; 12.9). On the whole, the christology in *Diogn.* is more elaborate than Justin, less sophisticated than Origen.[51]

(3) *Salvation.* For the author, salvation is God's "great and marvelous plan" communicated to God's child and executed through this child, somewhat akin to Reformed theologies of a *pactum salutis* between Father and Son (8.9–9.1). In all things, God is motivated by love and mercy (9.2; 10.1), salvation expresses his goodness and operates in his power (9.2, 6), with the apparent delay of salvation due to God's patience with human iniquity and ignorance (8.7; 9.1). When put in christological coordinates, salvation means sharing in the Son's "benefits" (8.11). This salvation can be abbreviated as the "kingdom" (9.1; 10.2), the "present season of righteousness" (9.1), the "mysteries of God" (10.7), and in the homilies as "grace" and the "Passover of the Lord" (11.5–7; 12.9).

Put negatively, salvation is from the "former season of unrighteousness" (9.1), where people become like idols (2.5), were enslaved to false gods (2.10), were characterized by undisciplined impulses and lust (9.1), powerless to help themselves (9.1, 6), mired in unrighteousness, lawlessness, guilt, injustice, godlessness, and corruption (9.2–5), and worthy of

---

[50] Contra Meecham, *Diognetus*, 26–7.
[51] Radford, *Diognetus*, 19–20.

judgment, punishment, and death, the real death, which is eternal fire (7.6; 9.2; 10.7). Put positively, salvation is expressed in several images, including an initiation into the mystery of Christian piety (4.6; 7.1), joining the Christian *genos* (5.1–17), entering the "kingdom" (9.1; 10.2), and being transformed in love for God and love for others (10.3–8). Salvation means one attains "life" (9.6) and "life in heaven" (10.7), as well as "knowledge" through faith (8.1, 6, 11; 10.3).

Salvation is very much at the divine initiative by God sending his Son, who comes with persuasion not compulsion, by calling rather than persecuting (7.2–5). Salvation is also by faith alone (8.6; 9.6; 10.1) and in the Son alone (9.4). *Diogn.* 9.2–5 provides one of the most penetrating descriptions of atonement and justification in all of patristic literature:[52]

> He himself gave up his own Son as a ransom for us, the holy for the lawless, the innocent for the wicked, the righteous for the unrighteous, the incorruptible for the corruptible, the immortal for the mortal. For what else but his righteousness could have covered our sins? In whom else was it possible for us, the lawless and ungodly, to be justified, except in the Son of God alone? O the sweet exchange, O the inscrutable work of God, O the unexpected blessings, in order that the lawlessness of many should be hidden in one righteous person, while the righteousness of one should justify many lawless ones. (trans. M. Bird)

The view of the atonement is certainly not "moral influence theory" and undoubtedly a "ransom" view of some variety.[53] Beyond that, the atonement is evidently substitutionary with the Son dying "for" sinners, not in the bland sense of merely benefiting them by his death, but specifically through an "exchange" (*anatallagē*) with the Son dying in place of others. If this substitutionary death is correlated with divine judgment against wickedness spoken about elsewhere in the letter, then the atonement also has an implicit penal aspect too (7.6; 9.2; 10.7). That said, the author's emphasis is on the effects of the atonement, not its mechanism.[54]

A looming question is whether the justification spoken about is strictly forensic or encompasses a broader suite of saving images.

---

[52] See Brandon D. Crowe, "Oh Sweet Exchange! The Soteriological Significance of the Incarnation in the *Epistle to Diognetus*," *ZNW* 102 (2011): 96–109.

[53] Meecham, *Diognetus*, 24; Jefford, *Diognetus*, 32.

[54] Radford, *Diognetus*, 40.

Brian Arnold has argued that *Diogn.* "presents a forensic view of justification that is rooted in grace and stems from substitutionary atonement" and "Sin was imputed to Christ via his substitutionary atonement and his righteousness was imputed to sinners for their justification."[55] We'd aver that there is certainly a forensic aspect since the Son's righteousness covers over lawlessness, it reverses one's status from wickedness to innocence, because a person's lawlessness is hidden in the righteous one and the Son's righteousness in turn justifies the lawless. However, there is no deployment of Pauline language for "counting/reckoning" (*logizomai*) of righteousness, no reference to union with Christ, and no mention of Christ's representative obedience.[56] Imputed righteousness at best is a possible corollary of the text, not part of its content. Plus, righteousness/justification language stands as the reversal, not only of guilt (*akakos*), lawlessness (*anomos*), and unrighteousness (*adikos*), but also of godlessness (*asebēs*), corruption (*phthartos*), and mortality (*thnētos*). In addition, "justification" (*dikaioō*) has its conceptual analogue in "be made worthy" (*axioō*) in 9.1 where the author contrasts human deeds, which render a person as "unworthy of life" with God's goodness and power, which render a person as "worthy" to enter the kingdom of God. While justification necessitates a forensic change in status from lawless to righteous, so too is a change implied in moral state from godlessness to being worthy of life, and from corruption to a fitness to receive immortality. Thus, justification/righteousness in *Diogn.* 9.2–5 functions – much like *dikaioō* does for Paul in Rom. 8.30 – as a metonym for God's redeeming and rectifying action in the Son.

In the homilies, salvation is due to God sending the "Word," (11.2–3), Mary's fidelity over Eve's disobedience (12.8), and the effects of "grace" in the church (11.5). This grace is reserved for "those who seek" (11.5), who love God "as they should" (12.1), and who have gained knowledge and seek life (12.6). Grace might even be a circumlocution for the Holy Spirit since grace rejoices over the faithful and should not be grieved (11.5, 7). The results of salvation are "understanding" and "knowledge" (11.5; 12.4–7). The saved are considered a "paradise of delight" in the sense of being spiritually fruitful (12.1).

---

[55] Brian J. Arnold, *Justification in the Second Century* (Waco, TX: Baylor University Press, 2018), 78, 101.
[56] Meecham, *Diognetus*, 25; Bird, "Reception of Paul," 87.

(4) *Church*. In *Diogn.* there is no attention given to church offices, ordination, or spiritual gifts, yet there is a rich account of the church.

Christians are "aliens" and "strangers" in their homelands, citizens of their own cities, but also citizens of heaven, making them mediators between two realms (5.5, 9). They dwell in the world, yet are not of the world (6.3). Christians are to the world as a soul is to a body, dispersed throughout it, and preserve it (6.1, 7). In addition, Christians are outwardly the same as others, but always different too, and their difference is always benevolent and virtuous (5.5–17). They love all people (5.11; 6.5–6) even as they are accused of misanthropy, hatred of the human race (cf. Tacitus, *Ann.* 15.44). They do not seek to lord it over others (10.5), but to become a god – in the sense of benefaction and beneficence – to their neighbors (10.6). "Theirs is," comments Bockmuehl, "a discriminating presence in the world, refusing its social orders any ultimate allegiance while contributing constructively to human welfare within them."[57] In addition, while they are persecuted, they persevere, and multiply (6.9; 7.8). Despite adversity they remain "unconquered" (7.7) and their survival is so miraculous that they are the proofs of God's presence (7.9). According to Benjamin Bunning, the author considers Christians to be exemplary exiles who outstrip Romans in their ability to meet Roman norms. But this is not a "serenely assimilationist" posture, rather, the author's stance is "an agonistic one, appealing to Roman ethical and cultural ideals as a platform upon which to valorize Christian alien identity and thus oppose its relegation to a site of reproach among the hierarchies of status and power that structure Roman society."[58]

The reference to Christians as a "new type of people" (1.1, *kainon genos*) and "another tribe" (5.17, *allaphyloi*) requires some context. Paul referred to Israel as a distinct *genos* (i.e., common lineage, ancestry, clan, people, family, etc., Phil. 3.5), yet he elsewhere implied that Messiah-devotees were a new *genos* since he divided people into the tripartite categories of Jews, Greeks, and the "church of God" (1 Cor. 1.22–5; 10.32). Paul reinterpreted the Jewish division of the world's inhabitants as either "Greek" or "Jew" in such a way as to create a third entity of the *ekklesia*, who are themselves comprised of Jews,

---

[57] Bockmuehl, *Jewish Law*, 218–19.
[58] Benjamin H. Dunning, *Aliens and Sojourners: Self as Other in Early Christianity* (Philadelphia, PA: University of Pennsylvania Press, 2009), 66.

Greeks, and Barbarians, yet are chiefly defined by a communal meta-identity of being "in Messiah" (Gal. 3.28; Col. 3.11; Rom. 10.12) even while they share in Israel's election (Gal. 3.29; Rom. 9.24–5). Paul's *ekklēsia* then are diverse with respect to ethnicity and social status, but nonetheless united in worship of the one God of Israel, co-sharers in Israel's Messiah, and partakers of the one Holy Spirit.[59]

The demarcation of Messiah-devotees as neither Jews nor Gentiles had momentous repercussions for the construction of Christian identity as a third entity over the next three centuries.[60] For instance, in 1 Peter, "Christians" are described as a "chosen *genos*, a royal priesthood, a holy nation, God's special possession" (1 Pet. 2.9; cf. *Mart. Pol.* 3.2; 14.1; 17.1; Justin, *Dial.* 119.2–4; 120.2; 121.3; 130.3; 135.3, 6; 138.2; Origen, *Hom. Ps.* 36; Eusebius, *Hist. Eccl.* 4.26.5). The categorization of Christians as a *genos*, a new *genos* no less, was taken up in the apocryphal *Kerygma Petri* (c. 100–150 CE), where it was said that Christians do not worship as the Greeks do nor as the Jews do, "but we Christians worship him in a new way as a third *genos*" (Clement, *Strom.* 6.41.6–7). Similar is Aristides' *Apology* (c. 125 CE), where the Greek version refers to three classes people, those who worship so-called gods (i.e., Chaldeans, Egyptians, and Greeks), Jews, and Christians; while the Syriac and Armenian refers to four classes of people, with barbar-

---

[59] See N.T. Wright, *Paul and the Faithfulness of God*, COQG 4 (London: SPCK, 2013), 1443–9; Love L. Sechrest, *A Former Jew: Paul and the Dialectics of Race*, LNTS 410 (London: T&T Clark, 2009), 164, 210; Michael F. Bird, *An Anomalous Jew: Paul among Jews, Greeks, and Romans* (Grand Rapids, MI: Eerdmans, 2016), 17–19, 51–5.

[60] See, e.g., Christine Mohrmann, "'Tertium Genus': Les relations Judaïsme, Antiquité, Christianisme reflétées dans la langue des Chrétiens," in *Études sur le latin des Chrétiens IV*, Storia e letteratura 143 (Rome: Edizioni di Storia e Letteratura, 1977), 195–210; Katharina Schneider, "Die Stellung der Juden und Christen in der Welt nach dem Diognetbrief," *JAC* 42 (1999): 20–41; Judith Lieu, *Neither Jew nor Greek? Constructing Early Christianity* (London: T&T Clark, 2002), 171–89; Lieu, "Identity Games in Early Christian Texts: The *Letter to Diognetus*," in *Ethnicity, Race, Religion: Identities and Ideologies in Early Jewish and Christian Texts, and in Modern Biblical Interpretation*, ed. K.M. Hockey and D.G. Horrell (London: Bloomsbury, 2018), 59–72; Denise Kimber Buell, *Why This New Race? Ethnic Reasoning in Early Christianity* (New York: Columbia University Press, 2005); Richard Valantasis, "The Question of Christian Identity in the Early Period: Three Strategies Exploring a Third Genos," in *The Feminist Companion to the New Testament Apocrypha*, ed. Amy-Jill Levine and M.M. Robins (Cleveland, OH: Pilgrim, 2006), 60–76; Dunning, *Aliens and Sojourners*, 67–77; Erich S. Gruen, "Christians as a 'Third Race': Is Ethnicity at Issue?," in *Christianity in the Second Century: Themes and Developments*, ed. J.C. Paget and J. Lieu (Cambridge: Cambridge University Press, 2017), 235–49.

ians, Greeks, Jews, and Christians (*Apol.* 2.2 [Greek] and 15 [Syriac]). In the late second or early third century, Tertullian puts "third people" (*tertium genus*) on the lips of pagan persecutors as an opprobrium toward Christians, "Death to the third people!" and his warning "Take care, however, lest those whom you call the third people should obtain the first rank" (*Scorp.* 10.10; cf. *Ad Nat.* 1.8). Later, Ps-Cyprian's *De Pascha* (c. 242–243 CE) bluntly states, "We Christians are the third people."[61]

The context of second-century identity construction explains why the author considers Christians to be a new *genos*, a new ancestral-group, even while alleging that they do not share ancestry or what we'd call nowadays ethnicity. So, whereas Suetonius accused Christians of being "a class of people given to a new and mischievous superstition" (*Ner.* 16.2, *genus hominum superstitionis novae et malefiacae*), *Diogn.* would reply, "New class of people? Yes! A superstition? No!" In his elaboration of Christian newness, the author stakes the particularity and superiority of Christians based on lionizing their differences and religionizing their identity. Christians are distinct from Jews and Greeks in ethos, while their identity transcends tribe, family, and people group. This is because their citizenship, their sense of belonging, is heavenly rather than civic, or as Judith Lieu calls it, "transfigured citizenship."[62] Christian identity is not a matter of dress, dwelling, diet, or dialect, but about *theosebēs* ("godliness") and *epitēduema* ("manner/ habit of living"), or, worship and way of life. Their identity is religiously salient while culturally hybrid. Christians possess a "mystery" rather than antiquity, a common piety rather than a shared *polis*, heaven rather than homeland, and ethics that transcend ethnicity. Christians might not be Greek, Roman, or Jewish as far as custom and worship goes, but they are neither seditious nor a superstition, rather, they comprise a new kind of human being defined chiefly by a new kind of worship. They are the new humanity for whom the world was made (*Diogn.* 10.2; cf. 4 Ezra 6.55; 7.11; *As. Mos.* 1.12; 2 *Bar.* 15.7; *Herm. Vis.* 8.1; *Gos. Thom.* 12; Justin, 2 *Apol.* 7; Origen, *C. Cels.* 4.23).

(5) *Eschatology. Diogn.* knows of three ages: first, a season of unrighteousness, which came to came to an end with the advent of the Son; second, a present season of righteousness when the Son revealed

---

[61] Cited from Sechrest, *A Former Jew*, 14.
[62] Lieu, "Identity Games," 71.

salvation and imparted knowledge of God (8.1, 11–9.2); and third, the future time of the "kingdom" (9.1; 10.2). In the future, there is also a future judgment with the Son as the appointed judge (7.6; 10.7). The entire epoch of hidden salvation, revelation, and judgment is the outworking of God's "marvellous plan" as communicated to the Son (8.9; 9.1).

16.6 FRAGMENT OF QUADRATUS

The fragment of Quadratus preserved in Eusebius reads: "But the works of our Saviour were always present, for they were true; those who were cured, those who rose from the dead, who not merely appeared as cured and risen, but were constantly present, not only while the Saviour was living, but even for some time after he had gone, so that some of them survived even till our own time" (*Hist. eccl.* 4.3.1–2). Eusebius included the fragment in his history because of its antiquity and proximity to Jesus' ministry. Eusebius also judged the apology to illustrate Quadratus' intellect and apostolic orthodoxy.

The fragment implies that some recipients of Jesus' healing ministry lived until Quadratus' own lifetime. Eusebius' *Chronicle* (preserved in Jerome's translation) also locates Quadratus in the immediate post-apostolic generation, calling him a disciple of the apostles. If Quadratus wrote during Hadrian's reign (117–138 CE), he could have met eyewitnesses of Jesus in his youth and written his apology as an old man in the first half of the second century.

Concerning authorship, historians face the problem that Eusebius' *Church History* mentions four Quadrati, who are variously taken to refer to one, two, or three different persons. In addition to the Quadratus fragment, Eusebius describes a certain Quadratus who was a prophet and successor to the apostles' evangelistic ministry, whose writing was extant in Eusebius' time (*Hist. eccl.* 3.37.1–4; 5.17.2). We may reasonably assume that this Quadratus is Quadratus the apologist, as both followed after the apostles and both left writings, and that Eusebius placed the description of the work alongside Hadrian's accession. Eusebius elsewhere describes Quadratus the bishop of Athens (*Hist. Eccl.* 4.23), whom Jerome conflates with the apologist (*Vir. Ill.* 19), though Eusebius gives no indication about when the bishop ministered. We think it unlikely that the bishop and apologist are the same person since Eusebius' *Chronicle* sought to record bishops, yet Eusebius does not mention that the apologist held a bishopric (Jer. *Chron.*

2.2140ab).[63] Thus, it is probable that Quadratus the apologist is also the prophet, but not the bishop.

There seems no reason to doubt the dedication to the emperor Hadrian, placing its date between 117 and 138 CE. Eusebius indicates more specific dates, which are unfortunately contradictory. If the *Church History* preserves a strict chronological sequence, then Quadratus' *apology* was written between 117 and 120 CE, as Eusebius mentions it immediately after Hadrian's accession. However, Jerome's translation of Eusebius' *Chronicle* alleges that Quadratus presented the apology to Hadrian when the latter was initiated into mysteries at Athens in 124/125 CE. In truth, both dates may be unreliable. The *Apology* may be grouped with Hadrian's accession topically rather than chronologically. Furthermore, Mosshammer writes that Jerome's struggle to discern in what order Eusebius' historical notices should be read means that events may be misplaced by up to three years.[64] For instance, the *Chronicle* narrates Quadratus' apology before a letter Hadrian wrote in 122/123.[65] It seems that the most precise we can be is to say that Quadratus wrote around the first decade of Hadrian's reign, and possibly in Athens.

Theologically, the fragment calls Jesus "our saviour" and emphasizes the efficacy of his healings. Quadratus' main concern is to defend the veracity and permanence of Jesus' miracles. Those whom Jesus healed and raised from the dead remained so, even after Jesus' death; their health and testimony endured. Quadratus seems to be responding to charges that Jesus' miracles were illusive, perhaps due to sorcery or magic. Justin Martyr addressed the allegation that Jesus worked miracles through magic arts (*1 Apol.* 30.1–4). He argues that Jesus' miracles were genuine since the prophets predicted them, and he invites the emperor to verify Christian claims to exorcise demons (*1 Apol.* 30.1–31.8; *2 Apol.* 5.5–6). In the late second century, the anti-Christian philosopher Celsus also claimed that Jesus did miracles by sorcery and that his disciples fabricated accounts of Jesus' miraculous powers (Origen, *Contr. Cels.* 1.6, 28, 68, 71; 2.13, 48; 8.45). This may be why Quadratus emphasizes the permanence of Jesus' miraculous powers and the ongoing testimony of supplicants as witnesses to his work, since

---

[63] Ehrman (*Apostolic Fathers*, 2.89) and Holmes (*Apostolic Fathers*, 691) also reject the identification of the apologist with the bishop.

[64] Alden A. Mosshammer, *The Chronicle of Eusebius and Greek Chronographic Tradition* (Cranbury, NJ: Associated University Presses, 1979), 63, 67, 81–3.

[65] Paul Foster, "The Apology of Quadratus," in *The Writings of the Apostolic Fathers*, ed. P. Foster (London: T&T Clark, 2007), 54–7; Grant, *Greek Apologists*, 34–5.

sorcerers were believed merely to trick the eyes with short-lived deceptions.

Irenaeus applies the same argument to miracle claims by heretics, arguing they produce phantasms while the apostles granted true healing (*Adv. Haer.* 2.31.2; 2.32.4). However, we think it more likely that Quadratus is responding to pagan allegations that Christian miracles were counterfeit, as it would be strange to bring an intra-Christian dispute before the emperor. Further, we reject Robert Grant's claim that Quadratus' apology was unsuccessful since later apologists did not repeat his arguments. We find Quadratus' argument replicated in Justin and Irenaeus, who apply the argument from enduring miracles to both internal and external contexts.[66]

Finally, it remains to consider the relationship between the two texts discussed in this chapter. Andriessen suggested that the fragment of Quadratus belongs in a lacuna of unknown length between *Diogn.* 7.6–7. In 7.1–6, the author describes the incarnation, waxing eloquent on how God sent the world's maker for the world's salvation. The passage mentions the Son's second advent, then breaks off, and resumes in 7.7–9 to argue that Christian martyrs' fortitude testifies to God's presence among them. Andriessen asserts that a discussion and proofs of the Son's earthly ministry must have followed the narration of the incarnation. He identifies Diognetus as Hadrian, and adduces in *Diogn.* references to Hadrian's initiation into the Eleusinian mysteries and prohibition of circumcision.[67] However, Andriessen's argument is mostly conjecture. The similarities with Hadrian are circumstantial. Many second-century apologies did not mention Jesus' earthly ministry, so the author of *Diogn.* need not have done so either. Andriessen's argument requires reading 7.7–9 as discussing Christ's return rather than God's presence with the martyrs, the more natural reading of the passage. Holmes points to a lack of stylistic similarities.[68] Where Quadratus' fragment has Jesus as the grammatical subject and primary actor, *Diogn.* always describes the Father as the primary actor, with the Son as his agent. Quadratus' fragment does not fit naturally within the gap in *Diogn.*, so we need to posit a large lacuna to enable the author to transition from Jesus' incarnation and judgment to the veracity of Jesus' miracles to the martyrs' fortitude. This is possible, but there is no

---

[66] So Foster, "The Apology of Quadratus," 58–9, contra Robert M. Grant, "Quadratus," *ABD* 5.583.

[67] Andriessen, "Authorship," 129–30, 133–4.

[68] Holmes, *Apostolic Fathers*, 688.

positive evidence that tells us it was so. The argument that Quadratus' apology is the *Diogn.* is an interesting suggestion, but there is insufficient evidence for it to be anything more.

16.7 CONCLUSION

Diogn. can be viewed as a peculiar puzzle when it comes to authorship, recipient, date, and textual integrity. However, if viewed as a piece of Christian apologetic literature with a homiletic appendix, the document is a sublime testimony to a God of love, the positive place of Christians in the world, and a poignant account of Christ's incarnation and atonement. In the case of Quadratus, though very brief, it attests to belief in the miraculous works of Jesus and to tradents who were eyewitnesses to Jesus' mighty deeds.

FURTHER READING

Bird, Michael F. "The Reception of Paul in the *Epistle to Diognetus*," in *Paul in the Second Century*, ed. M.F. Bird and J.R. Dodson. LNTS 412. London: T&T Clark, 2011, 70–90.

Crowe, Brandon D. "Oh Sweet Exchange! The Soteriological Significance of the Incarnation in the Epistle to Diognetus," *ZNW* 102 (2011): 96–109.

Foster, Paul. "The Apology of Quadratus," in *The Writings of the Apostolic Fathers*, ed. P. Foster. London: T&T Clark, 2007, 52–62.

"The Epistle to Diognetus," in *The Writings of the Apostolic Fathers*, ed. P. Foster. London: T&T Clark, 2007, 147–56.

Grant, Robert M. "Quadratus," in *Anchor Bible Dictionary*, ed. D.N. Freedman. ABRL. 6 vols. New York: Doubleday, 1992, 5.582–3.

Hill, Charles E. *From the Lost Teaching of Polycarp: Identifying Irenaeus' Apostolic Presbyter and the Author of Ad Diognetum*. WUNT 186. Tübingen: Mohr/Siebeck, 2006.

Jefford, Clayton N. *The Epistle to Diognetus (with the Fragment of Quadratus): Introduction, Text, and Commentary*. OAF. Oxford: Oxford University Press, 2013.

Meecham, Henry G. *The Epistle to Diognetus*. Manchester: Manchester University Press, 1949.

Young, Frances. "Greek Apologists of the Second Century," in *Apologetics in the Roman Empire: Pagans Jews and Christians*, ed. M. Edwards, M. Goodman, and S. Price. Oxford: Oxford University Press, 1999, 81–104.

17 The Fragments of Papias

STEPHEN C. CARLSON

17.1 INTRODUCTION

Papias of Hierapolis flourished in the early second century and wrote five books of *Exposition of Dominical Oracles* (*logiōn kyriakōn exēgēseōs*),[1] of which only scattered quotations from his readers survive, including Irenaeus, Eusebius, Apollinaris, and Andrew of Caesarea. Among these excerpts, we learn that Papias was commended by Irenaeus as a hearer of John and a colleague of Polycarp.[2] Eusebius mentions him too for his testimony on the origin of the Gospels of Mark and Matthew,[3] and this is the main reason why Papias holds our interest today. Yet his materialistic views about the millennial kingdom of Christ fell out of favor in the third century and ultimately led to the loss of his *magnum opus*. The largest edition of his remains to date is that of M.W. Holmes, which has twenty-eight separate "fragments" of Papias,[4] though my forthcoming edition for the Oxford Early Christian Texts series will have more than triple the number of items.

17.2 COLLECTING THE FRAGMENTS OF PAPIAS

Although Papias was missing from J.B. Cotelier's 1672 seminal edition of the Apostolic Fathers,[5] his fragments had already been collected by P. Halloix in 1633 when he published a book on the life and works of writers of the early Eastern church.[6] For Papias, Halloix printed five

---

[1] Eusebius, *Hist. eccl.* 3.39.1.
[2] Irenaeus, *Adv. Haer.* 5.33.4.
[3] Eusebius, *Hist eccl.* 3.39.15–16.
[4] Michael W. Holmes, *The Apostolic Fathers*, 3rd ed. (Grand Rapids, MI: Baker Academic, 2007).
[5] Ibid., 5.
[6] Pierre Halloix, *Illustrium ecclesiae orientalis scriptorium vitae et documenta* (Douai: Bogard, 1633), 635–49. Specifically, Halloix has treatments of Dionysius the

testimonia about his life and work from various sources and three fragments of his work, all taken from Eusebius, *Hist. eccl.* 3.39. Halloix's useful distinction between fragments and *testimonia* was abandoned by subsequent editors, so that contemporary editions do not distinguish between quotations from his work and mere mentions of Papias and his life. Every excerpt they print is a "fragment." As a result, these editions exhibit considerable heterogeneity in what they include of Papias. Sometimes the fragments are extensive quotations; sometimes they are brief paraphrases. Sometimes they are about the life of Papias; sometimes they mention his work. Some of the authors cited seem to have personal knowledge of Papias' work; others seem dependent on their predecessors. All in all, these fragments span more than a millennium of Christian literary history.

Given this diversity of material, different editions have adopted differing criteria for what to include in their collections. Some editions are maximalist in their criteria for inclusion, printing as many mentions of Papias by name they can find. The editions of E. Norelli (2005) with twenty-six fragments and M.W. Holmes (2007) with twenty-eight fragments are two recent examples of this approach.[7] Other editions of Papias are minimalist, printing only those fragments that pertain to the content and text of Papias' work. Examples of this approach are B.E. Ehrman (2003) with twelve fragments, and D.R. MacDonald (2012) with eight.[8] Owing to problems with the authenticity, reliability, and delimitation of the fragments, even these minimalist treatments of the fragments of Papias are aggressively inclusive with the material that should be included.

As in any collection of fragments, it is important to avoid misattribution. Some fragments assigned to Papias in some editions actually come from someone else, occasionally with names identical or very similar to his. For example, some editions print an excerpt on the four

Areopagite, Ignatius of Antioch, Polycarp of Smyrna, Hierotheus of Athens, Papias of Hierapolis, and Quadratus of Athens, two of which turn out to be fictitious.

[7] Enrico Norelli, *Papia di Hierapolis, Esposizione degli Oracoli del Signore: I frammenti*, Letture cristiane del primo millennio 36 (Milan: Paoline, 2005); and Holmes, *Apostlic Fathers.*

[8] Bart D. Ehrman, *The Apostolic Fathers*, LCL 24, vol. 2 (Cambridge, MA: Harvard University Press, 2003); and Dennis R. MacDonald, *Two Shipwrecked Gospels: The Logoi of Jesus and Papias's Exposition of Logia about the Lord*, ECL 8 (Atlanta, GA: Society of Biblical Literature, 2012).

women named Mary at the tomb of Jesus as one of the fragments of Papias,[9] even though Lightfoot long ago proved that it came from the medieval dictionary of the eleventh-century lexicographer, Papias of Lombardy.[10] Also misidentified is an Armenian comment on Jn. 19.39 about the fifteen kinds of aloes reported by the Geographer (i.e., the eighth-century Pseudo-Moses of Chorene) and someone with the oddly spelled name "Papēas," who was correctly identified by the original editor of the Armenian text as the fourth-century Alexandrian geographer Pappos.[11] Occasionally the misattribution lies not with the modern editor or the medieval scribe but with the ancient source. For instance, the seventh-century *Chronicon Paschale*, a chronicle of universal history from creation to its present day, records the martyrdom of Papias in Pergamum at the time of Polycarp's martyrdom (dated by the chronicle to 163 CE). Although Lightfoot demonstrated more than a century ago that the chronicle's entry stems from the chronicler's confusion between a martyr named Papylus in Eusebius, *Hist. eccl.* 4.16, and the more famous Papias,[12] it still finds life in some recent works as a supposedly reliable piece of information about his death.[13]

Problems of paraphrase and exactness of quotation are a major concern to the collectors of fragments, and Papias is no different. Sometimes it is not always clear whether a witness is quoting Papias or merely summarizing him. For example, the seventh-century Anastasius of Sinai in his commentary on the six days of creation, *Hexaemeron* 1.6.1, brings up the name of Papias among various allegorical exegetes of the creation account: "We take this opportunity to

---

[9]   Ulrich H.J. Körtner, *Papias von Hierapolis: Ein Beitrag zur Geschichte des frühen Christentums*, FRLANT 133 (Göttingen: Vandenhoeck & Ruprecht, 1983), no. 22; Reinhard N. Hübner, in Josef Kürzinger, *Papias von Hierapolis und die Evagelien des Neuen Testament*, EM 4 (Regensburg: Pustet, 1983), no. 24; and Norelli, *Papia*, no. 25.

[10] J.B. Lightfoot, "The Brethren of the Lord," in *St. Paul's Epistle to the Galatians: A Revised Text with Introduction, Notes, and Dissertations*, 2nd ed. (London: Macmillan, 1866), 265–6 n. 1, repr. in Lightfoot, *Dissertations on the Apostolic Age* (London: Macmillan, 1892), 25–6 n. 1.

[11] Évariste Prud'homme, "Extraits du livre intitulé Solutions de passages de l'Écriture sainte, écrits à la demande de Héthoum I, roi d'Arménie, par le vardapet Vardan," Extract 4, *Journal asiatique* (Paris: Impériale, 1867), 12. The Armenian fragment found its way into the editions of Erwin Preuschen, *Antilegomena: Die Reste der ausserkanonischen Evangelien und urchristlichen Ueberlieferung*, 2nd ed. (Giessen: Töpelmann, 1905), no. 20; Hübner/Kürzinger, *Papias*, no. 24; Norelli, *Papia*, no. 25; Holmes, *Apostolic Fathers*, no. 25; and Monte Allen Shanks, *Papias and the New Testament* (Eugene, OR: Pickwick, 2013), no. 25.

[12] J.B. Lightfoot, *Essays on the Work Entitled Supernatural Religion* (London: Macmillan, 1889), 148.

[13] E.g., Shanks, *Papias*, no. 16.

speak with the love of truth together with Papias the Great, the Hierapolitan, who was a pupil of the Beloved Disciple, and Clement, and Pantanetus [sic] the Alexandrian priest, and Ammonius the most wise, the exegetes of the earliest times and before the councils who considered the whole six days to be Christ and the church." How much Papias supports the proposition is unclear. What is clear, however, that the phrase is "Christ and the church" comes from "Paul's affirming tongue," as Anastasius put it, in Eph. 5.2. In other words, Anastasius expresses Papias' view in Pauline language; what Papias actually said is lost in this very general synopsis of many different exegetes. A similar problem affects a scholion of John of Scythopolis on the *Celestial Hierarchy* of Pseudo-Dionysius that "those who cultivated innocence in God were called 'boys,' as Papias shows in the first book of the *Dominical Expositions*, and Clement the Alexandrian in the *Pedagogue*."[14] Now the phrase "cultivated innocence in God" is not to be found in Clement's *Pedagogue* or anywhere in extant Greek literature, which suggests that the terminology is John's own. Moreover, it is not even clear that John has the term "boy" (*pais*) in mind for Papias, because he could have read from Eusebius, *Hist. eccl.* 2.15.2, that "Papias adds that Peter mentions Mark in his first letter," referring to 1 Pet. 5:13, where Peter uses the synonymous term "son" (*huios*) for Mark.

These examples raise another difficulty for collectors of Papias' fragments: derivation. In *Hexaemeron* 7b.5.5, Anastasius repeats his claim about the early exegetes of the creation account:

So the earliest exegetes of the churches, I mean, Philo the philosopher and contemporary of the apostles, and Papias the great, the pupil of John the evangelist, the Hierapolitan, and Irenaeus the Lugdunian, and Justin the martyr and philosopher and Pantanetus [sic] the Alexandrian, and Clement the Stromatist, and those associated with them spiritually contemplated the things concerning paradise to refer to Christ's church, among whom there are also the two Cappadocian Gregories, all-wise about everything, all of these saying for these reasons that paradise is also something spiritual.

Here Anastasius of Sinai lumps Papias in with such luminaries as Philo, Irenaeus, Justin, Clement, Pantaenus, and the two Gregories for

---

[14] See Paul Rorem and John C. Lamoreaux, *John of Scythopolis and the Dionysian Corpus: Annotating the Areopagite*, OECS (Oxford: Clarendon, 1998), 154.

allegorical exegesis of the creation account.[15] His citation of Irenaeus raises a concern because Irenaeus in *Adv. Haer.* 5.33.3 quotes Papias in support for his view of the recapitulation of creation upon Christ's return. Anastasius' knowledge of Papias as a transmitter of Christological exegesis can thus be derived from Irenaeus and as such does not provide secure, independent attestation of Papias' lost work. Indeed, many of the fragments printed in contemporary editions of Papias are derivative in nature. A good example – present in all the recent editions of the fragments except for MacDonald's – is Jerome's entry on Papias in his *Illustrious lives*, no. 18, whose information about Papias is dependent on Eusebius.[16] Although Jerome's witness is important evidence of the reception of Papias, it lacks independent value for the reconstruction of Papias' work.

Even if a fragment appears to be correctly attributed to Papias and not to someone else of a similar name and even if the information does not appear secondary, there is still the question of its reliability. One example is an old Latin prologue to John of the mid-to-late fourth century, which claims that "Papias by name, the Hierapolitan, a dear disciple of John, related in the *Exoterica*, that is, in the outermost five books, ... wrote down the gospel correctly while John was dictating it straight." This fragment is not only manifestly corrupt, mangling the title and meaning of Papias' work (it should be *Exegeseis* or something like that), but its information about Papias' role in the production of the Gospel of John is difficult to credit, possibly stemming from a misinterpretation of Irenaeus' statement that Papias was a "hearer of John" (*Against Heresies* 5.33.4). Indeed, this notice fits the fourth century better than the second. On the one hand, speculation about the amanuenses of the canonical gospels is a feature of the fourth and fifth centuries; but on the other, two earlier readers of Papias, Irenaeus and Eusebius, are silent about any involvement of Papias in writing down the Fourth Gospel, even though both had an interest in its authorship and authority.

Another case of doubtful reliability is a fragment found in a lost, early seventh-century Byzantine epitome of church history, usually attributed to the fifth-century Philip of Side, but more recently scholars have lost confidence in this attribution.[17] This epitome summarizes

---

[15] Anastasius, *Hexaemeron* 1.6.1 and 7b.5.5.

[16] Thomas P. Halton, *Saint Jerome: On Illustrious Men*, FC 100 (Washington, DC: Catholic University of America Press, 1999), 36–8.

[17] Compare Carl de Boor, *Neue Fragmente des Papias, Hegesippus und Pierius in bisher unbekannten Excerpten aus der Kirchengeschichte des Philippus Sidetes*, TU 5.2 (Leipzig: Hinrichs, 1888), 167–84, with Bernard Pouderon, "Les Fragments anonymes

what Eusebius conveys about Papias (*Hist. eccl.* 3.39), adding details of questionable reliability. For example, at the end of its treatment of Papias, one manuscript of the epitome adds the sentence fragment that "about those raised by Christ from the dead, that they lived until Hadrian." This note had been used to date Papias to the reign of Hadrian (117–138 CE), but it is more likely that there is a lacuna in the original editor's manuscript at this point and that the note actually pertains to Quadratus' apology (*Hist. eccl.* 4.3.2). As another example, the Byzantine epitome inserts this statement in the midst of its treatment of Papias: "Papias in the second volume says that John the theologian and James his brother were killed by Jews." As a fragment of Papias, the specificity of the reference is encouraging but the content is not. The term "theologian" is a late antique appellation for the apostle John, showing that at least some part of the quotation belongs to a later period than Papias. Nothing is otherwise known about John's martyrdom at the hands of the Jews from earlier writers, not even from those who have seen Papias' work. Furthermore, the epitome itself misrepresents its Eusebian source text in several places (e.g., misnaming the Ethiopian eunuch baptized by Philip as "Candace"). Papias could well have said something in his second book, but the epitome is too unreliable to know exactly what.

After the various testimonies to the text and content and Papias' work have been examined for their authenticity, independence, and reliability, only a handful of independent witnesses provide us with useful fragments about Papias' work: Irenaeus, Eusebius, Apollinaris of Laodicea, and Andrew of Caesarea. As we will see among the following fragments, the student of Papias must still contend with issues of delimitation – where the quotations start and finish. These results may seem minimalist, but they constitute a solid foundation for any study of Papias' life, thought, and work.

17.3 PAPIAS ON ESCHATOLOGICAL FERTILITY AND A DIALOGUE WITH JUDAS IN IRENAEUS OF LYONS

The earliest person to mention Papias by name is the late second-century Biblical theologian Irenaeus of Lyons, who wrote a massive

---

du Barocc. Gr. 142 et les notices consacrées à Jean Diacrinoménos, Basile de Cilicie et l'anonyme d'Héraclée," *Revue des Études Byzantines* 55 (1997): 169–92, and Pierre Nautin, "La continuation de l'«Histoire ecclésiastique» d'Eusèbe par Gélase de Césarée," *Revue des Études Byzantines* 50 (1992): 163–83.

refutation, popularly called *Against Heresies*, of his mainly Valentinian opponents. At the end of his fifth and final volume, Irenaeus quotes Papias in the course of an argument that the scriptural promises about the future kingdom of Christ are true, whether they come from the Father's Son Jesus in the New Testament or the Creator in the Old Testament. Irenaeus is particularly intent on showing that the two Testaments prove that, unlike the speculation of the Valentinians, the resurrection of the righteous will involve the resurrection of the entire person, both body and soul. In *Adv. Haer.* 5.33.1–2, Irenaeus argues that the promises of Jesus spoken in Mt. 26.27–9, Lk. 14.12–14, and Mt. 19.29 will be fulfilled in the times of his kingdom since they were not fulfilled in the times of his ministry. Then, in 5.33.3–4, Irenaeus turns to the promises of the Old Testament and argues that the same logic applies, specifically with blessing of Isaac upon Jacob in Gen. 27.27–9 that "God will give from the dew of heaven and from the plenty of earth an abundance of wheat and wine." Pointing that that this blessing was not bestowed upon Jacob, Irenaeus find confirmation of this Old Testament promise in the future with a saying of Jesus unattested in the New Testament:

> So the predicted blessing [of Isaac upon Jacob in Gen. 27.27–9] without contradiction refers to the times of the kingdom, when the righteous will reign upon rising from the dead <and honored by God through that resurrection>, when also creation, renewed and liberated, will produce an abundance of all kinds of foods "from the dew of heaven and the plenty of earth" (Gen. 27.28). Just as the elders who had seen John the disciple of the Lord remember hearing from him just how the Lord would teach about those times and say:
> "The days will come in which vines will germinate, each one having ten thousand shoots, and on each shoot ten thousand branches, and on each branch ten thousand twigs, and on each twig ten thousand clusters, and in each cluster ten thousand grapes, and each grape when pressed will yield twenty-five measures of wine. And when any of the saints grabs one of these clusters, another cluster will cry out: 'I am better, take me, bless the Lord through me.'"
> That likewise also a grain of wheat will produce ten thousand ears, and each ear will have ten thousand grains, and each grain will yield five double pounds of pure fine flour; and moreover other fruits and seeds and grass in accordance with the corresponding

proportion for them, and all the animals, using what they get from the earth as their food, will become calm and docile, subject to humans in all submissiveness. (cf. Isa. 11.6–9)

Now these things are also testified to in writing by Papias, a hearer of John and colleague of Polycarp, a man of old, in the fourth of his books, for there are five books composed by him. And he added,

"But these things are believable to those who believe. And when Judas," he says, "the traitor who did not believe and asked how then will such yields be accomplished by God, the Lord said, 'Those who will come to those times will see.'"

The extent of the attribution of this fragment to Papias is complicated by the fact that, strictly speaking, the fertility tradition is attributed, not to Papias by name, but to the "the elders who had seen John the disciple of the Lord." Irenaeus introduces Papias as someone passing on dialogue between Judas and Jesus only after quoting the fertility tradition. These facts raise the issue of delimitation because it is not immediately evident how far back, if at all, does the use of Papias extend. Although a few scholars reject Papias as the source of the fertility tradition as conveyed by Irenaeus,[18] most conclude that Irenaeus did find this tradition in Papias, and rightly so. Irenaeus introduces Papias' testimony with the phrase "these things are also testified to," using an anaphoric pronoun that must refer back to the fertility tradition he just presented. Moreover, the Judas dialogue itself contains several referring expressions ("these things," "such yields," and "those times") that are comprehensible in Irenaeus' cover-text only with regard to the fertility tradition. Finally, as the "hearer of John," Papias also qualifies in Irenaeus' eyes as an "elder who has seen John." Thus, there is considerable evidence in support of the conclusion that Papias' work contained the fertility tradition.[19]

---

[18] Antonio Orbe, *Teología de San Ireneo: Comentario al Libro V del "Adversus haereses,"* vol. 3, Biblioteca de autores cristianos 33 (Madrid: La editorial católica, 1988), 418; Richard Bauckham, "Intertextual Relationships of Papias' Gospel Traditions: The Case of Irenaeus, Haer. 5.33.3–4," in *Intertextuality in the Second Century*, ed. D. Jeffrey Bingham and Clayton N. Jefford, The Bible and Ancient Christianity 11 (Leiden: Brill, 2016), 37–50.

[19] Even Bauckham, "Intertextual Relationships," 39, concedes that Papias must have had a version of the fertility tradition that overlapped that of the elders in some way, though he thinks it is much shorter.

Scholars have long noted that Papias' fertility tradition shows striking parallels with earlier Jewish eschatological speculation about the age to come, and have generally concluded that the closest parallel is 2 *Bar.* 29.5.[20] There, Baruch receives a revelation of various mysteries of the end times, among which he is told that "Anointed One will begin to be revealed" (29.3) and that the land will be so productive that "the earth will give its fruits, one in ten-thousand; and one vine, there will be on it a thousand twigs, and one twig will make a thousand clusters, and one cluster will make a thousand grapes, and one grape will make a *kor* of wine" (29.5). This parallel is very close to Papias but lacks two developments in Papias: first, 2 *Baruch* does not detail the production of wheat and, second, the multiplicative factor for the viticultural productivity in 2 *Baruch* is merely one thousand, not the ten thousand of Papias. Both these developments in Papias can be traced to a paronomastic exegesis of the Hebrew text of the final clause of Gen. 27.28, "an abundance of wheat and wine," in which "abundance" (*rb*) can be read or interpreted as "ten thousand" (*rbw*).[21] Such a wordplay would have been opaque to Irenaeus with his poor knowledge of Hebrew, so the fact that Irenaeus sees Papias' fertility tradition so prominently as a fulfillment of the blessing of Isaac indicates that Irenaeus derived from Papias not only the tradition but also its exegetical application to Genesis. This fragment shows that Papias was a crucial vector for the transmission of Jewish eschatological speculation into the chiliasts of the second and third centuries.[22]

Irenaeus also furnishes us with information about the person of Papias. He identifies Papias as a "colleague of Polycarp," the long-lived bishop of Smyrna who flourished throughout the first half of the second century. Unlike Polycarp, Papias is described as a "man of old," which suggests that he was the older one of the two. Irenaeus also identifies Papias as a "hearer" or pupil of John, who for Irenaeus is the "disciple of the Lord," the evangelist, and the seer of Revelation. Modern scholarship doubts the identification of the authors of the Fourth Gospel and Revelation, as did Eusebius based on the critical acumen of Dionysius of Alexandria.[23] Yet for Irenaeus they were the one and the same John

---

[20] Summarized in Stephen C. Carlson, "Eschatological Viticulture in *1 Enoch, 2 Baruch*, and the Presbyters of Papias," *VC* 71 (2017): 37–58.

[21] The wordplay was first noticed by J. Rendel Harris, "A New Patristic Fragment," *Expositor* 5 (1895), 448–55, at 449.

[22] See generally, Charles E. Hill, *Regnum Caelorum: Patterns of Millennial Thought in Early Christianity*, 2nd ed. (Grand Rapids, MI: Eerdmans, 2001).

[23] *Eccl. hist.* 3.39.2–6, 7.25.

who, according to *Adv. Haer.* 2.22.5, taught in Asia until the times of
Trajan (reigned 98–117 CE). These notices combine to suggest that
Papias was instructed by his elders in the last decade or so of the first
century and then flourished in the first decades of the second century.
As it turns out, there is no other reliable notice contradicting this
admittedly imprecise dating for Papias.

The last part of Irenaeus' witness to Papias is an otherwise
unattested dialogue between Jesus and Judas about the future kingdom.[24] Given Papias' characterization of Judas, it is clear that he would
have considered Judas as not being able to make it to those times to see
the bountiful fertility of "those times." According to Irenaeus, this
fragment on Judas comes from the fourth of his five books. As it
happens, this is not the only extant reference to Judas in this book.

17.4 PAPIAS ON THE EXAMPLE OF JUDAS IN APOLLINARIS OF LAODICEA

Another mention of Judas in the extant fragments of Papias occurs in a
comment by the late fourth-century Apollinaris of Laodicea, who was
discussing the notorious problem of the two different deaths described
for Judas in the New Testament. Apollinaris' solution is that Judas
survived the hanging described in Mt. 27.5 only to meet his end as
related by Acts 1.18. To bolster this solution, he appeals to Papias for
information that Judas "lived on":

> It must be known that Judas did not die from the hanging (Mt. 27.5)
> but lived on, as he was taken down before choking to death. And
> this is made clear by the Acts of the Apostles, that "falling
> headlong, he burst open and his guts spilled out" (Acts 1.18). This
> is told more clearly by Papias, John's disciple, saying this in the
> fourth [book] of exposition of the Lord's oracles:
>> "Judas walked around as a great example of ungodliness in this
>> world, as his flesh got so bloated that he could not pass through a
>> place where a wagon passes through easily."
> Not even just the bulk of his head, for his eyelids, they say,
> swelled up so much that he could not see light at all, and his eyes
> could not be seen, even by a medical optical instrument: they had
> sunk so far below the outer surface. As for his private part, it

---

[24] There is a similar dialogue, though not with Judas, in Hippolytus, *Daniel* 4.60, but
this appears to be a recasting of Irenaeus' version into a new context.

appeared more disgraceful and bigger than anyone else's, and when
he relieved himself both pus and worms from every part of his body
passed through it, much to his shame. After many torments and
punishments he expired in his own field, they say, and from the
stench the area is deserted and uninhabitable even now; in fact,
until today no one can pass that place without blocking up their
nose with their hands. So much was the discharge from his flesh and
so far did it spread over the ground.

Unfortunately, Apollinaris' commentary is lost and this comment is
preserved only in textually divergent catenae, which differ on how
much of the quotation ought to be attributed to Papias. Most scholars
today take the maximalist position attributing the entire lurid
account of the death of Judas in grisly detail, but in my view only
the first sentence can safely be assigned to Papias.[25] In addition to the
positive signals in the text that Apollinaris has shifted his sources
with "they say," the gruesome demise of Judas here incorporates
many details of the death of the persecuting emperor Galerius in
311 CE from a condition that resembles Fournier's gangrene
(Eusebius, *Hist. eccl.* 8.16.2–5).[26] Corroborating these positive indications for the lateness of the details is the silence of Papias' earlier
readers, especially Eusebius, for any indication that Judas died in this
horrific manner.

Apollinaris locates Papias' comment on the terrible example of
Judas in the fourth book, which is the same book from which
Irenaeus obtained his dialogue between Jesus and Judas about who
will get to see those times. Although evidence is woefully lacking, it
is tempting to see these two fragments as coming from the same
basic context, since Apollinaris' fragment about Judas supports the
implication of Irenaeus' fragment that Judas was not worthy to see
the future fertility of the Messianic kingdom. In any case, Judas'
walking around as a great example of impiety would have occurred
after the handing over and quick crucifixion of Jesus, and this fragment is evidence that Papias' work includes information about post-
Easter events.

---

[25] So also J. Vernon Bartlet, "Papias's 'Exposition': Its Date and Contents," in H.G.
Wood, ed., *Amiticiæ Corolla: A Volume of Essays Presented to James Rendel Harris,
D.Litt. on the Occasion of His Eightieth Birthday* (London: University of London
Press, 1933), 15–44, at 36–9.

[26] See Antonis A. Kousoulis et al., "The Fatal Disease of Emperor Galerius," *Journal of
the American College of Surgeons* 20.10 (2012): 1–4.

17.5 PAPIAS ON THE ADMINISTRATION OF ANGELS IN ANDREW OF CAESAREA

Andrew of Caesarea was an early seventh-century bishop of Caesarea in Cappadocia who wrote a commentary on the Revelation of John. In the preface to his work, he lists Papias as among several others in supporting this controversial book of the New Testament: "the blessed Gregory the theologian and Cyril, as well as of the more ancient Papias, Irenaeus, Methodius, and Hippolytus, corroborate its trustworthiness." Despite this endorsement, Andrew quotes Papias only once, in connection with Rev. 12.7–8 ("And there was war in heaven; Michael and his angels, waging war with the dragon. And the dragon and his angels waged war and they did not prevail, and there was yet no place for them in heaven"), and the content of his quotation has only minimal contacts with the text of Revelation:

> It must be known that, just as it has seemed good to the fathers, after the creation of the perceptible world he who had been first entrusted with rule over the air was deposed by his arrogance and envy, just as the apostle says (Eph. 2.2). And Papias too in these words: "but to some of them, clearly the once-divine angels, he granted rule over the arrangement of the earth and commanded them to rule well" And next he says: "but it turned out that their order came to nothing."
>
> "And the great dragon was thrown, the ancient serpent, the one called a devil and Satan, the deceiver of the whole world, he was thrown to the earth, and his angels were thrown." (Rev. 12.9)
>
> Naturally; for heaven would not bear an earthly mindset, because darkness has nothing in common with light (2 Cor. 6.14)...

Here too the problem of delimitation appears. Some collectors of the fragments extend the quotation of Papias so as to include the statement about Satan,[27] but it is clear from the form of Andrew's commentary that this merely the lemma from Rev. 12.9 for the next entry of the commentary.[28] The effect of the shorter quotation is that the Papias quotation does not have a direct reference to Satan, but rather concerns the angels (characterized by Andrew as "once divine") who were

---

[27] E.g., Holmes, *Apostolic Fathers*, no. 11 (following Lightfoot's analysis).
[28] Norelli, *Papia*, 398–400.

appointed to administer the world. Given the brevity of the quotation, it is difficult to conceive in what context it was made, but the focus on the angels does not look so much like Papias commenting on the text of Revelation, but rather on a Septuagint form of Deut. 32.8 ("God set the borders of the nations according to the angels of God"), known to Justin, *Dial.* 131.1.[29] In 2 *Apol.* 5, Justin has a strikingly similar remark about the fallen angels, describing that these angels mixed with women and became the progenitors of demons, who enslaved the human race (cf. Gen. 6.1–4). Papias may well have a similar context in mind. For Papias' knowledge of Revelation, accordingly, the best place to look is Eusebius.

17.6 PAPIAS ON EARLY CHRISTIAN TEXTS AND TRADITIONS IN EUSEBIUS OF CAESAREA

Eusebius of Caesarea, the famous church historian, is a crucial witness to Papias, preserving more genuine fragments from his work than everyone else combined. The main collection of these fragments is located in Book 3, chapter 39, of his *Ecclesiastical History*, but Eusebius does mention Papias elsewhere. In his *Chronicle* under the year 100 early in the reign of Trajan, Eusebius coordinates information from Irenaeus on Polycarp and Papias: "Irenaeus relates that John the apostle remained alive until the times of Trajan; after whom his hearers became known, Papias of Hierapolis and Polycarp bishop of Smyrna." Here we learn that Papias hails from the city of Hierapolis in Phrygia, near Laodicea and Colossae, and in *Hist. eccl.* 2.15.2 and 3.36.2 Eusebius states that Papias was bishop of that city, though this office may be anachronistic.

Eusebius' interest in Papias concerns not the subject matter of Papias' book but rather his witness to the writings that will make up the New Testament. In particular, Eusebius is motivated to call the apostolicity of the Revelation of John into question by showing that Papias knows of more than one disciple of Jesus named John. In the course of doing so, Eusebius quotes extensively from Papias' preface, giving us insight into Papias' attitude toward oral tradition and some of his remarks about the writings of Mark and Matthew.

17.6.1 The Title of Papias' Work

Eusebius also preserves what is lacking in Irenaeus' notice about Papias: the title of his five-volume work. At the beginning of Eusebius' chapter

---

[29] Ibid., 407.

on Papias, *Hist. eccl.* 3.39, Eusebius quotes from Irenaeus and supplies the title:

> But of Papias there are five volumes in circulation, which are entitled *Exposition of Dominical Oracles* (*logiōn kyriakōn exēgēseōs*).

This title has engendered a considerable amount of literature on the nature of Papias' books, because Eusebius does not tell us more about the structure of the work, and the paucity of genuine and substantial quotations provides little insight into the genre of Papias' work. As a result, scholars have scrutinized every term in the title and come to a number of incompatible conclusions. Some take the position that it is a commentary on the sayings of Jesus, perhaps with some narrative elements, but others contend that it was a commentary on at least the Gospel of Matthew, or a commentary on Revelation, or a commentary on Messianic passages in the Old Testament, or a narrative of Jesus' words and deeds much like the Gospels.[30]

17.6.2 Papias on the Traditions of the Elders

Next Eusebius quotes from Irenaeus, who claimed that Papias was a "hearer of John." Eusebius argues that this John is not the apostle but someone else:

> These Irenaeus mentions as his only writings, as follows: "But these things are also testified to in writing by Papias, John's hearer and Polycarp's colleague, a man of old, in the fourth of his books, for there are five books composed by him." And this is what Irenaeus said.
>
> Yet Papias himself, according to the preface of his text, in no way presents himself to have been a hearer and eyewitness of the holy apostles, but teaches that he had received the elements of the faith from those acquainted with them, using this language:

[30] E.g., Armin Daniel Baum, "Papias als Kommentator evangelischer Aussprüche Jesu: Erwägungen zur Art seines Werkes," *NovT* 38 (1996): 257–76 (commentary on Jesus' sayings); Lightfoot, *Essays*, 158–9 (gospel commentary); Oronzo Giordano, "I commentari di Papia di Ierapoli," *L'Antiquité Classique* 39 (1970): 106–46 (commentary on Revelation); John Burslem Gregory, *The Oracles Ascribed to Matthew by Papias of Hierapolis: A Contribution to the Criticism of the New Testament* (London: Longmans, 1894) (Old Testament commentary); and Richard Bauckham, "Did Papias Write History or Exegesis?," *JTS* 65 (2014): 463–88 (historical biography).

I will not, however, shy away from including also as many things from the elders I had carefully committed to memory and carefully kept in memory, along with the interpretations, so as to confirm the truth for you on their account. For it is not in those who say many things that I delight (as many do), but in those who teach the truth; nor is it in those who remember the alien commandments, but in those [who remember the commandments] given by the Lord to the faith and coming from truth itself. But if anyone who had followed the elders ever came along, I would examine the words of the elders – what did Andrew or what did Peter say, or what did Philip, or what did Thomas or James, or what did John or Matthew, or any other of the disciples of the Lord – and what Aristion and John the elder, disciples of the Lord, were saying. For it is not what comes from books that I assumed would benefit me as much as what comes from a living and lasting voice.

At this point, it is worth calling attention to the fact that he lists the name of John twice, as he includes the first one with Peter and James and Matthew and the remaining apostles, clearly indicating the evangelist, but the other John he places separately among the others outside the number of the apostles, putting Aristion before him, and he clearly calls him a presbyter.

The payoff for Eusebius' analysis of the prologue is that, if there were two men named John, one an apostle and the other merely an elder, then the Revelation of John could have been written by the non-apostolic John and as a result did not belong to the canon.

In the course of making this argument, Eusebius quoted an extensive portion of Papias' prologue, which preserves for posterity some information about Eusebius' argument. Most striking to modern readers is the remark at the end of the prologue excerpt that Papias prefers the living voice to books. This should not be interpreted as a skepticism to the written word *per se*, but rather an invocation of a common ancient trope that the best instruction comes from a personal teacher.[31] In other words, the main function of this statement is to reassure the reader that Papias is well qualified to pass on the interpretations and traditions of his predecessors.

---

[31] Stephen C. Carlson, "Papias's Appeal to the 'Living and Lasting Voice' over Books," in *Rise of the Early Christian Intellectual*, ed. Lewis O. Ayres and Clifton Ward, AZK (Berlin: De Gruyter, 2019).

17.6.3 Papias' Oral Traditions Preserved by Eusebius

In the prologue quoted by Eusebius, Papias comments about the structure of his work. He states that it includes two types of content: first, "the interpretations" (*tais hermēneiais*) and, second, carefully collected oral traditions Papias learned from the elders. Unfortunately Eusebius does not however pay any attention to the "interpretations" that were the primary object of Papias' work (they appear to be individual expositions of dominical oracles), but he does relate a number of these oral traditions, as follows:

To the reports of Papias rendered above, it is worth attaching some other statements of his, in which he relates other, incredible stories as if they had come to him by tradition. That Philip the apostle spent time in Hierapolis with his daughters has been explained before; but it must now be noted that Papias was there at the same time and mentions that he received an extraordinary account from Philip's daughters, for he relates that a raising of a corpse happened at that time, and again another incredible thing, about Justus who had been surnamed Barsabbas, that he swallowed a poisonous dose and suffered nothing unpleasant by the Lord's grace. Now according to Acts this is the Justus whom the holy apostles put forward with Matthias after the ascension of the Lord and prayed over the replenishment of their number by lot in place of the traitor Judas, as follows: "And they put forward two, Joseph called Barsabas, who was surnamed Justus, and Matthias, and they said a prayer."

And the same writer set forth other things as coming to him from an unwritten tradition, strange parables of the Savior and his teachings and some other more mythical things, among which he says that after the resurrection of the dead there will be a thousand years when the kingdom of Christ will be set up upon this earth in bodily form, which I believe he got from misconstruing the apostolic accounts, not seeing that they were spoken by them in figures mystically. For it is apparent that he was a man of a middling mind, to judge from the words he says, except that he became part of the reason for why such a large number of the clergy after him had a similar opinion, who cited the man's antiquity in defense, as did Irenaeus or anyone else who appeared with similar views.

Two of the oral traditions conveyed by Eusebius concern events that seem to have occurred in the early church after Easter: one, the raising of a corpse in the time of Philip's daughters, and, two, the drinking of poison by Justus Barsabbas. In addition to these, Eusebius states that Papias' work contain "strange parables," and it seems likely that Eusebius had in mind at least the fertility tradition quoted by Irenaeus. At any rate, this discussion shows that Papias' chiliasm was problematic to Eusebius.

17.6.4 Papias on Early Christian Writings

Eusebius' interest in Papias goes beyond his transmission of oral traditions about first-century Christian figures and reaches his witness to the writings related to the formation of the New Testament. These include Papias' statement on the writings of Mark, Matthew, John, Peter, and one other text:

> We now need to add to these statements of his a tradition which he set forth about Mark who wrote the gospel as follows: "And this is what the elder would say: 'Mark, who had indeed been Peter's interpreter, accurately wrote down yet not in order as much as he remembered about what was either said or done by the Lord.' For he neither heard the Lord nor followed him, but later, as I said, Peter, who would give his teachings as needed, but not, as it were, making a compilation of the dominical oracles, so that Mark did not fail at all by writing some of them as he recalled." For he took care of one thing, to omit nothing of what he heard or falsify anything among them.
>
> So then these things were reported by Papias about Mark, but about Matthew these things were said: "So then Matthew compiled the oracles in the Hebrew language, but each interpreted them as they could."
>
> The same writer used testimonies from the former letter of John and likewise from that of Peter, and he set forth another story about a woman accused of many sins before the Lord, which the Gospel according to the Hebrews contains.

The material presented on the gospel of Mark has been subjected to an intense amount of scrutiny, but only a few points can be made here. First, although this testimonium comes from Papias, Papias himself is relating information he earlier obtained, so that the initial sentence about what the elder said about Mark goes back at least to the end of the first century. Second, Papias' comment "as I said" suggests that he said more about Mark than what is presented here. Since someone named Mark is also mentioned in 1 Pet. 5.13, a good candidate for this

additional information is the identification of this Mark with an interpreter of Peter (cf. Eusebius, *Hist. eccl.* 2.15.2). Third, the more straightforward sense of the Matthew testimonium, that Matthew composed a
work in Hebrew, does not apply to the canonical Matthew, which is a
Greek-language composition, and has engendered much speculation
about what Papias could have had in mind.

17.7 ANONYMOUS FRAGMENTS

Given the citation practices in antiquity, it is reasonable to expect that
some uses of Papias would be anonymous. From a methodological
perspective, however, these cases are difficult to identify, unless they
can be related to subject matter already securely assigned to Papias.
A good example of this is the third-century Victorinus of Pettau, who
wrote a commentary on Revelation and had this to say about his interpretation of the four living creatures of Rev. 4.4:

> Mark, Peter's interpreter who remembered what he taught in his
> office wrote down but not in order, and he began with the word of
> prophesy announced by Isaiah. ... Mark begins so: *The beginning of
> the gospel of Jesus Christ as it was written in Isaiah; he began with
> the Spirit flying up*, thus he also has the likeness of a flying eagle.

The detail that Mark wrote down "but not in order" what he learned
from Peter is striking and is paralleled in Eusebius' quotation of Papias
about Mark (see above). Since Victorinus predates Eusebius, he must be
independent of him, and as such Victorinus is a witness to the use of
Papias. It is possible that there is more of Papias to be found in
Victorinus, though Victorinus' failure to cite his sources makes the
identification of additional material difficult if not impossible.

17.8 CONCLUSION

The fragments of Papias have not always found a place in the Apostolic
Fathers, yet he certainly belongs there on chronological grounds. As an
older contemporary of Polycarp, he appears to be active during the reign
of Trajan (98–117 CE), and this is probably when he composed his five
volumes of *Exposition of Dominical Oracles*. Papias also belongs in the
Apostolic Fathers as a pivotal link from the last apostolic generation to
the rest of the second century, transmitting traditions from his elders,
including those from a certain John the elder and the daughters of
Philip. Though the genre of this work is not entirely clear from the

surviving fragments (it appears to be a commentary of some sort), what is clear is that Papias is an invaluable witness to Christian views about eschatology and the origin of the Gospels – especially that of Mark – in decades immediately following the composition of the Gospels. Unfortunately, almost all of his work is lost and much remains unknown about this enigmatic figure and his work.

FURTHER READING

Ehrman, Bart D. *The Apostolic Fathers*. LCL 24. Vol. 2. Cambridge, MA: Harvard University Press, 2003.

Hill, Charles E. "The Fragments of Papias," in *The Writings of the Apostolic Fathers*, ed. Paul Foster. New York: T&T Clark, 2007, 42–51 .

Holmes, Michael W. *The Apostolic Fathers*, 3rd ed. Grand Rapids, MI: Baker Academic, 2007.

Körtner, Ulrich H.J. *Papias von Hierapolis: Ein Beitrag zur Geschichte des frühen Christentums*. FRLANT 133. Göttingen: Vandenhoeck & Ruprecht, 1983.

Kürzinger, Josef. *Papias von Hierapolis und die Evagelien des Neuen Testament*. EM 4. Regensburg: Pustet, 1983.

MacDonald, Dennis R. *Two Shipwrecked Gospels: The Logoi of Jesus and Papias's Exposition of Logia about the Lord*. ECL 8. Atlanta, GA: Society of Biblical Literature, 2012.

Norelli, Enrico. *Papia di Hierapolis, Esposizione degli Oracoli del Signore: I frammenti*. Letture cristiane del primo millennio 36. Milan: Paoline, 2005.

Sources Index

OTHER SOURCES

Subject Index

Other Titles in the Series

Lightning Source UK Ltd.
Milton Keynes UK
UKHW020630210621
385893UK00013B/1148